If it's worth watchii it's worth nitpickin

Did you catch these X-FILES® bloopers?

1 Life after death? In the episode called "The Jersey Devil," what acting flub shows us the beast-woman's death is only make-believe?

2 Is it forgery? What is very odd about Mulder's signature on his resignation letter in that classic episode, "One Breath"?

3 The powerful story "Anasazi" is filled with great nits to pick. Among them—what makes you wonder if Scully's been taking a bodybuilding course?

4 "War of the Coprophages," a great creepy-crawly episode, obviously shook up the cast. What's wrong with Mulder and Dr. Bambi's inspection of the cockroaches with an illuminated magnifying glass?

Answers:

1 *After the police kill the beast-woman, Mulder uses his hand to close her eyes. Miraculously, her left eyelid shuts though Mulder's palm doesn't touch it!*

2 *It doesn't match his signature on his badge seen at the beginning of this episode.*

3 *Petite (5'3") Dana Scully shoots Mulder in the shoulder using only a one-handed grip, then apparently hefts around his unconscious body, all six feet 170 pounds of it. Can we get the name of her personal trainer, please!*

4 *Bambi and Mulder use the magnifying glass backward; the circular neon bulb is shining in their eyes, not on the specimen. Obviously, it isn't the bugs' bodies that have their attention.*

THE NITPICKER'S GUIDE FOR X-PHILES

Also by Phil Farrand

THE NITPICKER'S GUIDE FOR X-PHILES

Phil Farrand

A Dell Trade Paperback

A Dell Trade Paperback
Published by
Dell Publishing
a division of
Bantam Doubleday Dell Publishing Group, Inc.
1540 Broadway
New York, New York 10036

Developed and produced by Ettlinger Editorial Projects, New York.
Copyright ©1997 by Phil Farrand
Designed by Chris Kalb.

Library of Congress Cataloging-in-Publication Data

Farrand, Phil.
    The nitpicker's guide for x-philes/Phil Farrand.
    p.   cm.
    ISBN 0–440–50808–8
    1. X-Files (Television program) I. Title.
PN1992.77.X22F37   197
791.45'72—dc21   9714878
        CIP

Printed in the United States of America

Published simultaneously in Canada

December 1997

10 9 8 7 6 5 4 3 2 1

FFG

Dedicated to creators of quality science fiction television everywhere in general and to the creative staff of The X-Files *in particular—ingenious, quick-witted, vista-hopping, farseeing artisans—without whom there would be no* Guides.

Table of Contents

Acknowledgments

As with any creative project, the one you hold in your hands would not exist without the dedicated efforts of many, many people. Obviously there would be no *Nitpicker's Guide for X-philes* had Chris Carter and crew not created a fascinating new entry into the world of television science fiction—with its expertly honed characterizations and brain-tickling plots. To the multitudes who oversee every aspect during the production of each episode of *The X-Files,* I do thank you for creating a product worth watching. And, as I am fond of saying: Since it's worth watching, it's worth nitpicking.

As with previous *Guides,* Steve Ettlinger served not only as agent for this work but book producer as well. He coordinated William Drennan's copy editing, Carol Fitschen's manuscript preparation, Jeff Fitschen's page makeup, AEIOU, Margo Zelie and John Long's proofreading, and Jane Farnol's indexing. It's been great working with you, guys! This one makes five! (By the way, Steve's managing editor, Tim Smith also served above and beyond the call by using a CD-ROM to track down the existence of almost a hundred locations taken from episodes of *The X-Files.* Thanks for that extra effort, Tim!)

As with *The Nitpicker's Guide for Deep Space Nine Trekkers,* Kathleen Jayes lent her most capable pen as editor on this installment of the *Nitpicker's Guides.* Thanks again for making it so easy to do my "job," Kathleen. (Granted, sitting and watching television all day doesn't exactly qualify as strenuous work, but Kathleen has always commended herself with gentleness and dignity.) Thanks as well to

Michelle Filippo and the rest of the able individuals at Dell Publishing.

Gratefully—though it comes as no surprise to me, for I know their hearts—my wife, Lynette, and daughter, Elizabeth, still stand beside me and lend me their strength. For that, I am privileged.

Having caught the X-phile craze just a wee bit late, I was also pleased to have Kymberlee Ricke serve as research consultant for this *Nitpicker's Guide.* For years, Kymberlee has maintained a Web site called "The Netpicker's Guide to *The X-Files.*" As you have already guessed, she has been collecting the foibles of the series for some time now. If you have Web access and would like to visit her site, it's located at: "http://aea16.k12.ia.us/ricke/netpick-home.html".

In addition, Bob Potter of Tasmania, Australia, had begun his own nitpicking tome on *The X-Files* some time before he learned of my plans to do a *Guide.* In response, he very kindly sent me all the material he had amassed. Thanks for all the input, Bob! It was fun comparing your notes to mine and seeing how many things we both found quirky!

And since the series revolves around the Federal Bureau of Investigation, I thought it only fitting to contact the Bureau and inquire about a few items that wandered through my little nitpicker's brain as I watched the episodes. I found everyone I talked with there to be kind and considerate and I do thank them for their help. I should also let you know that I couldn't pass up the opportunity to ask if they actually *had* agents who routinely investigated claims of the paranormal (i.e., UFO sightings, government conspiracies, psychic divination, demon possession, past life memories, etc., etc.). Understanding the tongue-in-check demeanor of my question, they responded that they did not but suggested I talk with the Department of Defense!

Nitpicker Central's resident solar physicist Mitzi Adams continues to serve with distinction, though—given the terrestrial nature of *this* series—she had somewhat fewer responsibilities this time. As always, she quickly and meticulously answered—or tracked down the answers to—all my pesky questions. I'm always grateful for the help, Mitzi! (By the way, if you're interested in having a real scientist speak at your convention, you can contact the Public Affairs Speakers' Bureau at the Marshall Space Flight Center in Huntsville, Alabama.)

In addition—since the subject matter of this *Guide* lent itself to greater scrutiny in regard to medical issues—I enlisted the help of longtime Nitpicker's Guild member Robert J. Woolley, M.D., of St. Paul, Minnesota. Certainly, I make no boast that this Guide covers all the medical peculiarities in *The X-Files*—or even most. But Robert was considerate enough to comment on the issues I brought to his attention. Thanks for the help, Robert! (By the way—as with the information attributed to Mitzi—the fault is entirely mine if you take exception with any of Robert's comments. Sometimes ideas get lost in the translation. And while we're on the topic, yes, *The X-Files* normally does do a good job of staying medically accurate. But . . . we *are* all human!)

Thanks as well to Deb Mirek of Fullerton, California, for supplying the episodes I forgot to tape! It's good to know that *somebody* was out there "minding the store" before I realized that the series was going to be a hit.

Obviously, I am indebted as well to the other members of the Nitpickers Guild who sent in contributions for this *Guide*—even if it was "beyond the pale" of what was considered "nor-mal" for a Nitpicker's Guide. (Until this point, the *Guides* have always dealt with some incarnation of *Star Trek*.) I have done my best to give credit where credit is due. Unfortunately, space considerations never allow the inclusion of all the nits that members of the Guild send my way. To everyone who wrote, whether your nit made it in or not, thank you so for taking the time to share your thoughts.

Finally, as always, I am eternally grateful to you, Jesus Christ, for being my Life, my Way, and . . . my Truth.

Guild Acknowledgments

Greetings, fellow nitpickers! It is my happy privilege once again to thank you for your communications and provide at least a few with some well-deserved credit! Certainly, since the subject matter for this *Guide* is such a departure from previous *Guides* (more on that in the Introduction), there aren't as many laurels to be handed out this time around, but I *am* grateful for all those who took the time to write, even if every nit submitted wasn't included. (As I've often said before, if you sent along some nits that didn't get included, they probably weren't bad nits. They most likely weren't included simply because of space constraints! Likewise, if you recognize a nit that you sent in but your name doesn't appear on this list, it's probably because someone sent in that nit first. With more than 6100 members in the Nitpickers Guild—at the time of this writing—that is *bound* to happen.)

Below then are the names of nitpickers who submitted nits that were included in this *Guide*—they were the first ones to submit those nits. (If a number follows a person's name, it means that more than one of his or her nits made it into this *Guide*.)

Picky Napthiping!

Pauline J. Alama of Rochester, NY (2)
Stephen Archer of Battersea, England
Stephanie Bamberger of Sacramento, CA
Simon Beale (location unknown)
Michael Bradbery of New South Wales, Australia
Steve Brandon of Pincourt, Quebec
Jonathan Bridge of Taylorsville, UT (2)
Mario Bruzzone of Westlake Village, CA
Bob Canada (location unknown) (4)
Daniel B. Case of Woodmere, OH (5)
Amy Cat (location unknown)
Daphne Chong of New South Wales, Australia
Paul Cunneen of Rochester, NY
Jon Davidson of Paducah, KY
Liam de Bruun of Dublin, Ireland
Mike Ezzo of Mie-ken, Japan
David Glover of United Kingdom
Amanda Gordon of Colorado Springs, CO (2)
Jenifer Gordon of Westlake Village, CA
Maranda Gordon of Houston, TX
Geoffrey Gould of Verona, NJ
Jen Grady of Greensburg, PA
Jason Allan Haase of Pierce City, MO
Benoit Hebert of Quebec City, Quebec
Paul Jennings of Rock Rapids, IA
Jeffrey Koeppen of Monticello, MN
Samuel Lawrence of Ann Arbor, MI (2)
Murray Leeder of Calgary, Alberta (18)
Jennifer Loehlin of Austin, TX
Jason Liu of Libertyville, IL (8)
Alex Lum of Tasmania, Australia
Michael Marks of Eastchester, NY (2)

E. C. Marshal of Hampshire, United Kingdom (6)
Matthew Chase Maxwell of San Francisco, CA
Martin McCarthy of Dublin, Ireland
Travis McCord of Reno, NV (6)
David Mcgrath of St. John's, Newfoundland
Aidan McGuinness of Dublin, Ireland (4)
Debbie Mirek of Fullerton, CA (8)
Ronan Mitchell of Dublin, Ireland (9)
Abigail Nassbuam of Israel
John Ogden of Olathe, KS
Tina Pedigo of Sierra Vista, AZ
Joseph Pintar of New Hartford, NY
David D. Porter of River Ridge, LA (3)
Bob Potter of Tasmania, Australia (79)
Jack Reasoner of Adrian, MI
Trevor Ruppe of Hickory, NC (2)
Alexander Shearer of Berkeley, CA
Paul Steele of Fort Belvoir, VA
Jonathan Strawn of Albuquerque, NM (3)
Peer Sylvester of Hamburg, Germany
David L. Tayman of Toms River, NJ (3)
Elijah Ton of Carthage, MO
Shane Tourtellotte of Rutherford, NJ (4)
Autumn Tysko (location unknown) (2)
Rutger van Bergen of Vianen, Netherlands
Lynn Wertz of Springfield, MO (2)
Gareth Wilson of Christchurch, New Zealand
Robert Wooley of St. Paul, MN (10)
John Wyant of Hants, United Kingdom (2)

Introduction

Greetings, fellow nitpickers!

And, then there's . . . *The X-Files!* As some of you may know, four guides have preceded this one: *The Nitpicker's Guide for Next Generation Trekkers* (a.k.a. the *NextGen Guide,* released November 1993), *The Nitpicker's Guide for Classic Trekkers* (a.k.a. the *Classic Guide,* released November 1994), *The Nitpicker's Guide for Next Generation Trekkers, Volume II* (a.k.a. the *NextGen II Guide,* released November 1995), and *The Nitpicker's Guide for Deep Space Nine Trekkers* (a.k.a. the *DS9 Guide,* released December 1996). (Someday I plan to have an entire shelf of *Nitpicker's Guides*!)

Obviously, this *Guide* represents something of a departure for me. And there were those—upon hearing my plans for an X-phile *Guide*—who wondered if nitpicking could be extended to anything other than a space show like *Star Trek.* In short, the answer is: *YES!* Nitpicking doesn't originate in space, it originates in the human heart—both the cause of it and the effect. We're all human. We all make mistakes. As long as we're all human and we are going to make mistakes no matter *what* we put our hands to do, we might as well be real about it and acknowledge it and try to have a little fun with our imperfections! That's why I say, "Nitpicking is a celebration of being human." Nowhere in this *Guide* will you hear me say that "I the Great" could do a better job producing or directing or writing *The X-Files* than those who capably serve in that capacity. *I* know that no matter who creates a television series, it will *always* have nits! Think of it as "nitpicker job security."

Having said that, I should hasten to add that

I did consider many elements about *The X-Files* before I finally decided to pursue this project. As far as I'm concerned, when it comes to the alien conspiracy genre, there just ain't *nobody* better that the creators of *The X-Files.* But I have to be honest with you and say that there *are* episodes of *The X-Files* that lay outside my personal boundaries of good taste. It is true that, in most cases, even the episodes I consider too ghoulish or gruesome are still executed with a high degree of creativity and artistry. Even still—after the gore began to increase with the second season—I instituted a practice in my home of screening the episodes before I allowed my young teenage daughter, Elizabeth, to watch them. Since then, there have been a significant number of episodes that haven't "made the cut"! I feel very strongly that it is my responsibility as a parent to render this service. I have all the episodes on tape. When she's older, if she wants to watch them, that's fine! (Obviously, if you're a parent, you will no doubt have an entirely different list but just for information purposes, these are the episodes that I seem to remember "reserving": "3," "Aubrey," "Irresistible," "Die Hand Die Verletzt," "Fresh Bones," "The List," "2SHY," "Syzygy," "Grotesque," "Home," "Sanguinarium" and "Leonard Betts.")

By now, I would assume that most everyone reading this book would understand the basic format of a *Nitpicker's Guide.* For those of you who are new to this form of entertainment, let me offer my usual quick tour. (Even seasoned members of the Nitpickers Guild might want to give this a quick read. There are a few new sections.)

For each episode I list the title (gleaned from the official *X-Files* literature and website), date (if known), and a brief summary—in case you haven't seen that particular installment of *The X-Files*. I also add a few ruminations along the way: things that struck me about the episode, a bit of analysis here and there, other random thoughts. In addition, I offer some picks for great moments. There are two trivia questions just to test your knowledge of the episode. (In case you've never tried my trivia questions, don't get discouraged. They are supposed to be *hard*! I figure the other books have already taken the easy ones!)

In addition, each episode review has a section titled, "Onscreen Locations." For some reason, the creators of *The X-Files* decided not to list the episode titles on the episodes themselves. This causes a bit of a problem for reference books on the series. Many nitpickers have written to tell me that they keep the other *Guides* nearby when they watch *Star Trek*. Once they see an episode title, they look up the episode in the appropriate *Nitpicker's Guide* and read what I have to say before settling in for their own session of nitpicking. But how's a nitpicker supposed to find the episode in the *Guide* if there's no episode title?! Well . . . that's where "Onscreen Locations" comes in handy. I've listed every location displayed during the episodes (aside from "FBI Headquarters," and "Washington, D.C.") and compiled them into an "Onscreen Locations" Index. So, once you spot any onscreen text, you should be able to flip to the index, find that entry, and then get a page number that will take you to the episode! (I know it's convoluted, but I couldn't figure out any better way to do it.)

Now let's talk about the *good stuff* in the episode reviews!

Given the open-ended storytelling technique used in *The X-Files* (a.k.a. "the search for the truth"), I have added a new section to the reviews of this book called, "Unanswered Questions." In this section I voice some quandaries that I felt the creators *intentionally* left unsolved. Never one to flee a chance for humiliation, I will also float some possibilities for

your perusal. I do recognize that episodes to come might answer these questions, but I thought you might enjoy a peek inside the old nitpicker's brain as I tried to make some sense of the issues raised.

I have also added a section called "Geographical Inconsistencies" (at the suggestion of Daniel B. Case of Woodmere, Ohio). Since *The X-Files* is a reality-based show (i.e., the creators make every effort to convince us that the events in the episodes are occurring in our time and space), I thought you might like to know of the little irregularities here and there spotted by nitpickers who live in or have knowledge about the regions depicted in the episodes. Mostly, this section deals with simple facts as reported by Guild members. In addition, Tim Smith of Ettlinger Editorial Projects took a list of almost a hundred towns and address and ran them through a super-duper CD-ROM to determine the existence or nonexistence of towns such as Bellefleur, Oregon. (I know some of you are thinking, "Well, of course, Bellefleur, Oregon, doesn't exist! It's just a small town the creators made up!" But I would hasten to point out that Winthrop, Washington, exists—as well as Folkstone, North Carolina; Two Gray Hills, New Mexico; and Dogway, West Virginia, which Tim Smith describes as "a one-street town near the Virginia border.")

The remainder of each episode review is taken up with categories that have served well for the other *Guides*: Plot Oversights, Changed Premises, Equipment Oddities, and Continuity and Production Problems.

Plot Oversights is a catchall. Anything that concerns the plot, or won't fit anywhere else, goes here. Under Changed Premises you'll discover that sometimes information given in one show directly contradicts information in another. In Equipment Oddities I'll point out any problems that I and the other members of the Nitpickers Guild have found with the equipment and technology of *The X-Files'* universe. Lastly, the section on Continuity and Production

Problems will expose errors in the actual creation of the show—from microphone booms reflecting in picture frames and car windows to leaping hippopotami to neckties with minds of their own and the like.

If you happen to have the episodes of *The X-Files* on videotape, pull them out and grab the remote as you work your way through this *Guide*. If you find something I missed, disagree with a nit I picked, or even find an error in the *Guide* itself, drop me a line at the address at the back of this book. That effort will make you a member of the Nitpickers Guild.

Sprinkled among the reviews of episodes you will also find sidebars of various incarnations. These have enjoyed a continuing popularity among Guild members, and I trust you will find them interesting as well.

As always, the Nitpicker's Prime Directive remains in full force. For those who don't remember, the main rule of nitpicking reads, "All nits picked shall derive from sources the creators consider canonical." In other words, anything that Carter and crew claims actually happened or is authoritative can be nitpicked. Until we hear differently, that includes all the episodes of *The X-Files* and all the official reference books. (I haven't heard if Chris Carter has said that the novels and the comic books represent cases that have "actually occurred.")

A final exhortation. Some of you may know that there is a Nitpicker's Secondary Directive. It reads, "All nitpickers shall perform their duties with lightheartedness and good cheer." This whole nitpicking thing is about having some fun with our favorite television shows and movies. It is not about pointing fingers and assigning blame. "Lightheartedness and good cheer" should also be the way nitpickers approach X-philes who don't enjoy nitpicking. If people want to watch their show without knowing what's wrong with it: *Let them watch their show!* A true nitpicker doesn't have to tell everyone everything he or she knows all the time. If you see a nit and are in a room full of "nonnitters," just smile and drop me a note later.

Happy nitpicking! (Or "Ping! Chikin Pat Py!" if you prefer!)

FIRST SEASON

Pilot

Onscreen Locations

🅇 Collum National Forest, Northwest Oregon
🅇 Coastal Northwest Oregon
🅇 Raymond County State Psychiatric Hospital
🅇 Rural Hwy. 133, Bellefleur, Oregon

Ruminations

I make it my policy to treat pilot episodes with some measure of gentleness. Time passes between the creation of the pilot and the start of production for any series. It makes sense that the creators tweak a few things here or there after their first experience of bringing a new project to life. Among the obvious differences:

Mulder becomes more sophisticated in later episodes. He almost seems giddy and even geeky at times in the pilot. He also gives up his less-than-inspiring beginning as a graffiti artist. This is the only episode where we see him wielding a can of spray paint to make a giant "X" on the road. "Photographer Mulder" almost entirely disappears after this episode as well. (One wonders why—given the possibility of documenting what he sees in later episodes— but we'll get to that in due time!)

As a minor item, Scully undergoes a makeover by the next episode—new hair, makeup, clothes. Also, when Mulder asks if she's squeamish about getting a tissue sample from an exhumed body, Scully says that she's never done that before and does seem uncomfortable with the idea. In later episodes she becomes suddenly adept at examining the corpses that litter The X-Files. *In fact, during "Fallen Angel," we learn that Scully did her*

PLOT SUMMARY

In Washington, D.C., FBI Chief Blevins assigns Special Agent Dana Scully—trained as a medical doctor—to write field reports and provide a scientific analysis on Special Agent Fox Mulder. Formerly a psychological profiler for the Violent Crimes Section, Mulder has developed a consuming interest in the X-files, cases that the Bureau deems "unexplained phenomena." (Mulder's sister, Samantha, disappeared at age eight. Mulder believes she was abducted by aliens. He hopes the X-Files will prove this to be the truth.)

The next morning, Mulder and Scully fly to Bellefleur, Oregon, the site of a recent series of four unexplained deaths among the graduates of the high school class of 1989. Once there, the two FBI agents quickly discover more mysteries. The exhumed body of Ray Soames—the third of the four to die—looks more alien than human and contains a metal, nasal implant. Then wheelchair-bound Peggy O'Dell—also of the class of '89—is killed after running in front of a semitruck. Even stranger, Mulder and Scully determine that the most likely suspect in the deaths is Billy Miles, a young man who has just awakened from a three-year coma. Under hypnosis, Miles speaks of graduation night in 1989—of a light taking him to a "testing place" and of being ordered to bring the others. However, Miles also insists that the tests failed and that "they" wanted everything destroyed.

It is impossible for the pair to corroborate Miles's story, but clearly *someone* wants the evidence destroyed. By the end of the episode, Soames's body has disappeared; all photographs and X rays have been burned; the Raymond County prosecutor drops the case against Billy Miles; and the only remaining piece of evidence—the metal implant—is given to a mysterious cigarette-smoking man who locks it away in a secured warehouse at the Pentagon.

residency *in forensic medicine. But by far the most fundamental change in Scully's character is the much-appreciated choice by the creators to focus attention primarily on her mind rather than her body. The pilot contains a motel room scene where Scully undresses to take a shower. She discovers marks at the base of her back similar to those found on the dead young people. Panicked, she flees to Mulder's room, where she peels off her robe to stand clad only in her bra and panties as Mulder conducts an inspection. (And, yes, he seems to take his time and enjoy the work!)*

Granted, she's scared, but this is definitely not the Scully we come to know *as a dedicated, scientifically minded researcher who dresses impeccably and carries herself with dignity and aplomb. Trust me: After you watch all the episodes in sequence several times and then go back to view the infamous underwear scene, it's quite jarring.*

On the other hand, this episode has much to commend it as a pilot. The character roles are well formed. The open-ended storytelling technique first used here serves well for many years to come. And, of particular warmth to my little nitpicker's heart, the creators demonstrate some nice attention to detail. During the autopsy on Ray Soames, the generated screen text reads "10:56" and—lo and behold—the clock on the wall reads the same! Also, the first scene in the psychiatric hospital shows a nurse making a bed in the background. When Mulder and Scully return to the hospital for a second visit, this same nurse speaks with them.

Unanswered Questions

X *The* unanswered question of the pilot has to be: What really happened to these kids? At this point in the series—if we are to believe everything we see on the screen—we must conclude that there is *some* extraordinary form of phenomenon at work. According to Mulder's watch, nine minutes disappear. (More on that

in a minute.) Billy Miles is somehow magically healed of the marks on his lower back right before our eyes. And the man we will hereinafter call Cancerman places the nasal implant in a box marked "Evidence." This would imply nonparticipation in the event. (An explanation: Yes, I know William B. Davis's character is called "The Cigarette-Smoking Man" when referred to in *The Official Guide to The X-Files.* But there are several references in the actual episodes identifying him as "Cancerman." Besides, it's my book and I like "Cancerman" *better!*)

However, events in later episodes might give credence to the possibility that while the phenomenon at work in this episode is extraordinary, it might not be *extraterrestrial.* In "Deep Throat" we learn that the government has very advanced airships that can dart away and create sonic booms like the one heard at the end of the pilot. We also learn in "Nisei" and "731" that "someone" is conducting some type of genetic experiments on humans, which might explain Ray Soames's corpse. Finally, "José Chung's *From Outer Space*" seems to suggest that it is well within this "someone's" capability to both generate the illusion of missing time and convince test subjects that they have been abducted by aliens.

Geographical Inconsistencies

X Bellefleur, Oregon, doesn't exist.

Plot Oversights

X As nearly as I can determine from this and subsequent episodes, Dana Scully joined the FBI directly out of medical school. She taught forensic medicine for two years at Quantico (apparently attending the Academy at the same time) and was then assigned as a special agent to evaluate Fox Mulder and the X-Files. The kind folks at the real Federal Bureau of Investigation (hereinafter referred to as The Real FBI) tell me that this is farfetched and wouldn't happen!

☒ After the opening credits, we see Dana Scully entering an office. (We learn later that this is Chief Blevin's office.) He seems to command a fair amount of authority, yet he apparently has no secretary. The Real FBI says he would.

☒ After the introductions, Mulder shows Scully a picture of Karen Swenson, the fourth person to die under mysterious circumstances in Bellefleur, Oregon. She has the two marks at the base of her back. Then Mulder shows Scully pictures of two other individuals—found dead in South Dakota and Texas, respectively. They have the marks as well. Yet, at the end of the episode, we see that those conducting the experiments can remove the marks from a young person's body. If so, why do "they" leave them on other bodies? (Because if they didn't, Mulder wouldn't be on this case!)

☒ Along the same lines, if Ray Soames had a nasal implant, one would expect Karen Swenson to have one as well. And since Dr. Nemman—who covered up evidence in the previous death—wasn't the one who did Swenson's autopsy, why didn't the medical examiner find the implant?

☒ One also wonders why Mulder didn't attempt to have Peggy O'Dell or at least Billy Miles X-rayed for nasal implants after the first hospital visit. I realize the fathers wouldn't have allowed it, but Mulder looks enthralled at finding the first implant. It seems reasonable that he would hunt for more.

☒ And does anyone want to guess how mad Mulder is going to be when he finds out that Scully gave away the *only* piece of hard evidence they had concerning the case?

Changed Premises

☒ The knowledgeable and sensibly minded Dana Scully floats an interesting theory in this episode. She wonders if the young people offered some kind of sacrifice in the woods—if they were involved in a cult. This is the same person who will vigorously debunk any notion of occult sacrifices in "Die Hand Die Verletzt" and "Syzygy"—citing exhaustive FBI research. (Maybe she hadn't read the reports yet?)

Equipment Oddities

☒ Okay, let's talk about the exhumation of Ray Soames's body. Mulder and Scully drive up as a backhoe digs up the grave. Straps are placed around the coffin. As the backhoe lifts the coffin, a close-up shows that one of the straps is badly frayed and—*surprise*—it breaks, sending the coffin tumbling down a hill. Did no one *check* these straps before they were used? Or are the guys in this cemetery so used to working with *dead people* that they've forgotten about *lawyers* and *criminal negligence*?

☒ Not a nit, just an observation. "They" appear to improve their implant technology at some point after this episode. All subsequent implants are much smaller. I couldn't help but grimace at the thought of having that pencil-sized chunk of metal rammed up my nose! (Just how many bottles of Robitussin *did* those parents go through trying to alleviate their kids' congestion?)

☒ As Scully enters information on her laptop concerning Soames's autopsy, note the close-up of the screen. It looks like a cathode-ray tube, the kind found on *desktop* computers, not laptops.

☒ All right, let's talk about Mulder's watch. He and Scully are driving along. He looks at his watch. It says "9:03." There's a bright flash. The car dies. Mulder looks at his watch. It says "9:12." Speaking of this experience later in the

Trivia Questions

❶ With whom has Mulder worked utilizing regressive hypnosis?

❷ What is the number on the box in which Cancerman places the implant?

episode, Mulder says that time stopped and something took control of it. The terminology "time stopped" doesn't seem to fit. Aren't they really just "missing time," because if time actually *stopped*, why did his watch keep working? Timex, maybe? ("It takes a licking—*even from time-stopping aliens*—and keeps on ticking!")

Continuity and Production Problems

☒ No doubt this was intentional, but the badges shown in the opening credits read, "Federal Bureau of Justice, Department of Investigations," when the official title of the organization is the "Federal Bureau of Investigation." It is, of course, under the Department of Justice. Did the creators do this to discount the possibility of someone making fake credentials from the opening stills? Or did they imagine that someday they would want to *sell* credentials and needed the organization's name to be fictitious?

☒ When Scully goes down to the basement to meet Mulder, a camera pan treats us to our first look of the "I Want to Believe" poster. The text of the poster is clearly visible. In the very next shot, there is suddenly a pile of folders and miscellaneous papers below the poster, and some of them obscure the "BE" of "BELIEVE."

☒ On the plane ride to Bellefleur, Oregon, Scully reviews the cases of the four young people who died. She reads a newspaper article about the fourth victim, Karen Swenson. A close-up of the article names Dr. Nemman and seems to indicate that he was the medical examiner for Swenson. But later dialogue contradicts this. In fact, Mulder and Scully are on the case because Nemman *wasn't* the one who did the autopsy on Swenson. (In all fairness to the creators: Very little of the article actually appears on the screen. *Possibly* the section shown refers to Nemman as the ME on the previous cases.)

☒ When Mulder compliments Scully on realizing that Nemman didn't do the autopsy on Swenson, watch his hands. From one camera angle, he's driving with his left hand while his right hand draws a sunflower seed to his mouth. The camera angle changes and, instantly, Mulder's hands have reversed their respective roles. (Must be those lightning-fast FBI reflexes!)

☒ Only moments later, the rental car's radio and clock go wacky. But even stranger, the sun seems to develop swivel hips! From one camera angle we see Mulder, and the shadow on his face shows the sun angling in from his left. But the next shot of Scully shows the sun angling in from her *right*. Then the shot changes and the sun is—once again—on Mulder's side of the car. (Probably some solar version of the macarena.)

☒ When Dr. Nemman's daughter, Theresa, asks for protection, Mulder and Scully escort her to a café to talk. Moments later, her nose gushes blood. If you freeze-frame just before this happens you can see the tube that the creators cleverly ran down the bridge of her nose to produce the effect.

☒ Pay close attention after Mulder and Scully experience "missing time." They stand in front of their car. As they talk, water pours from their faces. This makes sense. They are, after all, standing outside in a rainstorm. Now look at the close-ups in the graveyard after they discover that someone exhumed the bodies of the first two victims. Notice the difference? Their faces are wet, but there are very few drips, though it's raining cats and dogs around them. (Some kind of weird atmospheric disturbance, no doubt. Either that or Mulder lives a charmed life.)

☒ In the very last scene of the episode, we see Cancerman turn into a long aisle between rows of tall metal shelves. He walks toward the camera and then stops to deposit the metal implant in a box. He turns toward the camera again and begins walking. The camera retreats all the way down the aisle and exits through a door that Cancerman then closes and locks. A few questions: Was Cancerman checking on something else in the room? He obviously took the scenic route to the box that he wanted. And if he entered by another door, *who opened the exit door?* The *cameraman?!* Or did someone leave the door open by mistake? This is supposed to be a secured facility—as evidenced by the card key entry system. ("Well, I don't know how evidence keeps disappearing, Mr. General, sir. 'Course, Philbert never remembers to shut the door, but *that* couldn't be it!")

Deep Throat

PLOT SUMMARY

When Colonel Robert Budahas, stationed at Ellens Air Base in Idaho, suffers a mental breakdown and is hauled away by military police, his wife—in desperation—reports the matter to the FBI as a kidnapping.

Mulder takes notice. The base supposedly received material from an alleged UFO crash in Roswell, New Mexico, in 1947. And since 1963 the base has reported six pilots "missing in action." Mulder suspects that the military has created some type of aircraft from UFO technology and that the craft is harming its test pilots in some way. He intends to use the kidnapping charge to find out more. Then an unidentified man ("Deep Throat") suddenly appears to warn Mulder off the case, further strengthening Mulder's determination.

Shortly after arriving in Idaho, however, Mulder and Scully learn that Budahas has mysteriously returned—though his wife claims it isn't really him. And by this time both agents have witnessed strange lights in the sky. Driven to investigate, Mulder sneaks onto the base. He is quickly apprehended, but not before seeing an advanced triangle-shaped craft. Unfortunately, the military wipes his memory even as Scully arranges for his release.

A week later, in Washington, D.C., Deep Throat reappears to tell Mulder that his and Scully's lives are in danger—that care and discretion are imperative.

Onscreen Locations

- ☒ Near Ellens Air Base, Southwest Idaho
- ☒ Marriette Field, southwest Idaho
- ☒ Outside Ellens Air Base

Ruminations

I believe this is the first episode where we see that Scully wears a small gold cross. In a lovely bit of continuity, the second-season episode "Ascension" will reveal that Scully's mother gave it to her for her fifteenth birthday.

Unanswered Questions

☒ What did Mulder see at Ellens Air Base? Was it a military craft based on UFO technology, or was it merely an experimental plane developed by the aerospace geniuses right here in the good old U.S.A.? In "Apocrypha" we do see an alien craft that is surprisingly similar to the one shown in this episode. Or is that just a matter of "Great minds think alike"? On the other hand, Deep Throat *does* comment in this episode that "they've" been on Earth for a very long time. (But as Mulder ponders at the end of "E.B.E.", which of his lies are we to believe?)

Plot Oversights

☒ Picture this. You come home to find a military SWAT team surrounding your home. This is the scene that greets Mrs. Budahas as the episode begins. And, after finding out that her husband has broken military protocol and stolen a vehicle, she stands quivering as the team assaults the house. Now, I realize that Mrs. Budahas is distraught, but personally I think I would be shouting "Wait, *wait,* don't smash in the door. Keys, I have *keys. KEYS!*"

☒ Granted, I personally don't know *a lot* of test

pilots but I was always under the impression that these guys were in *top* physical condition. Colonel Robert Budahas seems . . . well . . . downright *pudgy*.

☒ After obtaining a map to Ellens Air Base at a local diner, Mulder takes Scully on a UFO-spotting excursion. Uninterested, she falls asleep in the car. Soon "something" flies overhead—producing an intense shock wave that shatters the back window. Two questions: If the shock wave is that powerful, why doesn't it shatter the windshield as well? And what would a shock wave that powerful do to a person's ears?

☒ As Mulder and Scully watch the pretty lights in the sky, a helicopter chases them away. It also flushes out a pair of young trespassers who crawl through a hole in the fence surrounding Ellens Air Force Base. This happens sometime close to 9:13 P.M., according to the text on the screen. The next scene shows Mulder and Scully with the young people in a diner. The screen says "5:02 A.M." As if they have just settled in, Mulder and Scully begin to question the young couple. Now, even if Mulder and Scully watched the lights for an hour, that still leaves almost seven hours unaccounted for. Did they take the scenic route back to town? Or is it . . . (suspenseful music builds) . . . *missing time?* (Aaaaah!)

☒ After the interview with the young people, Scully scoffs at their testimony, asking Mulder if he saw their eyes—claiming that they were stoned. Yet the guy's eyes appear to be normal! (It was hard to tell with the young woman; her eyes *could* have been dilated.)

☒ And speaking of these young people, I am firmly convinced that they are being controlled by the faire pixies of Out There, a shadow organization ultimately dedicated to revealing the Truth. Consider the evidence. Mulder and Scully

first meet the young couple as they supposedly flee a helicopter. Yet, later in the episode, we learn that the teenagers' normal observation post is a forty-five-minute walk from the base perimeter. How likely is it that these young people outran a helicopter for that distance? Isn't it more likely that they were already on their way to intercept Mulder and Scully when the helicopter began its approach?

And later, when Mulder lets them know that he's planning to go to the infamous "Yellow Base," the female member of the duo shouts, "Don't go past the tall weeds." Yet the teenagers have just said that *no one* has ever gone to Yellow Base. If no one has ever gone that far, how would the young woman know where the tall weeds stop? Finally, as Scully holds an undercover military operative at gunpoint, the pair *just happens* to ride up to disclose Mulder's location so Scully can force the military to release him. Truthfully, doesn't this all seem just a bit *too* coincidental?

☒ And how did Mulder walk *ten miles* in broad daylight across a supersecret base and not get caught?

☒ While sneaking across a runway to get closer to Yellow Base, Mulder stops and stares dumbfounded as a triangle-shaped craft approaches. Then it zips away, and the military police charge his position in a jeep and van. Mulder turns and starts sprinting *straight down* the runway! Is there some reason he isn't heading back into the tall weeds to make his escape?

☒ After capture, Mulder is strapped to a gurney and wheeled through a hangar that houses an experimental craft. Granted, the military is going to wipe his memory, but this still seems odd. I had the privilege of taking the Spirit Tour at Whiteman Air Base in December 1996. In case you don't know, Whiteman AFB houses the B-2 stealth bombers. As a civilian, I could only approach to a distance of one hundred feet

Trivia Questions

❶ What was Paul Mossinger's code name?

❷ Who suggested that Verla McLennon's husband take up fly-fishing?

Trivia Answers
❶ Redbird.
❷ His brother Hank.

from the craft as it sat in its hangar. I was told that if I got any closer, the guards were authorized to shoot! (By the way, a B-2 pilot happened to be there with some friends and—with regard to my comments above on the physical conditioning of test pilots—*that* guy was *obviously* . . . rock-solid.)

Equipment Oddities

☒ And speaking of the back window that shatters, by the time Mulder unloads the teenagers' motorcycle from the trunk the next morning, you can see the back window is *intact*. No doubt Mulder carries a spare in his post-UFO sighting kit (PUFOSK) and installed it during the wee hours of the morning.

☒ I vote we give Scully the nickname "Barney" in honor of Deputy Fife from *The Andy Griffith Show*. At one point in this episode, Mulder and Scully are stopped by a bunch of guys in suits and sunglasses. The guys confiscate their guns and pull the clips. For some unknown reason, Scully has only one bullet loaded!

☒ I suppose I could comment on Scully leaving her weapon in an unlocked motel room as she goes to make a phone call, but I believe I shall postpone. (Maybe "Barney" shot her one bullet the day before and hasn't had a chance to reload?)

Continuity and Production Problems

☒ These guys on the SWAT team at the beginning of the episode must use some new kind of military math. The leader of the unit radios everyone that they are going to go on a count of five. We see a man charge the front steps and flatten against the exterior wall to the right of the front door. Two others approach with a battering ram. The first man holds up his hand and clearly mouths "five." Then he closes his

thumb and pinkie finger to make three followed by two and one. Excuse me, we seem to be missing . . . *four!* (It's so much fun to watch this scene because the actor doing the count realizes what he has done just as his hand closes to three. You can tell that he's ready to say "four," but he's already made the symbol for "three," so he stops and looks sheepish through the rest of the numbers.)

☒ This same numerically challenged SWAT team member is apparently "kicking challenged" as well! Moments after his "missing four" countdown, we see him attempt to kick open a door from a squatting position. He *barely* connects. Thankfully, the door obliges and swings open. (Not a good day for this guy!)

☒ Watch closely as the suited and "sunglassed" goons pull in front of Mulder and Scully's car. It screeches to a halt, and suddenly Mulder no longer drives and Scully no longer rides in the passenger seat. Frighteningly enough, they have been abducted and replaced . . . by *stunt doubles! (Double aaaah!)* For one thing, the guy's face is bigger and more rectangular than Mulder's, and for another, the woman's hair is a good inch longer than Scully's.

Squeeze

Onscreen Locations

☒ Baltimore, Maryland

☒ Crime scene, George Usher's office, Baltimore, Maryland

☒ F.B.I. Bureau, Baltimore, Maryland

☒ Lynne Acres Retirement Home, Baltimore, Maryland

☒ 66 Exeter St.

Ruminations

The date on this episode comes from the program used by Mulder to elongate Tooms's fingerprint. Information scrolls onto the screen indicating that Tooms was arrested on July 23, 1993.

Since I've never seen *Twin Peaks*, I'll have to rely on Jason Allan Haase of Pierce City, Missouri, for this next tidbit. According to Jason, there's a picture hanging on the wall in Mulder's basement office that's very reminiscent of the slain Laura Palmer. Given David Duchovny's role in that series, I certainly wouldn't be surprised if the set designers added this as one of their inside jokes. If you're a *Twin Peaks* fan, take a look. You can see the picture Jason noted in the scene where Mulder shows Scully the elongated fingerprints from previous murder scenes. As Scully backs away in her chair and stands, look for the picture near her head.

Plot Oversights

☒ At the beginning of this episode, Tom Colton tells Scully of a fellow agent who "lucked into" the World Trade Center bombing and was very influential in solving the case. In only two years,

PLOT SUMMARY Tom Colton—a classmate from the Academy at Quantico—asks Scully to look in on a baffling case in Baltimore, Maryland. In the past six weeks there have been three murders in which the killer ripped out his victim's liver with his bare hands but left no clear point of entry to the crime scene. Aware of an X-File with the same details, Mulder tags along and—much to Colton's chagrin—Mulder finds an elongated fingerprint on a small air-conditioning vent at the latest crime scene. Colton immediately dismisses the evidence, but Mulder finds that it matches prints taken from ten other murders: five in 1933, five more in 1963.

Utilizing a profile prepared by Scully, the FBI soon apprehends Eugene Victor Tooms. After passing a lie detector test, however, Tooms is released. Mulder knows it's a mistake. Once elongated, Tooms's fingerprints match those at the crime scenes. Events soon prove Mulder's theory as Tooms stretches himself to squeeze down a chimney and murder a fourth victim.

The next day, Mulder and Scully find a nestlike structure below Tooms's last known residence. It is here that he hibernates between killing sprees—sustained by the stolen livers. In revenge, Tooms decides to make Scully his last victim, but—thankfully—Mulder arrives in time to stop him.

the man has become a supervisory agent. The Real FBI tells me this probably *wouldn't* happen.

☒ The crime scene for the third victim, George Usher, seems a bit too clean. The adult human male body contains approximately six liters of blood. That's a lot. Given that Tooms rips apart his victims to extract their livers, one would expect a bit more carnage. One also would expect a trail of blood back to the vent. Tooms had to crawl up there, and it seems unlikely that the wall wouldn't have a few stains. (Of course, if there were a blood smear up the wall, it would be fairly easy to figure out how the murderer escaped!) On the other hand, perhaps Tooms is so fastidious that he brings a change of clothes and the appropriate number of plastic bags to store his new liver and soiled garments?

❌ In this episode Scully writes a psychological profile on Tooms. In fact, both she and Mulder engage in this activity frequently during the series. At The Real FBI, psychological profiles are created by the Child-Abduction and Serial Killer Unit (CASKU). It's part of the Critical Incident Response Group (CIRG) at Quantico, Virginia.

❌ The polygraph operator says that Tooms "nailed" his polygraph. She adds that he did not kill those two people. Excuse me, miss. Wouldn't that be *three* people at this point in the episode?

❌ And speaking of the polygraph, Mulder has the examiner ask Tooms two additional questions: "Are you over a hundred years old?" and "Have you ever been to Powhatan Mill in 1933?" (Actually the Powhatan Mill question comes in two parts: "Have you ever been to Powhatan Mill?" followed by "In 1933?") During the discussion that follows, Mulder determines that Tooms lied on the added questions, and he identifies them as questions 11 and 13. In fact, they are questions 12 and 14. (The examiner inquires about: 1. his name, 2. his residency, 3. his employment, 4. his intent to lie, 5. his education in general, 6. his medical education in specific, 7. removing a liver, 8. killing a living creature, 9. killing a human being, 10. Usher's office, 11. killing Usher, 12. his age, 13. Powhatan Mill, and 14. Powhatan Mill in 1933.)

❌ You have to appreciate a man who keeps his chimney nearly spotless. The fourth victim,

Thomas Werner, comes home, fixes himself a drink, and proceeds to light a fire (in *July*, no less, but that's another matter). By this time Tooms is already in his living room, having crawled down the chimney. Yet when we see Tooms, he's dirty but not *covered* in soot, as one would expect, and there's no trail from the fireplace to Tooms's hiding spot. (Of course, if there were, Werner might suspect something.)

❌ Following leads, Mulder and Scully interview a retired policeman who tried to solve the murders that Tooms committed in 1933 and 1963. All I can say about this guy is that he is *well* preserved. Yes, he's in a retirement home and looks to be confined to a wheelchair, but the man claims to have retired in 1968 after forty-five years of police work. That means he joined the force in 1923! Since police don't normally hire *children*, his birth year must be somewhere around 1903, making him approximately ninety years old in this episode.

❌ Soon after looking around Tooms's apartment, our heroes discover an opening that leads to a coal cellar and Tooms's hibernation nest. On a small table, Mulder finds a cache of trophies. (Tooms took them from the crime scenes.) For some reason, Mulder picks up one of the objects, thereby contaminating it with his fingerprints.

❌ As the exciting finale of the episode, Tooms attacks Scully in her apartment. Question: How did Tooms find out where Scully lived? (Oh, wait: He probably read it in *The Official Guide to* The X-Files!)

❌ After locating Tooms's abode, Mulder begins a stakeout, and Scully arranges for two agents to relieve him at 11:30 A.M. At some point after this—while it's still daylight—the dweeb Colton calls off the stakeout and tells Scully to go home. Which she does! Why doesn't she meet Mulder at 66 Exeter Street at seven-thirty that evening to tell him what happened? Is she prohibited from *driving by* the location? And, once she returns home, she calls Mulder's answering machine, claiming that she's furious that Colton shut down the operation. If she's "furious," why hasn't she called Mulder on his cell phone?! This has to be *hours* after Colton told her he called off the stakeout.

☒ Toward the end of the episode, the creators fudge a bit on the timelines. We see Scully start a bath at her apartment. Then we see Mulder discover that Tooms is going after Scully next. (He sees her necklace among Tooms's collection.) At this point, he's in Baltimore. Back at Scully's apartment, she finishes running the water for her bath when some of Tooms's bile guck drips on her hand. (That'll teach him not to slobber when he's "peeping.") Scully runs for her gun, and Tooms quickly attacks. Moments later, Mulder bursts in to save the day. Now—according to *The Official Guide*—Scully's apartment is in Annapolis (although "Grotesque" seems to indicate that it's in Washington, D.C.). My map says that there are *twenty-two miles* between Baltimore and Annapolis. How did Mulder get there so fast?

☒ I really was appalled with the scene that shows the old detective learning of Tooms's arrest by *reading* the paper. He provided Mulder and Scully with *critical* corroborating evidence on the case, and they didn't have the *decency* to pay him another visit and tell him of Tooms's capture in person?

Equipment Oddities

☒ Tooms gains entry to Usher's office by unscrewing the vent cover from the inside. Two items here. First, Tooms unscrews only *one* screw and removes the cover. The other three aren't attached to anything? (I guess we should mark this up to shoddy workmanship.) Second, how is Tooms unscrewing even this one screw? Normally, the holes for the screws on an air han-

dling vent reside *outside* the area enclosed by duct because the screw has to be screwed into something like a wall stud.

☒ The function of eyeglasses is to bend light and focus it correctly on the retina. If you take any pair of prescription eyeglasses and use them to catch a reflection, you'll see that the image is distorted. Oddly enough, the glasses that Mulder wears in this episode (when he first tells Scully about the matching fingerprints) show no distortion in the reflection. The lenses appear to be flat pieces of thin glass, which means they have no prescription. So why does Mulder wear them? Just to look cool?

☒ The telephone junction box at Scully's apartment building is interesting. It's labeled with the occupants' names! I suppose that makes it easier for would-be burglars to know which wire to cut. (By the way, some have taken the number below Scully's name, "403," to be her apartment number, but Scully's door clearly reads "35" when Mulder bursts through.)

☒ Mulder must use "anti-stretchy-guy" handcuffs. For some mysterious reason, the same guy who can squish himself through the tiniest space can't slip out of the handcuffs after Mulder slaps them on.

Continuity and Production Problems

☒ When we first see Usher's office, a close-up centers on an area near the phone. There's a Sno-Globe and a hippopotamus nearby. Then the camera angle changes and the hippopotamus leaps across the desk! A coffee cup takes its place. Good thing, too, because moments later, Usher picks up the cup.

☒ I covered the lack of blood at Usher's office under Plot Oversights since it directly affected the plot, but there's another item about the

FIRST SEASON

Trivia Questions

❶ According to this episode, who works as a supervisory special agent for Foreign Counterintelligence's New York City bureau?

❷ What did Tooms take as a souvenir in the Walters murder?

Trivia Answers
❶ Marty Neil.
❷ A hairbrush.

13

Squeeze

crime scene that seems odd. Usher takes his coffee mug into the hall, fills the mug, and returns to his office. Very shortly after entering the room, Tooms attacks. Later we see the mug lying on its side at the edge of Usher's desk. There *is* a puddle of coffee on the carpet, but nowhere else. How did this happen? If somebody attacked me, that coffee cup would get *launched*. It *might* land on the desk, but there would be coffee everywhere. It definitely would not look like someone set the mug near the edge of the desk and then tipped over the mug with the *greatest* measure of gentility!

X The sound effects guys got a little "dub-happy" as Mulder approaches Scully during a stakeout. When she snaps her gun into position, they added the sound for racking the slide. (Now, I suppose the recoil spring on her pistol might be broken, causing the slide to flop around, but if that's the case, she needs to have it repaired immediately!)

X The canister of matches near Thomas Werner's fireplace seems to have a mind of its own. Just before Tooms attacks, Werner kneels and opens the wire mesh that hangs in front of his fireplace. At this point the matches rest on the hearth to the right of the fireplace opening. A reverse angle shows Werner leaning back, but

when we return to the previous shot, the matches have somehow migrated to a spot on Werner's left.

X Does the hole in the wall that leads to Tooms's nest seem a bit *oversized* for a guy who can stretch himself through tiny air handling ducts?

Conduit

Onscreen Locations

🗶 Sioux City, Iowa

🗶 FBI Regional Headquarters, Sioux City, Iowa

🗶 Lake Okobogee, Iowa, Campsite 53

Ruminations

The date for this episode comes from the cover sheet on a fax that Mulder sends to the ubiquitous "Danny."

Also, I believe this is the first episode where we get a hint that Scully carries a cell phone as well. In her hotel room, we see her gun, handcuffs, her writing pad, and the phone on a dresser. (I suppose we could wonder why Mulder didn't try her cell phone in the last episode as he raced to her apartment to warn her about Tooms.)

It's not really a nit, but this episode has some strange timing in the dialogue between Mulder and Scully. On the way to Lake Okobogee for the first time, Mulder and Scully discuss Kevin. The dialogue stops dead and then both actors seem to be scrambling to get to their lines. It struck me as unusual the first time I heard it, and it still does after multiple viewings.

On the other hand, there is a very nice sequence of dialogue at the end of this episode as we listen to a regression hypnosis session in which Mulder tells of Samantha's disappearance. As we see Mulder start to cry, seated in a church, we hear how a voice told Mulder that his sister would be okay. The therapist asks Mulder if he believes the voice. Mulder replies, "I want to believe," giving the poster in his office a new layer of meaning.

PLOT SUMMARY

In Sioux City, Iowa, Mulder and Scully investigate the disappearance of Ruby Morris. Her mother, Darlene, claims Ruby was abducted by aliens. The Sioux City sheriff believes Ruby ran away. For a time, it appears that the sheriff is right. Another young woman, named Tessa, comes forward to claim that a biker-bartender named Greg Randall had gotten Ruby pregnant and that he and Ruby were planning to meet the night she disappeared. Mulder and Scully soon discover that Tessa is the one who is pregnant and that she murdered Randall the night Ruby disappeared.

With Ruby still missing, Mulder returns to the case's most baffling element. Ever since Ruby disappeared, her little brother Kevin has scrawled long strings of binary code (1s and 0s). He claims to receive the information from television. Strangely enough, analysis reveals the seemingly random numbers are actually fragments of digitized pictures and music—even a portion of a secret satellite transmission. Mulder believes that Kevin was touched in some way by the abduction, and in short order the young boy produces a multipage binary portrait of his older sister. Then Ruby unexpectedly returns. For Mulder, it's a prime opportunity to learn more about alien abductions. Medical evidence *does* indicate a prolonged period of weightlessness. Unfortunately, Darlene won't allow any further investigation, and Ruby says "they" told her not to tell.

Plot Oversights

🗶 After meeting with Darlene and Kevin, Mulder takes seventy-seven pages of Kevin's manuscript to the local FBI office and faxes them to Washington. In short order the National

Security Administration (NSA) shows up because a portion of the information contained an excerpt from a highly classified Defense Department satellite transmission. At five-thirty in the morning, NSA agents burst into Scully's motel room, demanding to know Mulder's location. In the first place, the camera shot of the room shows us that Scully left her gun all the way across the room on a dresser instead of keeping it on her nightstand. Why? Why bother to carry a weapon if you aren't going to keep it nearby to defend yourself? Second, why is the NSA barging into Scully's room looking for *Mulder?* When we see Mulder, he has his shirt off and his hair's all messed up—apparently he was sleeping. If he was sleeping, he was probably in his room at the motel. (Okay . . . he *might* have been somewhere else, but there's no indication of that, so *go* with me on this!) If he's in his room, why didn't the NSA check there first? Are they just trying to wake up as many people as possible? (Or do they know something we don't? Wait. Never mind. Forget I brought it up.)

🅇 Scully needs to brush up on her CPR. After Ruby is returned, we see Scully doing chest compressions on the young woman, but she never bothers to follow up with mouth-to-mouth resuscitation. Even stranger, Scully comments that Ruby is "unconscious but alive." If she's "alive," wouldn't she have a heartbeat? And if Ruby has a heartbeat, why is Scully pumping on her chest?

Equipment Oddities

🅇 At the beginning of this episode, we see Darlene Morris sleeping in a camper, with Ruby and Kevin outside, around a campfire. Everything starts to shake. Dishes fall out of the cabinet. Kevin hollers. Darlene leaps up and grabs the doorknob but it sears her hand. The implication is that the "something" outside has heated the metal doorknob. There's only one problem. Moments later, Darlene runs down the metal stairs of the camper in her bare feet, and she seems just fine. So either the metal cooled very quickly, or the "something" heated the doorknob but not the stairs.

🅇 So let's talk about Kevin's binary dictation. (A *really* nice plot idea, by the way!) It looks like Kevin gets about twenty-four 1s and 0s to a line. And when the head NSA guy pulls a stack of papers out of Kevin's drawer, it appears that there are twenty-seven lines per page. In addition, Agent Atsumi of the FBI regional office indicates that they scanned seventy-seven pages. Sounds like a lot, doesn't it? Seventy-seven pages, each with twenty-seven lines, each with twenty-four binary digits.

Well . . . it's not! Since there are eight bits (1s and 0s) to a byte, each line of Kevin's tome corresponds to about three bytes. If there are approximately twenty-seven lines per page, that's about eighty-one bytes per page. Multiply that by seventy-seven and you get about six kilobytes. Supposedly in those six kilobytes there are—among other things—a reproduction of a work by da Vinci, a *digital video* clip, and an excerpt from a Brandenburg concerto. When the Brandenburg concerto plays, the computer screen shows us a graph of digitized audio that plays for four seconds. Just to be fair, let's say that the sample rate is fairly low and slow. CD-quality digital stereo music requires two channels that use sixteen bit samples taken at a rate of approximately 44,000 samples *per second*, but let's say that this music was digitally recorded in mono, with an eight-bit sample at only twelve thousand samples per second. At that rate we would blow through Kevin's *entire* seventy-seven-page manuscript in . . . half a second. And while it *might* be possible to reproduce a portion of da Vinci's Universal Man in black-and-white and utilize only six kilobytes, I assure you that—without some kind of amazing fractal compression scheme—there is *no way* that six kilobytes of data could reproduce the DNA video shown on the computer screen!

☒ After Mulder and Scully discover the body of Greg Randall at Lake Okobogee, a forensics team comes to the gravesite. Watch the photographer: he not only has a lens-mounted ring flash on his camera, he has a handheld flash as well. Surprisingly enough, *neither* go off when he takes a picture. Yet he continues to take pictures off-camera, and there's *never* any corresponding flash of light!

Continuity and Production Problems

☒ As Scully and Mulder walk down the hall at the end of the episode, watch the small cross Scully wears. When the shot changes to a close-up, it suddenly jumps inside her shirt.

Trivia Questions

❶ What is the name of Darlene Morris's ex-husband?

❷ What are the date and time of Tessa's appointment with Dr. Fowler?

Trivia Answers
❶ Charles.
❷ August 7, 2:30 (presumably P.M.).

The Jersey Devil

PLOT SUMMARY Hearing Scully tell of a homeless man found in the woods near Atlantic City with his arm chewed off—apparently by a human predator—Mulder immediately concludes that it is the work of the Jersey Devil, a beast-man and topic of a long-standing, unsolved X-File.

Unfortunately, the Atlantic City Police Department has decided to treat the case as a homicide. The officer in charge "politely" asks the pair to leave, but—of course—Mulder stays. He finds a park ranger named Peter Brouillet, who admits seeing a creature like the Jersey Devil four years ago. Mulder also finds a homeless man who says he's seen it recently. That night, Mulder sees something as well, only to be apprehended by the Atlantic City police and given an "invitation" to return to Washington.

Then Brouillet calls with news that he has found the body of a beast-man—dead for six to eight months. Realizing that what he saw was actually the beast-man's mate, Mulder returns to Atlantic City with Scully, eventually locating the beast-woman before she retreats into the woods. Unfortunately, the police soon find her as well and shoot her like a rabid animal. When postmortems on both bodies indicate the probability of offspring, Mulder speculates that the beast-woman was merely protecting her young. As the episode ends, we see she was.

Onscreen Locations

- ☒ New Jersey, 1947
- ☒ Atlantic City Morgue
- ☒ Outskirts of Atlantic City
- ☒ University of Maryland

Ruminations

The date for this episode comes from the toe tag on the homeless man, Roger Crockett.

By the way, did you notice that the same actor plays the 1947 dad at the beginning of this episode and the present-day dad at the end?

Did Chris Carter give himself a cameo at the beginning of this episode? One of the policemen in the opening sequence looks a lot like him!

Geographical Inconsistencies

☒ This episode prominently features dense woods that seem to run right up to the edge of Atlantic City. Geoffrey Gould of Verona, New Jersey, assures me that Atlantic City has the Atlantic Ocean on one side and miles and miles of swamps and wetlands on the other. There are no forests with hard-packed dirt for flooring. (Geoffrey also commented that the back alleys shown in this episode look like none he's ever seen in Atlantic City.)

Plot Oversights

☒ Not to be gruesome, but one wonders why the beast-woman chewed off the homeless guy's *arm*. After all, there is more meat on a thigh, right? (And what about a rump roast? To quote Mulder, "With a little twist of lemon, if you'll pardon the expression, it's to die for.")

☒ Along the same lines, hasn't this beast-woman ever heard of a doggie bag? Granted, no one expects her to eat an entire human in one sitting, but why leave the remains for the park ranger to find? Why not drag it back to home, sweet home for leftovers?

X There's some confusion over the actual days of this episode. Kicked out of the morgue, Mulder suggests to Scully that they make a weekend of it in Atlantic City. Scully declines and promptly finds the car keys in her hand. Mulder has decided to stay anyway. Reacting, Scully complains that it's a three-hour drive back in Friday night traffic. From this, it's safe to assume that Scully believes it's Friday. Yet, at the beginning of the episode, Scully states that the homeless man was found "yesterday," and only a bit later Mulder walks among the homeless, shouting that Crockett was murdered "two days ago." Now, Crockett's toe tag carries a date of August 29, 1993. It doesn't matter whether this is the date of his death or date when his body was discovered, because August 29, 1993, was a *Sunday.* So Mulder and Scully had to arrive in Atlantic City on either a Monday or a Tuesday.

X The sidebar "Whose Truth Is Out There" examines the approaches used by Mulder and Scully when they speak of "The Truth." To the creators' credit, they are *very* thorough in their understanding of these characters and how their personal belief structures cause them to react to various situations. As discussed in "Whose Truth," Mulder's obsession often drives him to act in ways that are counterproductive to his goals—taunting those who don't believe as he does. For example, in this episode, Mulder searches for some evidence of the Jersey Devil and interviews a homeless man who says that he's seen the creature. During the interview, the homeless man shows Mulder a crudely drawn picture of the Jersey Devil. Mulder—in typical Mulder fashion—seizes on this tenuous piece of evidence simply because he *believes* it contains truth. So far, so good. It does seem reasonable that Mulder would do this. A short time

later, however, Mulder actually presents this document to the police chief of Atlantic City to strengthen his case during an argument! (This is when I started laughing.) And he actually looks serious when he does it!

X After rescuing Mulder from the drunk tank, Scully takes him to see Dr. Diamond, one of her professors at the University of Maryland. While discussing the food chain, Mulder suggests the existence of a human who has reverted to animalistic behavior—like the Jersey Devil—something akin to a carnivorous Neanderthal. He wonders if this creature would occupy the space *above* humanity on the food chain. Diamond seems to agree. I find this an odd conclusion. Why would humanity's highly evolved traits suddenly be worthless to protect us just because some biped carnivores happened along? Wouldn't our intelligence still give us an edge? And what of our *highly evolved* machetes, machine guns, hand grenades, and tactical nuclear warheads? Those would be good for a grunt or two, wouldn't they?

X This same Dr. Diamond—a professor of anthropology—makes a fascinating statement as the search begins for the beast-woman. He tells Mulder that if the beast-woman is a primate, she would have a natural fear of heights. *Primates* have a natural fear of heights?! That must be why you *never* see monkeys climbing trees!

X During the search for the beast-woman, the searchers make an amazing amount of noise. For some reason, the searchee—the same creature who bolted into the night at the first whiff of a human—hangs around long enough to have her encounter with Mulder. (I suspect that she likes him. After all, she does need a new mate. And Mulder *does* seem intrigued by her wardrobe—which, if you recall, is *nothing at all!*)

FIRST SEASON

Trivia Questions

1 What is the first name of the woman who examines the body of the homeless man?

2 What is the name of Scully's date?

Trivia Answers
1 Glenna.
2 Rob.

"Keep that up, Mulder, and I'll hurt you like that beast-woman."

—**Scully** *to Mulder after he wonders if she has a life, since she canceled a date to accompany him to the Smithsonian.*

☒ In addition to Mulder's odd use of the crude drawing, mentioned above, this episode also contains an odd character bit from the other side of the spectrum. During the final race to get to the beast-woman before the police kill her, Mulder actually *stops* in the forest and *waits* for the others in his party to catch up. Does this seem typical for Mulder? Wouldn't he normally set his face toward the goal and forget about the others?

☒ It's appalling, I tell you, *truly . . . appalling!* In this age of deficit spending and huge government debt, it's almost unbelievable to see the kind of gross, unnecessary fiscal flagrance as displayed by Mulder (and Scully!) at the end of this episode. Mulder says that he has an appointment at the Smithsonian to speak with an ethnobiologist. Presumably this appointment is at the Museum of Natural History. Yet Mulder *requisitions a car!* A check of any Washington, D.C., map will show that the Museum of Natural History is *one block south* of the J. Edgar Hoover Building! (And even if the appointment is elsewhere among the Smithsonian buildings, most are close to the Mall, and D.C. has a wonderful subway system called the Metro. Or is Mulder *too sophisticated* to ride the Metro?)

Continuity and Production Problems

☒ Given my ineptitude in the matter, I rarely comment on matters of style, but my daughter, Elizabeth, found Scully's white hose at the beginning of this episode unsatisfactory given that *nothing* else in her ensemble complements them.

☒ After the police kill the beast-woman, Mulder approaches, kneels down, and uses his hand to close her eyes. Miraculously, her left eyelid closes though Mulder's palm doesn't even come close to touching it!

Shadows

Onscreen Locations

☒ HTG Industrial Technologies, Philadelphia, PA

☒ Bethesda Naval Hospital, Bethesda, Maryland

☒ Broad Street, Philadelphia, PA

☒ National Bureau of Medical Examiners, Philadelphia, PA

☒ University of Pennsylvania Hospital, Tissue Bank

☒ Monroe Mutual Insurance Co., Omaha, Nebraska

Ruminations

The date on this episode comes from the automated teller footage that Mulder and Scully watch, athough, technically, the start date for the pair's involvement is a day later, since they seem to meet with the NSA sometime in the early morning hours of September 23, 1993 (most likely around 6:00 A.M.).

During this episode, Kyte visits her boss's grave. After she leaves, Mulder and Scully walk up and examine the area. They ask the groundskeeper about Howard Graves and his relationship to Sarah Lynn Graves (buried right beside him). The groundskeeper then proceeds to give them a detailed history of how Sarah Lynn died as a child—including the fact that Graves's wife divorced him a year later and is buried on the other side of the cemetery! I gotta tell ya—this guy was creepin' me out! You have to wonder how he got all this information. (Maybe he's just one of those guys everyone talks to?)

PLOT SUMMARY

Unexpectedly, Mulder and Scully are called to the Bethesda Naval Hospital morgue to view a pair of corpses. Both bodies show residual electrostatic charge. Both have throats crushed from the inside out. Two tight-lipped agents from the NSA ask if Mulder and Scully have encountered the phenomena in the X-Files. Mulder says no but manages to lift a pair of prints before leaving. He thinks the men were killed by psychokinesis and wants to investigate further.

Using the prints, Mulder and Scully trace the dead men—members of a terrorist group called Isfahan—to Philadelphia and locate the crime scene. Surveillance footage from a nearby automated teller shows the men attacking Lauren Kyte. Kyte's boss, Howard Graves, recently died. Isfahan has been purchasing restricted technology from Graves's company, but Graves was about to confess to the authorities so Graves's partner, Robert Dorlund, had him killed. Now Graves's ghost is protecting Lauren to keep Dorlund from harming her.

Instead of chasing after supernatural shadows, Scully uses Lauren's belief that her boss has returned from the grave to talk the young woman into cooperating. She agrees to help them search for evidence detailing the sales to Isfahan. At first they find nothing. Then, in spectral frenzy, Graves trashes Dorlund's office and cuts open a wall covering to reveal an all-important diskette.

Plot Oversights

☒ Two hours after the men from Isfahan attack Kyte, a young couple wanders by the crime scene. Looking for a place to stay the night, they decide to climb up a fire escape. The young man lifts the young woman, and she begins tugging on the fire escape ladder. Eventually she dislodges the two bodies of the men from Isfahan. The young people scream and run away. Oddly enough, when Mulder and Scully arrive in Philadelphia, the scene begins with a shot of the fire escape, and you can see right through the metal grating. So why couldn't the young people see those two bodies before they fell?

🅇 Not only do Mulder and Scully determine that Lauren Kyte is their next lead by examining the video of the automated teller, they also discover a streaked image to the left of Lauren as she is attacked by the two men from Isfahan. Scully believes that the image belongs to the person who protected Kyte from harm. In the subsequent interview, Scully hands Kyte a printout of the frame that contains the image. But the image is really nothing more than a smear. How can Scully expect Kyte to identify it? (I half-expected Kyte to roll her eyes and say, "Why, sure I recognize that person. It's Mr. Blurry from down the street!")

🅇 Leaving Kyte's house, Mulder and Scully enter their rental car. The doors suddenly lock. The engine revs. The car puts itself in reverse and fires backward for some undetermined distance before smashing into another vehicle. Then Mulder looks up and Kyte closes her curtains. The creators make it look like Kyte could still see them, but—while there's no way to prove that she couldn't—I find it very difficult to believe that she could because of the angles involved. (I know it. I just *know* it! Hey, if it's good enough for Mulder . . .)

🅇 At this point in the series, Mulder is the one who gets the ringside seat for the spectacular paranormal displays. Scully is left to her science. At times, though, the creators' efforts to ensure this formula seem a bit forced. In this episode, Mulder and Scully arrive at Kyte's house as Graves has his way with two thugs.

Kyte provides a screaming accompaniment. As the car stops, Mulder leaps into action, racing inside. Scully twiddles with her seat belt. And twiddles. And twiddles. By the time she finally makes it to the house, the show is over. (Guess we'll never have to worry about her getting out of one of those child-safety harnesses! See "The Calusari.")

Equipment Oddities

🅇 The use of videotape in *The X-Files* has always made me happy—specifically, rocking the tape back and forth, freeze-framing, step advance, all things that are near and dear to my little nitpicker's heart. In this episode, Mulder and Scully examine the videotape from an automated teller and find a streaked image that appears during Kyte's attack (the personable and kind "Mr. Blurry" mentioned above). Ever the eagle-eyed observer, Mulder spots it immediately and rewinds the tape to time index 9:45:24. However, if *you* rewind *your* tape and step-advance through the same footage that Mulder watches before he spots this image, you might discover something astonishing. The streak isn't there at first! It appears only *after* Mulder rewinds the tape! (See now, *that's* why he's a special agent for the FBI and I only sit in my basement and watch television. I can't see it the first time through, but Mulder somehow knew that if he rewound the tape it would magically appear!)

🅇 The crucial piece of evidence needed to charge Dorlund is a diskette. It's hidden in an upholstered wall covering. Yet, there doesn't seem to be any way to get *to* the diskette without cutting open the wall. Was that just his safety-safety-safety backup?

Continuity and Production Problems

🅇 Howard Graves's headstone deserves a bit of

GREAT LINES
"My advice to you: Don't get rough with her."

—**Mulder** *to the NSA just before they interview Lauren Kyte. (From the smirk on Mulder's face you can almost hear him thinking, "I know something you don't know.")*

scrutiny. It records his death on October 5, 1993. Interestingly enough, the two guys from Isfahan attempt to mug Lauren Kyte on September 22, and Graves supposedly died "a couple of weeks" *before* that, not after!

☒ Near the beginning of the episode, Mulder and Scully interview Kyte in her home. The first time she opens her door, the latticework behind our dynamic duo is covered with leaves. Near the middle of the episode, Mulder charges up the stairs of Kyte's home as Graves murders two assassins. There's a lightning flash that shows the latticework is still covered with leaves. Sometime between these two events, Mulder takes a surveillance photo of the house. Guess what? The latticework doesn't have any leaves! (Yes, there is enough time for Kyte to rip out all the foliage and replant it a few days later . . . but why would she?)

☒ I love the guy who helps Mulder and Scully analyze the photo of Kyte's house. Watch his reaction when Mulder observes that Howard Graves might still be dead, even though they are staring at a picture of the man. While Scully gives Mulder a puzzled look, the guy at the desk stares straight ahead. (No doubt he's thinking, "And that's why they call him 'Spooky,' friends and neighbors.")

Trivia Questions

❶ When is Howard Graves's birthday?

❷ What was the final destination of Howard Graves's liver?

PERSONAL FAVORITES

I've said it before, I'll say it again: I'm not sure why these nits and "odd little moments" are some of my favorites. Some I caught the first time through. Some came only after multiple viewings. Some were submitted by proud members of the Nitpickers Guild and confirmed with a smile as I saw them, too. I hope you enjoy them as well!

1 *Four? We don't need stinkin' four!* During the teaser of "Deep Throat" a military assault team breaks into the home of Colonel Robert Budahas. At the front door, an officer gives a silent countdown. He mouths "five" and then draws his thumb to his pinkie finger to hold up three fingers. A befuddled look crosses the actor's face when he realizes what he has done but he stays with the scene, finishing the countdown before the troops break down the door.

2 *I prefer white meat.* Like surgeries, medical autopsies are performed using scalpels with single-use, disposable blades. In "Miracle Man," Dr. Scully takes a more novel approach. We join the scene as she sharpens a long butcher knife (shwick, shwick)! Honestly, it looks like she is getting ready to carve up the Thanksgiving turkey.

3 *This isn't going to be on the test, is it?* "Sleepless" contains a scene set at Quantico. Scully is lecturing on the effects of electrocution. A body lays before her. Students stand on the other side of the table. The camera pans around a particular young female student who appears to be taking notes. Except . . . the pages in her notebook are completely blank! Obviously, she's decided that Scully's lecture is *decoy* information.

4 *Is this a secret message to X-philes everywhere?* In case you missed the call to arms, the American flag in Skinner's office is hanging upsidedown when Scully meets with him during "End Game."

5 *When the moon is in the seventh house . . .* During "Fearful Symmetry," Mulder tells zoo administrator Willa Ambrose that the reason her abducted animals aren't being properly returned is because of "astrological variance." Evidently, the alien who was operating the teleportation controls was having a bad horoscope day!

6 *No comment.* There's an odd moment in "Humbug." Scully is attempting to arrest Dr. Blockhead and secure his hands behind his back with handcuffs. Being the escape artist that he is, Blockhead slips out, spins, and locks Scully in her own bracelets before fleeing. Well . . . almost. Using frame advance, an interesting tidbit comes to light. As Blockhead bolts into the night, *only one* handcuff is actually attached to Scully's wrist. The other swings free. The very next time we see Scully, however, she is fashionably attired with *both* handcuffs secured to her wrists, and Scully appears to the be only person who could have accomplished this intriguing deed. (There is really *nothing* I can say at this point that wouldn't get me into trouble, so I believe I shall postpone.)

7 *They kill chickens, don't they?* I'm fascinated by the town of Dudley, Arkansas. During "Our Town," we learn that the good townsfolk have discovered the secret to long life. And what do they do with this amazing knowledge? They work in a chicken processing plant! Not that there's anything *wrong* with working in a chicken processing plant. It's just not the type of thing that I'd want to do for the rest of my *very long* life!

8 *I'm kneeling and I can't get up.* Surprisingly enough, "Our Town" contains another of my personal favorites! At the end of the episode, the townsfolk prepare to make a stew out of Scully. They secure her head in a metal device that's supposed to hold her tight. From all appearances, however, Scully should be able to jerk her head loose. But . . . she doesn't! She remains on her knees—looking scared.

9 *I suppose some would say it's better than HBO!* In "Tunguska," we get our first look at Skinner's new apartment building. It looks identical to the building that housed an escort service in "Avatar." In addition—during that episode—Skinner was "entertained" by one of its prostitutes. Hmmm. I wonder why Skinner chose this *particular* building for his new residence. (I know the creators attempt to hide the fact that it's the same building, but. . . .)

10 *Aura Photography Sleight-of-Hand.* During "Leonard Betts," Dr. Charles Burks demonstrates the amazing properties of aura photography to Mulder and Scully. Except, he cheats! He slips an undeveloped piece of film into a tray of liquid and then reaches *under* that piece of film to extract an already doctored image.

Ghost in the Machine

PLOT SUMMARY

When Benjamin Drake—CEO of Eurisko—is found murdered, Special Agent Jerry Lamana asks his old friend Mulder to assist with the investigation. Though all the clues point to Eurisko's disenfranchised founder, Brad Wilczek, Mulder believes that the central operating system (COS) of Eurisko's World Headquarters building is actually responsible. Wilczek's goal was to create a thinking computer. Benjamin Drake had threatened to close down the project, and Mulder speculates that COS killed Drake in an act of self-preservation. Lamana and Scully are happy to support the more conventional suspect, and Lamana leaves to make the arrest.

Meanwhile, Wilczek heads to the Eurisko building, determined to learn what really happened. Aghast, he watches COS kill Lamana as well. Wilczek then confesses to both crimes, knowing that a thinking computer—no matter how murderous—would be the Holy Grail to some elements of the military. By taking the blame, he hopes that no one will suspect COS. In short order, Mulder visits Wilczek in prison and convinces him that COS must be destroyed before it can kill again. Wilczek writes a virus. Mulder and Scully deliver it—despite the obstacles. Then Wilczek disappears, kidnapped by those who would capitalize on his work. And COS? At first it appears destroyed, but as the episode ends, some part of it comes back to life.

Onscreen Locations

- ☒ Eurisko World Headquarters, Crystal City, Virginia
- ☒ Federal Detention Center, Washington, D.C.

Ruminations

The date for this episode comes from Scully's field journal entry.

Plot Oversights

☒ Does it strike anyone else odd that Benjamin Drake—CEO of a major corporation such as Eurisko—would type his own correspondence, as he does at the beginning of the episode? Must be a "hands on" guy!

☒ I'm a bit confused by the attempt to discontinue the COS project. It evidently runs the entire World Headquarters of Eurisko. Wouldn't the discontinuing of COS result in a massive overhaul of the building? Or does Drake merely wish to discontinue new research when it comes to COS? And if Drake is simply going to discontinue the research, then why does COS feel threatened enough to kill? It seems to be learning just fine on its own.

☒ Scully poses a strange question in her field journal. She wonders if Brad Wilczek is a genius and writes that she doesn't know. Well, let's see. Mulder said the guy had an IQ of 220 so, um, yeah, sounds like he's a genius, Scully!

☒ There's an old, unkind joke that made the rounds a few years back. Question: How do you know if a blonde's been using your computer? Answer: There's Wite-Out on the screen. Unkind as it is, that joke popped into my brain during a scene from this episode. Mulder and Scully have just proven that Wilczek's voice is the voice on the last telephone call Drake received before he died. They perform this feat with a computer spectrogram that can identify individual speech patterns. Telling Lamana of this new evidence, Scully drives home her point by reaching up and *drawing* on the computer monitor with a red marker! (Leading to the new incarnation of the joke: How do you know if *Scully's* been using . . .)

🔏 Why does Lamana struggle to get to his feet when COS sends the elevator rocketing *downward?* Wouldn't he almost *float* off the floor?

🔏 Honestly, did anyone else think, "What are you doing, Dave?" near the end of this episode? (HAL from *2001: A Space Odyssey.*)

Equipment Oddities

🔏 Granted, everyone is for energy conservation, but the *invasiveness* of the computer control in this building has an obsessive/compulsive air about it. Evidently COS controls the stopper in Drake's sink! (Just before he's electrocuted, Drake walks into the bathroom and finds his sink overflowing.) No wonder this project is losing money! How much did it cost to fit every sink with a little servomotor so COS would lower the stopper?!

🔏 And while we're engaged in bathroom humor, why is a card key necessary to enter *and exit* the CEO's private bathroom? What self-respecting CEO would put up with a computer making an entry in a database every time he visited the rest room? (Not only that, COS apparently takes *pictures* of you while you're in there!)

🔏 On a related subject, Benjamin Drake dies when he attempts to put his override key in a slot beside the door. COS sends an electrical charge into the lock and launches him backward ten feet through the air. One has to wonder what idiot on the Buildings and Zoning Commission of Crystal City, Virginia, approved the placement of

a high-voltage power conduit so near this panel. This is definitely not your standard 110 volts. (I've been crossways with 110 volts before, and it doesn't do this!) Even 220 won't throw you across the room. Even stranger, the dialogue seems to indicate that the voltage was routed *through* an integrated circuit panel! Most integrated circuits run on 5 and/or 12 volts, not 500.

🔏 In one scene, Scully finishes a field journal entry at her home. She reaches toward the screen and there is the distinct click of a mechanical switch. She gets up, turns off a lamp, and wanders into her bedroom. Along the way, you can see that the monitor's indicator light is off. Then the camera pans back to the computer and the monitor's indicator light is somehow back on. In short order, the computer comes to life because COS wants to read Scully's field journal. The obvious question is: How did COS—residing in Crystal City—turn on Scully's home computer? (All right, enough with the wisecracks about COS sending it erotic data! Sorry, sorry. We now resume our regularly scheduled *family* programming.)

True, Scully *might* have a remote activation device on her computer—allowing her to call her home from far-flung, exotic locales and download her field journal. But here's what's really strange about this sequence: The telephone never rings. Later in the episode, Scully discovers that COS has tapped into her computer because her telephone rings and when she picks up the receiver, she hears data transmission tones. Why then doesn't the telephone ring the *first* time COS pays an uninvited visit? Answer: Because Scully can't know about COS intrusion at this point for the plot to work. So all the ringers in Scully's apartment conspire against her and forget to operate! (No doubt they read the script.)

🔏 Attempting to prove that Wilczek murdered Drake, Scully reviews a series of lectures Wilczek gave at the Smithsonian. She uses a

Trivia Questions

1 At what age did Brad Wilczek start Eurisko?

2 With which congressman did Mulder consult concerning Wilczek's whereabouts?

Trivia Answers
1 Twenty-two years old.
2 Congressman Klebanow.

DAT (digital audio tape) recorder, but the sound effect used for rewinding is definitely from an analog tape recorder.

☒ Knowing that COS murdered Drake, Wilczek goes to the Eurisko building to instruct his creation in the ways of gentility and kindness. Lamana follows and soon plays patty-cake with an elevator. (The elevator wins.) During this sequence, Wilczek attempts to save Lamana's life by rushing to the main breakers for the computer and turning them off. It does no good. Wait a minute: How can a computer possibly keep running after its main breakers are shut off? Did it somehow *rewire* itself?! (Or . . . did the building super—who's really a military man—think ahead far enough to rewire the breakers *just in case* Wilczek tried to annihilate COS?)

☒ Evidently, the same Buildings and Zoning Commission that approved gigawatt power conduits running next to access panels also made an exception for Eurisko when it came to emergency stops on elevators. Normally, COS couldn't kill Lamana by sending the elevator hurtling downward because the *mechanical, non-computerized* stops would engage and keep the elevator from falling any farther.

☒ After Lamana dies, we see Mulder sitting in his darkened office watching his friend plummet to his death. Mulder's hand—clutching the ever-useful remote control—rises, and the screen changes to show Wilczek pleading with COS. Then Mulder rewinds the tape, and the tape continues to show Wilczek pleading with COS. What happened to the footage of Lamana? Does Mulder have some kind of multichannel VCR that can record two video signals on the same tape? (Those FBI guys get all the cool toys.) Or is he actually running two decks with two tapes and he has them perfectly synced? (It *is* possible. I do it when I'm comparing footage from two different episodes.)

☒ Why doesn't COS have audio on its video feeds? It's not like Eurisko was trying to save money. They put little motors on the sink stoppers, for crying out loud!

☒ And who's *brilliant* idea was it to install turbojet engines in the air handling ducts?! Attempting to gain access to the twenty-ninth floor, Scully climbs into the ductwork. COS decides to thwart her effort by engaging the blowers—blowers that have so much power they send Scully hurtling toward her doom. Do you know much airflow you have to have to suck a one-hundred-pound woman across an air handling duct?

☒ The building super—who is supposedly also a trained military operative—makes an astonishingly simple blunder when disarming Mulder. He tells Mulder to drop the clip on his weapon, but he never has Mulder rack the slide. If Mulder has a round chamber, he can still fire.

☒ And *finally*, I find it incredible that COS can still function even a bit—as it does at the end—with its circuit boards lying in piles around the room!

Continuity and Production Problems

☒ Watch closely as HAL—I mean COS—gives its death performance. The building super looks at Scully and then looks back, but it's the same footage both times. The creators just ran it backward for the second segment.

Ice

Onscreen Locations

X Arctic Ice Core Project, Icy Cape, Alaska,
  250 miles north of the Arctic Circle

X Doolittle Airfield, Nome, Alaska

Ruminations

Well, this is an exciting episode, isn't it? Lots of good performances all the way around!

The date on this episode comes from the AICP transmission. November 5, 1993, was a Friday. At Doolittle Airfield, Scully seems to suggest that it's now Wednesday. If it is the following Wednesday, then the actual mission begins on November 10, 1993.

Plot Oversights

X The unflappable Dr. Scully seems a bit stunned by the spectacle that greets the investigative team once they arrive at the AICP. She walks through the doorway, surveys the carnage, and wonders, "Where do we start?" Mulder suggests that they thoroughly document the scene. Isn't this standard operating procedure? Scully is acting like she has never been part of a criminal investigation.

X Obviously the investigative team wasn't worried about any type of airborne contagion. Arriving at the AICP, they wander in without breathing apparatus. What really amuses me is when the medical doctor on the team (not Scully) later admits that the parasite could infect others through the air, yet—when he wants to leave—he makes the valiant claim that the

PLOT SUMMARY When a transmission from the Arctic Ice Core Project (AICP) shows a man mumbling "We're not who we are," Mulder and Scully are dispatched with three scientists to Icy Cape, Alaska. The team finds that all of the AICP personnel suffered violent deaths. The only survivor—a dog—is extremely aggressive, biting the team pilot, "Bear," while being subdued. Afterward, Scully notices movement beneath the dog's skin. Soon Bear begins acting aggressively as well, refusing to submit to any tests though the team has begun to suspect some kind of parasite. As Mulder and Scully force Bear to cooperate, the team notices the same type of movement under his skin. They manage to extract a worm, but the process kills Bear. Further investigation reveals that AICP unknowingly retrieved an organism from deep within the arctic ice. Once introduced into a mammalian body, the parasite triggers the production of acetylcholine—a hormone that produces violent behavior.

By this time, no one is sure which of the team members are infected, but after a rousing romp of "Worm, Worm, Who's Got the Worm?" the survivors return to Doolittle Airfield and relative safety. Mulder then states his intention to revisit the site. He believes the parasite has extraterrestrial origins. Unfortunately, "someone" has already torched the AICP installation.

team probably isn't infected because they have taken "all the necessary precautions"!

X Mulder shows his kinder, gentler side in this episode. When Bear's physical health comes into question, Mulder takes a vote to decide what they should do. Mr. "I'm Right, I Just Know It" taking *a vote?* This is new.

X At one point, Mulder and Scully must restrain Bear, and Mulder calls for a rope to tie up the pilot. Obviously Mulder left his handcuffs at home, though he's on an official investigation for the FBI.

X During the procedure to restrain Bear, the team notices movement under the skin at the back of Bear's neck. Specifically, there's this big knot moving back and forth. It's supposed to be the parasite, but when the team finally extracts the worm, it's difficult to imagine that the little worm caused a lump that large. (Unless it kept its back arched the entire time!)

X And speaking of worms in necks, Scully reports that the AICP men had worms lodged deep in their brains in the hypothalamus. This causes a small puzzlement. If the worm lodges in the hypothalamus, what was it doing crawling around the back of the neck? Granted, the worm in Bear might just be trying to get its bearings. ("Let's see, which way to the brain. *That* way? No, no, that's not right. Maybe it's *this* way. No . . .") But the dog has been infected for some time, hasn't it? It's been at the AICP all by itself for at least five days. (Of course, if the dog's worm had already made it to the dog's brain, the investigative team wouldn't have seen it crawling at its neck and made the connection to Bear!)

X One also wonders how Scully found these worms in the hypothalami of the AICP team members in the first place. Did she just happen to bring along a skull saw? ("Don't leave home without it!") Or did she use the crowbar that we see in several scenes?

X And does anyone else find it amazing that this parasite—a parasite that quite possibly has extraterrestrial origins—knows precisely where to lodge itself in the mammalian brain to stimulate the production of the hormones it needs?

X Not to be unkind, but the investigative team doesn't score very high marks when it comes to dealing with contagions. First they stroll into an unknown hazardous area without any protection against an airborne threat. Then they all get tired and decide to sleep in the beds formerly occupied by the *infected* members of the AICP. Note that this is *before* they figure out how the parasite is transmitted. Does this seem like a good idea?

X And here's something else I don't understand about this whole worm deal. Supposedly the parasite stimulates the production of acetylcholine—a hormone that produces violent behavior. So you've got the five guys on the AICP, and they kill each other. That makes sense. Then the worm gets into the dog and Bear and they get violent. That makes sense. Next, the worm gets into Dr. Da Silva, the only other female member on the investigative team. Yet, Da Silva can maintain the appearance of sanity though her system is supposedly flooded with a violence-inducing hormone. This allows her to lure the team's geologist out of his bed, slit his throat, and stuff him in the freezer without anyone else seeing or hearing her. Good thing, too, because if Mulder and Scully found her killing the geologist, then it would have been a short show! Only when her infection is discovered does Da Silva exhibit the same violent behavior as the rest of the worm victims.

X I'm tellin' ya, that Scully has one tough constitution. Complaining about the heating system, the medical doctor on the team grouses that it's forty below outside but inside, "it's sweltering." Granted, he might be exaggerating, but we're still talking a swing of a hundred degrees or so. Yet when Scully opens the door to toss the bullet clips into the snow, she doesn't even grimace.

Not to beat a dead worm, but this whole business of putting another live worm into an already infected body makes me twitch. Supposedly, the two worms kill each other. Well, okay, but, um, in the first place, an individual worm evidently produces larvae that infest the bloodstream of the host. Presumably these larvae grow to adulthood at some point. Do *these* adults fight with each other, or do they all just "get along"? And if a second adult worm is introduced into the host and the two adult worms kill each other, what's to stop the larvae from growing up and reinfecting the host? And isn't it just a bit too convenient that these worms always battle to mutual annihilation? One *never* dies before the other?

And as long as we are parading a dead worm through the streets of Nitpickerdom (honestly, I *really* did enjoy this episode), how about the following weirdness? The team puts a second worm in the dog. The dog gets better. The medical doctor says the dog *passed the worms in his stool.* To which I replied, *"What?!"* How did the worms get into the digestive tract? Last I heard, they were heading for the brain. (Must have taken a wrong turn at the esophagus.)

Equipment Oddities

It's fun to watch the gun props as they are passed around. The black Tarus that Mulder carries for the first few shows is passed off to the head of the AICP team for this episode, and Mulder inherits the Glock 19 that the building super carried in the previous episode. This causes some problems, however. Just before finding the dead geologist, Mulder accidentally walks into the room that contains the caged dog. It barks and startles Mulder. (It fails, however, to wake any of the other team members, for some mysterious reason.) Mulder reacts, snapping his weapon into position. If you listen closely you can hear the distinctive sound of a hammer

cocking. Except . . . the Glock 19 has an *internal* hammer. You can't cock it with your thumb, like other semiautomatic pistols. You cock it by racking the slide or pulling the trigger.

In addition, a Glock 19—while an excellent weapon—is not standard issue for the FBI. The Real FBI tells me special agents normally carry a 9-millimeter Sig-Sauer P228.

Same problem as in the previous episode. Scully drops the clip on her pistol and the clip on Mulder's before she throws them outside, but she doesn't rack the slides to eject the live round that both weapons probably have chambered. (It's also a bit unbelievable that during this whole discussion about guns—initiated by the paranoid doctor—no one remembers that the AICP weapons are stashed in a nearby drawer.)

Continuity and Production Problems

Just before Scully tosses the bullet clips outside, Dr. Da Silva stands, and her sleeves are bunched around her forearms. The shot changes, and suddenly Da Silva's sleeves are down.

Trivia Questions

1 Where did Danny Murphy serve as professor of geology?

2 What is Dr. Da Silva's first name?

Trivia Answers
1 University of California at Sacramento.
2 Nancy.

31

ice

Space

PLOT SUMMARY

Michelle Generoo, Mission Control communications commander for the space shuttle program, secretly meets with Mulder and Scully to voice her suspicions of a saboteur at NASA. After a scrubbed launch two weeks prior, an unknown informant sent her an X ray of a damaged part. If the shuttle *had* flown, it probably would have exploded.

In Houston, Mulder and Scully meet with Colonel Marcus Aurelius Belt, longtime astronaut and the person responsible for launch decisions. He takes offense at the very idea that anyone connected with the shuttle program would be a saboteur, but he does allow the pair to stay for the launch. At first, all appears to go well. Then strange problems plague the ship. The shuttle crew even report some kind of ghost hovering outside the craft. Hearing this, Belt breaks down and flees to his office. During an Apollo mission he encountered something similar while on a space walk. Ever since, the thing has lived within him, forcing him to sabotage the space program. Mulder does manage to garner enough information from Belt to return the shuttle and its crew safely to Earth, but—determined to stop the entity within him—Belt soon leaps to his death, leaving Mulder and Scully to ponder what he meant when he raved, "They don't want us to know."

Onscreen Locations

- ☒ Jet Propulsion Laboratory Pasadena, California, 1977
- ☒ Shuttle Space Center, Cape Canaveral, Florida
- ☒ Houston Mission Control
- ☒ Houston Space Center
- ☒ Shuttle Orbiter passing over Canada
- ☒ Kirtland Air Base, Albuquerque, New Mexico

Unanswered Questions

☒ Who are "they"? Belt claims that "they" don't want us to know. How do these aliens fit into the aliens featured in episodes such as "Colony" and "End Game"? The alien in this episode actually possessed Belt's body and took the form of an apparition—something we've never seen again in relation to the other aliens on the show. Did this group of aliens get tired of trying to keep us from "knowing," so they left? Given the seemingly radical differences between this alien and the one in the next episode and the aliens of "Colony" and the alien of "Piper Maru," one wonders if Earth isn't near an off-ramp for an intragalactic hyperspace bypass! (With apologies to Douglas Adams.)

Plot Oversights

☒ In the episode teaser, Marcus Aurelius Belt tells a reporter that the winds on Mars blow across the landscape at three hundred miles per hour, ten months a year. Mitzi Adams tells me that the winds on Mars actually range from about five to thirty meters per second, or about seventy miles per hour at maximum.

☒ I also talked with Mitzi in general about the shuttle program. Certainly, whenever television attempts to re-create NASA, there are plenty of discrepancies. (There are even discrepancies between The Real NASA and the fake one portrayed in the wonderful movie *Apollo 13*. If a big-budget movie has those kinds of nits, certainly a television program will as well.) There was one item, however, that I felt should be noted, since it's an ICBN. (That's a nit that destroys the entire plot!) This episode features Michelle Generoo as the Mission Control communications commander. She appears to be the person responsible for communicating with the astronauts on the shuttle. Mitzi tells me that in real life, this role is filled by a person who goes by the title of capcom. The capcom is an astronaut who sits at a console in Houston. No mention is made of Generoo ever serving as an astronaut. In addition, when Belt wigs out, Generoo seems to take command and starts barking orders. In real life, the flow of command would be: mission director, then flight director, then capcom. So even if Belt is mission director, there should be another individual in line before authority passes to Generoo—if she is even the capcom, that is. Mitzi didn't recognize the term Mission Control communications commander.

X During one particular scene, Mulder and Scully follow Generoo in a rental car as she drives to Houston Mission Control. Unexpectedly, the alien face rushes out of the fog, sending Generoo's car careening off the road. Moments later—as evidenced by the still-spinning back wheels—Mulder and Scully arrive on the scene. *Dr.* Scully apparently forgets her medical training, because she allows Mulder to drag Generoo out of the car without a peep of protest. Then she tells Generoo, "Don't try to move," but quietly watches as Mulder hefts the woman to her feet. Scully performs no exam beyond what she can see superficially. She performs no first aid and seems nonplussed that Generoo may have serious injuries exacerbated by Mulder's attentions.

X Having identified the problem with shuttle communications as a digital processor, Mulder, Scully, and Generoo head for a computer room.

Finding a lowly technician, Mulder barks that he wants a search—that no one should come in or out of the building without proper clearance. I guess NASA *normally* has a policy of just letting *anyone* wander through their buildings?!

X It's grungy nitpicking time! Houston Mission Control cuts off telemetry to the shuttle at 2:55:20. Generoo claims that sixty seconds have elapsed before they reestablish contact. But a shot of the clock after this statement reads, "2:56:09." That would be *forty-nine* seconds.

X Mulder decides that he and Scully need to find evidence of a saboteur. They begin looking through "tens of thousands" of documents. Now, come on, is there *really* any chance that they could find something that *everyone* else has missed? Not only that, NASA evidently employs some kind of sophisticated filing system that is incomprehensible to laymen (and laywomen) like you and me. One shot shows Mulder with folders strewn around him. Three of these folders carry the numbers "10," "17," and "47." Oddly enough, when Scully looks through a set of folders on a shelf moments later, Folders 10, 17, and 47 exist there as well! And the rest of the folders are arranged on the shelf in some sort of ingeniously inventive system. Reading left to right, the folders are numbered 64, 82, 10, 7, 47, 17, and 74. Can you make any sense of this numbering scheme?

X I'm confused by the ending. Belt leaps to his death—crashing through a hospital window (which in itself is a feat)—and somehow annihilates the alien who inhabits him. But earlier in the episode, the alien left Belt's body and traveled up to the space shuttle. So why didn't the alien just drift away when Belt jumped? And even if it rode Belt all the way to the ground, why would a fall like this damage a ghost? (Granted, we don't know much about this creature, but Mulder knows even less, and he concludes that Belt "took it with him.")

Trivia Questions

1 What is the room number of Belt's residence?

2 According to Generoo, how many orbits did the shuttle complete?

Trivia Answers
1 1266.
2 Thirteen.

33

Space

Equipment Oddities

☒ When Belt decides to cut "telemetry" to the shuttle, Mission Control loses voice communication. This seemed very odd to me, and I asked Mitzi about it. She was kind enough to talk to a few people at NASA, and she confirmed that "telemetry" refers to data, not voice contact, so there really isn't a good reason why cutting telemetry would lead to the inability to communicate.

☒ After the launch of the shuttle, Mulder and Scully prepare to leave Houston. As they walk down the corridor of their hotel, Generoo rushes up to tell them that there are problems. Why didn't she call Mulder on his cell phone?

Continuity and Production Problems

☒ Obviously NASA has a right to protect its trademarked logos, and just as obviously they didn't give their permission for the creators to use them during this episode!

☒ The accident scene discussed above also features a miracle reminiscent of the Red Sea. Just before the accident, it's raining hard. By the end of the commercial break, the rain has stopped. Mulder drags Generoo out of the car and, during her attempt to stand, she kneels on the grass— *on dry ground!* Her light-colored pants show no water marks as Mulder helps her to their car.

☒ Belt returns to his condo. The door opens. He walks down a short hall, and it sounds like a beeper goes off, but Belt never reacts. Were the creators trying to give us the impression that Houston Mission Control needed him, or did someone else's beeper go off on the set?

☒ Albuquerque, New Mexico, must be built *entirely* of pop-up buildings. At the end of the episode, we watch the shuttle land. Then the scene cuts to a "live" shot of the shuttle, and buildings magically appear in the background. Then the scene cuts back to the footage, and the buildings disappear!

Fallen Angel

Onscreen Locations

☒ Townsend, Wisconsin
☒ U.S. Space Surveillance Center, Cheyenne Mountain, Colorado
☒ Budget-Rest Motel, Townsend, Wisconsin
☒ Operation Falcon Field Headquarters
☒ Mill Road High School Emergency Evacuation Center
☒ U.S. Microwave Substation B21
☒ County Hospital, Townsend, Wisconsin
☒ Lake Michigan Waterfront, Dock 7
☒ Office of Professional Responsibility Hearing

Ruminations

Those of you who watch Millennium probably will recognize the visual effect used at the beginning of this episode when the alien pilot flashes Deputy Wright. I watched only the first four or five episodes of Millennium, but I spotted the similarity almost immediately!

Isn't Max Fenig a great character? I love the whole Gypsy feel to the guy, wandering around the country, investigating the paranormal. There's also an excellent bit of foreshadowing concerning his character when he and Mulder first meet. Mulder wonders what makes Fenig so sure that there's "something out there." In response, Fenig just chortles and scratches behind his right ear—an area that we later learn holds a scar that Mulder identifies as common to abductees. (Yes, it is true that at this point in the episode, we don't know if Fenig knows that he's been abducted, but that makes the gesture all the more interesting.)

PLOT SUMMARY

Acting on information from Deep Throat, Mulder travels to Townsend, Wisconsin, without authorization. A UFO has crashed nearby, and the military has dispatched Colonel Calvin Henderson with a team to retrieve this "fallen angel." At the crash site, Mulder is quickly apprehended. Confined to a temporary stockade, he meets Max Fenig—another seeker who somehow knew to travel to Townsend even before the crash. The next day, Scully arrives to escort Mulder back to Washington. Section Chief McGrath has called an Office of Professional Responsibility (OPR) inquiry over Mulder's conduct. He wants to close down the X-Files and kick Mulder out of the Bureau.

Meanwhile, the alien pilot eludes capture, exposing its pursuers to high levels of radiation that result in fifth- and sixth-degree burns. As another UFO appears in the skies over Townsend, the alien pilot then makes contact with Max Fenig. In a lakeside warehouse, Mulder locates Fenig just in time to see him taken away by a shaft of light.

Returning to Washington, a belligerent Mulder reports to the OPR inquiry, knowing the men on the committee are about to terminate his work with the FBI. Reprieve comes from an unexpected source: Deep Throat countermands the decision. He explains to Section Chief McGrath that one should always keep his friends close . . . but his enemies *closer*.

Unanswered Questions

☒ Was Deep Throat lying when he called Mulder an enemy? Your guess is as good as mine! It's true that Deep Throat will be killed trying to protect Mulder during "The Erlenmeyer Flask," but that will probably be done by a group not associated with Deep Throat's group. Will we ever know Deep Throat's ultimate purpose with respect to Mulder? (I realize Deep Throat gives Mulder a heartwarming speech during Mulder's out-of-body experience in "The Blessing Way," but I'm hesitant to base anything on that!)

Plot Oversights

X Preparing to search for the downed UFO, Mulder listens to a news report about the immediate evacuation of all twelve thousand residents of Townsend, Wisconsin. But Mulder is listening to the report in a Townsend motel! Did the military just *forget* to evacuate the motel manager? Given the circumstances, one would think that the military would "encourage" *everyone* to leave.

X Personally, I was surprised that there were trees standing around the impact site. The UFO hit the ground doing eight hundred miles per hour. Wouldn't that produce a considerable shock wave?

X A doctor tells Mulder and Scully that the men who first encountered the UFO were brought to the hospital dead, with fifth- and sixth-degree burns covering 90 percent of their bodies. Scully compares this type of damage to those Japanese unfortunate enough to be at ground zero when the United States of America dropped an atomic bomb on Hiroshima. I have an amazingly informative book in my library called *The Making of the Atomic Bomb* by Richard Rhodes. Near the end of this tome, Rhodes chronicles the demise of those within one-half mile of the Little Boy fireball, saying that they "were seared to bundles of smoking black char in a fraction of a second." He also recounts how one survivor noted that "a human being who has been roasted becomes quite small, doesn't he?" Strangely enough, none of those we see brought to the emergency ward

after an encounter with the alien pilot in this episode exhibits anything *close* to this kind of horrific annihilation.

X Discovering the scar behind Fenig's right ear, Mulder asks Scully to examine it but incorrectly indicates that it is behind Fenig's *left* ear.

X Discussing Max, the enigmatic Dr. Scully says that the drug Mellaril is used exclusively to treat schizophrenia. According to my sources, it is also used to treat anxiety, tension, and sleep disorders, among other things.

X Toward the end of the episode, two soldiers attempt to apprehend Fenig. The alien pilot responds by flashing them with some kind of energy. Mulder and Scully find the bodies a few moments later. Without even taking a pulse, *Dr.* Scully somehow intuits that both soldiers are dead!

X Finding Fenig in a warehouse on the waterfront, Mulder sends Scully outside to stall the military. Scully walks out a doorway. Military men rush up, grab her, and then plant explosive charges on the overhead door to the left of the doorway that Scully just used for an exit. Scully's door wasn't good enough? It *was* open. Just wanted to make a little boom-boom for fun? (I also love the way the military guys run up with this big box and we see that there're only two strips of explosive *way* down in the bottom!)

X As Mulder attempts to help Fenig, the alien pilot races up and sends Mulder flying through the air. I guess we should be grateful that the alien didn't toast Mulder like all the rest, even though there is a flash just before Mulder makes like Peter Pan.

Equipment Oddities

X I'm all for the military cutting expenditures, but as long as the military already *has* a piece of equipment, it should be properly maintained. Near the beginning of the episode, we visit the U.S. Space Surveillance Center at Cheyenne Mountain, Colorado. Watch the monitor in the upper left-hand corner of the screen during the establishing shot. The image jumps and flickers. It is obviously in dire need of attention.

■ Ever played with a laser pointer? It makes a nice little dot wherever the beam lands, but unless the room is filled with smoke, you usually don't see a red streak from the pointer to the dot, do you? How then can we see the red laser beams that make up the laser fence in this episode?

■ After arriving in Townsend, Scully escorts Mulder out of military confinement and back to his motel room. There, Mulder discovers that someone has rifled his belongings. Hearing a sound coming from the bathroom, Mulder approaches the door as Scully pulls her weapon. Notice how the tip of the barrel looks like it's sticking out about one-half inch. In fact, the slide on the pistol is pulled back. Either the slide is *locked* back because Scully doesn't have any bullets in her gun (I wonder when "Barney" shot her one bullet this time? See "Deep Throat."), or the slide is *jammed*. In either case, it's not a good situation, and Scully needs to do something to make the pistol operable. Thankfully, the weapon miraculously corrects itself a few seconds later.

■ Operation Falcon seems to have one extremely valuable piece of equipment. It is some type of telescope that can actually detect the normally invisible alien pilot. Oddly enough, Operation Falcon seems to have only *one* of these scopes. It's usually handled by someone far from the action. That's unfortunate, because in situations where it would come in really handy, the grunts on-site have no choice but to spin around looking for something they can't see! Sure would be nice if the guys who are actually hunting the alien could *see* their prey, wouldn't it?

Continuity and Production Problems

■ The episode opens with flames in the forest and screen text stating, "12:57 A.M. Day 1." A few minutes later we see a night shot of a motel and the screen reads "Budget-Rest Motel, Townsend, Wisconsin, 12:57 A.M. Day 1." Yet, in moments, we learn that Mulder is already *at* the motel and that Deep Throat directed him to the motel earlier in the day! Since Deep Throat tells Mulder about the UFO *after* it crashes (and it crashes at 12:57 A.M. on Day 1), how can it be "12:57 A.M." on "Day 1" when we see Mulder in Townsend? The simple answer is: It's not "Day 1," it's "Day 2." But that doesn't work either, because Mulder has to get to Townsend, check into a motel, and get back out into the woods to be captured by the military and spend the night in a cage—*all* on Day 1! (Here's the timeline: The UFO crashes around midnight on Day 1. Operation Falcon goes into operation at 1:00 A.M. on Day 1. Deep Throat meets with Mulder sometime during the day on Day 1. Mulder travels to Townsend and sneaks into the woods as darkness falls on Day 1. The military catches him, and he meets Max Fenig in the evening of Day 1. Scully comes to get him on the morning of Day 2. Mulder later finds Fenig in his motel room. Fenig takes Mulder to his trailer and plays the recording he made of the original police calls concerning the downed UFO. Fenig says that he intercepted the transmissions two nights ago. Fenig is abducted on Day 3. Mulder has his OPC hearing on Day 4.) The establishing night shot of the motel simply shouldn't be there.

■ When the alien pilot finds Fenig, his ear begins to bleed. The blood drips onto a pillow. A short time later, Mulder and Scully enter Fenig's trailer and find the stained pillow. Except . . . the blood pattern has changed.

Trivia Questions

❶ What code does Colonel Henderson recite as he institutes Operation Falcon?

❷ Where does Max Fenig fill his prescriptions?

3 7

Fallen Angel

Eve

PLOT SUMMARY

Mulder suspects alien involvement when two men die simultaneously by exsanguination (the removal of blood). But after he and Scully discover that the daughters of the two supposedly unrelated men look like twins, Deep Throat provides another explanation. He speaks of the Litchfield Experiments—a program of genetic engineering in which scientists designed and raised eight boys named Adam and eight girls named Eve. The children were strong, intelligent, and much too prone to psychosis.

During the experiment, two Eves escaped. One of them, Eve 7—under the name of Sally Kendrick—continued the work by using a reproductive clinic to locate host families for the clones. The identical daughters are actually Eve 9 and Eve 10. Eve 7 soon kidnaps them. Logically, Mulder and Scully suspect that Eve 7 and Eve 8—working together—killed the men. In fact, the girls themselves poisoned their fathers, and Eve 7 wants to determine what went wrong. By the time Mulder and Scully arrive, however, Eve 7 is dead as well. Looking innocent, the girls call it suicide, but—just in time to save Scully's life—Mulder deduces the truth and the daughters are committed to an institute for the criminally insane.

They don't stay long. As expected, a scientist comes to release them. She is Eve 8.

Onscreen Locations

- ☒ Greenwich, Connecticut
- ☒ Fairfield County Social Services Hostel, Greenwich, Connecticut
- ☒ Reardon Crime Scene, Marin County, California
- ☒ Luther Stapes Center for Reproductive Medicine
- ☒ Whiting Institute for the Criminally Insane
- ☒ Cellblock Z
- ☒ Pt. Reyes National Seashore, 40 mi. north of San Francisco

Ruminations

The date on this episode comes from the medical examiner's report on Joel Simmons, Teena Simmons's father. It records his date of death as "Nov. 07 / 93." Also—referring to the crime scene—Mulder says that the rain "yesterday" would have washed away any trace evidence. In addition, near the end of the episode, Eve 7 indicates that she keeps close tabs on the girls. Apparently the events of this episode took place within days of the fathers' deaths.

A small milestone to note: I believe this is the first episode in which Scully gets a call on her cell phone.

And I do have to admit that once the episode revealed that the girls killed their dads because of a chromosomal predisposition, I made a note to have my daughter tested for that "exsanguinate your father" gene!

One more fun little item that I didn't notice until I had watched this episode for the fifth time. Watch the background as Mulder orders the soft drinks in the Hi-Way 49 Café. There's a whole pack of kids who enter the building. Are these the kids who later leave on the school bus that the young Eves attempt to use as a distraction? If so, kudos to the creators for continuity! Nicely done.

Plot Oversights

☒ Both fathers died because they lost four liters of blood. That's a lot of blood. Where did it go? There's no sign of it at either crime scene. (Yes, I am quite capable of offering several theories, but I can't think of one that isn't ghoulish, so I believe I shall postpone.)

☒ Operating on the theory that Joel Simmons was murdered by aliens, Mulder interviews daughter Teena about the events of that day. Specifically, he asks about strange sounds and lights. When Teena offers that there was red lightning, Mulder asks if she can tell him more about the red lightning. Then he asks if she has ever seen anything like that before, and Teena replies that the men from the clouds were after her dad. Mulder looks like he's straining for all he's worth not to jump up and down shouting, "Yes! Yes! *Yes!* YES! I knew it!" But somehow he manages to calmly ask Teena to explain why the men were after her dad. Teena then stoically offers that they wanted to exsanguinate him.

I reproduced this exchange because Scully totally dismisses this conversation—claiming that Mulder asked leading questions. I don't get it! How are these leading questions?

☒ This episode is replete with the young Eves telling the adult Eves, "We just knew." How did you "this"? How did you "that"? "We just knew." Okay, so why did Teena Simmons try to get away from Eve 7 when Eve 7 came to fetch her? Didn't she "just know" that Eve 7 would bring her to her clone?

☒ According to the screen text, Eve 7 kidnaps (abducts?) Teena Simmons from the Fairfield County Social Services Hostel at approximately one o'clock in the morning, Eastern Standard Time. Later that day, Scully tells Mulder that Simmons was taken at eleven o'clock the night before. Obviously Scully is using Pacific Standard Time, because she's in California. Only

one problem: 1:00 A.M. on the East Coast is 10:00 P.M. on the West Coast, not 11:00 P.M.

☒ At the Whiting Institute for the Criminally Insane, Mulder and Scully visit Eve 6, who is confined (actually, straitjacketed and hobbled with leather cuffs). As the episode ends, Eve 8 comes to the institute to release the two girls. Given that all the Eves look identical, why didn't anyone tell Eve 8, "Say, you look just like Eve 6!"? Well—according to the episode—none of the staff has ever gotten a good look at her! Yet, in the interview, Eve 6 states that she has been trussed as they see her for two years already in 1985. *1985!* That means Eve 6 has been at the institute since 1983-ish. She has been there for a *decade,* and no one has ever gotten a good look at her?! (I sense a bit of plot trickery here. By the way, Harriet Harris does a *fabulous* job with this character!)

☒ We are not impressed with the job Mulder and Scully do while manning the stakeout of the Reardon home. *Somebody* must have taken a walk around the house at *some* point. And during that walk, why didn't anyone notice the driveway that leads to the rear of the house? Obviously no one even thought there was a *possibility* that the kidnapper would use the back alley for an escape route. Otherwise he or she would have noticed that Eve 7 left her car parked back there *with the lights on!*

Equipment Oddities

☒ Mulder must have turned on the map light in the rental car he and Scully use while staking out the Reardon home. There's *a lot* of light coming from inside their car. No doubt he didn't want to deny us the chance to see their stylish faces as he and Scully discuss the case. And I'm sure—being an accomplished and feared agent—he knows that *spotlighting* their presence will send all potential perpetrators

Trivia Questions

❶ Where was Cindy Reardon born?

❷ How long does the Hi-Way 49 Café serve breakfast?

Trivia Answers
❶ San Rafael General Hospital.
❷ Forty-nine hours a day.

39

Eve

fleeing in terror at the realization that the FBI is on the job!

Continuity and Production Problems

X There's some odd lightning on Mulder's face as he and Scully watch a videotape of Sally Kendrick in Mulder's hotel room. The camera angle is set so the television takes up the left portion of the screen. In the right portion, an adjacent mirror reflects the images of Mulder and Scully. Watch Mulder's face. "Something" flashes on and off. (Portable strobe, maybe? Is he enrolled in a disco course at Georgetown and has a big final coming up so he brought it along to study?!)

X In the same scene, keep your eye on the television. Note how close it sits to the mirror. The tape ends. Scully makes a comment. Mulder turns to reply. Look over Mulder's shoulder. The television has somehow moved a foot to the left!

X Having kidnapped both of the girls, Eve 7 sits down to have a little chat with them over a fast-food meal in a motel room. Note that all the cups are made of paper. The girls poison Eve 7, and in short order the police break down the door. Now there are glasses on the table, and the girls say that Eve 7 mixed digitalis with soda

and wanted them to drink it. What happened to the paper cups? Did the girls get the glasses from the cupboard? Why not use what was already on the table? Is there some unwritten mass-suicide rule (that the girls "just knew") that says you have to use real glass or the authorities will become suspicious?

X Near the end of the episode, the two girls lead Mulder and Scully on a merry chase through a muddy parking lot filled with semi-trucks. Then Mulder and Scully race into the Hi-Way 49 Café. Amazingly enough, the soles of their shoes leave no footprints whatsoever! They must have taken a few extra moments in the middle of this heated chase to wipe really well before they ran into the building! (I suppose that's just the kind of considerate people they are. Of course, one is forced to wonder when Scully is going to figure out that sprinting through an obstacle course is normal fare for an X-File case. When is she going to take the hint and start wearing sensible shoes? Or is it *possible* that those cute little pumps really *do* run like sneakers?)

Fire

Onscreen Locations

☒ Bosham, England, 70 miles southwest of London

☒ Cape Cod, Massachusetts

☒ Boston Mercy Hospital

☒ Venable Plaza Hotel

Plot Oversights

☒ The episode begins with an elderly gentleman saying good-bye in public to his much younger wife. He tells her that he loves her, and she replies that she loves him. This supposedly occurs in Bosham, England, but Bob Potter tells me these public displays of affection are uncharacteristic for the British.

☒ In this episode, Scully works in the basement area devoted to the X-Files even when Mulder isn't around (although she does have another scene where she works "somewhere" else). So when is she going to get her name on the door?

☒ How did Cecil L'ively know the Marsdens' *exact* destination? The Marsdens decided to come to the States because Lord Marsden's life was in danger. Presumably they took some precautions in releasing their whereabouts, yet L'ively travels to Cape Cod and murders the caretaker almost *two weeks* before the Marsdens arrive.

☒ Commenting on the pampered upper crust of British society later in the episode, Scully grouses that "these people probably don't even tie their own shoes." Oddly enough,

PLOT SUMMARY

Scotland Yard inspector Phoebe Green comes to Washington seeking Mulder's help on a baffling case. (They are old "acquaintances" from Mulder's Oxford days.) Someone has been murdering royalty using accelerant-assisted fires. After narrowly escaping one such fire, Lord Malcom Marsden has rented a house for his family on Cape Cod. Unfortunately, the arsonist has learned of their plans and already assumed the role of the home's caretaker. He is Cecil L'ively, a man with an extraordinary ability to start fires by force of will. By the time the Marsdens arrive, L'ively has painted the walls with rocket fuel.

Growing too confident, L'ively soon errs, impulsively setting a bar on fire. Recognizing the trademark intensity of the blaze, Mulder takes a statement from a survivor and asks her to work with a sketch artist. Meanwhile, Scully finds L'ively's name by comparing the employment records of those murdered and confirms through immigration that he is in the country. Working together, Mulder, Scully, and Green then save the Marsdens from harm but not before L'ively is badly burned in the process—a victim of his own accelerant. What follows stuns even the military's arson specialists, for though L'ively's body is covered by fifth- and sixth-degree burns, his rapid regeneration promises full recovery in as little as a month.

when the Marsdens arrive at Cape Cod, they are attended only by their driver/bodyguard. Lady Marsden even makes tea at one point! Getting a little worried about the hired help, are we? Or, just *roughing* it to keep with the spirit of "the colonies"?

GREAT MOMENTS

This episode has some absolutely gorgeous rippling-fire special effects at the end after L'ively sets the upstairs hallway ablaze.

⌧ I have to say it: I am shocked and appalled at the flagrant waste of taxpayer dollars in this episode by the enigmatic Dr. Scully. Finishing her profile on L'ively, she calls Mulder on his cell phone. Note that she appears to be at FBI headquarters, and she uses *her* cell phone to call *his* cell phone! So not only did we, the taxpayers, have to pay for the long-distance charge and *his* cell phone charge, we also had to pay for *her* cell phone charge just because she didn't feel like walking down the hall and picking up a land line!

⌧ Aside from all of the other ponderments about Phoebe Green ("Why is she in the States in the first place? And if she's here to protect the Marsdens, why is she hanging around with Mulder? And, and, and . . ."), there is also the matter of her attire at the gathering for the Marsdens in Boston. She wears a shiny, black strappy number that does not afford her much mobility. How does she expect to apprehend any criminal who might appear? With a wink and a saunter?

⌧ Scully is confused when she tells Mulder about her investigative efforts. She claims that L'ively's name appeared on a list of recent visas issued by the British government. Anyone who's ever traveled to other countries will tell you that the country of *destination* issues the visas, not the county of origin. (I know. Pick, pick, pick, pick, pick.)

⌧ People are funny. The Marsdens, Scully, Green, and Mulder rush into a room at the end of the episode after some drapes catch fire. Everyone stands and watches. A painting ignites. Everyone stands and watches. Mulder beats the flames. Everybody else stands and watches. The bedspread ignites. Everybody stands and watches. "Everybody out!" Mulder shouts. Suddenly, everyone else realizes they should leave the room! Good thing Mulder gave clear, concise instructions. Otherwise everyone else might have stood there watching the fire until they burned to death!

⌧ To beat the aforementioned flames, Mulder uses a towel that later ignites because its been coated with accelerant as well. Um . . . if the towel has rocket fuel on it, why didn't it ignite when Mulder used it on the flames? Ever tried to beat out a fire with a gasoline-soaked rag? (And don't try that at home! It was a *rhetorical* question.)

Equipment Oddities

⌧ Not a nit, just an observation. Mulder must have recently been approved for some kind of office renovation funds. In this episode he has a new floor-to-ceiling glass divider, and his basement dwelling seems to be a bit larger. In addition, Mulder appears to be storing some of his extra furniture in his basement office at FBI headquarters. When Scully asks him if "the game's afoot," notice the wooden chest of drawers laying sideways on top of his filing cabinets. Wouldn't the drawers dump out their contents every time Mulder tried to open one?

⌧ Okay, so there's this hotel in Boston. And it's got this fire alarm system that has indicators for every floor. The only problem is, *nothing happens* when there's a fire on the fourteenth floor—aside from a little light glowing on a panel tucked away on a lower floor. Scully has to run and tell a bellhop that there's a fire, and only then does the alarm sound. Does this seem like a good system? (*"Beauford! I told you that you have to stand there and watch that panel 'cause if that there little light lights up, there's a fire, and that's the only way we'll know about it!"*)

⌧ Scully needs to get a new watch. As she waits for a fax of the composite of the man who set the bar fire, a close-up shows that the analog portion of her watch reads 5:05 while the digital portion reads 4:22. That's not really a problem. Lots of people have trouble getting those dual-time watches synchronized. Here's the real problem: *Moments* later, you can see that the analog portion of Scully's watch reads a completely different time! (It's tough to tell exactly what time the watch reads, but it isn't even close to 5:05. Put your tape into slow motion after Scully says "Right," and you'll hit a series of frames where the hands of the watch are fairly well lit. It looks like 4:43 to me.)

 It's amazing the things one can learn while watching *The X-Files*. In this episode, Scully can't contact Mulder on his cell phone because he's on his way to Cape Cod. Yet, in "Anasazi," Mulder communicates with Scully just fine from New Mexico. In other words, New Mexico has better cell-phone service than Massachusetts! (And speaking of this attempt to reach Mulder, why doesn't Scully call the house the Marsdens are renting? She must know where it is. She drives right to it!)

Continuity and Production Problems

 Shortly after the Marsdens arrive on Cape Cod, L'ively finds the Marsdens' dog digging up "Bob the dead caretaker" in the backyard. L'ively gives the pooch a boot as the camera looks down from above on the freshly dug hole. Nothing shows except dirt. Miraculously, moments later, there's a hand sticking out of the dirt just in time for us to see it! (And another thing: Why would L'ively bury Bob so close to the house when the place is surrounded by dense woods? Why not take the body farther off the beaten path?)

 In this episode, Scully builds a profile on the arsonist. Listen carefully as she comes to the end of her voice-over and you'll hear two beeps, spaced five seconds apart. Coincidentally, the second beep occurs just before a man

walks into Scully's area and hands her some immigration information. The beeps sound like some sort of audio cue to help Gillian Anderson time her narration.

 Near the end of the episode, we learn that L'ively set fire to the Marsdens' driver/bodyguard as he retched into a toilet. Now—aside from the fact that this would send a horrible stench into the rest of the house and no one seemed to notice—if you watch closely you'll see that the dead, charcoaled guy is *twitching!*

 During the house fire, Mulder makes like a hero and breaks down a door that traps the Marsden children. Strangely enough, all the medium-wide shots show that the door is set back from the wall (it opens in), whereas the close-up shows that the door is flush with the wall (it opens *out*).

 The footage of Scully making an addendum to the X-File opened by Mulder is actually taken from "Squeeze." In that episode it occurs as Scully works on her profile of Tooms. There's even a photograph of poor, dead George Usher on her desk.

Trivia Questions

1 Which British member of Parliament died six months prior to this episode in a car bomb explosion?

2 What is the name of the bar L'ively burns to the ground?

Trivia Answers
1 Reggie Ellicott.
2 Hennesey's.

ROMANCE
TOTE BOARD

1 Number of times Mulder goes out on a date: one and one half

2 Number of times Scully goes out on a date: three

3 Number of times Mulder poses in his underwear for Scully: one

4 Number of times Scully poses in her underwear for Mulder: one

5 Number of hints the creators give that Mulder has a penchant for erotica: nine

6 Number of women who "jump" Mulder: two

7 Number of men who are attracted to Scully: twelve

8 Number of times Mulder appears in his red Speedo: one

9 Number of times we see Scully putting on bowling shoes: one

10 Number of times Mulder and Scully are mistaken for a couple: two

11 Number of public displays of affection between Mulder and Scully: twelve

12 Number of times Mulder and Scully shower together: one

13 Number of times Mulder spends the night with Scully: two

References

1 In "Little Green Men," we learn from Mulder's answering machine that he stood up a woman who subsequently calls him a pig. He gets half credit for at least agreeing to the date. In "Irresistible," Mulder drags Scully to Minneapolis on a ruse to take her to a Vikings vs. Redskins game in the Hubert H. Humphrey Metrodome. In my book, that's a date!

2 In "The Jersey Devil," Mulder interrupts Scully's dinner with "Rob." In "Irresistible," Scully agrees to go with Mulder to the Metrodome. In "Never Again," she has Edward Jerse take her to the sleazy Hard Eight Lounge. (Other possible contenders: Scully's lunch with Tom Colton in "Squeeze" and the "weird bank robbery date" in "Lazarus." See "Lazarus" for more details.)

3 After succumbing to smoke inhalation in "Fire," Mulder parades around his hotel room in black boxers. (Of course, he appears to be buck naked in the shower when Scully finds him near the beginning of "Demons.")

4 Flustered by the events of "Pilot," Scully flees to Mulder's motel room and peels off her robe so he can inspect her back.

5 At the beginning of "The Jersey Devil," Scully finds Mulder gazing at the centerfold of a woman who claimed to be abducted by aliens. As Mulder peruses a criminal profile in "Beyond the Sea," Scully sneaks up behind him and says that the last time she saw him that engrossed he was reading the *Adult Video News*. When chided for not reading the August edition of *The Lone Gunman* during "Blood," Mulder responds that it came the same day as his subscription to *Celebrity Skin*. Just before getting the call that Scully has returned in "One Breath," Mulder watches some kind of videotape in the dark. He repeatedly rewinds the tape and in the background we hear heavy breathing, kissing, and a lusty female voice saying, "We should stop." Near the beginning of "Excelsis Dei," Mulder comes into his darkened office and finds Scully at his desk, watching a videotape. He freezes for an instant and then says whatever tape she found in the VCR wasn't his. Scully retorts that's good because she put it back in the drawer with all the other videotapes that aren't his. After returning from the dead in "The Blessing Way," Mulder tells Frohike that he's going to have to wait a little longer for Mulder's video collection. (This comment in itself would be fairly innocent except for the other references and the fact that Mulder has identified Frohike as a pervert.) In "D.P.O.," Mulder and Scully find a girlie magazine in Darren Oswald's room. Scully expresses surprise that Mulder hasn't "read" that issue yet, and Mulder replies that he has. When Scully finds Mulder watching an odd-looking video in "Nisei," she comments that it isn't his usual brand of entertainment. After being rigged with a videocamera in "Pusher," Mulder wonders if he can pick up the Playboy Channel. In "Small Potatoes," Van Blundht checks Mulder's messages and finds one from "Chantal." She says that it's been so long since they've spoken and she's missed hearing his sexy voice. She informs "Marty" that just for him they have dropped their rates to forty cents a minute and $2.99 for the first minute. (I realize that some of these are inconclusive, but . . . putting them all together paints a fairly complete picture!)

6   The beast-woman in "The Jersey Devil" and Detective White in "Syzygy."

7   Mulder (and no one can tell me he isn't), Rob from "The Jersey Devil," Brother Andrew from "Genderbender," Jack Willis from "Lazarus," Frohike from "E.B.E." et al., Donny Pfaster of "Irresistible," Lanny from "Humbug," Leonard Trimble from "The Walk," José Chung from "José Chung's *From Outer Space*," Gerald Schnauz from "Unruhe," Edward Jerse from "Never Again," and Eddie Van Blundht from "Small Potatoes."

8   He steps out of a pool wearing them in "Duane Barry."

9   Scully dons them near the beginning of "Elegy." (Oo, baby.)

10   By Hal Arden in "Excelsis Dei" and Fred Neiman in "Small Potatoes."

11   Scully rubs Mulder's hair as well as squeezes his hand in "Little Green Men." Mulder and Scully hug at the end of "Irresistible." Mulder hugs Scully at the end of "Paper Clip." They hold hands twice in "Pusher." Scully hugs Mulder at the end of "Herrenvolk." Mulder and Scully hug after he returns from Russia in "Terma." Scully hugs Mulder's neck at the end of "Paper Hearts." Mulder and Scully hug near the end of "Momento Mori" and Mulder kisses Scully on the forehead. Scully hugs Mulder's back at the end of "Demons." (Okay, a couple of these weren't very "public," but they were displays of affection!!)

12   Near the end of "Die Hand Die Verletzt."

13   Mulder slept over at Scully's during "Anasazi" and spent the night in Scully's hotel room during "José Chung's *From Outer Space.*"

Beyond the Sea

PLOT SUMMARY When a young couple is kidnapped from their car, death-row convict Luther Lee Boggs professes psychic ability. Meeting with Mulder and Scully, Boggs proposes an exchange: information on the couple for a reduction to life imprisonment. Mulder suspects deceit. He believes Boggs has orchestrated the kidnapping. At first Scully agrees, but as she leaves the prison conference room, Boggs begins to sing, "Beyond the Sea"—a song she heard only hours before as the ashes of her newly deceased father were sprinkled into the ocean. Captain William Scully never gave his approval to his daughter's career choice of the FBI over medicine. She desperately yearns to know if he was proud of her.

Whether by channeling or collusion, the FBI does locate the kidnapped young woman using Boggs's information. Unfortunately, Mulder is shot during the raid, and Scully must manage the case alone. She attempts to get Boggs his deal but fails. Knowing that she tried, Boggs tells her where to find the young man and even provides a warning that saves her life. Afterward, he invites Scully to his execution. He says he'll let her talk to her father only then. Scully refuses, finally realizing that she already knows what she only *thought* she needed to hear. Her father was, after all . . . her father.

Onscreen Locations

- ☒ Jackson University, Raleigh, North Carolina
- ☒ Central Prison, Raleigh, North Carolina

Ruminations

Great episode! When I was contemplating an X-phile's Guide, I worried that I would have

difficulty putting together a complete collection of episodes on tape. I hadn't watched the program from the beginning, and I was certain I had missed most of the episodes from the first season. Quite simply, I could think of very few episodes that had that "new series" smell—stiff dialogue, stiff acting, lack of focus. Imagine my surprise as I started cataloging my tapes and realized, "That was a first-season episode?!" "That was, too?!" In the end, I discovered I had seen almost all of the shows aired thus far and was missing only six episodes on tape. That little exercise demonstrated to me how quickly The X-Files hit its stride. First-season episodes such as "Deep Throat," "Squeeze," "Ice," and "Eve" feel like an old X-Files T-shirt—comfortable, experienced, washed so many times it wears just the right way.

To me, "Beyond the Sea" is another example of how well formed The X-Files' formula was from the beginning. It is a compelling forty-five minutes as Scully's world shifts out of phase and the scientist is suddenly confronted with a realm beyond anything her analysis can quantify. She knows what she saw. She knows that her father appeared to her after he died and was trying to tell her something. Into this confusion comes Boggs—evil, desperate, willing to exploit, to deceive, to do anything to escape his sentence. It's agony for Scully to admit even to herself that this vile creature might have what she needs, and yet the ache drives her back to him too many times. I especially love the scene where Scully roars into Boggs's cell to tell the murderer that she'll be the one to pull the switch if Mulder dies. Just two people in a room, but the stuff of great television!

On more mundane matters, the date on this episode is inferred from two scenes. William Scully taunts his daughter about the fact that she still has her Christmas tree up. And when we first see the kidnapped young people—Elizabeth Hawley and James Summers—Hawley tells Summers that she thought about him all Christmas day.

In the realm of fun continuity, watch as Mulder walks out of his office at the beginning of this episode. Max Fenig's NICAP cap is hanging on the coat rack. (See "Fallen Angel.") No doubt Mulder is keeping it for him until he returns. (Even if Max did have a second one made. See "Max.")

Plot Oversights

☒ Here's the scenario: Mom and Dad Scully leave Scully's apartment after enjoying an evening with their daughter. At one forty-seven the next morning, Scully gets a call from her mother. Dad Scully had a massive coronary *an hour ago* and has died. Sorry. Don't believe it. Scully is trained as a medical doctor. Obviously, Mom Scully is proud of her daughter. Doesn't it seem almost inconceivable that proud Mom—when faced with a *medical* crisis—wouldn't get on the horn to her *medically* trained daughter at the first available *instant?* From the sound of the phone call, all efforts at resuscitation are over, and Dad Scully has been pronounced dead. Now, if the phone call came while the doctors were struggling to *revive* him, *that* I would believe.

☒ Where's Melissa Scully during William Scully's burial at sea? Did the creators know that Scully had a sister at this point in the series? (To the creators' credit there are two additional families standing beside Dana and her mom. Probably these are Dana's two brothers. Both appear to be married, and the older brother has two children.)

☒ After Mulder is shot, one wonders why Scully doesn't address his wound with some

haste. Granted, she takes off her coat to help him stay warm and keep him from going into shock, but the wound seems serious from the attention later given him at the hospital. This would imply some type of accelerated blood loss and would normally invoke a high-priority response from a *medical doctor.* (Interestingly enough, when Mulder and Scully discover Farraday after his alligator attack in "Quagmire," Scully *immediately* and *earnestly* goes to work to stop the bleeding.)

☒ There is a reason that a gun has sights. You pull the weapon up to your eye so you can look through the sights to your target and—if you don't jerk too much and the sights are adjusted properly—you hit the spot where you aim with a bullet. When firing on the kidnapper, Scully holds her pistol too low to align the sights properly. Consequently she shoots him in the side, and he runs away. (And, no, I don't think that's where she was aiming! This situation doesn't call for fancy shooting. The guy has an ax, and a hostage. In this situation, you *put the guy down.* In fact, while you're at it, you fire twice, not once.)

Changed Premises

☒ At the funeral, we learn that William Scully proposed to his wife after he disembarked his ship following the Cuban Missile Crisis. Given William Scully's involvement in the navy, it seems reasonable to assume that Dad Scully was part of the naval "quarantine" of Cuba. During a news conference on November 20, 1962, President Kennedy announced he had instructed the secretary of defense to lift the quarantine. It is likely then that William Scully proposed sometime in late November 1962. In addition, we know that Scully was born February 23, 1964. (We get the date from "Lazarus," because Scully has the same birthday as Jack Willis, and we get the year from Scully's tombstone at the beginning of "One

Trivia Questions

1 At what age did Scully steal one of her father's cigarettes and smoke it?

2 Where is the Blue Devil Brewery located?

Breath.") Also, "Roland" establishes that Scully has an older brother, and "One Breath" introduces us to Scully's sister Melissa. A flashback in "Piper Maru" shows Melissa to be the older sister (unless, of course, Melissa is *really* tall for her age). So between November 1962 and February 23, 1964, Mom Scully gave birth to *three* children. Sixteen months for three kids. Right!

Equipment Oddities

X Prior to the previous episode, Mulder's office gained a glass partition. For this episode, a door magically appears. From the initial encounter between Mulder and Scully in "Pilot," we learn that as you walk into the basement office, there are file cabinets on your left. A wall travels for a short distance before connecting to another wall. Against this sidewall, Mulder has a small work area and he sits, hunched over, looking at slides. The sidewall is slathered with photos and paraphernalia, including the "I Want to Believe" poster. In "Beyond the Sea" this sidewall now includes a door to some unknown nether region. (The "I Want to Believe" poster has moved, and there's a lot more stuff lying around, but that's to be expected.) In addition, the wall containing the entrance door gets a second door (although you can see it much better in "E.B.E.") and there's a new work area that

Scully seems to claim as her own by depositing her briefcase on the desk. (Would it do any good for me to wonder why her name isn't on the door yet?)

X Either Mulder is doing really well for a dead guy, or the hospital in North Carolina is in dire need of new equipment! During one of Scully's visits, the sound effects technicians dutifully put in the beeping of a heart monitor, but the heart, blood pressure, and respiration monitor itself—positioned on the other side of Mulder's bed—is *completely flat-line!*

Continuity and Production Problems

X Right after Scully locates Boggs's "angel of stone," the part in her hair jumps to the other side of her head. Thankfully, it returns to its senses moments later and jumps back! (The editor spliced in a piece of film backward. You can see that the rearview mirror has suddenly leaped to the wrong side as well.)

X After being shot, the kidnapper runs away holding his left side. Apparently he forgets where he was shot, because moments later it looks like he's running along holding his *right* side.

Genderbender

Onscreen Locations

☒ Crime Scene, Germantown, Maryland, outside Washington, D.C.

☒ Steveston, Massachusetts

Unanswered Questions

☒ Are the Kindred aliens? At first, the answer would seem to be, "Of course!" They can change gender at will (with retracto hair, no less). They disappear into the night, and a crop circle is found in their hayfield. But what about the human DNA found in their pheromones? Also, during the search for Mulder and Scully, two of the Kindred speak in an underground cave—unaware that Mulder listens nearby. They speak in *English*. One would expect something a bit more exotic from aliens.

Geographical Inconsistencies

☒ Steveston, Massachusetts, doesn't exist.

Plot Oversights

☒ Mulder needs to brush up on his geography just a tad. Telling Scully of the murders, he steps to an overhead map transparency and begins circling the cities in which a victim was found. He eventually reaches Washington, D.C. Unfortunately, because of the way the map is made, there are two large dots near the word "Washington"—one near the beginning of the word; the other below and toward the middle. Mulder circles the latter. If he had remembered that an almost straight line runs through Boston, New York, Philadelphia, and Washington, D.C., he would have known that the *other* dot was the correct one to circle.

PLOT SUMMARY When five people die in the throes of passion in cities across the Northeast, Mulder and Scully travel to Steveston, Massachusetts, to speak with the "Kindred." The Kindred live simple, reclusive lives, making stone pottery from a white clay unique to the area. Oddly enough, the clay was identified on a body in Washington, D.C.

The group agrees to the visit but soon proves adept at getting questions answered without answering any in return. Later that evening, Mulder takes a second look. Soon he finds a lifeless body of a male member of the Kindred that is somehow changing into a female. And Scully learns from one "Brother Andrew" that "Brother Martin" has committed the murders. When she asks how, Andrew merely rubs her hand for a moment before the two tumble into bed. Only Mulder's intervention saves Scully from terminal embarrassment.

The Kindred generate vast amounts of pheromones, an aphrodisiac so powerful it can lead to a heart attack. In addition, the Kindred can change gender at will, making them difficult to identify. Eventually Mulder and Scully do locate Martin in Washington, D.C.—only to have the Kindred suddenly appear and spirit him away. And by the time the pair return to Steveston, the Kindred have vanished, leaving a crop circle as the one clue to their departure.

X And speaking of this map, Mulder indicates that Martin left victims in Boston, Hartford, Philadelphia, and Washington, D.C. So . . . this sex-crazed maniac skipped *New York?!*

X You have to admire the work ethic of the Kindred. When Mulder and Scully arrive at their compound, puddles show that it's lightly raining. Yet the Kindred are working in the fields. They are chopping wood. They even have clothes hanging out to dry!

X Following the dinner with the Kindred, Mulder tells Scully that he believes they are hiding something. As proof, he claims that he could see it in their eyes, in the way they looked at each other. While that might be true, there's a far less nebulous reason to suspect the Kindred. They never asked why Mulder and Scully had come to their compound in the first place. They just seemed to know that the pair had just cause for suspecting that a murderer had departed from their midst. And, how would the Kindred know that Mulder and Scully had just cause unless they realized that a murderer *had* recently departed from their community?

X When asked by Brother Andrew how the victims died, Scully reports that they all died of "cardiac arrest." Wait a minute: Didn't the guy in Washington, D.C., blow an artery? (I asked Dr. Robert Woolley about this. He thought Scully should have been more specific but added that in *generic* terms, almost *everyone* dies of cardiac arrest. He noted, "Except for brain death of people on respirators, death in every state is defined as the 'irreversible cessation of cardiac and respiratory function.' In other words, you're not dead until you have cardiac arrest." Robert added that listing "cardiac arrest" as the cause of death is useful until the real cause can be determined. Then *that* becomes the official cause of death. In this episode, Scully knew before she went to Steveston that the victims showed high levels of pheromones that directly contributed to their deaths. So wouldn't the pheromones be the actual cause of death?)

X I think we should all take a moment to express our gratitude to Brother Martin for launching into an unsolicited soliloquy just at the right moment to move the plot forward near the end of the episode. If he had done it after having sex with the guy at the *beginning* of the episode, it would have totally ruined the tension of the plot.

X After speaking with "the man who would be Krycek" (see below), Mulder and Scully learn that a victim's credit card was used to order takeout in a downtown hotel about eight blocks from the hospital. Arriving on the scene, we hear Scully calling for backup. Two questions: Why didn't she call for backup as they left the hospital? And why didn't they wait for the backup after they called for it? (Then again, maybe it *was* a good thing they didn't wait, because the backup never shows!)

Equipment Oddities

X On the way to the Kindred encampment, Mulder and Scully get lost in the woods. Mulder struggles to figure out which way is west. What happened to his compass? Isn't that part of his handy-dandy post-UFO sighting kit?

X You have to wonder where Brother Martin shops. I mean, here's a guy who changes into a much smaller woman and back at will. Just where do you find things like expand-o-matic boots and stretch-to-fit panties? (At least he doesn't have to bother with the drudgery of buying razors to shave his legs. Evidently he can retract his hair at will. For those of the feminine persuasion among my kind and gentle readers, I would imagine *that* is an enviable trait!)

X Just before Mulder kicks open the door in a seedy motel, you can see a sign in the upper right-hand corner of the screen that reads, in part, "No Cheques Cashed." No doubt this was once a fine French-style establishment, because here in the States we spell that middle word "checks." (As opposed to some parts of Canada, where it's spelled as shown. In case you don't know, *The X-Files* is shot in Vancouver.)

Continuity and Production Problems

☒ Well, there's one good thing that comes from all this heaving and sweating and dancing in the dark. Toward the end of the episode, Brother Martin—doing his only moderately attractive impersonation of a female—seduces a young man at a local club. They retire to the guy's car, where they moan a lot until a policeman wanders by and stops them. Martin gets out, beats up the cop, and runs away. The young man in the car then has a seizure from his contact with Martin but survives. Later, in the hospital, he tells Mulder and Scully of his experience and dejectedly observes that hustling the club scene used to be so simple. (He's appalled because he saw Martin run away and thinks that the woman he took to his car was actually a "he.") Evidently this same young man decided to mend his ways and apply to the FBI because by next season we are going to meet him again as . . . *Alex Krycek!* (Okay, so maybe some good *didn't* come out of it. Maybe it *would* have been better for Martin to kill the guy!)

☒ I am always amazed by the amount of light in the forest at night during these *X-File* episodes.

Especially in *this* episode, where Mulder and Scully are out in the middle of nowhere and there supposedly isn't any electricity around. (Then again, I suppose it *would* be pretty boring to stare at a black television screen!)

☒ During the inspection of an odd cave on Kindred property, Mulder hears footsteps. He runs one way and sees shadows approaching on the wall. He turns and runs the other way, but there is a second group of people coming from that direction. He resumes his original course and then leaps into a cubbyhole just as the first set of Kindred round the corner. Note that the leaders of this group have their lanterns lit. Yet, only moments earlier, the shadow of a lantern fell on the wall. If the lantern is lit, shouldn't there be a bright spot in the middle of the shadow—if there is a shadow at all?

☒ Escorting Scully out of the Kindred communal house after her encounter with Brother Andrew, Mulder looks up to see a group of Kindred blocking his path. Sister Abby steps forward to rebuke him but then steps back and allows the pair to leave. Mulder nods before helping Scully on toward the woods. Watch Mulder's right arm. From one angle, it's wrapped around Scully's shoulder. From the other, he holds her hand.

☒ During this same encounter, it's raining hard during one of the reaction shots, yet no one gets wet.

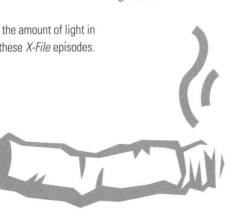

Trivia Questions

❶ Who was the first murder victim?

❷ What is the name of the person who chokes at dinner?

🔢 51

Genderbender

Lazarus

PLOT SUMMARY

At Maryland Marine Bank, Scully assists Agent Jack Willis with a stakeout to catch a pair of bank robbers whom Willis has tracked for months: Lula Phillips and Warren Dupre began a torrid romance while she was in prison. After Phillips's release, Dupre joined her life of crime. Now an anonymous tip has supplied the location of the pair's next heist. Soon Dupre appears, and gunfire erupts. Willis and Dupre are seriously injured.

At the hospital, both men die, but after thirteen minutes, medical personnel revive Willis. Then, two days later, he flees the hospital without explanation after taking the wedding ring from Dupre's dead body. When Willis finally reappears, Mulder tries to convince Scully that Willis isn't Willis—that his body has somehow been taken over by Dupre's spirit. Scully scoffs at the idea, but as she and Willis finally apprehend Phillips, Willis turns on Scully, forcing her into handcuffs. Willis then contacts Mulder and makes demands for Scully's release. However—unknown to Dupre—Willis is a diabetic. And as Scully attempts to administer insulin to keep him from dying, Phillips intervenes. She doesn't want him saved. She supplied the original tip to the FBI, hoping Dupre would die during the robbery. In the end, Dupre kills Phillips just before Willis's body dies for good.

Onscreen Locations

- ☒ Maryland Marine Bank
- ☒ Bethesda Naval Hospital
- ☒ University of Maryland, Department of Biology
- ☒ Crime scene, Desmond Arms Resident Hotel

Ruminations

The date on this episode is inferred from the fact that Scully and Willis share the same birthday (February 23) and Scully comments that her birthday isn't for two months. However, since "Beyond the Sea" seems to occur after Christmas 1993 and "Genderbender" comes after that episode, this episode would have to begin very close to December 31, 1993—if the episodes are shown in the order they "actually" occur.

I groused at the lovely—though enigmatic—Dr. Scully in "Beyond the Sea" for not finishing the job when she fired on Lucas Henry. She atones for that transgression in this episode. After Dupre shoots Willis, Scully quickly puts Dupre on the floor with a triple tap. (Now, if she had only fired as Willis jerked the shotgun into position . . . sorry, sorry.)

Plot Oversights

☒ In "Tooms," Scully tells Tom Colton that she is officially assigned to the X-Files. Yet in this episode we see her assist her former boyfriend on a stakeout. Several questions arise from this. It's possible that Willis asked her to help. ("Dana, how have you been? Listen, I'm about to face down two extremely violent bank robbers. Wanna come?") But why aren't there more than just the two of them at the bank? Was this some kind of weird date? And what about positioning a few agents outside? Willis knows the bank robbers took turns driving the getaway car. Was he really content to let one of them escape? Or . . . did no one believe that he had a hot tip for the location of the next heist, and the Bureau wouldn't give him any resources, so he called his old girlfriend? (Willis does call someone on his concealed communications unit, but we never see the other guy. I think Willis was just faking it!)

☒ According to Scully, Jack Willis was her instructor at the Academy, and the two of them dated for a time. The Real FBI tells me that this would not be allowed.

☒ Dr. Scully misspeaks when discussing Willis's sugar intake toward the end of the episode. She claims that consuming soda has given him "hypoglycemia" (low blood sugar). In fact the closed captioning correctly identifies his condition as "hyperglycemia" (high blood sugar). As a doctor, Scully *would* know the difference, but maybe the pressure has gotten to her.

☒ Amazingly, Willis's shotgun wound to the stomach seems to have no bearing on the entire last half of the episode. There is even one scene when this neglect in continuity becomes comical. When Scully finally identifies Willis as a diabetic, Phillips wonders if that's why his stomach has been hurting so badly. Scully counters that abdominal pain *is* the first sign of pending diabetic coma. Phillips touches Willis. He winces. We're all supposed to nod and realize that Willis is in trouble. Only one problem: Phillips grabs Willis very near his bullet wound. If I had been shot just a few days before and someone started groping the area, I think I'd *wince,* too! (And I'm not even a diabetic!)

☒ Phillips's actions deserve a closer look. This is a woman who has ratted on her husband to get him killed so she could take the money and run. Then the guy has the audacity to steal a body and come back from the dead! (No doubt *this* put a serious kink in her day.) Then she discovers that his stomach is very tender and he needs insulin to survive. Exactly what happens next is a bit sketchy, but apparently she and Willis release Scully and the three of them rob a drug-store. Returning to the hideout, Phillips stops Scully from administering the insulin. She wants Willis dead. Well . . . if she wants Willis dead, why didn't she just slug him in the stomach, cuff him, and start a death watch? Why rob the pharmacy in the first place? When he died, she could resume her plan to *take the money and run!* (Of course, if Phillips didn't help Willis rob the pharmacy, then Mulder wouldn't have been able to narrow the search area.)

☒ Mulder makes a simple math error in this episode. He says that they have an area of three square miles to search, roughly a thousand households. He also says that with a hundred officers canvasing—with each officer covering thirty homes an hour—they can cover the area in three hours. Not quite. If each officer can cover thirty homes per hour, each officer can cover ninety homes in the allotted time. If Mulder has a hundred officers at his disposal, that means the officers can cover *nine thousand* homes in three hours, not a thousand. In other words, with a hundred officers, each officer would have to canvass only ten homes. At a rate of two minutes per home, they could get the job done in twenty minutes.

☒ Near the end of this episode, Mulder returns Willis's watch to Scully. She says that she gave it to him for his thirty-fifth birthday three years ago. According to the dialogue in this episode, Willis was born in 1957. His thirty-fifth birthday would have been February 23, 1992. As stated above, this episode occurs in December 1993. Willis was about to turn thirty-seven. That means Scully gave him the watch *two* years ago, not three. (Unless she gave him a "Happy thirty-fifth" watch on his thirty-fourth birthday, but that would be an X-File in itself!)

Equipment Oddities

☒ Either someone needs to check the heart monitors at Bethesda Naval Hospital or Willis is

Trivia Questions

❶ Which apartment did Lula Phillips rent from landlord Multrevich?

❷ What was the name of Lula Phillips's warden?

Trivia Answers
❶ Apartment 207.
❷ Jackson.

53

Lazarus

incredibly fit. Just before he gets out of his hospital bed, the scene shows respirator baffles. A heart monitor beeps in the background. There are seven beeps over a period of twenty seconds. That works out to a resting heart rate of *twenty-one* beats per minute! (Even more amazing, the heart monitor continues to beep after Willis walks away from the bed. Presumably he's already detached the leads.)

🗶 Was anyone else amazed that Dupre's ring just happened to fit Willis? (And while we're on the subject, here's one I'll leave for you to peruse, gentle reader. Watch closely in the medium-wide shot as Willis attempts to take the ring off Dupre's finger. Does it look *really* loose to you?)

🗶 Willis is on the firing range, practicing for his handgun recertification. The scene begins with a close-up of the target, and there are four bullet holes. Four more shots are fired, making a total of eight marks on the target. Then the scene cuts to Willis, who fires his weapon five more times. Now, if I've done my math correctly, that would be thirteen shots. Strangely enough, when Willis retrieves the target, there are still only eight holes! Either he completely missed

the target on the last five rounds or every one of them went through an existing hole. Both possibilities seem unlikely.

🗶 Even more odd, as Willis signs a birthday card for Scully, you can see that Willis's best shot—a near-perfect bull's-eye—has disappeared. Does the FBI use some kind of self-sealing paper for these targets? (I've heard that the Bureau's standards are high, but this is ridiculous!)

🗶 Much hand-wringing fills this episode over Scully's kidnapping. Specifically, Mulder seems very frustrated that Willis is using Scully's cell phone. He claims that this makes the call untraceable. As a good friend of mine would say, "Hogwash!" *It's a transmitter!* Do the creators expect us to believe that the FBI doesn't have equipment to triangulate on a transmitter? And, at the very least, can't the FBI locate the cell tower that processed the call? Wouldn't that narrow down the search a bit? (Cancerman had no trouble pinpointing Mulder's position in "Anasazi," but . . . then again, he probably has access to some super-duper-heterodyne-magnascopic-liquid-helium-cooled-thingamabob.)

Young At Heart

Onscreen Locations

❌ Tashmco Federal Correctional Facility, Pennsylvania, 1989

❌ National Institutes of Health, Bethesda, Maryland

❌ Janie Taylor Memorial Recital Hall, Washington, D.C.

Ruminations

This episode may contain the first contact between Mulder and Cancerman. Near the end of the episode, Mulder watches as medical personnel attempt to save Barnett's life. There is a man in a suit shouting in Barnett's ear— trying to find out where Barnett hid Ridley's research. Scully comes in, and Mulder says that the man in the suit is probably CIA. It's hard to get a good look at the guy, but he seems very similar in appearance to Cancerman. And though William B. Davis is not credited anywhere in the episode, The Official Guide to The X-Files *lists him as having appeared in this episode. I suppose we could wonder why Scully doesn't recognize him, but it* has *been more than a year and a half since she saw him during the pilot episode.*

Plot Oversights

❌ Mulder has a flashback to his testimony at Barnett's trial. Obviously he doesn't quite remember it as it was. He finishes his testimony and is dismissed before the attorney for the defense declines to cross-examine. Then Mulder makes a little speech and the judge is

PLOT SUMMARY Called to a crime scene, Mulder and Scully view a note left for Mulder—apparently from a cold-blooded murderer whom Mulder helped convict named John Barnett. Strangely enough, according to prison records, Barnett died four years back. A fellow prisoner at Tashmco Federal Correctional Facility named Crandall claims otherwise. Crandall tells Mulder and Scully that he saw Barnett blinking on the night that prison doctor, Joe Ridley, pronounced him dead after cutting off Barnett's hand.

In time, Dr. Ridley contacts Scully and reveals the purpose of his illegal research. For decades he has sought a way to reverse the aging process and stimulate the body into regrowing lost limbs. Barnett was Ridley's greatest success. Gene therapy has transformed Barnett into a young man. It also regrew the severed hand, even if it isn't altogether human. Now Barnett has stolen Ridley's research and is negotiating with the government for immunity and cash. Meanwhile, Barnett is determined to kill Mulder's friends one by one and then Mulder himself. Eventually Barnett tries to shoot Scully—unaware that the FBI has already prepared for his attack. Wearing a bulletproof vest, Scully is unharmed, and when Barnett takes a hostage, Mulder fires first to keep him from harming anyone else. Shortly afterward, Barnett dies, taking the location of Ridley's research to his grave.

reduced to tapping her little gavel while she tells Mulder what a naughty boy he is for not being quiet. (If the courtroom scene portrayed here is the way it *really* happened, Barnett's judge must have taken the "Judge Ito Correspondence School of Judicial Courtroom Conflict Resolution.")

X Did anyone else find it a bit contrived that the one prisoner who saw Barnett on the night of his "death" *just happened* to be the guy Barnett named in his will so that Mulder and Scully could find out who he was and interview him?

X There must be a book out there called *Everything You Ever Wanted to Know About the Good Guys* that evil slime buckets can purchase at local drugstores to implement their nefarious schemes. In this episode, not only does Barnett secure the home address of Mulder's former supervisor Reggie Purdue (and kill him), he also somehow locates the apartment of our favorite medical-doctor-turned-FBI-agent! And if that wasn't bad enough, Dr. Joe Ridley—having just returned after an extended stay in South America—manages to walk straight to her door! Good thing, too, because it's necessary to move the plot along! (I suspect both these individuals had help. But from whom? Cancerman? The faire pixies of Out There?)

X Okay, so Scully knows there's a murdering maniac out there. And she knows that this maniac is after Mulder's friends. Yet in one scene we see her typing on her computer at home and her gun is halfway across the room on the fireplace mantel. Now, I realize that I do not measure up to the brave and valiant standards of FBI agents, but I can assure you that if I were in this situation, the gun would be within reach *all* the time!

X And speaking of this scene, Scully hears a squeak, at night, alone, in her apartment, with a maniac on the loose, and she sits there and thinks for a few seconds. Me? Gun in hand! All lights on! Shoot *anything* that twitches!

X Realizing Barnett has compromised Scully's answering machine and now knows that Scully will attend a cello recital that evening, Mulder decides to set a trap. Before the recital, he briefs a contingent of FBI agents, reminding them that they aren't sure of Barnett's current appearance. He also tells them that Scully should not leave their sight. Well . . . they may not know what Barnett looks like, but they *do* know by this point that he has a *mutant hand*. Doesn't it seem like a good idea to tell the agents to look for somebody with a deformity or someone who seems intent on hiding his or her right hand?

X Moments later, we see that Barnett has somehow taken over the identity of the piano tuner. As he tries to tune the piano, the cellist sits beside him, sawing away. Most of the piano tuners I know prefer quiet while they do their job!

X So, did anyone ask Kathy—the young woman who is going to give the cello recital— if she wanted to turn her performance into a potential bulletfest? Recitals are nerve-racking enough without having to wonder if one of your friends is going to be murdered in the middle of your finale!

X Lucky for us that Barnett shot Scully in the chest. The last time Barnett shot an FBI agent, he shot the agent in the face!

X And speaking of Scully getting shot, the other agents in the room don't seem to be paying attention. Scully herself has to yell, "Gun!" when Barnett pulls his gun. What happened to all those guys who were supposed to keep an eye on her?

X Fair is fair. I derided Special Agent Scully for holding her weapon too low to use the sights when she fired on the kidnapper in "Beyond the Sea." Mulder makes the same mistake in this episode just before he shoots Barnett. (Also, he holds the gun with one hand, when a dual grip is more steady. But . . . I *suppose* if he is such a crack shot that he can pick off a guy who is thrashing around with a hostage and he can do it one-handed, and he can do it without using the sights on his weapon, then . . . more *power* to him!)

Equipment Oddities

☒ Evidently the black earpiece that Mulder wears for communication during the surveillance of the concert hall has a cloaking device. You can see the black earpiece in his right ear as he races into the concert hall and Barnett takes a hostage. You can see it during the short stand-off between Mulder and Barnett. Then the camera cuts to a close-up just before Mulder shoots, and the earpiece disappears!

Continuity and Production Problems

☒ Major continuity gaff! Realizing that the person who robbed the jewelry store might be his old nemesis, Mulder plunges back into the guilt he felt after allowing Barnett to kill an FBI agent during his apprehension years before. Mulder even goes to watch the agent's son practice on a football team. Walking back to his car, Mulder passes a young man seated in the front row of the bleachers. The man wears a parka with the hood pulled tight around his face. Inside his car, Mulder finds an envelope containing pictures and a death threat. Mulder immediately realizes it's from Barnett and shouts to the air that he will "get" Barnett. The creators then show us an extreme close-up of the young man's eye. It is fogged over, and later footage establishes that Barnett's eyes look exactly like this young man's eyes. There is no question that the creators expect us to make the connection that this young man in the parka *is* Barnett. Here's the problem: as Mulder walks by the young man, the scene clearly shows his right hand. It's normal, when it should be the three-fingered salamander hand shown later. (Evidently the creators didn't want the extra expense of applying the prosthetic for this scene. And why should they? After all, *no one* would notice, right? Wink, wink.)

☒ There's an odd bit of dialogue just before Deep Throat brings Mulder up to speed on Ridley and Barnett. Deep Throat enters a bar. He walks up to Mulder's table and sits. There's plenty of ambient noise, but not enough to obscure Deep Throat's first words. He says, "I know why you've contacted me. Listen, I'll explain." He then waves his hands as if he's saying something else when the shot suddenly cuts to a close-up of Deep Throat. He continues, "I am not particularly proud of the way . . ."

At this point, Deep Throat sounds like the Deep Throat we all know and love, but those first two sentences are uncharacteristically "chatty." (Deep Throat normally chooses his words with some reservation.) It's almost as if we weren't supposed to hear Deep Throat's initial words but the ambient noise wasn't mixed loud enough to provide sufficient cover.

☒ Watch the medical person who is supposedly doing chest compressions on Barnett at the end of this episode. He doesn't even look like he's trying!

FIRST SEASON

Trivia Questions

❶ What is the name of the FBI agent whom Barnett shot in the face?

❷ Where did Dr. Ridley spend the past three years?

Trivia Answers
❶ Steve Wallenberg.
❷ In Belize.

57
Young At Heart

E.B.E.

PLOT SUMMARY

Drawn to Reagan, Tennessee, by a truck driver's UFO sighting, Mulder and Scully are baffled when local police ask them to leave. Looking for answers, Mulder takes Scully to meet the men behind *The Lone Gunman*, a newsletter dedicated to exposing conspiracies. Unfortunately, they offer no tangible assistance. Then Scully finds a surveillance bug in her pen, and Mulder decides to contact Deep Throat.

Deep Throat provides a transcript that indicates a UFO was recently shot down over Iraq. At the same time, Scully learns that the truck driver served in Special Operations during the Gulf War. Mulder surmises that the military has recovered an extraterrestrial biological entity from the wreckage and is transporting it across the country. Although misled by Deep Throat, our intrepid pair eventually traces the driver to a power plant in Mattawa, Washington. Sneaking into the building, they are soon discovered, but Mulder bolts and almost reaches an isolation chamber before he is captured. Deep Throat then reappears, saying that it wouldn't have done him any good. Since the Roswell Incident in 1947, the nations of the world have had a standing agreement to exterminate any apprehended extraterrestrial biological entity (EBE). Deep Throat claims the entity is gone and Mulder does confirm that the chamber is empty. He later wonders, however, which of Deep Throat's lies he should believe.

Onscreen Locations

- ☒ The skies of Iraq, 37th Parallel
- ☒ Hakkari, Turkey, NATO Surveillance Station, Turkey/Iraq border
- ☒ Route 100, Reagan, Tennessee
- ☒ Police station, Lexington, Tennessee
- ☒ Dulles Airport, Washington, D.C.
- ☒ McCarran Airport, Las Vegas, Nevada
- ☒ Junction of Highways 90 & 283, Washington State

Ruminations

Did anyone notice as Dr. Scully scrutinized a photograph in this episode with a magnifying glass? Did anyone notice that she was trying to discern if it was real or fake? Could we say that the refined, intelligent Dr. Scully was nitpicking the photo? If so, I hereby induct her as an honorary member of the Nitpickers Guild!

On a creepier note, this episode reveals that Mulder has a telescope in his apartment—pointed out a window! Just what would he be doing with that device in that location? Is there a beautiful woman in the apartment complex across the street whom Mulder likes? (You can see it as Mulder escorts Scully into his living room to look at the surveillance bug he's just found.)

The date on this episode comes from Deep Throat's comments to Mulder in their first meeting during this episode. Deep Throat comments that pitchers and catchers are reporting that week for spring training.

Unanswered Questions

☒ Did the semitruck *ever* contain an extraterrestrial biological entity? According to the footage of the episode and the data gathered by Mulder's post-UFO sighting kit, a UFO *did* approach the vehicle in Tennessee, but does that automatically mean that the trailer contained either alien wreckage or an alien pilot? If the truck actually carried extraterrestrial cargo, why didn't the UFO recover the material when it appeared in Tennessee? Or did it? Or was it scared off by the driver's shotgun? (Not likely.) Also, if the truck actually carried extraterrestrial cargo and the driver was an ex-Black Beret, why did he report the incident to local authorities? Why draw attention to himself? And why would those involved in the conspiracy raise questions by creating a manifest listing the trailer weight as thirty-one hundred pounds when weigh stations all along the highway would judge it two thousand pounds heavier? And why use a truck *at all*? If the extraterrestrial cargo was actually recovered in the recent past from Iraq, it had to travel by air for some portion of the journey, right? Why not just *fly* it to Washington State? Or did the military fly it to Washington and the truck was a decoy all along—not only for the benefit of human observers but also for the benefit of those who would look down from the skies? (Deep Throat and his colleagues might be more devious than we think. Wheels within wheels.)

🗙 Does Deep Throat's superior know that he's supplying information to Mulder? Deep Throat claims that his life is endangered by his activities, but he is an accomplished liar. And, in this episode, he supplies Mulder with a fake picture that he says was prepared by the "very best." If those of the conspiracy are preparing documents to mislead Mulder, isn't there a possibility that Deep Throat is working with his superior's approval?

Geographical Inconsistencies

🗙 Reagan, Tennessee, doesn't exist.

Plot Oversights

🗙 Amazingly enough, after finding that Scully's pen has been bugged, neither Mulder nor Scully seem to have any clue that there might be *more* bugs until Deep Throat suggests it. (Ding, ding!)

🗙 On the other hand, during an attempt to throw off those who would follow her, Scully first buys a round-trip ticket to Chicago and pays for it with her credit card. Then she tells the lady behind the counter that she wants to purchase another ticket and she'll pay cash for this one. That makes sense. The conspirators can no doubt track her credit card expenditures. But why doesn't she say that she wants to purchase the ticket for a "friend" and use an alias?

Equipment Oddities

🗙 The episode opens with an Iraqi fighter pilot's confrontation with a UFO. Flying along, the pilot sees an object in the night sky. He looks down, but nothing shows on his radar. He calls his base, and their radar screen shows only the fighter. Then the UFO flashes the plane, and the base radar screen suddenly shows *four* objects. One of them is probably the fighter, but what are the other three? (I suppose one of the remaining three could be the UFO—becoming visible during an attack run. That still leaves two unaccounted for.)

🗙 In the continuing saga of the basement office, you might note that a table has been added to the main work area. Interestingly enough, Scully appears to work at Mulder's desk yet again during this episode. (Of course, she *still* doesn't have her name on the door!)

🗙 There's a fun moment in this episode after Scully meets the Lone Gunmen. Back in the basement office, she tells Mulder that they are the most paranoid people she's ever encountered. She says they delude themselves into

Trivia Questions

❶ Where did Frank Druce serve during the Gulf War?

❷ What names did Mulder and Scully use to gain entry to the power plant?

Trivia Answers
❶ Mosul, northern Iraq.
❷ Tom Braidwood and Val Stefoff.

"I think it's remotely plausible that someone might think you're hot."

—**Mulder** *to Scully after she scoffs that she doesn't understand how Mulder can find anything the Lone Gunmen say remotely plausible. (Frohike had twice observed that she was "hot.")*

believing that they are important enough for someone to eavesdrop on their lives. All the while she has been trying to get her pen to work and decides to switch cartridges. Making her final pronouncement on the mental state of the Gunmen, she pulls the old cartridge out of the pen to discover that it is covered in circuitry and has been broadcasting her observations! (Fun stuff!)

While the scene is well executed, there are oddities involving this pen. Earlier, we see Mulder and Scully at the rental car counter. A woman asks to borrow Scully's pen and then returns it. Evidently the creators want us to believe that this is when the "Dark Force" (to use a Lone Gunmen term) switched Scully's pen with the one that had the bug. First, is the pen "standard government issue," or did the woman who switched the pen have an entire purse filled with all kinds of different pens? Or did she just carry around spare cartridges for every make and model of pen and was sure she'd have enough time to unscrew the pen, replace the cartridge, and put it back together before Scully noticed? Or does the Dark Force know so much about Scully that they know exactly what kind of pen *she* carries?

Second, if the Dark Force wanted to plant a bug on Scully, why pick a pen? Isn't it going to get stuffed down inside something when people are traveling? (Just how incredible is the Dark Force's microphone technology? I could see placing a surveillance pen in a penholder on someone's desk, but handing them one as they are about to board a plane?) By the way, in an incredibly strange twist of fate, after Scully receives the surveillance pen, she *holds it in her hand* during the bus ride! She doesn't slip it inside her suit jacket. She doesn't drop it in her briefcase. It's almost as if she knows that it's bugged and she knows that we, the viewers, will want to see that it could record their conversations.

Third, if the Dark Force is going to go to all this trouble to bug Mulder and Scully, why don't they give her a pen *that writes?!* Scully discovers

the bug only because the pen doesn't work. (On the other hand, if the cartridge actually had some ink in it, we couldn't have the fun scene. I realize that there's a great deal of electronic equipment crammed into the tube and there may not be room for ink but come on, we're talking about the Dark Force here. They can do anything!)

🅧 After Deep Throat says there are more bugs, Mulder tears into his apartment. Don't these bugs generate some kind of electrical interference that can be tracked with some kind of handheld scanner? Wouldn't the FBI have equipment to detect surveillance devices? (Or is Mulder so paranoid that he wouldn't trust the equipment?)

🅧 And speaking of surveillance equipment, why doesn't the Dark Force install a video camera in Mulder's apartment? Why just audio?

🅧 To gain access to the secret facility in Mattawa, Washington, Mulder calls the Lone Gunmen to hack some credentials. He calls on his cell phone! Obviously he wasn't paying attention during "Fallen Angel," when Max Fenig showed him a surveillance device that could jack into cellular pathways—a device in use by the CIA. Good move, Mulder.

Continuity and Production Problems

🅧 Eventually Scully locates the semitruck traveling northwest on "I-90." Moments later we see her and Mulder waiting on the side of the road to follow. In time, the truck passes and Mulder pulls onto the highway. Screen text—shown moments earlier—even indicates that this is the "Junction of Highways 90 & 283." While there *is* a junction of I-90 and 283 in Washington State, this little scene has several production problems.

When we join the scene, there's a very odd effect on Scully's passenger window. At first it looks like rain, but on close inspection it looks like bad video! (It's all grainy.) There's also a hard black line around Scully's hair that would indicate that the footage in the window was composited onto the footage of Mulder and Scully in the car in post-production.

In addition, our favorite FBI agents are supposedly waiting on the edge of "I-90"—an *interstate* highway. Yet, when the car pulls out, there's a local-looking intersection to the west. (Presumably this is Highway 283.) All the interstates I've ever traveled have exchanges with on-ramps and off-ramps to control the flow of traffic to and from the highway.

Finally, just as Mulder and Scully pull onto the highway, keep an eye on the back passenger window. If you freeze-frame the tape, you might see some camera equipment (a light, a boom, a reflector panel).

 Scully practices her sleight-of-hand in this episode. After finding the abandoned, jack-knifed semitruck, she and Mulder head for the trailer. Mulder climbs inside as Scully holds a flashlight in her right hand. The shot changes, and Scully starts to climb inside as well, except the flashlight has magically disappeared. (No doubt she slipped it into her sleeve!)

 And while we are on the topic, you remember the trailer? The one that's hauling auto parts weighing thirty-one hundred pounds? Keep an eye on the boxes as Mulder plows through them. Does anyone out there believe that there's *anything* in those boxes?

FIRST SEASON

GREAT MOMENTS

I love Deep Throat's little chuckle and shrugging expression at the end of this episode as Mulder observes that he's trying to decide which lie to believe. It seems to contain equal parts of appreciation for Mulder's intelligence, and conceit in Deep Throat's own ability to tangle an impenetrable web of illusion.

E.B.E.

Miracle Man

PLOT SUMMARY

When local authorities in Kenwood, Tennessee, suspect a faith healer named Samuel Hartley is murdering petitioners, the FBI sends Scully to investigate. Naturally, Mulder tags along. Kenwood County sheriff Daniels is convinced that Samuel has killed the victims with a touch, but Scully is skeptical. Beyond circumstantial, there is no evidence, and Samuel's adopted father, Reverend Calvin Hartley, has blocked any autopsies of the bodies.

When the pair finally speak with Samuel, Mulder and Scully find a young man who believes he has corrupted his gift and now suffers under God's judgment. He does, however, tell Mulder that he can see the pain he carries over the loss of his sister. This jarring revelation convinces Mulder of Samuel's gift and his innocence. Soon Scully confirms Mulder's suspicions. Someone poisoned the victims, and a quick check reveals the sale of cyanogen bromide to Leonard Vance, a member of the ministry, raised back to life by Samuel after dying in a fire, though he has remained horribly disfigured ever since. Unfortunately, by this time, Samuel is already dead, beaten to death in his cell as police turned a blind eye. Then the case takes one final odd turn. Several witnesses say they saw Samuel apparently come back to life after his body disappears from the morgue.

Onscreen Locations

- ☒ Kenwood, Tennessee, 1983
- ☒ Miracle Ministry, Kenwood, Tennessee
- ☒ Kenwood County Courthouse
- ☒ Kenwood County Hospital
- ☒ Kenwood County Jail

Ruminations

Not that you asked, but as long as I have your attention—and the creators brought up the subject in this episode—I thought I'd pass along a couple of pointers for those of you who have never been to an evangelical "miracle" service. If the head guy makes statements like "Samuel (or Bob or Tom or Dick or Harry or any other human) can heal you. Samuel will heal you," leave the tent. Likewise, if you see the "healer" guy pushing people to get them to fall over, leave the tent. And for certain, if the powers-that-be not only take an offering at the door but pass the plate as well, LEAVE THE TENT!

Plot Oversights

☒ Mulder gives Scully a stack of physician-documented cases showing impressive recoveries such as spontaneous remission of cancer and regenerated nerve growth after post-trauma paraplegia (i.e., someone got up out of their wheelchair for real). All were supposedly healed by Samuel. Yet, when we see the tent where the "miracle services" are being conducted, it appears to seat only two hundred or so people. I can assure you—given Hartley's publicity-hound demeanor—that if Samuel had consistently performed the kind of healing mentioned in this episode for *ten years*, the tent would be a lot bigger! Hartley would need room for *thousands!*

☒ After arriving in Kenwood, Scully notes that autopsies were not done on those who died at the miracle services. The sheriff says that the ministry blocked the examinations. That night, Mulder, Scully, and the police go out to the graveyard to exhume a body. Hartley's followers approach, lead by Vance. In the next few moments, we learn that the woman had no family, and we watch the police just give up and walk away (ostensibly to fetch Samuel, but they never come back to finish the job). Wait a minute: If the woman had no living relatives, who blocked the autopsy? I realize that the coroner is a member of the ministry, but he must answer to somebody. Why didn't the sheriff force him to do the autopsy? Also, why did the police give up so easily? They have jurisdiction. Dig up the body. If anyone gets in the way, *arrest* that person! The sheriff has Samuel *beaten to death* in his cell by the end of the episode. He doesn't seem like the type to avoid a little conflict! (Of course, if we learn the victims have been poisoned at this point, it would be a short show.)

🅧 Mulder must be reading from the *Reader's Digest Condensed Version of the Bible*. After Samuel's arraignment and subsequent descent of locusts on the courtroom, he holds a book and quotes from Exodus 11:13–15. Except the actual passage reads, "And Moses stretched forth his rod over the land of Egypt, and the Lord brought an east wind upon the land all that day, and all that night; and when it was morning, the east wind brought the locusts. And the locusts went up over all the land of Egypt, and rested in all the coasts of Egypt; very grievous were they; before them there were no such locusts as they, neither after them shall such be. For they covered the face of the whole earth, so that the land was darkened; and they did eat every herb of the land, and all the fruit of the trees which the hail had left: and there remained not any green thing in the trees, or in the herbs of the field, through all the land of Egypt." Compare *that* to what Mulder reads. (By the way, Scully makes a little joke after this, wondering if the slaying of

the firstborn is next. I know it was meant as a jab at Mulder, since he is the firstborn of his family, but just for the sake of information, the plague of darkness came after the plague of locusts.)

🅧 Scully really, *really* needs to take a refresher course on CPR. A young woman named Margaret Hohman dies at the miracle service, and Scully just watches. To her credit, Scully does at least take a pulse *this* time before pronouncing the poor woman dead but she should have dragged Hohman out of her wheelchair and at least *tried* to resuscitate her.

🅧 And as long as we're talking about Scully, she makes a very odd leap of logic as she types her field journal entry. She first states that they have conclusive evidence linking Vance to the courtroom infestation of the locusts and the poisoning deaths of the three victims. She also writes that Vance's guilt over what he had done drove him to commit suicide, effectively ending the investigation. Then Scully says that—in light of this information—it's doubtful that there have ever been any miracles in Kenwood. *What?!* How do Vance's actions lead to the conclusion that there weren't any miracles? What about the *physician-documented* cases of spontaneous recovery?

Equipment Oddities

🅧 When the sheriff of Kenwood equated his town to "Hicksville," he wasn't kidding. The autopsy scene starts with Scully sharpening this big knife (shwick, shwick). She looks like she's getting ready to carve up a turkey! (shwick, shwick) This is very odd, because Deb Mirek tells me that autopsies—like all surgeries—are normally done with scalpels that have single-use *disposable* blades (no shwick, shwick). And besides, even if this town is so small it can't afford disposable blades, hasn't the administrator ever heard of *Ginsu* knives? (They *never* need sharpening!)

Trivia Questions

❶ Name one of Scully's favorite movies.

❷ Who bring the news to Sheriff Daniels that Samuel Hartley is dead?

63

Miracle Man

Continuity and Production Problems

X Early in the episode, Vance comes to the hotel where Mulder and Scully stay to invite them to speak with Hartley. Note the door across the hall. It reads, "104." At the end of the episode, Mulder comes to Scully's room to tell her that Samuel's body is missing. Note the door across the hall. It reads, "14." (The actual numbers might be off, since my copy of this episode is a little fuzzy, but there're definitely three numbers in the first instance and two in the second. Normally, hotels maintain a bit more consistency.)

TRIATHLON TRIVIA ON CHARACTERS

MATCH THE CHARACTER TO THE DESCRIPTION TO THE EPISODE

CHARACTER	DESCRIPTION	EPISODE
1. Aaron, Brother	A. The FBI first profiler	a. "Pusher"
2. Berenbaum, Dr. Bambi	B. Told Mulder about the manitou	b. "Syzygy"
3. Biddle, Sullivan	C. Works for the Philadelphia office of the CDC	c. "Shapes"
4. Brandt, Alice	D. Hoped to earn the "virgins'" favor	d. "Teliko"
5. Bruin, Dr. Simon	E. Scully found a metal implant in his nose	e. "Red Museum"
6. Burkholder, Gus	F. Daniel Trepkos's girlfriend	f. "The Walk"
7. Burst, Detective Frank	G. An elf gave him an idea	g. "Terma"
8. Chaney, Special Agent Sam	H. Talked to death by Robert Modell	h. "Unrequited"
9. DeBoom, Jay	I. Finds cockroaches honest	i. "Unruhe"
10. Diamond, Dr.	J. Signed John McAlpin's death certificate	j. "The Jersey Devil"
11. Dmitri	K. Was unable to find Brad Wilczek	k. "El Mundo Gira"
12. Estrada, Erik	L. Sarah Kavanaugh's fervent love	l. "3"
13. Eve 6	M. He was on Neech Manley's list	m. "Aubrey"
14. Fenig, Max	N. Anthropologist who sought ape-woman	n. "The List"
15. Foyle, Dr.	O. Left his heart in San Francisco	o. "Genderbender"
16. Freely, Quinton	P. His heart was cooked by lightning	p. "The Blessing Way"
17. Green, Phoebe	Q. "Roach's" real name	q. "Beyond the Sea"
18. Hale, George Ellery	R. Member of the Right Hand	r. "Piper Maru"
19. Hammond Jack	S. Scotland Yard scamp	s. "Pilot"
20. Herman, Doug	T. Russian host for Flukeman	t. "Never Again"
21. Ish	U. Edited Cancerman	u. "The Field Where I Died"
22. Jacobs, Amy	V. Sells paint to cover bald spots	v. "War of the Coprophages"
23. Jarvis, Owen	W. Choked at the dinner table	w. "Firewalker"
24. Jesse O'Neil	X. Gerald Schnauz's second victim	x. "Young at Heart"
25. Kallenchuck, Geraldine	Y. Bit a guard in the eye	y. "Fire"
26. Klebanow, Congressman	Z. Talked Scully back to life	z. "One Breath"

27. Li Oi-Huan	AA. Attacked Mulder with a knife	aa. "Revelations"
28. Lorre, Garret	BB. John Lee Roche's "fourteenth" victim	bb. "Musings of a Cigarette-Smoking Man"
29. Lowell, Mrs.	CC. Kidnapped by Carl Wade	cc. "Ghost in the Machine"
30. McLennon, Hank	DD. Divorced Edward Jerse	dd. "D.P.O."
31. McRoberts, Mrs.	EE. Eladio Buente's alias	ee. "Eve"
32. Owens, Nurse	FF. Suggested his brother take up fly-fishing	ff. "Irresistible"
33. Parmelly, Vincent	GG. Kevin Kryder's guardian angle	gg. "Blood"
34. Peskow, Vassily	HH. Tried to kill Scully with a cancer "treatment"	hh. "Hell Money"
35. Pomerantz, Dr. Mark	II. Mulder's first ASAC	ii. "The Host"
36. Popeil, Ron	JJ. Worked with Lenoard Betts	jj. "Paper Hearts"
37. Purdue, Reggie	KK. Was a partner to Krycek	kk. "Momento Mori"
38. Roth, Walden	LL. Had a bad hot tub experience	ll. "Little Green Men"
39. Savalas, Cindy	MM. Does holotropic breathwork	mm. "Fresh Bones"
40. Scanlon, Dr. Kevin	NN. Belonged to NICAP	nn. "Deep Throat"
41. Soames, Ray	OO. Was stationed at Parris Island	oo. "Oubliette"
42. Sparks, Addie	PP. Killed Dr. Charne-Sayre	pp. "Fallen Angel"
43. Terle, Catherine Ann	QQ. Her dog mistook her for dog food	qq. "Clyde Bruckman's Final Repose"
44. Wilkes, Michelle	RR. Richard Odin's real name	rr. "Sleepless"
45. Willig, Henry	SS. Got a haircut from Donny Pfaster	ss. "Leonard Betts"

SCORING

(BASED ON NUMBER OF CORRECT ANSWERS)

0–10	Better start reviewing your tapes!
11–19	Consider yourself a fan of *The X-Files*.
20–29	Consider yourself a *diehard* X-phile!
30–45	You might want to investigate a twelve-step recovery program for television addicts!

CHARACTERS ANSWER KEY: 1. W o **2.** I v **3.** L u **4.** X i **5.** C d **6.** R h **7.** H a **8.** A m **9.** D b **10.** N j **11.** T ii **12.** EE k **13.** Y ee **14.** NN pp **15.** J mm **16.** Q f **17.** S y **18.** G ll **19.** P dd **20.** R e **21.** B c **22.** CC oo **23.** GG aa **24.** F w **25.** KK r **26.** K cc **27.** O hh **28.** LL l **29.** QQ qq **30.** FF nn **31.** AA gg **32.** Z z **33.** M n **34.** PP g **35.** MM p **36.** V q **37.** II x **38.** U bb **39.** DD t **40.** HH kk **41.** E s **42.** BB jj **43.** SS ff **44.** JJ ss **45.** OO rr

Triathlon Trivia
on Characters

Shapes

Onscreen Locations

- Two Medicine Ranch, Browning, Montana
- Trego Indian Reservation, Northwest Montana
- Grove Medical Clinic, Browning, Montana

Plot Oversights

- During the initial interview with Mulder and Scully, Jim Parker pleads his case that he thought Goodensnake was an animal. As evidence, he encourages them to look at his son's wounds. Surprisingly enough, it's Mulder who hops up to gaze at the claw marks on Lyle's shoulder. I would have expected Scully to pay some attention to this. And, if she had hesitated, I also would have expected Mulder to ask her to examine Lyle as well. Doesn't he usually ask her medical opinion on this type of thing?

- Ish tells Mulder about the creature that is on the prowl. I love the way Ish describes it. He says it's a spirit that the Algonquins call a Manitou. Um . . . so what do the *Tregoes* call it? (This would be like me saying, "Come on into my living room and have a seat on the piece of furniture some Canadians call a chesterfield.")

- Also, Ish tells Mulder that he saw a man turn into a beast—saying that even after the transformation the creature still had the eyes of a human. Strangely enough, when Lyle transforms, his eyes are the *first* things to change! (I guess the Manitou affects people in different ways.)

- Does Ish have the only "stealable" truck in the

PLOT SUMMARY Hearing that rancher Jim Parker has killed a Native American, named Joseph Goodensnake—believing that Goodensnake was a wild animal attacking his son Lyle—Mulder volunteers for the case. Mulder knows that the incident occurred near Browning, Montana, site of the very first X-File. After a series of vicious attacks during World War II, authorities shot what they thought was a wild animal. They found a dead *human* body. Over the years, the killings have continued—unexplained.

On the Trego Indian Reservation, Mulder and Scully speak with Sheriff Tskany, but Trego beliefs allow only a cursory exam of Goodensnake's body. Still, it reveals that Goodensnake had fangs like a mountain lion. The following night, Jim Parker is torn to shreds, and the next morning Scully finds Lyle naked in a nearby field. As Scully takes Lyle to the hospital, an older Native American named Ish tells Mulder of the Manitou, an evil spirit that can change a man into a beast—passed on to anyone whom the beast attacks. Almost too late, Mulder realizes that the Manitou has possessed Lyle, and in short order it erupts after Scully drives Lyle home. Thankfully, Mulder and Tskany arrive in time to kill the resulting beast.

As the pair depart, Ish ominously informs Mulder that he expects to see him again . . . in about eight years.

whole reservation?! After Mulder learns of the Manitou from Ish, there's a noise outside. Mulder, Tskany, and Ish all run outside and find Gwen Goodensnake—Joe's sister—trying to steal Ish's truck. This is quite fortunate because it allows Gwen to disclose important information to move the plot along, but it seems a bit too

GREAT LINES

"Well, they told me that even though my deodorant is made for a woman, it's strong enough for a man."

—**Mulder** *to Ish, after Ish comments that he could "smell" that Mulder was an FBI agent a mile away. (Nominated by Jonathan Strawn of Albuquerque, New Mexico.)*

convenient that Gwen would just *happen* to try to steal Ish's truck just as Ish concluded his story!

☒ A doctor tells Mulder that the blood tests on Lyle Parker have come back and show something disturbing: the presence of Jim Parker's blood. The doctor says it could have gotten there only through ingestion. I talked with Dr. Robert Woolley about this. He said that for this to be true, we nitpickers would have to grant the creators several assumptions. The blood cells would have to be absorbed rather than digested —perhaps through a laceration in Lyle's mouth or a bleeding stomach ulcer. Then Lyle and Jim Parker's blood types would have to be compatible so Jim's blood cells wouldn't be destroyed by Lyle's immune system. And finally, the Grove Medical Clinic in *Browning, Montana,* would have to have an "incredibly sophisticated test to detect these extraneous cells." Offhand, Robert couldn't think of a test that would accomplish this, but he said it would be plausible that such a test could exist *somewhere.*

☒ Toward the end of the episode, Scully brings Lyle home from the hospital, after which Lyle begins to metamorphose. Thinking he's merely ill, Lyle goes to the bathroom and begins a series of convulsions. Through the locked bathroom door, Scully informs him that she wants to take him back to the hospital, but Lyle responds that he'll be all right. Then he commences a fair amount of groaning and howling. Scully—still standing on the other side of the door—apparently takes no mind of these odd sounds and merely attempts to gain entry by dismantling the doorknob mechanism.

Now, some nitpickers have viewed this scene with a measure of derision, saying that Scully should be able to hear Lyle's groaning and howling from within the bathroom and should therefore be aware of the hideous transformation occurring mere feet away. I believe a broader analysis of this incident will yield a different conclusion. It must be remembered that Scully

holds a degree in medicine. Undoubtedly she has spent a significant amount of time at hospital facilities and has a fair degree of knowledge about those establishments. (She has demonstrated this knowledge numerous times in the episodes of *The X-Files.*) It seems clear to me then that—while the understanding Dr. Scully heard the groaning and howling from the bathroom—she has probably concluded that it is the result of the intense gastronomic discomfort normally associated with the digestion of hospital food. Being the refined, cultured person she is, Scully is simply too polite to say anything! (I know. I know. It was a *long* way to go for the punch line!)

☒ And aren't we *all* delighted that Scully survived Lyle "jumping" her—without external intervention—even though *all* previous encounters of this kind have been fatal?

Equipment Oddities

☒ It's a small, grungy little detail (aren't they all) but at the beginning of the episode, Lyle unbuttons his shirt to show Mulder his wounds, and it looks like whoever applied Lyle's bandage did a lousy job! It doesn't even cover the entire wound. This is odd because Lyle presumably was treated at the same clinic that ministers to him toward the end of the episode. Yet, at the end of the episode, we see that the bandage is done correctly.

☒ Gotta hand it to those Tregoes! Them folks know how to *build a fire!* During the cremation of Joe Goodensnake, a tribal elder touches a torch to the pyre and nothing happens. Then the fire literally *erupts. Whooosh!* Must have borrowed some rocket fuel from Cecil L'ively! (See "Fire.")

☒ Why isn't Scully carrying her cell phone? Mulder calls the hospital, looking for her. Learning that she has already left, he voices his intention to call the Parker ranch. Did her phone get broken at some point and the creators didn't tell us, or is this just a case of technoamnesia?

Continuity and Production Problems

 After speaking with the Parkers, Mulder and Scully go to the corral to inspect the crime scene. Ever the observant sleuth, Mulder finds a set of tracks that change from man to beast in one step. This is when I frowned. The prints look very clean and precise. It's almost as if "some-one" had a plaster print made of the beast and stuck it straight down into the mud before pulling it up to make the next impression. (I suppose the beast could have been *hopping* across the corral. No doubt it was listening to that new aerobic exercise album Richard Simmons created *just* for werewolves, *Howling to the Oldies.* After all, the poor creature *has* had a steady diet of beef for the past few months, and we all know what that can do to the svelte waistline of a figure-conscious predator.)

But all seriousness aside, the descriptions of this transformation from man to beast—both narrative and visual—reveal a pain-filled, agitated process, not the instantaneous transformation demonstrated by the prints.

 Mulder seems to be having a bad hair day. Keep an eye on his part as he and Scully watch the preparations to cremate Joe Goodensnake's body at the funeral pyre. Just as Sheriff Tskany arrives, a reaction shot of Mulder shows that his part has suddenly jumped to the right side of his head! (Hate it when that happens.)

 As Lyle turns into a beast, his left hand rakes down a shower curtain and rips it to shreds. Yet a moment later we see his left hand, and his nails look short and normal. So, how did he rip the shower curtain?

 The FBI manufactures the most amazing flashlights. Searching the Parker home for Lyle after locating Scully, Mulder holds his gun *in front of* his flashlight, and yet the reverse shot shows a perfect circle of light traveling across the wall.

FIRST SEASON

Trivia Questions

1 Where was Richard Watkins killed?

2 Where was Ish fishing just before he saw the Manitou?

Shapes

Darkness Falls

PLOT SUMMARY

When thirty loggers disappear from Olympic National Forest—suspected victims of ecoterrorists—Mulder volunteers for the case. An X-File has similar details. In Washington State, Mulder and Scully travel to the loggers' base camp with Forest Service official Larry Moore and logging company employee Steve Humphreys. Unfortunately, spikes strewn over the road by ecoterrorists soon disable Moore's truck, and the group is forced to hike the remaining distance.

At base camp, the group finds that all the equipment has been sabotaged. They also find a human body wrapped in a cocoon, hanging in a tree. Ecoterrorist Doug Spinney then appears with a fantastic story. He claims that bugs are responsible for the loggers' deaths. (Apparently the loggers released the bugs by illegally felling an old-growth tree. The insects are everywhere but attack only when darkness falls.) Humphreys scoffs but soon dies as well. The next morning, Spinney convinces Mulder to let him retrieve a jeep. He promises to drive back to the camp and rescue them. After a tense night, Spinney does return as Mulder, Scully, and Moore retreat down the mountain. In short order, Spinney's jeep falls prey to his own road spikes. Horrified, everyone squirms as the bugs attack and entomb them in fibers. Spinney dies but miraculously the others survive, rescued from their cocoons by a biohazard team responding to the group's prior call for help.

Onscreen Locations

☒ Olympic National Forest, Northwest Washington State

☒ High containment facility, Winthrop, Washington

Ruminations

Not a nit because people actually do talk this way, but I smiled when Spinney described a Douglas fir tree as standing in one location "since before time." Later dialogue establishes that the tree is approximately five hundred years old. Granted that's a ripe old age but hardly "before time."

Unanswered Questions

☒ Just how many of these tiny bugs are there? The ring from which they come doesn't look very large, but they capture and kill *thirty* men who are retreating down the mountain. Surely these guys—manly men that they are—covered five or ten miles before nightfall. Is the swarm really *that* big? Apparently! The bugs also got to Spinney's two surviving friends, and their camp was *two valleys away.*

Plot Oversights

☒ One wonders why Larry Moore didn't attempt to call for help as soon as his truck was disabled. After all, at *some* point *someone* is probably going to need to offer them assistance. It was only a four-hour drive up the mountain. Why not just holler for help, get some other tires, and finish the journey? (Because then our heroes couldn't get stranded!)

☒ Okay, so let's talk about the body that Mulder, Scully, and Moore find cocooned some ten feet (or more) off the ground. From all the dialogue in the episode it sounds like everyone believes that the bugs put him up there. I've read all kinds of theories on how this could be possible. I've seen the calculations about what a body weighs once it's been dried out. I know that some have speculated that the cocoon threads might shrink and loft the body into the air. I'm sorry. I *just don't get it.*

For one thing, Spinney says that he saw his buddy taken right off his feet and devoured alive. This would imply that the bugs can gang up and lift a man into the air from a standing position. Does this seem reasonable? These are tiny little bugs! Just for the sake of argument, let's say that they are smart enough to work together. Let's say that they completely cover all the horizontal surfaces of a man as he stands in place. (It won't do any good to cover the vertical surfaces, because the bugs would be sideways, and their wings are not designed to give them any significant vertical thrust in that position.) No matter how tightly packed the bugs are on the man's body, each one will still have to lift a weight equal to a cylinder whose circumference is defined by the size of the bug and whose height is defined by the distance to the ground! I simply don't believe that a bug has the capability to lift that much weight. I know insects often can lift several times their body weight, but we're talking "manly men at the height of their manliness" here! This would be like a fly carrying a six-foot piece of string! Not only that, the "cargo" is bound to be thrashing around while the bugs attempt this gymnastic feat, creating all sorts of air-current disturbances that would be very difficult for these tiny bugs to overcome. And *besides* once the bugs get the guy airborne, how do they *steer* him? Do all the other bugs line up and flash their tails to create a flight path?! (No doubt one of them is designated to wear headphones and wave teeny-tiny flashlights.)

But let's say that Spinney was lying. He really didn't see the bugs lift his friend off the ground. Let's say the bugs killed him on the ground, sucked the life out of him, and then lofted him into the air to cocoon him. (Even through all the examples of cocooning that we witness occur while the body is *hydrated*, and Scully herself says that the bugs probably cocoon their victims so they can oxidize the proteins later. In other words, the cocoon is a "doggie bag.") Even if the body is dehydrated and then lifted, you still have to have an incredible amount of coordination and sophistication for these bugs to lift and hold a body in place while other bugs wrap, tuck, and fold.

And if the body was supposedly wrapped on the ground and the silk shrank to lift it into the air, how did the bugs wrap under the body? Did they roll him over?! ("Okay, everybody on *three!*")

Having said all that, I will admit that there is one explanation for all this that I do find at least remotely plausible. Cutting down trees isn't exactly an occupation that requires genius-level intelligence. (Not that there's anything *wrong* with being a logger, and I know that *many* loggers are smart, witty, fine, upstanding members of society.) However, it is *inevitable* that *any* group will be blessed with at least one individual who doesn't qualify for Mensa. I'm guessing that this cocoon guy—seeing the bugs descend on all the others—decided he would outsmart the bugs and climb a tree. Once there, he held on for dear life in a state of rigid panic until the bugs entombed him, and that was that. After all, Mulder, Scully, and Moore did find only *one* body in a tree. What I *can't* figure out is why Mulder and Scully find it remotely plausible that the bugs were responsible for lofting the guy up there!

✗ Sure was a good thing that Spinney and his pals put sugar in *every single* gasoline can but the one needed to supply the generator!

✗ After deciding it might be poetic justice that the loggers released the thing that killed them by illegally cutting down old-growth trees, Spinney wanders off into a dark room in the

Trivia Questions

❶ Give the first and last name of a logger who dies.

❷ Whom did Doug Spinney see devoured alive?

Trivia Answers

❶ Bob Perkins. (The opening scene does mention a "Dyer," but Steve Humphreys identifies Bob Perkins by his first and last names.)

❷ Steven Teague.

bunkhouse at night. Maybe I missed some subtlety here, but I thought going into the dark during this episode was . . . a *bad* thing.

🅇 Of course, instead of letting Spinney go back to his encampment alone, Mulder could have suggested that everyone go with him.

🅇 And they could build a fire to ward off the bugs.

🅇 And while they are putting plastic over the windows to keep the bugs out, they probably should do something about the big gaps in the wallboards. (You can see daylight through the cracks!)

🅇 For some reason, near the end of this episode the bugs suddenly decide that the light isn't so bad after all and swarm Spinney as he stands in front of the headlights of his jeep. To my eyes at least it looks like there's every bit the same amount of illumination as there was in the room with only one dinky lightbulb. (Some have suggested that the bugs swarmed Spinney's backside because it was shadowed, but everybody's backside was shadowed in the room with the one lightbulb, and nothing happened to them! On the other hand, one wonders why Spinney didn't just keep driving even after the flats. Granted it's not the best thing to do in a car, but this is an extraordinary situation, and the road did seem smooth enough to allow it for a time at least.

🅇 Not a nit, just an observation. The big closing moment comes as we are left to wonder if the government will be able to eradicate the bug infestation. Yet, at the beginning of this episode we learned that a group of loggers disappeared from the same area in 1934. Did they die because of the bugs as well? And if so, what happened to *those* bugs? Are they still out there or did they just die off, and given enough time we won't even have to worry about it?

Changed Premises

🅇 Ya know, Mulder does *really* well in this episode for someone who hates bugs—as we find out in "War of the Coprophages."

Equipment Oddities

🅇 I am *really* surprised that somebody didn't bring along a portable shortwave during this excursion. I believe that's what Mulder and Scully take along for their "Firewalker" mission. Maybe this case taught them a lesson!

🅇 And speaking of communication devices, Humphreys gets fed up and says he's going to hike back down to Moore's truck to get on the horn and call for help. This seems sensible. The next time we see him he's trying to hot-wire the truck to get it started. One question: Why doesn't he just connect the wires to supply voltage to the accessories and make the call? Is the radio *gas-powered*? Why does he need to start the truck?

Continuity and Production Problems

🅇 The approximately five-hundred-year-old Douglas fir cut down by the logging company is rough-cut in all the wide shots, but when the scene cuts to a close-up the center is suddenly smooth.

Tooms

Onscreen Locations

☒ Druid Hill Sanitarium, Baltimore, Maryland
☒ Lynne Acres Retirement Home
☒ Smithsonian Institute, Forensic
   Anthropology Lab
☒ 66 Exeter Street, Baltimore

Plot Oversights

☒ Tooms really must have enjoyed his time at the hospital. Given his abilities and the food slot in his door, I see no reason why he couldn't have escaped at any time.

☒ At the beginning of Scully's visit, Briggs comments that if they don't stop Tooms now, Scully will be his age before Tooms murders again. If I were Scully, I'd take that as an insult. Dialogue in "Squeeze" indicates that Briggs is approximately *ninety* years old! Is his saying that he believes Scully is *sixty*? (Tooms comes out of hibernation every thirty years.)

☒ Scully tells Mulder that it's FBI policy to assign two pairs of agents to a stakeout on rotating twelve-hour shifts. Mulder retorts that this is "Article 30, Paragraph 8.7." According to The Real FBI, it isn't! (I know, cheap shot!)

☒ Tired of Mulder's interference, Tooms decides to frame our favorite hopelessly obsessive agent on an assault charge. He sneaks into Mulder's apartment at night through a heater vent by somehow unscrewing the cover from the inside. (See "Squeeze" for more information.) A few points to ponder about this scene: Isn't it amaz-

PLOT SUMMARY To Mulder's amazement, Eugene Victor Tooms (see "Squeeze") is released after less than a year in an institution. Without authorization, Mulder begins a round-the-clock surveillance to ensure that Tooms will not murder again. Mulder also dispatches Scully to find hard evidence linking Tooms with any of the earlier murders. Scully, in turn, seeks out retired detective Franks Briggs. Briggs had investigated the Powhatan Mill murders in 1933 and the second set of murders in 1963. When questioned, Briggs recalls that one of the bodies was never found in 1933, although a piece of a liver was discovered at the Ruxton Chemical plant during construction. Using EMP (Extra-Muldery Perception: the ability to jump to the right conclusion without any help from Mr. Intuition himself), Briggs not only guesses the location of the sixty-year-old body but also leads Scully to the remains buried in cement. After excavation, analysis positively matches Tooms's teeth to gnawmarks on the skeleton's collarbone.

Unfortunately, by this time Tooms has evaded surveillance, framed Mulder for assault, murdered his psychologist, and returned to his hibernation nest beneath a newly revitalized 66 Exeter Street. Mulder and Scully *do* track down Tooms and grind him up in an escalator, but as the episode ends, Mulder tells his ever-faithful partner that he can sense a change approaching for them.

ing that Tooms—*inside* the heater vent—knows exactly when to stop unscrewing the screw as Mulder rouses from his sleep in the other room? And isn't it thoughtful of Tooms to give us a dramatic entrance by leaping into Mulder's living room doorway from the *right* just as the music swells? Especially since the vent by which he entered Mulder's apartment is to the *left* of the doorway. (Maybe he decided to root around in Mulder's refrigerator before doing the deed. "Yeah, *buddy.* I not only *framed* you, I also ate your leftover *pizza!*) And isn't it also *extremely* considerate of Tooms not to make Mulder his fifth and final victim?! (Think about it: If Tooms had killed Mulder and snacked on his liver, he could have gone back to his little abode beneath the elevator and slept happily for another thirty years. Granted, Scully would have been ticked, but Mulder was the one who figured out the location of Tooms's hideout.)

☒ The police use an interesting technique when they come to arrest Mulder. They walk into his apartment without any explanation and begin searching for evidence. Paint me blue and call me silly, but I thought police had to have a search warrant for this type of thing! Of course, it *could* be that the police know this is illegal search and seizure and they are intentionally collecting the evidence in an illegal manner, hoping to have it thrown out of court since Mulder is a fellow law enforcement official.

☒ Gotta hand it to those Baltimore construction crews. "Squeeze" took place near the end of July 1993. This episode occurs sometime in March 1994 (given that this episode is bracketed by episodes that both occur in March 1994). In those short eight months, some company managed to tear down Tooms's old building and erect a beautiful new one on the same site!

☒ The end of the episode has Tooms chasing Mulder through escalator machinery. With Scully's help, Mulder manages to scramble onto the main floor of the building just as Tooms crawls under the bottom end of the escalator. Frantically, Mulder lunges for a button at the base of the escalator's handrail. The machine revs into action and crushes Tooms. This seems excessive. Mulder is already out of the hole.

Scully has a gun. If Tooms tries to leap out of the hole, Scully could shoot him. Why does Mulder murder this guy?

Changed Premises

☒ Shortly after this episode begins, Tooms takes part in a hearing that returns him to society after less than a year under psychiatric supervision. Several things about this hearing seem to contradict events in "Squeeze." At the hearing we learn that a doctor can find nothing physically out of the ordinary with Tooms. We learn that he is confined to the sanitarium *only* because of his attack on Scully. And we learn that he was never charged in any of the other murders and no evidence was found linking him to those murders. *How can this be?*

In "Squeeze," Scully said that preliminary exams revealed "quite abnormal development in the muscular and skeletal systems." They also showed a "continually declining metabolic rate" well below the levels registered in deep sleep. Now, everything looks normal. If Tooms can mask his extrahuman capabilities, why didn't he do it for the exams in "Squeeze"?

And what about the trophies that Mulder found at 66 Exeter Street? He found Scully's necklace there, and Tooms then attacked Scully. Doesn't that establish a link between Tooms and the location? In addition, I find it hard to believe that *some* forensic evidence at the scene could not definitively link Tooms to the nest location as well. He licked all the newspaper strips to make his nest, for crying out loud! Doesn't saliva contain DNA?

Once 66 Exeter Street is established as Tooms's abode, don't the trophies link him to the murders? Consider only one of those trophies. The fourth victim in 1993 was Thomas Werner. Tooms took a fireplace doodad from his house. We see Werner touch the doodad before Tooms kills him. That means it has Werner's fingerprints on it. Tooms never wears gloves, so it probably has Tooms's fingerprints on it as well.

Doesn't that link Tooms to Werner? Would the trophy he took from George Usher's office do the same? Granted, a jury might find it hard to believe that Tooms committed the murders in 1963 and 1933, but it seems like there's plenty of evidence to pin him with the murders in 1993! Did someone screw up and make all the evidence inadmissible?

🗙 Tooms's behavior changes in this episode as well. In "Squeeze," Tooms stalked his victims in voyeuristic fashion. In this episode he starts walking directly at a woman in broad daylight with murderous intent.

🗙 Giving Scully the facts of the X-File in "Squeeze," Mulder states that there were ten murders in the Baltimore area with undetermined points of entry, and *each victim* had his or her liver removed. The ten murders that Mulder refers to come from the 1930s and the 1960s. Based on this pattern of five murders in 1933 and another five in 1963, Mulder can conclude during "Squeeze" that the murderer has two more to go in 1993. However, in *this* episode Briggs reveals that only *four* of the victims were found in 1933. Why the discrepancy? Answer: Because the creators wanted to give Scully something to do, so they "forgot" that all five bodies had been found in 1933, according to the previous episode, and created the subplot with Briggs. (And yes, nitpickers do notice these things!)

Equipment Oddities

🗙 Evidently Dr. Monte has the same eyeglass prescription as Mulder. (See "Squeeze.") As Monte finishes visiting with Tooms at the beginning of the episode, you can see that the reflection in his eyeglasses is perfectly flat and smooth.

🗙 Speaking of the escalator scene mentioned above, Tooms appears to be directly beneath the bottom end of the escalator. When Mulder starts the escalator, it looks like the stair sections wrap around, crush Tooms, and yank him backward. Two problems: Concerning the big button that Mulder pushes at the base of the escalator handrail, isn't that normally an emergency *stop* button? Also, if the stair sections are dragging Tooms backward, wouldn't the escalator be going *down* and not *up,* as shown in the wide shot?

Continuity and Production Problems

🗙 Good old Tooms, he's such a *kidder!* The episode opens at the Druid Hill Sanitarium. In time, the camera stops at Tooms's door. Zooming in on the food slot, we see Tooms lean forward as light illuminates his face from below. It seems unlikely that he has a nightlight plugged into the base of the door, so we must assume that someone gave him a flashlight and he has it shining up at his face. No doubt he's also thinking, "Oooo, I'm a creepy guy. I'm a creepy guy!"

🗙 Toward the end of the episode, Dr. Monte comes to visit Tooms in his foster home. We see Tooms tearing a newspaper into strips. With each motion, we hear an elongated "scritch" sound. As he begins to tear a new strip, there's a knock at his door. Tooms stops and looks up. A reverse angle shows Dr. Monte entering. Then the camera returns to Tooms, and now we see that the paper strip he holds is almost completely torn, yet there was no accompanying "scritch." Is this just another of Tooms's incredible capabilities? Has he *actually* perfected—gasp!—the *stealth paper tear?!* (Insert dramatic music here.)

FIRST SEASON

Trivia Questions

❶ What type of sandwich did Scully bring for Mulder to eat during his surveillance of Tooms?

❷ What is Mrs. Green's first name?

Trivia Answers
❶ Liverwurst.
❷ Susan.

Born Again

PLOT SUMMARY

Mulder and Scully travel to Buffalo, New York, after Police Detective Barbala leaps to his death from an interrogation room window. At the time, he was interviewing a little lost girl named Michelle Bishop. Oddly enough, Michelle claims a man pushed Barbala—a man later identified from a composite sketch as long-deceased police officer Charlie Morris. Further investigation reveals strange links between Morris and Michelle, including the fact that Michelle often mutilates dolls in the same way Morris's body was found—eye gouged out, arm cut off.

Soon another man dies with Michelle nearby—former police officer Leon Felder. During a drug sweep of the city nine years back, Morris, Barbala, Felder, and Tony Fiore participated in a major drug bust. Barbala, Felder, and Fiore wanted to keep the money they confiscated, and when Morris objected, Barbala and Felder drowned him in his own fish tank. They then mutilated his body to make it look like a gangland hit. At that time, Morris's spirit took possession of Michelle. Now he wants revenge.

Knowing Tony Fiore is the last remaining member of the group, Mulder and Scully rush to his home. They find him cowering in pain before Michelle. But when Fiore confesses and his wife asks for mercy, Morris spares his life—and vacates the little girl he has traumatized for eight years.

Onscreen Locations

- ☒ 14th Precinct House, Buffalo, New York
- ☒ Brylin Psychiatric Hospital, Buffalo, New York
- ☒ Fiore Residence, Kenmore, New York
- ☒ Buffalo Mutual Life, Main Office, Buffalo, New York
- ☒ FBI Regional Headquarters, Buffalo, New York

Ruminations

The beginning date on this episode comes from a log sheet that Scully examines as she and Mulder attempt to find the links among the four police officers. The ending date comes from Mulder's final log entry.

Geographical Inconsistencies

☒ Daniel B. Case of Woodmere, Ohio (who used to live in Buffalo, New York) tells me there is no commuter train that runs between Buffalo and Orchard Park, as mentioned in this episode, and if there were, it probably wouldn't take thirty minutes to traverse the distance. In addition, the bus route shown does not exist. Also, Buffalo, New York, has no Chinatown.

Plot Oversights

☒ How did Mulder and Scully arrive at the 14th Precinct in Buffalo, New York, so quickly? When we return from the opening credits, the site of Barbala's death seems very "fresh," yet Mulder and Scully are already on the job!

☒ Leon Felder missed his calling. Instead of a police officer, he probably could have been a world-class track star. The fastest runners in the world compete in the hundred-meter and two-hundred-meter races and can sprint at a rate of approximately ten meters a second. Remember that figure. To kill Felder, Morris waits for the man to disembark a bus; Morris then tangles Felder's scarf in the bus and causes the bus to accelerate as it pulls away from the curb. Frantic, Felder runs alongside, pounding on the side of the bus, screaming. We see the speedometer on the bus pass fifteen miles an hour, and we hear the bus *accelerate* even more. Felder runs alongside the bus. The bus sounds like it *continues* to accelerate. Felder *still* runs alongside the bus. Finally—*seven seconds* after the speedometer crosses fifteen miles an hour—Felder stumbles and chokes to death as the bus drags him along. Just for the sake of argument, let's say that the bus averaged twenty miles an hour during those seven seconds. How fast was Felder running? Well, twenty miles per hour is thirty-two kilometers per hour. A bit of math with reveal that Felder is doing almost *nine meters a second* (32,000 divided by 60 to get "per minute," and 60 again to get "per second"). Now, remember, this guy is a retired cop who sits at a desk all day selling disability insurance. I'm thinking that if this guy had applied himself, who knows what he could have accomplished? (Especially with a pair of gold running shoes!)

🅇 One wonders how much attention Ms. Bishop pays to her troubled daughter. The little girl seems to disappear on a regular basis, and the mother is clueless until someone informs her. One would expect—at least from the latter portion of the show—that Ms. Bishop would notice when her daughter runs off and would seek Mulder and Scully's assistance in the matter. (Unless, of course, Michelle has some kind of Svengali-like hold over her mother. "No, Mother, I vill *not* clean out the litter box." *You* vill clean out the litter box, and *you* vill not notice when I leave. Look deep into my eyes . . . *deeeeeeep* into my eyes.")

🅇 How are the X-Files numbered? Does Mulder use some mystic Zen method of identification? At the end of the episode he gives a case number of "X-40271." All well and good. It's a new case. It should have a high number. Except . . . when Mulder opened a file for Cecil L'ively sometime during "Fire," *that* case number was "11214893"! Why are the numbers going *backward?!*

Equipment Oddities

🅇 Early on, Mulder comes to the Bishop home with a composite artist to work with Michelle and develop a sketch on the man she claims pushed Barbala out the window. First, why is the composite artist working with a full-size computer when a laptop would serve just as well? Does he really lug this thing around to each appointment, or is this a special case? Second, when Mulder asks if the pusher had dark hair like his or light hair like hers, Michelle replies that the man had light hair like hers, but the tint on the hair seems to lighten by only one shade.

🅇 Two seconds disappear from the video of Michelle Bishop's hypnosis session between the time it's recorded and the time Mulder views the tape. (And did you notice that Mulder *rewound* the tape and viewed the scene over and over? And did you notice that he used frame-advance? And do you know what that means? He's a *nitpicker* in his heart of hearts!) During the actual hypnosis, Michelle says that she is twenty-four, and three seconds elapse before she starts screaming, "No! We can't!" In the replay, there's not only a glitch in the video but two of those seconds disappear as well. Now, remember that the video guy says he checked the "windup profile" and the tape was up to speed. That means the tape *continued to roll* through the video recorder during that portion of the interview. So what happened to the two seconds?

Trivia Questions

1 Against what group did police score "very heavy busts" nine years ago?

2 Who performed the autopsy on Charlie Morris?

Trivia Answers
1 Woo Shing Woo. (I just like saying that! "Woo shing woo, woo shing woo . . .")
2 Dr. Yamaguchi.

Continuity and
Production Problems

☒ After the composite sketch is identified as Charlie Morris, Mulder and Scully visit his former partner, Tony Fiore. Watch the composite sketch as Mulder talks to Fiore through the barely open front door. Mulder holds it up for Fiore to see. Then the shot changes and suddenly Mulder is holding it sideways.

☒ Not a nit, just an observation. Creators of every persuasion always seem delighted whenever they can shoot footage inside a precinct house. Invariably there is at least one prostitute paraded in front of the camera. (It adds to the realism, don'tcha know? And it means the creators get to spend time on the set with a young woman thusly attired.) This episode is no different. Coming back from the commercial break after Felder's death, we see an officer escorting the obligatory prostitute past the camera and, of course, it has to be done in such a way that, for a time, her hips *fill* the screen. Honestly, if that lens got any closer, the actress would have to sue the cameraman for sexual harassment! (Boys will be boys.)

Roland

Onscreen Locations

☒ Mahan Propulsion Laboratory, Washington Institute of Technology, Colson, Washington

☒ Heritage Halfway House, Colson, Washington

☒ FBI Regional Headquarters, Seattle, Washington

☒ Mahan Propulsion Laboratory, Building 214

☒ Avalon Foundation, Washington Institute of Technology, Colson, Washington

Ruminations

The date on this episode comes from a computer screen that shows the modification date for a file Roland worked on after murdering Keats.

There are times when reality doesn't respond to intuition. Finding themselves locked inside the wind tunnel that is used to test the prototype engine, Drs. Surnow and Nollette both immediately head for a wire mesh near the wind tunnel's air intake area. This positions the engine directly behind them. They then wait until the engine generates enough flow pressure to rip them off the mesh. This always puzzled me because I couldn't understand why the scientists didn't go stand beside the engine in the space between the edge of the fan and the sidewall. Granted, there's nothing to hold onto there, but it just felt like it would be a good thing to do. (I knew it. I just knew it . . . to use a Mulderism.) Being highly unskilled in the area of fluid dynamics myself, I shrugged it off. In the process of compiling this Guide, I talked with my friend Greg Ojakakangas. He's a physics professor at Drury College here in Springfield. While he couldn't definitively answer the question of the best location to stand in in such a situation, he did suggest that I take a shoebox and a vacuum cleaner and run

PLOT SUMMARY

When a scientist is chopped to death by a prototype jet engine, Mulder and Scully come to investigate. (Dr. Surnow was actually the second scientist to die while working on the project to achieve Mach 15. The first—Arthur Grable—died in a car accident six months before.) Then another project scientist dies when someone shoves him into a vat of liquid nitrogen and smashes him to the floor. At both crimes scenes, Mulder and Scully find calculations that no one will claim. Most intriguing, the pair soon discover that Roland Fuller—a mentally challenged custodian—is actually Arthur Grable's twin.

Mulder concludes that Grable's consciousness is forcing Roland to commit the murders despite the fact that Grable's head has been *frozen* since his car accident. Certainly, Grable would have cause to be angry. The sole surviving scientist, Dr. Nollette, stole Grable's work after his death, and once Nollette realizes what's happening, he even sabotages Grable's cryonics capsule.

Aware of Nollette's treachery, Grable redoubles his efforts to complete the project—using Roland like a puppet to achieve Mach 15 with the prototype engine. Then he locks Nollette in the laboratory's wind tunnel. He intends to slice and dice him just like Surnow, but Mulder and Scully intervene and save Nollette's life. And Grable's consciousness? It finally expires as the temperature of his capsule rises to minus 150 degrees.

my own experiment! I did so and I'm guessing that it really isn't going to matter where the scientists stand once that Mach 15 engine gets up to speed. The corners of the room are going to fill with high-pressure vortices that would probably shove the scientists into the low-pressure area that runs from the air intake to the engine. From there, it's a one-way trip to the afterlife via airmail. (Score one for the creators!)

There are little things that make my nitpicker's heart glad. To access the "Arthur" file on the computer, Mulder instructs Scully to enter the password "15626." Careful analysis using slow motion and freeze-framing shows that she does indeed enter "15626." We like this!

At one point, Mulder goes to Heritage Halfway House to see if Roland can describe what's happening to him. Finding that Roland is unwilling to talk about his dreams, Mulder discloses that he himself had a dream the night before. He says that he was swimming in a pool and could see that his father was underwater. But when he dove down, the water stung his eyes. Then there was another man at the pool, asking questions that upset Mulder. He had to leave, and he couldn't find his father. It occurs to me that this might be the first hint the creators give us of William Mulder's collusion with the Consortium (the men whom we first see meeting in a room on 46th Street in New York City during "The Blessing Way"). It's easy to imagine that the pool in which Mulder swims is the "Truth." His father lies deep in that truth and Mulder is attempting to reach him, but the possibility of his father's involvement stings his eyes. The other man enters (Cancerman or Mulder's own consciousness?) with questions whose answers make Mulder even more uncomfortable, and he turns away. Perhaps Mulder's subconscious has strung together the disparate facts and reaches the disturbing conclusion that his father had a hand in Mulder's sister Samantha's disappearance but his conscious mind isn't ready to allow that possibility just yet.

Geographical Inconsistencies

🄧 Colson, Washington, doesn't exist.

Plot Oversights

🄧 Does anyone else find it fascinating that Scully just happens to wear a patterned blouse on the day that she and Mulder visit Roland for the first time? Before and after this, Scully normally wears solids (in fact, she does for the rest of this episode as well). Yet, on this particular day, she wears a blouse with stars. Hmmm. Stars. *Roland* likes stars, and we learn about his savant capabilities because he counts the stars on Scully's blouse with just a glance. But there's really no way she could have known that this would happen unless she read the script. So her choice of a patterned blouse in this situation *must* have been just a coincidence. . . .

Equipment Oddities

🄧 Sometimes technology geeks do the *strangest* things. The wind tunnel in this episode features a door that opens and shuts *solely* under computer control. I realize it's whiz-bang-neato-keeno-sexy-cool—and the scientists probably sing the *Star Wars* theme every time it opens—but did *no one* stop to think of the safety implications of a wind tunnel without an *emergency exit?!*

🄧 And what about the terminal *inside* the wind tunnel? Surnow dies because he enters the wind tunnel to view the information it holds. Why couldn't he access this information from the terminals in the control room?! Why weren't the wires on the data sensors made a *little* longer so this workstation could be located with the others? Or is this how the scientists ensure that they get their exercise?

X The FBI really has some incredibly sophisticated photo-manipulation programs. In this episode a technician takes a picture of a full-bearded Arthur Grable and removes the beard to reveal the jawline even though the jawline is shaped differently from the line on the edge of the beard! Was this a guess hazarded by the software that *just happened* to be *perfect?* And another thing: When Mulder tells the technician to remove Grable's eyeglasses, the man's head suddenly gets *fatter!* Why would removing glasses make a man's head bigger? (There's a punch line in here somewhere, but it eludes me at the moment.)

X Grable's head thaws out near the end of this episode as scientists attempt in vain to keep the temperature in his capsule from rising. I'm sure there's a good reason, but why doesn't someone grab a can opener and dump in more liquid nitrogen? (In the next episode we see an alien embryo preserved in liquid nitrogen, and there doesn't seem to be any sophisticated regulatory equipment to keep it cold.)

Continuity and Production Problems

X I believe the footage of the surveillance camera focusing near the end of this episode comes from "Ghost in the Machine," although there's no reason why the lab couldn't have exactly the same type of camera.

X A compliment first and then a nit. As Roland enters the final instructions to send the engine to Mach 15, note the abrasion on his right hand. It resides just where it would be if a pencil or pen had rubbed the skin raw. This seems very realistic. After all, Arthur has been forcing his twin to write furiously for hours. Unfortunately, this well-placed and lovely detail disappears when we see Roland in the next scene. Watch his hands while he folds his shirt in the halfway house just before he tells Tracy good-bye. No abrasion. No scab. Nothing.

FIRST SEASON

Trivia Questions

1 Where were Arthur and Lewis Grable born?

2 Who was in charge of the Avalon Foundation?

The Erlenmeyer Flask

PLOT SUMMARY In a cryptic late-night call, Deep Throat tells Mulder to watch a news report about a fugitive's high-speed escape. Enhancing the video, Mulder and Scully trace the offending vehicle to a scientist named Berube. Though uncooperative, Berube dies that night under suspicious circumstances.

Searching through Berube's lab the next day, Mulder finds a flask labeled "Purity Control." Subsequent testing by Scully's associates indicates that the flask contains extraterrestrial DNA. Meanwhile—at Berube's residence—Mulder finds keys to a building that houses five humans floating in tanks. But by the time he returns with Scully, everything is gone. Deep Throat then appears, telling them that they've found the place where the first human/alien hybrids were created. Now that one has escaped—a scientist named Secare—the covert group behind the research is destroying all the evidence.

On a hunch, Mulder returns to Berube's residence and finds Secare hiding in the attic. Unfortunately, so do the group's henchmen. They kill the hybrid and capture Mulder, only to learn that Deep Throat has helped Scully steal a frozen alien fetus. Deep Throat secures Mulder's release by returning the fetus, but he pays for his actions with his life.

The season concludes with Skinner shutting down the X-Files and Cancerman visiting a warehouse in the Pentagon to deposit the recovered fetus for safekeeping.

Onscreen Locations

🗶 Emgen Corporation, Gaithersburg, Maryland
🗶 Georgetown University, Microbiology Department
🗶 Berube Residence, Ardis, Maryland
🗶 Fort Marlene, High Containment Facility

Ruminations

This is a great episode. What a fabulous way to end the first season! I'm sure you noticed the parallelism between the end of this episode and the end of the pilot. Both feature a late-night call from Mulder to Scully, both show the time changing from "11:21" to "11:22." Both end with Cancerman storing a vital piece of evidence in a warehouse in the Pentagon.

Aside from all the normal X-Files stuff in this episode, there's one scene I find particularly appealing. Mulder and Scully are fumbling along, trying to follow a trail of scant evidence to Berube's lab. As Mulder interviews the recalcitrant scientist, Scully absentmindedly puts her finger up to a cage. She knows better. She just isn't thinking. The monkey inside reacts and angrily charges forward. Jumping back, Scully receives a well-deserved rebuke from Berube. Out in the hall, Mulder is still hot to follow up on the next lead, but Scully puts her foot down and unloads on him. When I saw this the first time, I thought, "Exactly right! Excellent characterization." She's embarrassed. She did something stupid. She knows it. And Mulder's willingness to keep stumbling along on what seems like a fool's mission is another irritant she doesn't need in her life at the moment . . . so she lets him have it! (And to Scully's credit, she does apologize for it later.)

Unanswered Questions

✖ After appearing to fill in the pieces for Mulder and Scully, Deep Throat nods to Scully and says that they have met "ever so briefly." When? Did I miss this meeting? The only time I can ever recall Deep Throat and Scully being near each other is at the end of "E.B.E." But during that encounter, Deep Throat was walking away into the fog. I didn't think that Scully even got a good look at his face. Is there something the creators aren't telling us?

Geographical Inconsistencies

✖ Ardis, Maryland, doesn't exit.

Plot Oversights

✖ This episode establishes that the body fluids of the alien/human hybrid are toxic, yet at the beginning of the episode, several police stand directly over the fluid on a pier and they seem fine.

✖ The episode also establishes that the alien/human hybrid can breathe underwater. At the beginning of the episode, Secare jumps into the water. At least a day later, the boats dragging the bottom of the harbor give up and depart. Nearby, Secare then surfaces. Question: If Secare can breathe underwater, why didn't he just swim away and find an out-of-the-way place to come ashore?

✖ The clean-up crew for the alien/human hybrid group doesn't seem very efficient in one respect. One of their men comes to Berube's lab to kill him, yet the next day Mulder finds a flask filled with alien DNA. It's even labeled "Purity Control"—the password to gain access to the frozen alien fetus in the high-security facility. Surely this clean-up guy would know what Berube was working on and what evidence should be destroyed and would recognize the term "Purity Control." So why is the flask still there? (Because if it wasn't, the plot couldn't move forward!)

✖ Sometimes Mulder confuses me. Here he is—after breaking into the newly deceased Dr. Berube's home—riffling through the aforementioned man's desk, sitting with his back to a window *with the blinds open!* Now, I don't know about you, but if I were breaking and entering, I think I would take a few more precautions!

✖ It's really too bad that Mulder decided to quit carrying a camera several episodes back. Think of the wonderful pictures he could have taken during *this* episode.

✖ Even more startling, Mulder makes it back to his apartment, only to be greeted by a ringing phone. It's Scully, and she's been trying to reach him. He explains that he left his cellular phone in his car. *Why* did he suddenly decide to stop carrying his cell phone?

✖ In one of the great scenes in this episode, Scully uses credentials supplied by Deep Throat to gain access to a frozen alien fetus at the High Containment Facility at Fort Marlene. She slides out a large round container and opens the lid to extract the fetus from liquid nitrogen. So, um . . . how did she get the little guy *out of the building?* That sucker has been in liquid nitrogen, it's going to be *brittle* and it's going to be *cold!* Ramming it under your trench coat is a surefire way to set your feet to dancing. Scully *is* carrying her thin leather briefcase, but the little guy is going to leave a big lump in it. (I suppose she could have a cardboard box in her briefcase.) On a related topic, one wonders why the guard allowed her to leave with it in the first place. Do people check the little guy in and out all the time? Deep Throat refers to the fetus as the "wellspring." This would indicate it's important. You usually don't allow scientists to cart around something important without strict procedures

FIRST SEASON

Trivia Questions

❶ What is the full license plate number of Berube's car?

❷ What is the address of Zeus Storage?

Trivia Answers
❶ 253 AYF
❷ 1616 Pandora Street.

"Okay, Mulder, but I'm warning you. If this is monkey pee, you're on your own."

—Scully *to Mulder after he hands her the flask labeled "Purity Control" in Berube's trashed laboratory and asks her to find out what it is. (At this point Scully isn't convinced that they should even be continuing with the investigation in the first place, and after one of Berube monkeys tried to take her finger off, she doesn't want to have any more to do with them!)*

for handling. (I do have a favorite explanation for how Scully got the alien fetus out of the building. I'm thinking she dressed it up in doll clothes and carried it out under her arm! There's just something about that image that makes me smile. "See my pretty dolly? It's the new Tickle-Me Alien. Of course, when you *do* tickle it, it spews toxic liquid all over you, but I like it anyway. It's *cute!*")

✗ Obviously Scully hasn't made it to that refresher course in CPR yet. After the dark conspiracy returns Mulder, she checks his pulse with her thumb! This is a no-no. Your thumb has its own pulse, and it's possible to confuse your pulse with the pulse of the patient.

✗ So I guess the alien dude wasn't needed any longer for experiments? The episode ends with Cancerman putting the little guy into storage instead of returning it to Fort Marlene.

Equipment Oddities

✗ Obviously Scully isn't worried about the dark conspiracy forces listening to her conversation with Mulder about the oddities of the substance found in the flask at Berube's trashed lab. Both she and Mulder are on cell phones, and already they have seen that the intelligence community has equipment to jack into the cellular pathways. A bit later, the scientist whom Scully

---

GREAT MOMENTS

Though Scully needs refresher courses from time to time in the episodes to come, her epiphany—as she gazes at the frozen alien fetus—caps a series of events that I think of as "The Reeducation of Dana Scully." It is a wonderful moment when the center of her world shudders and reorients to the reality of extreme possibilities.

---

works with dies in a horrible auto accident that kills the entire family. In addition, all the evidence of what the scientist and Scully found disappears. Hmmm. I wonder how the dark conspiracy *ever* found out what Scully was doing. (It's just a mystery, I tell you!)

Continuity and Production Problems

✗ The opening car chase of this episode supposedly takes place near Washington, D.C., but there are a few moments when you might feel like turning to your dog to say, "Oh, Toto! I don't think we're in Maryland anymore!" First, watch as two cars pull into a train yard; you should be able to spot at least two instances of a logo that reads "CN." That stands for "Canadian National." Second, just as we hear the dispatcher respond to the police unit's call for assistance, the scene cuts to a close-up of a rearview mirror. Between the top of the mirror and the top of the windshield, a sign zips by. If you put the tape in slow motion you should be able to read, "Vancouver Drydock Company Ltd." (Score one more for Vancouver—home for production of *The X-Files!*)

✗ This episode reveals an important piece of information about those involved in dark conspiracies of the U.S. government. The Postal Service is cooperating with them. (Gasp!) In fact, the Postal Service has given them their own special zip codes to ensure that their mail gets delivered promptly, with maximum efficiency. During his first visit to Berube's house, Mulder confirms that he's at the right location by pulling some mail from the mailbox. A close-up on an envelope reveals that Dr. T. A. Berube lives at "2650 W. 1st, Ardis, Maryland 149376." Obviously those involved with dark conspiracies get *six* digits in their zip codes as opposed to the normal *five* (not to mention that Maryland zip codes normally start with a "2")!

Whose Truth Is Out There?

Epistemological Thoughts on the Games Mulder and Scully Play

If there is any one statement that succinctly summarizes *The X-Files*, it would have to be the trademarked catchphrase, "the truth is out there." Those five simple words evoke images of an ultimate goal, an arduous quest, a determined spirit. These ideas alone probably could have carried the series. Thankfully, Chris Carter and company saw more than just the first level in those words and gave us a fascinating pair of characters in Mulder and Scully, who speak to the essence of an age-old philosophical conflict—one that is often categorized as "faith versus science." As you already know, Mulder plays the believer and Scully plays the scientist in this weekly reenactment of the conflict. However, that simple categorization—while it is useful—doesn't quite fit the complexities that the creators have birthed in their two lead characters. For Carter and company—whether intuitively or analytically—understand that "truth" can twist in odd ways within the human spirit and that we as fallible creatures often choose the path to the "truth" that best *serves* us rather than the path that will ultimately lead us to our destination.

In discussing *The X-Files* with others, I have often found confusion over the actions of our intrepid pair. I've heard nitpickers complain about Mulder's illegalities; about the "believer's" behavior not befitting a *real* FBI agent. While willing to attribute *these* elements to his obsession to find "the truth," nitpickers soon turn to other perplexities—episodes such as "Revelations" where Mulder suddenly turns into the skeptic. Or "Paper Hearts," where Mulder instantly abandons everything he "believes" about his sister's abduction and fully commits to a mundane, terrestrial explanation. Scully has her share of peculiar episodes as well when held to a rigid embodiment of the disinterested researcher. In "The Erlenmeyer Flask" she encounters hard scientific evidence for the existence of extraterrestrials. She even holds what appears to be an alien fetus in her hands. Yet, only ten episodes later, in "Red Museum," she—a scientist—questions the scientific findings. And in "Oubliette" she even accuses Mulder of protecting Lucy Householder "beyond the point of reason" when, in fact, dispassionate reason and logic would demand a conclusion that Householder had no role in the kidnapping. (Scully believes that Householder is involved because she had Amy Jacobs's blood on her fast-food restaurant uniform. But dozens of witnesses placed Householder at the restaurant at the time of the kidnapping. Those same witnesses would confirm that her uniform was clean prior to her collapse. In addition, Householder was taken *straight* to the hospital and held overnight. Apparently her uniform was taken at that time and submitted for testing. There was simply *no* opportunity for Householder to encounter the kidnap victim.)

Are these examples simple inconsistencies

in the characterization? Did they just slip through because no one was paying attention? For me, the answer to both questions is a resounding "No!" If there's one thing *The X-Files* has done consistently right in episode after episode, it's the accurate characterizations of Mulder and Scully. Here's why.

Humans find many disciplines in their pursuit of "the truth." Chris Carter and company have chosen two different approaches for their lead characters—that of subjective truth versus objective truth.

Mulder is a subjectivist. For the most part, when he says, "The truth is out there," what he really means is, "Someday, what I believe will be shown to be the truth, and everyone will know that I was right all along." In other words, *he* establishes truth simply because he believes that a certain thing is true. Note the words of his soliloquy describing his life at the beginning of "Colony." He says that he has lived with a "fragile faith built on the ether of vague memories from an experience that I could neither prove nor explain." He adds that his sister was abducted by what he believes were extraterrestrials and that belief has sustained him, fueling him to his quest for truths that are as elusive as the memory itself. Having just come from an encounter with an extraterrestrial in the Arctic Circle, Mulder lies immersed in a tub, barely alive, while his narration continues—stating that what happened to him on the ice has justified every belief; that if he dies, it will be with a certainty that his "faith has been righteous."

As a subjectivist, Mulder not only decides what is true by intuition, he also expects others to realize immediately the brilliance of his leaps. I could write dozens of pages documenting this trait, but suffice it to say that *The X-Files* is replete with Mulder jumping to conclusions with little or no evidence and then justifying his beliefs with the statements "I know it" or "I'm sure of it"—often deriding Scully because she's not willing to make the same leap as he. And when she does open herself to "extreme possibilities," as in "Beyond the Sea," *he* decides that they are the *wrong* possibilities (because he has come to a different conclusion) and chastises her for it!

Interestingly enough, because Mulder expects near-instantaneous approval for his theories (they are "true," after all, at least in his mind), he has little patience to educate those who do not believe as he does. In "Squeeze" he tells Scully that he runs into so many people who don't believe that sometimes he can't resist playing with their minds. At the beginning of "Tooms," Mulder has an opportunity to testify that Tooms should remain in custody. Instead of attempting to prove the believable—that Tooms recently murdered four people—Mulder immediately goes for the fantastic, trying to convince the panel that Tooms is a mutant. (The result is Tooms's release.) Likewise, he pontificates belligerently in front of a Senate subcommittee at the end of "Tunguska," when a more reasoned approach would bring him closer to his goal. But then again, he's not really interested in persuading or convincing. He expects that his statements should be enough to definitively establish "the truth." After all, he's *Mulder!*

In addition, Mulder's subjectivism often exhibits scant concern for the human element in his quest. In "Born Again" he campaigns to have a little girl rehypnotized, disregarding what effect it might have on her. He's more interested in "proving" transmigration of the soul. Near the end of "Oubliette" he actually smiles when he hears that Lucy Householder drowned in the back of a car because it shows that his intuition was correct. (Yes, Mulder seemed to demonstrate compassion toward Householder in this episode, but compassion for what purpose? Ultimately, I would contend that Mulder's emotions are based on the hope that Householder will prove the extreme possibility of psychic connections.) And during the emotionally powerful ending of "Never Again," as Scully explains that not everything is about him, Mulder responds, "Yes, but it's . . ." before falling to silence.

Not surprisingly, Mulder's subjectivism also mates him with strange bedfellows. There is an old saying, "The enemy of my enemy is my friend." Mulder finds extreme possibilities in *anything* ridiculed by the those who ridicule him. He even validates the concept of Roky Crikenson's screenplay, *The Truth About Aliens,* in "José Chung's *From Outer Space*"—despite its inclusion of Lord Kinbote, a red, Cyclops-like alien who speaks in King James English, and the graphic depictions of underworld sex orgies! And what about "Quagmire"? In that episode, Mulder and Scully chase after Big Blue—a Loch Ness-type sea monster. Why? Because—to pull a quotation from the end of the episode—Mulder "sees hope in such a possibility." In Mulder's mind, if Big Blue exists, so do aliens. In fact, Scully's statements in "Quagmire" accurately describe his condition when she observes that everything takes on a warped significance to fit his megalomaniacal cosmology. (An interesting side note here: Mulder also rejects Melissa Scully's New Age espousals in "One Breath." Perhaps they're too "mainstream" for him?)

Worst of all, though, Mulder's "subjective truth" is only as strong as his emotional state. Becoming depressed in "Little Green Men," he begins to wonder if his sister's abduction really happened. And—as mentioned above—he is willing in "Paper Hearts" to abandon all the evidence of extraterrestrial involvement in his sister's abduction ("Colony," "End Game," "Paper Clip," "Herrenvolk") because he has begun to believe that she was taken by a serial murderer.

On the other hand, Scully is an objectivist. When *she* says "The truth is out there," she means that "the truth" exists *whether she believes in it or not,* and its very existence is a call to discovery through careful investigation. She takes the reductive science approach: Gather the evidence, analyze it, develop a hypothesis, test the hypothesis through experimentation, adjust the hypothesis to account for the results. In "Pilot," Scully tells Mulder that she finds it "fantastic" that there are answers beyond the realm of science. She adds that the answers are there, "you just have to know where to look."

No matter what Scully encounters, she must always return to objectivism, because it gives her a sense that there is order and persistent principles in the universe (and we'll see in a moment why that's important). At the conclusion of "End Game," sitting beside Mulder's bed, Scully narrates that many of the things she has seen have challenged her belief in an ordered universe, but this uncertainty has only strengthened her need to know, to apply reason to those things that seem to defy it.

To her credit, Scully's objectivism allows her to understand Mulder. She's not afraid to demand more proof from him. She accurately identifies the blinding quality of his obsession in

"E.B.E." And she even redefines her vocabulary to help him understand the thing for which *she* searches. Sitting in an empty hospital room after the death of her sister in "Paper Clip," Scully tells her partner, "I've heard the truth, Mulder. Now what I want are the answers." This statement comes on the heels of an episode that provided evidence for two contradictory "truths." Mulder has concluded that alien abductions are vehicles to create an alien/human hybrid. Scully has concluded that alien abductions are cover stories for the monstrous experiments conducted *by* humans *on* humans. By the end of the episode, Scully realizes she and Mulder will forever argue over this "truth," so she turns her attention away from such futility. Now she wants hard *data.*

There is only one problem with Scully's objectivism. It relies on a fundamental—and potentially flawed—assumption. To be an objectivist, she not only believes that "the truth is out there," she also must believe that the human mind has the *capability* to comprehend it (hence the need for an ordered and persistent universe). Count on it. *Anything* that pricks this assumption of human competence will evoke fear and uncertainty in Scully. In the same bedside narration mentioned above, Scully acknowledges that several aspects of the case covered by "Colony" and "End Game" remain unexplained and suggest paranormal phenom-

ena. She then adds that she *is convinced* that to accept those conclusions would be to "abandon all hope of understanding the scientific events behind them." This is the reason why Scully *must* reject the reasonable and logical conclusion that Householder was *not* involved in the kidnapping of Amy Jacobs during "Oubliette." To accept the evidence that Amy Jacobs's blood *magically* appeared on Householder's uniform—without any possible scientific theory or methodology to explain it— would be to allow the possibility that "truth" lies beyond the realm of human understanding. That thought strikes *terror* in her heart, for with it, objectivism comes undone.

Unfortunately for Scully, the caseload of *The X-Files* often leads our favorite FBI agents into domains that do not readily respond to scientific investigation, and—at times—it even leads them into areas that do not lend themselves to Mulder's divination. But then, these journeys *are* by design, are they not? And Chris Carter and company have used them to supply us with some fascinating mind candy.

(By the way, there is another discipline in this *ultimate* pursuit of life. It's called "revealed truth," and it posits a final Truth that resides beyond the bounds of human intuition and investigation—a Truth so fundamental and transcendent that it cannot be known unless it chooses to communicate with us.)

Whose Truth
Is Out There?

SECOND
SEASON

Little Green Men

Onscreen Locations

☒ Arecibo Ionospheric Observatory, Arecibo, Puerto Rico

☒ Longstreet Motel, Washington, D.C.

☒ F.B.I. Academy, Quantico, Virginia

☒ Watergate Hotel & Office Complex

☒ Chilmark, Mass., November 27, 1973

☒ U.S. Naval Observatory, Washington, D.C.

☒ Miami International Airport

Ruminations

The date in this episode comes from a passenger manifest that contains the name George E. Hale—an alias used by Mulder.

In this episode, Mulder says that he attended Deep Throat's funeral using eight-power binoculars from a thousand feet away. One wonders if he wandered over to the gravesite after everyone left to finally learn the name of his benefactor!

I couldn't help but snicker as Senator Matheson spoke with Mulder about Bach's Brandenburg Concerto, No. 2. Matheson comments on the beauty of the piece. (And don't get me wrong, it is beautiful.) He then goes on to make a very terracentric statement. He says that if another civilization listens to the music, they would think that Earth must be a wonderful place. Well . . . maybe. On the other hand, the aliens might be tone deaf and hear the concerto as an aggressive avalanche of sound designed to numb the senses of anyone who listened to it! Enraged over this unknown enemy's encroachment into their territory and fearing that the brain-sucking composition was designed to prepare them for invasion, the aliens would, no doubt, mount a preemptive strike to destroy the manufacturers of such a heinous weapon.

By the way, many nitpickers found Scully's choice of a trench coat in Miami International Airport amusing—given the normal temperature of southern Florida. But they also recog-

PLOT SUMMARY

The days after the shutdown of the X-Files grind by. Scully teaches at Quantico. Mulder works "white bread" cases—bank fraud and the like, listening via wiretap to men lusting over exotic dancers. Without the resources of the Bureau, he has given up. Then Senator Matheson calls Mulder to a meeting. There has been "contact" at the radio telescope in Arecibo, Puerto Rico, and little time remains to gather evidence before a UFO retrieval team sanitizes the location.

At Arecibo, Mulder finds printouts that show contact with extraterrestrial life. He also finds a worker named Jorge Concepción—obviously frightened by something. When that "something" approaches again, Concepción runs away and soon dies in the jungle from unknown causes. "Something" approaches a second time. Filled with terror, Mulder blockades the door and even tries to shoot a little green man who appears, but his gun malfunctions.

Later, Mulder wakes, with Scully hovering over him. She's been searching for him ever since he disappeared from work. Enthralled, Mulder begins to tell her of the proof he has found. Then he hears the retrieval team approaching in the distance. There's a harrowing escape before the pair return to Washington, but the tape they bring back as evidence is blank. Still, Mulder has found the will to continue.

nized that the creators had to conceal Gillian Anderson's real-life pregnancy somehow.

Unanswered Questions

☒ What really happened at Arecibo? Was it aliens? If so, they seem to be new to the area. They rebroadcast transmissions from *Voyager* as a kind of cosmic handshake, and everyone who talks about the signal makes it sound like first contact. (Yet more visitors from the intragalactic hyperspace bypass to add to the ones we've already seen?) On the other hand, is it possible that the events at Arecibo were created by *terrestrial* intelligence? As Mulder himself observes, are these events just an elaborate joke played on those who want to believe? Consider this: The episode opens with Mulder in a blue funk. It ends with him committed to continuing his obsession. In "Herrenvolk" we learn that Cancerman considers Mulder's involvement "vital" to "the project." Is it possible that Cancerman staged the encounter at Arecibo as a carrot to dangle in front of his suddenly mulish rebel? ("José Chung's *From Outer Space*" seems to say that the government possesses functioning UFOs and they are flown by military men dressed like aliens.)

Geographical Inconsistencies

☒ The Arecibo Observatory at Arecibo, Puerto Rico, *does* exist. But—while it *was* in the midst of an upgrade during July 1994—it never was shut down, as portrayed here. (If you would like more information and you have access to the World Wide Web, you can visit the National Astronomy and Ionosphere Center's Web site at www.naic.edu.)

Plot Oversights

☒ Surprisingly enough, just after Mulder jolts awake from his remembrance of Samantha's abduction, Senator Matheson's aide opens the door to Mulder's apartment and tells him they are going to "the Hill." So . . . did Mulder forget to lock the door of his apartment? Or does Senator Matheson have a key?

☒ Matheson and Mulder must know something about the intelligence community. Both assume that if they talk low in his office, no one will be aware of the conversation. This indicates that they believe any surveillance will be audio only. If Matheson has access to sensitive information and Cancerman thinks he is enough of a threat to bug his office, why not hide a videocamera in there as well? (Then again, maybe Matheson is part of the whole "carrot charade" as well! See above.)

☒ Attempting to locate Mulder's whereabouts, Scully comes to his apartment, only to discover that a pair of agents have it under surveillance. When questioned, Scully says that she has come to feed Mulder's fish and makes a show of going to the fish tank. Strangely enough, the actual fish appear to be missing! (Either that or they are all taking a nap in the back corner.)

☒ Mulder finds Jorge Concepción in a lavatory inside the control room of the Arecibo Observatory. Actually, Mulder finds him in a lavatory inside the *locked* control room of the Arecibo Observatory—a control room that was *locked* from the outside with a chain! Did the guys who secured the building leave poor Concepción in there by accident? Or is there another entrance? And how long has this guy been here? And is the plumbing still working?

☒ After Concepción dies, Mulder records his observations of the body in case decomposition sets in later and obscures the evidence. Interestingly enough, he does this with Concepción almost fully clothed. Not that I'm volunteering for the job, but wouldn't it be better to examine the naked body in detail?

☒ And speaking of this scene, Mulder nears the end of his observations as the ground begins to quake. "Something" is approaching a second time. For a person so consumed with finding more evidence, Mulder does something very strange: He shuts off his hand-held tape recorder! Granted, that little thing might not pick up much, but it might pick up *something*.

☒ As Mulder comes back to consciousness after his close encounter, Scully hovers over him. She looks very relieved and says that she "was sure" he was dead. Did she bother to check his pulse?

☒ Why does Mulder take only *one* reel of tape from the control room? Why not the printouts as well?

Changed Premises

☒ It's a minor thing, but Mulder refers to "little green men" in this episode (hence the title). Yet in "Squeeze," Mulder went out of his way to tell Tom Colton that Reticulans weren't green, they were gray. (I'm surprised that Scully didn't mouth off about this in an attempt to lighten Mulder's mood.)

☒ When did Mulder figure out that he wasn't in bed when his sister was abducted? From "Pilot" and "Conduit," we learn that Samantha disappeared out of her bedroom at night and that Mulder was in bed at the time and he couldn't move. Yet, in this episode, we have a very detailed recollection that shows Mulder and Samantha playing Stratego in the living room when the abduction occurred. In addition, *this* Samantha looks older than either the picture of Samantha we see in "Conduit" or the little girl who appears to Mulder in "Miracle Man."

Equipment Oddities

☒ I want a keyboard like the one Mulder has on his computer. Scully comes to his apartment and turns on his computer. She quickly discovers that his hard drive is password-protected. For her first guess she types "SPOOKY" and hits the Enter key. Appropriately enough, we hear six key clicks and then see her press Enter. For her second attempt, she tries "SAMANTHA." This time we hear *ten* keystrokes. Granted, the last one is the Enter key, but that still leaves eight letters and nine key clicks. Then Scully tries "TRUST-NO1." Again, eight letters, nine keystrokes (not counting the Enter key). Amazingly enough, the computer seems to know which keystroke to discard to give Scully what she wants instead of what she types!

☒ Even more odd, Mulder has a printer that is clearly labeled as a bubble jet printer, but it sounds exactly like a laser printer and spits out paper at an incredible rate! (Almost like the creators just put a preprinted piece of paper in the bin and hit the form feed button. Hmm.)

☒ Too bad Mulder quit carrying a camera several episodes back. He sure could have used it on this mission.

☒ At the very end of the episode, Mulder listens again to the blank tape he brought back from Arecibo. Dramatically, he leans forward, straining for any missed nuance. Um . . . is there a reason why he doesn't use the *headphones* that hang around his neck?!

Continuity and Production Problems

☒ For some reason, the light level suddenly increases at the Arecibo control room just after Scully arrives and Mulder wakes from his close encounter. It happens just after Mulder gets up from the floor and begins telling Scully about all the evidence he has found. Watch as he says, "On the tapes . . . the tape."

Trivia Questions

❶ To what *Offspring's* song does Tuesday perform?

❷ Who was Mulder's music appreciation teacher?

Trivia Answers
❶ "Come Out and Play."
❷ Professor Ganz.

The Host

PLOT SUMMARY

Unexpectedly, Skinner dispatches Mulder to Newark, New Jersey, for what seems to be a simple homicide. Mulder balks, believing that Skinner is trying to demoralize him. After all, the body rests facedown in a sewer. But then, a sanitation worker is attacked by something that leaves a giant bite mark; an anonymous phone call reveals that Mulder has a friend at the FBI and someone shoves a tabloid newspaper under Scully's door that tells of a monster attacking a sailor on a Russian ship. Scully soon identifies the body found in the sewer as the sailor.

The case appears solved when a worker at a sewer processing plant in Newark traps a giant wormlike creature with humanoid features. But, the worm—a.k.a. Flukeman—soon escapes, and Mulder must hunt it down—energized by a second anonymous phone call, asserting that success in the case is imperative to the reinstatement of the X-Files. And if that wasn't enough, Scully soon realizes that the creature is using humans as hosts for reproduction.

Mulder does stop Flukeman's return to the sea—killing it in the process—and later analysis shows it was born in the radioactive soup of Chernobyl before traveling on the Russian ship to the New Jersey shore. Unfortunately, as the episode ends, we see that the creature has already produced an offspring.

Onscreen Locations

- ☒ Atlantic Ocean, two miles off the coast of New Jersey
- ☒ Longstreet Motel, Washington, D.C.
- ☒ Newark, New Jersey
- ☒ Middlesex County, Sayreville, New Jersey
- ☒ FBI National Academy, Quantico, Virginia
- ☒ Newark County Sewage Processing Plant
- ☒ Middlesex County Psychiatric Hospital
- ☒ Lake Betty Park

Geographical Inconsistencies

☒ Screen text in this episode identifies the Newark County Sewage Processing Plant. New Jersey has no Newark County. The city of Newark resides in Essex County.

Plot Oversights

☒ Discussing the case with Mulder, Scully identifies the parasite that she found inside the Russian sailor as a "Turbellaria"—commonly known as "a fluke or flatworm." She then goes on to say that this type of worm has a scolex, a sucker-like mouth with four hooker spikes. I discussed these "facts" with Elizabeth Harrison, a former biology teacher and she did a bit of research for me. According to Elizabeth, "flatworm" is the most generic term that Scully uses. There are several classes of flatworms, among them Turbellaria. However, turbellarian are not flukes and do not have scolexes! In addition, flukes are in the class Trematoda (a.k.a. trematodes) and they don't have scolexes either! (They hang on to their host with one or two muscular suckers.) If the flatworm that Scully extracted from the Russian sailor really has a scolex then it's a tapeworm (which are in the class Cestoda)—not turbellarian, not a fluke and we should probably call the monster in this episode Tapeman instead of Flukeman! (But that doesn't sound nearly as cool, does it?)

☒ Flukeman escapes from his first capture because the Justice Department wants him transferred to an institution for a full psychological evaluation. At the time, he's being held in the Middlesex County Psychiatric Hospital. Noticed the name of the place? "Middlesex County *Psychiatric* Hospital"? No doubt there's a *really* good reason that the *psychiatric* evaluation couldn't be done there! (Ever heard of the infamous short-show syndrome?)

☒ After submitting his report on Flukeman, Mulder learns that the sanitation worker died because of injuries received when Flukeman attacked. Incensed, Mulder pontificates that if he and Scully had been on the case from the beginning, they might have been able to save the man's life. How? Mulder gives this little speech only thirty-five minutes into the episode. *The X-Files* usually has people dropping like flies until the last ten minutes or so! (Okay, okay. If you want a more reasoned objection, try this on: Mulder isn't even convinced that the case has any merit until *after* Scully does the autopsy and the sanitation worker is attacked. By that time, events are already in motion for the man to die. And since this is a new mutation, I don't think Mulder would have a preexisting X-File on Flukie.)

☒ I realize that I do not measure up to the grand and valiant standards of U.S. marshals, but I can tell you for sure that if I were transporting Flukeman and I looked back and saw that he had freed himself from a gurney, I *would* wait for my backup to arrive and I *especially* would not open the back door of the ambulance on a dark, secluded highway!

☒ Mulder has the most amazing luck. Near the end of the program, an official from the Newark County Sewage Processing Plant attempts to shut off an overflow channel and tumbles into the water. Flukeman attacks. Mulder tries to reach for the sanitation official but eventually dives in to save him. By this time, Flukeman has finished mating. Yet—instead of lunging for the next tasty morsel—Flukeman heads out the pipe that leads to the ocean. Guess Mulder wasn't his type!

Changed Premises

☒ Just last episode, the creators treat us to a scene in which Scully starts an autopsy for a group of students at the Academy. We join her as she says it is advantageous to begin an autopsy with the removal of the cranium. Yet, in this episode, the creators give us an overhead shot of the Russian sailor's body well after Scully has begun her autopsy, and sailor-boy's head is still intact (i.e., she hasn't removed his cranium yet). Why wasn't it "advantageous" to begin with the cranium in this case? (Or—in the last episode—was Scully simply trying to set a new personal best for the time it takes her to make a student hurl?)

Equipment Oddities

☒ Moments before being attacked, a Newark sanitation worker climbs down a ladder and wades through stomach-high sewage to arrive at a damaged piece of wire mesh. He wears chest-high waders. Then Flukeman yanks the guy underwater. Moments later, the guy surfaces. Much thrashing follows. His coworker throws him a rope and hoists him up to a platform that sits approximately two feet above the waterline. What's wrong with this scene, you ask? Did I mention that the guy wears *waders*? Wouldn't they *fill* with water, making it nearly impossible to drag the guy out (even counting adrenaline)? Even more odd, when the coworker flops his injured friend onto the platform, the waders have somehow emptied themselves of water! Nary a trickle spills onto the flooring.

Trivia Questions

❶ Who was Mulder's contact in Newark?

❷ What is the phone number for A&A Anderson Tank Cleaning Service?

✖ After the apprehension of Flukeman the first time, Mulder and Scully visit him in the Middlesex County Psychiatric Hospital. Afterward, Scully tells Mulder that she has identified the body of the Russian sailor. She shows Mulder a picture of the man's arm. It contains a tattoo. But why does the picture of the arm show so much more decomposition than was present on the arm during the autopsy? Wasn't this photo taken during the autopsy? And if not, why not? Wouldn't a tattoo be a somewhat important and transient piece of data to document?

Continuity and Production Problems

✖ For the most part, the creators do a good job hiding Gillian Anderson's pregnancy. The closing moments of the episode, however, provide a shot when it's obvious that *something* is different about our normally svelte medical-doctor-turned-FBI-agent. Watch as Scully walks around a bench to sit beside Mulder. (Evidently, the director tired of headshots.)

✖ The creators seem to have a fondness for the sewer grate they shot for the footage at the beginning of "Squeeze." They shoot it again for the closing footage of this episode. (At first I thought it was the same piece of film, but the crawl rate is different. Then again, maybe they sped it up?)

Blood

Onscreen Locations

☒ Postal Center, Franklin, Pennsylvania
☒ Civic Center, Franklin, Pennsylvania
☒ Venango County Sheriff's Office
☒ FBI National Academy, Quantico, Virginia
☒ Franklin Community Hospital, Franklin, Pennsylvania
☒ Franklin Community College

Ruminations

Was "someone" actually controlling the murderers through nearby electronic devices, or were the messages merely a result of drug-induced psychosis? I almost added this "unanswered question" to my review of "Blood," but there is one piece of evidence that definitively supports a less conspiratorial theory for the events in this episode (at least in my opinion). If "someone" was sending messages to the assailants via the electronic devices, the devices would have to be physically capable of generating those images. In three cases—the zip-code machine shown at the beginning of the episode, Mrs. McRoberts's microwave, and Ed Funsch's digital watch—the readouts are obviously seven-segment displays normally used to represent numbers. These readouts cannot generate a capital "K."

To generate the messages shown, "someone" would have to replace all the electronic devices used by a given individual with identical, but internally enhanced, devices that could relay the orders "KILL 'EM ALL." This seems improbable. More likely, each person's phobias created a fear response in the normal course of

PLOT SUMMARY A rash of bizarre murders by previously law-abiding citizens in Franklin, Pennsylvania, sends local police to the FBI for help, but even Mulder is quickly stymied. For the first time, he struggles to develop a profile on who will kill next and why. The only real connection in the crimes is the destruction of an electronic device at each site.

Then a woman named McRoberts murders her mechanic. When questioned, McRoberts attacks Mulder with a knife—told to do so by her microwave—and the local sheriff is forced to shoot. Scully's autopsy shows McRoberts's adrenaline levels at two hundred times normal. It also reveals a high concentration of a compound Mulder later identifies as LSDM—a chemical designed to invoke a fear response in insects. That night, Mulder witnesses illegal crop spraying—becoming drenched with LSDM in the process. Although Scully can document no side effects, Mulder is convinced that the chemical heightens a person's paranoia and that "someone" is conducting a test—controlling those exposed through messages transmitted via electronic devices. The county supervisor thinks Mulder is crazy, but he agrees to halt the spraying. Thankfully, only one more person goes berserk, and Mulder subdues him without great loss of life. But after the incident, Mulder's cell phone suddenly spits out a series of tones as it proclaims, "All done. Bye-bye."

his or her life (just as it had in days past). After exposure to the bug spray, however, the stress-related hormones reacted with LSDM to create a hallucinogenic state that caused the individual to believe that he or she was receiving messages from nearby electronic devices. (In fact, the creators are careful in this episode to document just such a progression!) So—to answer Scully's suspicion—yes, Mulder is paranoid!

Geographical Inconsistencies

☒ As Ed Funsch listens to a public announcement concerning a cholesterol screening that is being given to all individuals in the area, the announcer states that "Franklin and Venango counties" are participating in the important program. I believe the announcer meant to say, "Franklin and Venango *county*" are participating. There is a Franklin County in Pennsylvania, but it's *a hundred miles* from Venango County—the home of the city of Franklin. (Ain't U.S. geography grand?)

Plot Oversights

☒ The episode opens at a "postal center" in Franklin, Pennsylvania. We see envelopes being stuffed and sealed for some kind of mass mailing. The addresses on the envelopes appear to be generated by computer. The zip codes whiz by in no particular order. (Remember that. It's important.) The letters then drop into a machine where they stop, one at a time, in front of a human operator. Glancing at the envelope, the operator keys-in the zip code. (By the way, the speed shown for this last process is correct! I called the post office and—although letter-sorting machines are fast becoming obsolete—the kind supervisor I spoke with thought he remembered a rate of fifty to fifty-five letters *per minute!*) Once told the zip code of the letter, the machine routes it to the appropriate slot so the letter can be bundled in bulk and sent to that location.

There is one enormous question that jumps from this scene for anyone who has worked with mass mailings. *Why* are the zip codes out of order on the envelopes? This is obviously a mass mailing. The U.S. Postal Service provides signif-

icant savings in postage if the mailing is delivered to it in a certain way. All letters bound for a certain destination must be bundled together. The easiest way to accomplish this is to generate the mailing labels from the name-and-address database *sorted by zip code.* After the envelopes are stuffed and sealed, it is a simple matter—though still tedious—to go through and create the bundles. Generating addresses that are out of zip code order simply makes no financial sense! It wastes time and resources. Now, if the creators had shown us just the letter-sorting machine with an assortment of personal letters, this scene would make sense. Or if they had shown a mass mailing being prepared, this scene would have made sense. But combining a mass mailing with a letter-sorting machine is a problem, because the two normally don't go together. At least in my experience! (The addresses shown are, of course, bogus!)

Equipment Oddities

☒ Yet another amazing performance from an electronic keyboard. In the opening scene, Funsch sits at a machine that shows him a quick succession of envelopes. His job is to read the zip code and key-in the first five digits on a small keypad. In each case, we see the envelope, we see Funsch's hand on the keypad, and then we see the resulting zip code pop up on Funsch's display. There's *no question* that the number he enters is *supposed* to be the number on the display. The letter to Candice Field carries a zip code of 13090. Yet Funsch appears to enter "95422." Next, a letter to Barry Backus has a zip code of 14414. Funsch simultaneously presses the "1" and "4" buttons followed by "2" and then "5." In both cases, the machine *automagically* arrives at the correct zip code! (And dare you think this is *too* nitpicky, I would offer that Scully herself uses freeze-frame-advance to analyze video and extract an exit code for the boxcar in "731"—on a keypad, no less! Granted, I realize Scully's endeavor was for a more high and noble purpose but, hey, that's why she's a hero and I'm a nitpicker.)

☒ Funsch tries to use an automated cash machine. He inserts his card and enters his PIN, but he does not appear to complete the transaction before flying into a rage and running away. Yet moments later, a guard approaches, pulls Funsch's card from the slot, and the screen asks if he would like *another* transaction. Did Funsch just happen to pound on the right buttons to complete his first transaction? (And how much money did he transfer to the Swahili Preservation League?)

☒ This is very odd. During the last episode, Scully wore eyeglasses that had some curvature to the lenses. (In other words, they were real eyeglasses that *actually* had a prescription. They are easiest to see as Scully sits in front of her computer, perusing information on flatworms.) In this episode, the eyeglasses she wears are perfectly flat and thin. (You can see them clearly as she reads of Mulder's difficulties in developing a profile on the murders, especially when the camera pans around her head and she mutters that she was wondering when Mulder would get around to mentioning aliens.) Why the change? Did Scully's eyes suddenly improve?!

☒ Mrs. McRoberts attacks her mechanic because a diagnostic computer tells her that the mechanic is a liar and he's going to rape and then kill her. I can't offer any opinion of the "rape and kill" part, but I think the diagnostic computer was dead-on when it pegged him as a liar! The mechanic tells her that her car should be generating 168 horses at 6,200 rpm's. So far, so good. Then he starts her car using the diagnostic machine, and the display supposedly shows that the car is at 6,200 rpm's but isn't generating 168 horses. He then goes on to tell her all the things that he will need to fix. All this time the car *idles*—occasionally revving a bit in the back-

ground. I think I can say with some certainty that Mrs. McRoberts's engine *is not* running at 6,200 rpm, as the computer states. It would be whining *like crazy* at 6,200 rpm's. Therefore, the mechanic has tampered with the computer and rigged it to give false readings so he can do unnecessary repairs!

☒ At one point, Mulder confers with the Lone Gunmen. The scene in question begins with Frohike using an illuminated magnifying glass to examine a fly brought in by Mulder. Byers and Langly stand nearby. Evidently the creators thought they needed more light on Frohike's face or they didn't want the circular fluorescent bulb of the magnifying glass pointed at the camera because Frohike is using the thing *backward!* (The creators do this twice more—in "Fearful Symmetry" and "War of the Coprophages.")

☒ At the end of the episode, Mulder pulls out his cell phone and we hear him enter ten numbers in quick succession and then press a final button. (Presumably this last one is the "send" button.) Only moments pass before we hear that Mulder has called Scully. One wonders why he doesn't have her number loaded into speed-dial.

Continuity and Production Problems

☒ For most of this episode, the creators do a good job matching the appearance of the "KILL 'EM" messages to the normal displays of the equipment. Unfortunately, Mrs. McRoberts's microwave display falls far short of the mark. Compare the display shown as she opens the microwave to the close-up of the display seen by Mulder.

Trivia Questions

❶ What are Franklin's two main fruit crops?

❷ What fear fuels Mr. Taber's rampage in the elevator?

Sleepless

PLOT SUMMARY In New York City, a sleep disorder specialist named Saul Grissom dies because he believes he's burning to death. Later, a veteran falls to the ground lifeless, killed by imaginary bullets. Mulder wants the case, but it belongs to Special Agent Alex Krycek, and Mulder must begrudgingly accept the young agent as a partner in order to investigate. (Scully is still assigned to teach at Quantico.)

The pair soon learn that both victims were stationed at the Marine Corps training facility at Parris Island. Then Mulder's anonymous supporter (identified only as Mr. X in the official literature) calls for a meeting. X gives Mulder a file on sleep eradication experiments performed on soldiers during the Vietnam War. The resulting squad had the highest kill ratio of the war but soon ran amok. Now, a soldier named Augustus D. Cole is avenging the deaths of innocent Vietnamese—hunting the remnants of the squad and the doctors who created them. Sleepless for twenty-four years, Cole can project alternate realities so intense they kill. In time, Mulder and Krycek stop Cole from murdering the project's other doctor, but Cole then commits suicide by convincing Krycek that he has a gun trained on Mulder. Afterward, all evidence on the experiments disappears.

And as the episode ends, Krycek meets with Cancerman—giving him the file Mr. X gave Mulder, telling Cancerman that Scully is a much larger problem than first described. Cancerman retorts that every problem has a solution.

Onscreen Locations

☒ New York City
☒ FBI Academy, Quantico, Virginia
☒ Grissom Sleep Disorder Center, Stamford, Connecticut
☒ FBI Library, New York City
☒ Brooklyn, New York
☒ V.A. Medical Center, North Orange, New Jersey
☒ Long Island Expressway
☒ Bronx Station
☒ Metropolitan Transit Authority, Bronx Station

Ruminations

There should be a date on this episode. As the episode begins, a report on Grissom's television says that the Dow Jones Industrial Average fell almost 14.5 points, to 3837, bringing the blue chip index's losses over the past three days to just under 100 points. Unfortunately, my local library's reference materials on the Dow only run through 1991! I looked through the library's microfilm collection of The New York Times, *and the closest I could find to this information was November 3, 1994, when the DJIA closed at 3738.13 after losing 26.24 points. But that date is far out of range for this episode. The date on "Little Green Men" is July 7, 1994. The date on "Duane Barry" is August 7, 1994. "Sleepless" should fall between these two. (By the way, I heartily agree with Mulder's comments in "Squeeze." Those microfilm machines make me seasick!)*

There are some nicely played moments in this episode as our intrepid pair react to the introduction of Alex Krycek. I love the way

Mulder and Scully huddle together to discuss Grissom's autopsy, speaking in hushed, conspiratorial tones, obviously excluding this interloper from their partnership.

Good foreshadowing at the close of this episode, too! Cancerman makes his retort and then lowers his cigarette to crush it out in an ashtray.

Geographical Inconsistencies

X Screen text identifies a North Orange, New Jersey. As fate would have it, New Jersey boasts an Orange, an East Orange, a West Orange, even a South Orange but—you guessed it!—no *North* Orange.

Plot Oversights

X Here's the scenario: The government wants a better soldier. They make a group of Marines who don't need to sleep. It's a top-secret project. They send these guys to Vietnam. The guys go berserk, and at Phu Bai they kill three hundred children. So what does the government do? At some point they bring the guys back to the States, discharge them from the military, and let them go back into society! Does this make sense? Granted, the government's actions rarely make sense, but if the project was so top secret, why not "erase" this problem? If the military didn't want anyone to know what it had done, why in the world would it ever allow these guys back into civilian life?

X Halfway through the episode, Mulder and Krycek interview Salvatore Matola—one of the last remaining sleepless soldiers. During the conversation, Matola tells Mulder and Krycek that, in time, they stopped taking orders from the company commander in Saigon. Krycek reacts with amazement. He can't believe the entire squadron "went AWOL." Stephanie Bamberger—a confessed Marine brat—tells

me that Marines don't go AWOL, they go UA (unauthorized absence). (Not that Krycek would necessarily know this!)

X After locating the second doctor who worked on the project, a man named Girardi, Scully calls Mulder to tell him that Girardi is arriving in New York at seven-thirty. Stuck in traffic, Mulder has her send a picture of Girardi to the train station. At seven-thirty-three, Mulder and Krycek make a dramatic entrance by running into the terminal with Girardi's picture in hand. I guess it was too much trouble to call the FBI's regional headquarters in New York City and ask them to send over a couple of agents to take Girardi into protective custody. And apparently it was too much trouble as well to call for reinforcements, even though Mulder knows that a *killer* is after Girardi. (Or has Mulder completely alienated the good folks at the New York City regional headquarters by now?)

X Sometimes Mulder and Scully give up at the oddest times. Near the end of the episode, both discover that someone has stolen both their copies of the top-secret report from Mr. X. Scully moans that without the report Skinner won't authorize an investigation. Wait a minute: What happened to Salvatore Matola? Mulder and Krycek interview him halfway through the episode because he's one of the last sleepless soldiers. There's nothing to indicate that the man has died. Wouldn't he be a prime piece of evidence? Put the guy in a room and watch him for two weeks straight! If he doesn't go to sleep and he has a military record and he has a scar at the base of his neck, wouldn't that be enough corroboration of his testimony for the FBI to launch a full investigation? And wouldn't a CAT scan reveal that he had undergone brain surgery?

Equipment Oddities

X Evidently Mulder's been doing a little redeco-

Trivia Questions

1 What is the name of the firefighter who reports that Grissom's call is a false alarm?

2 Just before dying, Henry Willig watches a home shopping channel. What is the price on the offered ring?

Trivia Answers
1 Lieutenant Regan.
2 $677.

101

Sleepless

rating in his apartment. During "E.B.E.," Mulder arrived home to find Deep Throat waiting for him in his living room. As Mulder walks through his front room you can see that there's a door separating the two areas. Yet, in this episode, the creators shoot the same area of Mulder's apartment from the same angle and now the door has disappeared. Not only that, the physical opening looks taller!

☒ During Scully's log entry halfway through the episode, a close-up of her computer screen shows a paragraph that begins, "This is consistent. . . ." Two lines down, Scully is typing the phrase "serotonin levels in the blood." Oddly enough, the insertion bar is flashing at the beginning of the paragraph, not where Scully is typing! In addition, it appears that this paragraph is separated from the rest of the text on the page, but in a subsequent wide shot, the computer screen shows only one block of text.

Continuity and Production Problems

☒ Even though Alex Krycek was posing under the alias of Michael during "Genderbender," one still wonders why Mulder doesn't recognize him when he approaches Mulder's desk in this episode. (Okay, so maybe Mulder doesn't want to embarrass the guy.)

☒ Some things never change. We first see Scully in this episode as she teaches at the Academy. A body lies, covered with a sheet. Scully lectures on the effects of electrocution. Opposite her, six students—all dressed in white lab coats—take notes in their little books. At least they are *supposed* to be taking notes! As the camera pans around the body, we see that the young woman on the end has decided that none of this stuff will be on the exam anyway, so she's just *faking* it. Her pages are completely blank!

Duane Barry

(Part 1 of 2)

Onscreen Locations

☒ Pulaski, Virginia, June 3, 1985
☒ Davis Correctional Treatment Center, Marion, Virginia
☒ Downtown Richmond, Virginia
☒ Jefferson Memorial Hospital, Richmond, Virginia

Unanswered Questions

☒ I will deal with the whole unanswered question of Duane Barry and his connection to the conspiracy in the next episode, but there is one puzzlement that should be addressed here. How did Barry make it to Richmond, Virginia? According to screen text, he was confined in Marion, Virginia. That's all the way across the state! Wouldn't authorities set up roadblocks almost immediately and seal the town of Marion? Or did Barry have help getting to the travel office?

☒ And why would the metal strip taken from Barry's abdomen make the cash register at a *grocery store* go crazy? Are those scanners really calibrated for an identification strip that's only five microns across?! (In case you don't know, a "micron" is one-*thousandth* of a *millimeter!*) Does this mean that *grocery* stores are participating in the conspiracy as well? Is that why they offer so many different tabloid newspapers at the checkout stands with their ridiculous covers and stories? Are the tabloids nothing more than a fiendishly clever disinformation campaign—designed to bring to ridicule anyone who might uncover . . . *the truth?* (Aaaaah!)

PLOT SUMMARY

When Duane Barry—a mental patient who claims to be an abductee—takes hostages in a travel office, the Bureau assigns Mulder to negotiate. Barry believes the aliens are coming back for him. Escaping from an institution, he has kidnapped his psychiatrist as a substitute to give the aliens. Unfortunately he couldn't remember where he was originally abducted, so he stopped at the travel office for directions.

What Mulder doesn't realize at first is that Barry was an FBI agent. A background check by Scully further reveals that years ago, a gunshot destroyed a portion of Barry's brain. Scully suspects that Barry is a pathological liar, capable of great deceit. By the time she arrives on the scene, however, Mulder is *inside* the office with Barry. Thankfully, a strike team safely extracts Mulder and the psychiatrist, though Barry is critically injured in the assault and must undergo surgery.

Then Mulder learns that the surgeon who operated on Barry found pieces of implanted metal. Scully takes one for analysis, and that evening, on a whim, she drags it across a grocery scanner. The register goes crazy. Flustered, she hurries home to call Mulder. As she starts to leave a message on Mulder's answering machine, Duane Barry—having escaped from the hospital—attacks her.

Plot Oversights

☒ Not really a nit, just a ponderment: When Mulder first speaks with Barry, he reads from a handwritten script. At one point he looks up to get the names of the hostages from a nearby blackboard as negotiation commander Lucy

103

Duane Barry

Kazdin points to them one at a time. Strangely enough, he already has the names listed on his pad! Why would he take his eyes off the script? Just so Kazdin could play Vanna White?

❎ After shooting a hostage, Barry allows medics to enter the travel office. Mulder and another agent don bulletproof jackets and go inside. Barry frisks both of them and then allows them to get to work. I have a hard time believing that Barry didn't feel their personal body armor during his examination. The guy used to be an FBI agent! Surely he knows what a bulletproof jacket feels like under a person's clothing. Why then doesn't Barry make Mulder take off the jacket so he can wear it? (He seems to take other precautions to guard his well-being. By the way, it's also a bit odd that Barry doesn't check the medical kit. He just takes Mulder's word that it doesn't contain a gun.)

❎ Scully's rapid arrival in Richmond seems highly implausible. After she storms into the room, she says that she just flew down from Washington. Yet consider the sequence: Kazdin wants a picture of what's happening inside the travel office. An agent begins to drill a hole in the wall. Scully calls from some office (probably her office at Quantico, since that's where she works at this point in the series). She learns that Mulder is inside the building with Barry and becomes upset. There's a commercial break. Then we see the agent drill through the drywall in the travel office. He inserts the videocamera. The picture shows up on a nearby monitor. Across the street, the tactical commander for the operation rushes up with a printout of the video and—as Kazdin looks at it—there's a commotion because Scully has barged in.

Now, if the sequence of events as shown in the episode is true, Scully somehow rushed to a Washington, D.C., airport (she claims to have flown down from Washington), flew to Richmond, rented a car, and drove to the travel office in the time it took for agents to complete

the drilling, insert a camera, print out a frame, and take it to Kazdin. Does this seem reasonable? I suppose if we really wanted to be generous, we could say that the whole video surveillance process took . . . *fifteen minutes?* Washington to Richmond, *fifteen minutes?*

❎ There's a startling lack of medical personnel as Barry escapes from the hospital after being shot. Silly me, I thought the whole purpose of monitoring equipment was to alert the nurses to a problem with a given patient. Yet, Barry rips off all his sensors and *no one* shows up to find out why?

❎ Also, why doesn't Barry take the policeman's gun in the hospital? He steals the guard's gun in the institution at the beginning of the episode. He evidently takes Scully's gun at the end of the episode (according to the dialogue in "Ascension"). He seems to have an affinity for guns. So . . .

❎ And while we're "reasoning" things out, why doesn't Scully call Mulder's cell phone during the closing scene of this episode? Why talk to his answering machine if she's so freaked? Technoamnesia, maybe?

Equipment Oddities

❎ A power station blows, and Kazdin says they've lost power up and down the entire block. Barry goes on a rampage and starts firing. Frantic, Mulder calls the travel agency. Barry answers the phone. Only one problem: Barry is using a cordless phone, and the base unit doesn't have any power, so the phone wouldn't work!

❎ I love the scene where we see an agent begin to drill a hole in the drywall to establish video surveillance on the travel office. A camera pan shows us the spotlight that illuminates the wall where the drill agent works. Then it continues down to a table that contains the building plans, and we find that another agent has *so little* light he has to use a *laser pointer* for illumination! Isn't a flashlight standard issue for all special agents? Sure seems that way after watching *The X-Files!* At the very least, Krycek could fetch the one that Mulder has in his car.

☒ Not sure on this one. You can decide for yourself. At the end of the episode, Scully calls Mulder's answering machine. Both in the first close-up and in the later wide shot of the device, you should be able to see that the phone jacks are empty! (In other words, the thing isn't connected to a telephone line.) There *is* a power cord coming out of the back. And there *is* another cord that seems to exit the machine in a very odd place (no idea what *that* is), but no telephone wire. Maybe this particular brand of answering machine has a built-in telephone cord? (That seems very odd, given the low cost of modular telephone jacks and patching cables.)

Continuity and Production Problems

☒ Near the end of the episode, we see Barry's medical monitoring equipment as beeps sound in the background. The beeps seems to have a mind of their own. They aren't synced with anything on the monitors! (Well . . . they are synced with the little heart on the first monitor in the beginning, but then they go out of sync. Somebody should have overdubbed this manually to make sure the two stayed locked.)

Trivia Questions

❶ What is the first name of the bald-headed hostage?

❷ Who enters Travel Time with Mulder?

Trivia Answers
❶ Bob.
❷ Agent Janus.

105

Duane Barry

Ascension

(Part 2 of 2)

PLOT SUMMARY Though ordered off the case by Skinner, Mulder feverishly works to discover where Duane Barry has taken Scully. He remembers Barry saying he ascended to the stars during his abduction and intuits that Barry is bound for a resort called Skyland Mountain. Unfortunately, Krycek quickly passes this information to Cancerman.

At the resort, Mulder finds an ecstatic Duane Barry, who proclaims that he's free—that "they" took Scully instead of him. And even after Mulder grabs him by the neck, Barry sticks to his story. Then Barry mysteriously dies, and the autopsy—performed by a military pathologist—indicates Barry was strangled. Sensing a frame, and searching for support, Mulder tries to speak with Senator Matheson, but Mr. X appears and tells him not to bother. Matheson can't help him now. The situation is beyond them all. On the way back to Bureau headquarters in Krycek's car, however, Mulder notices Cancerman's cigarettes in the ashtray. The next morning Mulder charges Krycek with the murder. Unfortunately, when Skinner calls Krycek to his office, he learns that the young agent didn't report for duty and his home phone has been disconnected.

Furious that Krycek has disappeared and there's nothing he can do about it, Skinner does what he can—what he says "they" fear the most. He reopens the X-Files.

Onscreen Locations

☒ Route 229, Rixeyville, Virginia
☒ FBI Headquarters, Video Production Unit
☒ Route 221, Warrenton, Virginia
☒ Skyland Mountain Summit

☒ FBI Academy Morgue, Quantico, Virginia
☒ Downtown Washington, D.C.
☒ Office of Senator Richard Matheson

Ruminations

Just one of those little tidbits of information that a nitpicker plucks along the way. Screen text tells us that Mulder arrives at his apartment at "11:23 P.M." After he comes to Scully's apartment, subsequent screen text reads, "11:46 P.M." This indicates that the distance between Mulder and Scully's apartments is less than twenty-three minutes by car.

An oddity next. The creators of The X-Files *seem to enjoy hiding little pieces of information for X-philes to find. Dates are a good case in point. Sometimes, you can find them on computer screens, sometimes on log sheets, sometimes on medical examiners' reports. This episode should have had a simple date to locate. One scene shows us a close-up of Duane Barry's toe tag, and there is something scribbled in the date field. For some reason, however, it seems intentionally obscured. This is puzzling, because it should be a simple matter for the creators to establish a date for this episode. It occurs only days after "Duane Barry," and that episode carried a date of August 7, 1994.*

Unanswered Questions

☒ Was Duane Barry acting alone? Or did "someone" oversee the entire affair? Once Mulder divines Barry's destination, Krycek calls Cancerman and informs him of Mulder's progress. (At least that's the impression the creators leave us with, given the camera sequence.) This would indicate that Cancerman is a passive observer, simply waiting to capitalize on the situation. In this scenario, Cancerman's men rush to Skyland Mountain and abscond with Scully after this phone call. On the other hand, Barry *did* go straight to Scully's house . . . from *Richmond, Virginia,* where he was hospitalized. *This* indicates that Barry was directed to Scully's residence in some manner. (In fact, I can't come up with another explanation for Barry's actions. At the most, he only saw Scully in passing as he was loaded into the ambulance.) But if Cancerman and his associates had a hand in orchestrating Barry's behavior, when did the concert begin? At the Davis Correctional Treatment Center in Marion, Virginia? With the assignment of Mulder to the case? Once Barry was hospitalized?

X Why kill Duane Barry if there was nothing to hide? (Okay, I can't take credit for that one. Mr. X floated this question to Mulder but refused to supply an answer.)

Geographical Inconsistencies

X As Mulder tumbles from the roof of the Skyland Mountain tram, note the very large body of water behind him: unfortunately I can find no such large body of water on any map of the Blue Ridge Mountains area.

Plot Oversights

X People in a hurry do the strangest things. Reaching the top of the mountain, Mulder quickly locates the car Duane Barry used to transport Scully to the area. Moments later, Mulder pops the trunk and finds Scully's necklace. Here's what's interesting. On arrival—according to the crime scene—Barry leaped out of his car, left it running with the driver's

side door open, and ran to extract Scully from the trunk. Then—on his way to hand Scully over to the *sinister* aliens; on his way to *rid* himself of the *terror* he had lived with for more than a decade; on his way to *secure his final freedom*—he paused to shut the lid.

X People under stress do the strangest things as well. Mulder leaves Krycek behind as he takes the tram to the top of Skyland Mountain. He tells Krycek that no matter what happens, don't let the operator stop the tram. Now, let's continue from Mulder's perspective. The tram nears the top and screeches to a halt. Suddenly it goes into reverse and nearly slings Mulder to his death. Mulder reaches Barry but is *mere moments* too late. Scully is gone. Surprisingly enough, the next time Mulder sees Krycek, Mulder doesn't even mention the incident. He doesn't ask what happened. He doesn't observe that the moments he spent hanging around on the tram might have been the moments that would have allowed him to rescue Scully. He just goes on to the next item. Is this the obsessive Mulder we all know and love? (I would have expected him to go postal on Krycek, just as he did with Barry.)

X And what about this: You borrow someone's car. He doesn't smoke. You drive it around the block a few times. You get out. You get back in. Suddenly you notice that there are freshly burned cigarettes in the ashtray. This is what happens to Mulder when he borrows Krycek's car. (We know Krycek doesn't smoke from the look on his face as Cancerman puffs away in his automobile and from the fact that Mulder is surprised to find cigarettes in the ashtray.) What's wrong with this picture? Wouldn't Mulder *smell* the cigarettes long before he found them? The ashtray was cracked open a bit. Wouldn't that allow the distinctive odor of burned cigarettes to permeate the car?

X Mulder figures out that Krycek works for

Trivia Questions

1 What number hangs over the entrance to Scully's apartment building?

2 What's the phone number for Skyland Mountain?

Cancerman near noon the day after Scully disappears. Yet it isn't until the *next* morning that he brings his suspicions to Skinner. Evidently he had something better to do?! (No doubt the latest issue of *The Adult Video News* had just arrived. See "The Romance Toteboard.")

Changed Premises

☒ This may not be a nit, depending on how you interpret Mulder's comments near the end of the episode. At the top of Skyland Mountain, Mulder finds Scully's necklace in the trunk of the car Barry stole. It is a small gold chain with a little cross. In a later meeting, with Dana's mom, Mulder pulls it out of his pocket and says—referring to the cross—"That's something I never considered about her. If she was such a skeptic, why did she wear that?" Taken alone, these comments would lead a person to believe that Mulder had never seen Scully wearing the cross before. Except . . . Scully wears it practically the *entire* first season. He's been around this woman for a year and he never noticed?! (Strike one against the male's powers of observation!)

Equipment Oddities

☒ In "Blood," we first saw Mulder use a camera with a laser focusing system. The user draws two dots together on the image he or she wishes to photograph and snaps the picture without the normal requirement of looking through the viewfinder. (Evidently the camera

not only uses the two laser beams for sighting but for focusing length as well.) The camera makes another appearance in this episode as a forensics team gathers evidence from Scully's apartment after her kidnapping. Specifically, we see the camera placed *two inches* from Scully's damaged phone, and a picture is taken. Aside from the fact that the photographer doesn't use the laser dots to sight the photograph, the composition of the shot looks more suitable for an art display than a criminal investigation!

Continuity and Production Problems

☒ Someone needs to replace the lightbulbs in the stairwell of Senator Matheson's office building. Either that, or they need to pay the electric bill. In the middle of the day, Mulder goes to the building to speak with Matheson. Mr. X intercepts him. Behind X we can see that there is a window. Yet, when Mulder joins X in the stairwell, everything is suddenly dark. (Must have been an unscheduled total eclipse of the sun!)

DAMAGE TOTE BOARD

1. Number of episodes in which someone dies or is found dead during the teaser: fifty-four
2. Number of times Mulder gets shot: four
3. Number of times Scully is attacked in the bathroom: five
4. Number of times a car runs into a tree: two
5. Number of times Scully retches: one
6. Number of times Mulder smokes: one
7. Number of times female characters slam into a wall: five
8. Number of episodes in which Scully is subjected to bondage: seven
9. Number of times Mulder is whipped: one
10. Number of episodes with decapitated heads: three
11. Number of times Mulder shoots a stuffed animal: one
12. Number of times animals fall from the sky: two
13. Number of times Scully ruins a pair of shoes: one

References

1. "Pilot," "Squeeze," "The Jersey Devil," "Shadows," "Ghost in the Machine," "Ice," "Eve," "Fire," "Beyond the Sea," "Genderbender," "Lazarus," "Miracle Man," "Shapes," "Darkness Falls," "Born Again," "Roland," "The Host," "Sleepless," "3," "Firewalker," "Fresh Bones," "Fearful Symmetry," "Humbug," "The Calusari," "F. Emasculata," "Soft Light," "Our Town," "D.P.O.," "Clyde Bruckman's Final Repose," "The List," "2SHY," "Nisei," "731," "Revelations," "War of the Coprophages," "Syzygy," "Grotesque," "Teso Dos Bichos," "Hell Money," "Avatar," "Quagmire," "Wetwired," "Herrenvolk," "Home," "Teliko," "Unruhe," "Sanguinarium," "Terma," "El Mundo Gira," "Leonard Betts" (most likely the patient in the ambulance died), "Synchrony," "Zero Sum," "Elegy," and "Gethsemane."

2. By Lucas Henry in "Beyond the Sea." By Augustus Cole in "Sleepless" (sort of). By Scully in "Anasazi." By an apparently self-inflicted wound to the head in "Gethsemane." (Supposedly. At the time of this writing it is the end of the fourth season, and according to Scully, Mulder is dead. Somehow, given that David Duchovny is slated for a fifth season with the show *and* a movie, I find his death a bit hard to believe!)

3. Tooms does it in "Squeeze." Incanto does it in "2SHY." An assassin knocks out Scully in the

bathroom near the end of "Avatar." Jerse does it in "Never Again." And, Psycho-Nurse Innes does it in "Elegy."

4   During "Fresh Bones" and "The List."

5   After her bedtime experience with Brother Andrew in "Genderbender."

6   During the interview with Darren Peter Oswald in "D.P.O."

7   Nurse Charters in "Excelsis Dei." Scully in "End Game." Scully in "The Calusari." Scully in "Never Again." Scully in "Gethsemane."

8   "Lazarus," "Ascension," "Irresistible," "Die Hand Die Verletzt," "Humbug," "Our Town," and "Unruhe."

9   By a Russian in "Tunguska."

10   "Our Town," "The List," and "Leonard Betts."

11   During "Shapes."

12   Frogs in "Die Hand Die Verletzt" and birds in "Syzygy."

13   After stepping in alien body goo during "Colony."

Damage
Tote Board

3

Onscreen Locations

☒ Hollywood Hills, Los Angeles, California
☒ Los Angeles, California
☒ Club Tepes, 8115 Hollywood Blvd.
☒ 8426 Melrose Ave.
☒ 1533 Malibu Canyon

Ruminations

The date on this episode comes from Mulder's calendar. Entering his office after the reinstatement of the X-Files, he takes down the plastic dustcovers and flips to the thong-bikini-clad Miss November—purveyor of the land's finest P. Bunyon Brand handsaws. (Watch the episode; you'll understand.)

I believe that this was the first episode of The X-Files *I refused to let my daughter watch. She was twelve at the time. The previews were enough to convince me that the creators had decided to begin frolicking in the deep end of the gore.*

Plot Oversights

☒ After the requisite slaughter scene to open the episode, we next see Mulder returning to his basement office and removing the plastic draped over the desk and hung from the walls. His actions raise several ponderments. First, we see that Mulder left his desk completely intact—pencils, paper, *name plaque.* He didn't *need* any of this stuff as he worked for months at a desk upstairs? Or did he make the FBI supply him with duplicates?

Second, "Ascension"—the episode in which

PLOT SUMMARY Mulder travels to Los Angeles after a brutal murder and exsanguination. The crime fits a triple-murder in Memphis as well as another triple-murder in Portland. Apparently the culprits believe they are vampires, needing large quantities of blood to sustain themselves, and will kill twice more before leaving L.A. To supplement their killing, Mulder believes they hold jobs at local blood banks and pilfer the supply unnoticed. In short order, Mulder arrests a night watchman at one such blood bank. The man, named John, seems absolutely convinced that he is a vampire—among a trio of vampires—with all the attendant attributes of lore. He admits the murders but refuses to testify against his two companions—another man and a woman. Convinced that John is delusional, Mulder is stunned when the young man burns to a char after exposure to sunlight.

An ink stamp on John's hand leads Mulder next to Club Tepes. There, he meets Kristen Kilar. At first Kristen seems to be one of the killers, but later she reveals that she is John's former girlfriend—pursued by the trio of vampires from city to city. Then John reappears, claiming it's really true, that he *will* live forever. He tries to talk Kristen into stabbing Mulder so she can become a vampire as well. Instead, Kristen battles with the trio, eventually sacrificing herself to kill them so Mulder can live.

Scully is abducted—occurs sometime in early August. At the end of that episode, Skinner reopened the X-Files. According to Mulder's calendar, this is November. That's three months! What's he been doing all that time? Granted, he may have taken a leave of absence to look for Scully, but he would still need a base of operations and all his *stuff* is in this basement office. Plus, it would make much more sense for Mulder to avail himself of the Bureau's resources in the hunt. Wouldn't it be easier to do that if he was working out of the basement?

And finally, speaking of Mulder's calendar, does anyone else find it interesting that a progressive organization such as the FBI would allow a girlie calendar to be prominently displayed in one of its offices? Maybe no one has complained yet! (It certainly doesn't seem to bother Scully—which is *another* thing that we men like about her!)

 Yet more evidence that Mulder uses some kind of Zen numbering system with respect to the X-Files. Scully's X-File—created three months ago—carries a case number of 73317. But the "Trinity Killers" file—a file started approximately nine months *earlier*—carries a case number of X256933VW.

 Arriving on the crime scene of the first murder in Los Angeles, Mulder finds the Scripture reference "John 52:54" scrawled on the wall in the victim's blood. Mulder confidently quotes the verse and then snidely observes that the vampires have the same feeble, literal grasp of the Bible as big-haired preachers. Take heart, Special Agent Fox Mulder, I can say with confidence that you *certainly* won't ever be charged with having a *literal* grasp of the Bible! The reference on the wall is *not* the reference for the verse you quote! In fact, the first time I saw this scene, I turned to my wife and said, "John doesn't have fifty-two chapters!" The *correct* reference for the verse that Mulder quotes is John 6:54.

 Once John refuses to talk about his two partners, Mulder confines him to a room with high barred windows. Ominously, we see the sun inching toward John as he frantically paces. At first glance, the events of this episode seem to indicate that morning approaches. The only problem is: If the sun was rising it would be

crawling *down* the wall, not sneaking across the floor. For the light to slip across the floor, the sun would have to be setting. But if the sun is setting, what did Mulder *do* all day? Interrogate John the Recalcitrant? (I suppose Mulder could have chosen a room with a westward exposure and rigged up a large reflective surface outside the window to bounce the eastern rays of the rising sun into the window, but how would *that* look on his expense report? "Item: One six-by-twelve-foot mirror. Reason for purchase: To demonstrate the delusional nature of a vampire's claims. Effectiveness of expenditure: Failed to produce desired results. Subject burned to a crispy critter.")

 Question: If Kristen is attempting to run away from the trio of vampires, why is she going to a bar that they are likely to frequent?

 Telling Mulder her story, Kristen says that she met John in Chicago and adds, "You know him as the son." How does Kristen know that Mulder knows this? He tells her that he knows she is running from "them," but he never addresses them as the "Trinity Killers." Lucky guess?

Equipment Oddities

 The strides being made in this day and age when it comes to lightbulb technology are truly stunning. After John's capture by Mulder, the episode cuts to an interrogation room. John writhes on the floor, screaming for them to turn out the lights. Two detectives from the Los Angeles Police Department sit at a table and stare, unimpressed with the show. Mulder enters with a desk lamp sheathed in red plastic. It has a gooseneck and the standard cone-shaped bulb cover that directs the light in a given direction. Mulder sets the lamp on the table, facing John, plugs in the lamp, and walks back to the door to turn off the overhead lights. Note the hard shadow on Mulder though the lamp on the table is *facing away* from him. With the room

GREAT LINES
"Not if drawstrings come back into style."

—**Mulder** *to John after John asks him if he wants to live forever.*

now bathed in red light, John says that he'll only talk with Mulder. The two detectives are happy to oblige. A wide shot shows them rising from the table. Notice that the lamp faces away from them, but somehow it *still* manages to light the two detectives so they cast hard shadows on the wall! Must be that amazingly advanced wrap-around lightbulb technology. (And no, the room does not appear to have a wall of one-way glass that could act as a reflector.)

 Evidently, Mulder bought a longer chain for Scully's cross. In this episode he wears it around his neck, and the cross rests on his sternum. But when Scully wore the cross earlier, it barely reached beyond her collarbone.

 Note to self: Find out the name of the contractor who built Kristen's house and make sure he or she never builds anything for you! Kristen pours a stream of gasoline from the garage to the entryway, and when she lights it, the entire place goes off like a *bomb!* (Must have used some of that newfangled *explosive* concrete and lumber soaked in nitroglycerin.)

Continuity and Production Problems

 Well, it's good to know that the conspirators take care of their own. In "The Erlenmeyer Flask," it appeared that a thug killed Dr. Berube for being too successful in creating an alien/human hybrid. Evidently the conspirators only *faked* his death. They gave him a new identify and got him a job as a medical examiner in Los Angeles! It's understandable that Mulder doesn't recognize him. Berube shaved off his beard and modified how he talks a bit, but it's the same guy!

 Shortly after meeting Kristen at Club Tepes, Mulder tells her that he needs to know what she is. As she takes his hand, the music changes to a hard-throbbing beat—tripled by

the drums, bass, and guitar. It's nearly impossible not to feel the tempo of this song, yet the gyrating, leather-bustiered, black-capped, dog-collared dancer in the background *hasn't . . . got . . . a clue!* She's not even *close!* (No doubt, she's deaf from swiveling around every night in her chain-link cage amid the pounding music. Someone forgot to tap her on the shoulder when the new set began.)

 Checking Kristen's former residences, Mulder finds that she once lived at "4057 Sweetgum Lane, Memphis, TN 88151." The zip codes for Memphis, Tennessee, run in the 381 range. The zip code shown is for someplace in New Mexico.

 Fleeing the trio of vampires, Mulder rushes Kristen around the rear of her BMW as it sits parked in the garage of her house. At most, there are two feet between the car's bumper and the closed garage door. Moments later, the female vampire rips Mulder from the car and onto the hood. Then, demonstrating her absolute mastery of automobile handling, Kristen hops into the driver's seat, revs the engine, jams the transmission into reverse, and punches the accelerator—slinging Mulder and the vampire onto the floor—before she shoves the transmission into drive and delivers the vehicle to the front of the garage with such force that it impales the female vampire's head on a *one-inch* wooden dowel rod. *Most* amazing about all this maneuvering is that it occurs without any noticeable damage to the *still* closed garage door, and afterward the car appears to be in *exactly* the same location as it was prior to Kristen's *incredible* display. (And I do mean that in the most *literal* sense of the word.)

Trivia Questions

1 How old was James Ellis when he died?

2 What was the name of the first victim in Los Angeles?

One Breath

PLOT SUMMARY When Scully suddenly reappears—comatose and in critical, degenerating condition—Mulder is determined to bring those responsible to justice. Through Skinner, he locates the residence of Cancerman—determined to find some answers. Yet even with a gun to his head, Cancerman only smirks. He believes that *he* is Mulder's only chance to learn the truth and tells Mulder if he dies, that opportunity dies as well. Frustrated and guilt-ridden—believing he is responsible for Scully's condition—Mulder offers his resignation. Skinner refuses to accept it. Then, Mr. X appears with his own form of comfort. He tells Mulder that he cannot supply the reason why Scully was taken. It's too close to him. But he has arranged for the men who took her to search Mulder's apartment. The men believe Mulder will be away on a trip. Mr. X wants Mulder there to defend himself with *terminal* force, administering the only justice possible.

Mulder eventually chooses otherwise. He goes to the hospital to be with Scully instead. And when all seems hopeless, miraculously, she recovers. Then, as the episode ends, Scully asks for nurse Owens—the nurse she remembers from her coma, the nurse who talked her back to life. Oddly enough, though Mulder saw nurse Owens hovering over Scully, the hospital personnel don't recognize the name.

Onscreen Locations

⊠ Northeast Georgetown Medical Center, Washington, D.C.

Ruminations

I love this episode! One great scene after the next, chock full of great performances and con-

flict. (And how 'bout that bow tie on Frohike?) The images of Scully in the boat are so simple and yet add so much to the overall feel of the episode. And such a nice idea for the title! It comes from Scully's out-of-body experience as her father comes to talk with her. He explains that though he always thought life transpired at the proper pace—never too fast or too slow—there came a moment when he realized he might never see his daughter again, and he felt as if his life had become the length of one breath.

Just for the record, this episode is the first time Mulder puts an "X" in the window to summon Mr. X. It's also the first time we hear of "The Thinker." (He'll reappear in "Anasazi.")

Didja notice? Didja? Huh? Huh? Didja notice? The Lone Gunmen tell Mulder that he is welcome to come over Saturday night. They are all hopping on the Internet to "nitpick the scientific inaccuracies of Earth 2." Kymberlee Ricke tells me that this comment was a direct result of an X-File *producer* visiting her Web site!

It's the details that impress me about The X-Files. At the very end of the episode, Mulder returns Scully's cross necklace. Scully takes it, turns her head, and smiles at her mom precisely as she should. After all, her mother gave it to her, and a real-life person would *react* to that connection after coming so close to death.

Unanswered Questions

⊠ Who was nurse Owens? Was she merely a disgruntled alien who was upset that the conspirators had damaged Scully so, a being who chose to intervene though the powers-that-be wanted Scully dead? Or was she more? Was she a force for good—an angel, even? Certainly, given the nearly impossible task ahead for our intrepid agents, it would be comforting to know that "out there" somewhere, there was *some* force for good willing to step in and set things right when evil turns especially cruel.

Plot Oversights

☒ There is a conspicuous lack of brothers in this episode, given Scully's nearness to death. Aside from the flashback story told at the beginning, they aren't even mentioned! (Although they apparently *did* attend their father's funeral. But in that case, *Melissa* was missing. Hmm. Bit of tension in the family, perhaps?)

☒ During a visit to the hospital, Mulder notices that a man has stolen a vial of Scully's blood. He chases the guy down and eventually apprehends him. Strangely enough, Mulder doesn't cuff him! This allows the guy to attempt an escape that Mr. X then thwarts by killing the man.

Equipment Oddities

☒ Skinner takes an interesting approach to the lighting of cigarettes in his office. He posts a "Thank You for Not Smoking" sign on his desk and then leaves an ashtray on an end table.

☒ Mulder must be one of those people who have a religious conviction against viewing brand names. As he prints out his resignation, you can see a piece of tape directly over the area that would normally contain the logo for the printer's manufacturer. Unless I miss my guess, the area that's obscured reads "Hewlett-Packard."

☒ At some point, the basement office of the X-Files . . . *moved!* I noted in "Beyond the Sea" that the office had acquired another door, but this episode finally provides tangible evidence that it's actually in a different location. After refusing to accept Mulder's resignation, Skinner tells Mulder about his out-of-body experience

while serving in Vietnam. Notice the pattern of light as Skinner leaves. There's an enormous shaft of illumination coming from the left side of the door. It's almost as if there's an open stairwell that leads directly to an outside door and the sun is shining down it. Yet, in "Pilot," we see Scully walking to Mulder's office, and it's the final turn just before the dead end of the hallway. (Precisely as it should be!)

☒ When Melissa Scully comes to Mulder's apartment, his door reads "4." That's interesting, considering the fact that Mulder looked out his apartment window in "Deep Throat" and he was clearly *not* at ground level! Shouldn't it read "24" or "34" or "44"? (Actually, in just a few episodes, it will read "42." See "End Game.")

☒ Why doesn't Scully get a blanket at the hospital? For almost the entire episode, she just lays there, clothed only in her hospital gown. Poor thing. Seems like she'd be cold.

Continuity and Production Problems

☒ The episode begins with Margaret Scully inspecting a gravestone for her missing daughter. At the bottom, the stone reads, "The Spirit is the Truth, I John 5:07." It's a nice selection, given the "search for truth" theme of *The X-Files*. There are two oddities here, however. The normal way of writing this reference would be "I John 5:7." For another, all of my Bibles say that the phrase "The Spirit is the Truth" should more appropriately be ascribed to the sixth verse—not the seventh verse—of First John, chapter five. (The whole verse is: "This is he that came by water and blood, even Jesus Christ; not by water only, but by water and blood. And it is the Spirit that beareth witness, because the Spirit is Truth.")

☒ You may recognize the African-American nurse at the beginning of this episode from a

SECOND SEASON

Trivia Questions

❶ What brand of cigarette does Cancerman smoke?

❷ According to Mulder's resignation letter, what is Skinner's middle initial?

115

One Breath

first-season episode such as "Shadows," in which she played a medical examiner named Dr. Ellen Bledsoe.

X Not a nit, just an observation. (And I shall endeavor to do this with some measure of gentleness.) This episode contains a touching scene with Scully dressed in white, laying on a table as her father approaches in a naval uniform to tell her it's not time for her to die. Beginning with an overhead shot of Scully, the camera drops and rotates to the side. During this sequence—indeed, during the entire episode—Scully seems, how shall we say, more *developed* than in previous episodes (and we are not just talking a *minor* difference here). Just what kind of experiments *were* those fiends in the conspiracy conducting?

X After Frohike stuffs Scully's medical charts down his pants, we see a close-up of one page of the documents, and there's a date in the upper left-hand corner that looks like it reads "01/03/94." This simply can't be right, since we know that Scully was abducted sometime after

"Duane Barry," and that episode carried a date of August 7, 1994.

X For some unfathomable reason, the signature that Mulder uses to sign his resignation looks *nothing* like the signature on his badge seen at the beginning of this episode. Could it be—gasp—that Mulder has been invaded by another consciousness, much like Jack Willis was in "Lazarus"?

Firewalker

Onscreen Locations

☒ California Institute of Technology, Volcano Observatory, Pasadena, California

☒ Cascade Mountain Range

Ruminations

The dates on this episode come from Mulder's field journal entry at the end.

Also, this episode makes particularly good use of "The Flashlight Effect" (a look that occurs in almost every episode of The X-Files). Searching the base camp just after arrival, Mulder walks down a hall with windows on both sides, and the flashlight beam reflects off the glass in all sorts of interesting ways.

Finally, in many ways, this episode is a counter part to the first season episode "Ice." Both episodes begin with a strange video transmission. Both episodes feature a secluded environment. Both episodes encompass a parasitic intruder whose existence lays outside the bounds of accepted biological systems (the worms of "Ice" like to swim in ammonia and are probably extraterrestrial, the fungi of "Fire" live in a volcano and are probably a silicon-based life-form). In addition, both episodes contain team members compromised by said organisms and the threat of infection hangs heavy throughout. The formula for the episode certainly worked the first time the creators used it. Why not use it again?

Plot Oversights

☒ After Mulder, Scully, and a scientist from the

PLOT SUMMARY Mulder and Scully travel to Mount Avalon. A volcano research team stationed there hasn't responded as scheduled, and the last video transmission shows a man named Erikson laying dead. Led by Daniel Trepkos, the team was using the robot "Firewalker" to gather information from the heart of the volcano. Once on site, Mulder and Scully find the equipment smashed and the remaining team members—Jacob Ludwig, Peter Tanaka, and Jesse O'Neil—twitching with paranoia. Trepkos has already fled, and the team members blame him for the damage, saying he became unbalanced after Firewalker's descent. Trepkos's own notes reveal a startling discovery. Trepkos believed that the robot brought up a silicon-based life-form. Unknown to Mulder and Scully, that life-form is actually a parasite that grows in the human body—bursting out to launch a cloud of infectious spores when it reaches maturity. Ludwig, Tanaka, and O'Neil already have the parasite, and Trepkos is simply trying to stop its spread.

Soon the parasite bursts from Tanaka, but Mulder is spared because Tanaka has tumbled into a deep ravine. Then Trepkos kills Ludwig to keep him from spreading it, and Scully barely escapes infection from O'Neil by shutting her in a room. In short order, a military biohazard team takes control of the situation, placing Mulder and Scully under a thirty-day quarantine. Trepkos returns to the volcano.

California Institute of Technology named Adam Pierce disembark at the volcano research base camp, the helicopter that brought them departs for points unknown. Why not stay a while? One Firewalker team member is dead. Others might be injured. Is it so unreasonable to think that an

immediate transport might be needed? (Of course, if the helicopter *hadn't* departed, the show would have taken place elsewhere, because Scully would have evacuated the Firewalker team members fairly quickly.)

X Trepkos kills Pierce shortly after he arrives, on the chance that Pierce might be infected with the parasite. Later in the show, Trepkos kills Ludwig because he *is* infected with the parasite, and then he sets fire to Ludwig's body to finish the job. So . . . if Trepkos thinks that he needs to burn the corpses to incinerate the parasite, why did he leave Pierce's body in the woods? Why not drag him back to the volcano and torch him?

X Here's the deal: Tanaka tumbles into a ravine. This thing punches out of his neck. The spores spew everywhere. He's laying there on his back looking . . . well . . . *gross*. Yet, in the next scene, we see the body wrapped in plastic in some kind of isolation chamber at the base camp. You have to wonder: How did he get here? Who actually went down into the ravine and retrieved the body after Tanaka dusted it with an infectious agent? Remember, at this point, *no one* knows how the parasite is spread, yet obviously *somebody* skittered down there and wrapped the guy in plastic. ("*I'm* not going down there, *you* go down there." "*I'm* not going down either." "I know! Let's get *Scully*. She'll do anything to prove she's just as brave as everybody else!")

X And speaking of managing bravely in the face of desperate circumstances, Mulder leaves Scully with the task of completing Tanaka's autopsy to find out more about the parasite. You might recall that this is a base camp for a *volcanic survey* mission. Did Scully bring along some scalpels just in case they were needed? ("Don't leave home without them.") Or did she do the deed with a pickax?

X Mulder and Ludwig go to the volcano looking for Trepkos. The pair enter the volcano's steam caves when suddenly a flare races through the air and buries itself in Ludwig's back. Ludwig thrashes around. Ludwig groans. Ludwig falls down. Ludwig dies. All this time, Mulder stares and stares and stares some more. He even turns his back on the area from which the flare originated! This allows Trepkos enough time to march up and point the flare gun at our favorite glassy-eyed agent. The only thing I can figure is that Mulder is enthralled with the possibility that he's about to meet Mr. Rock-Buddy ("Your Silicon-Based Friend"). I mean, *I* certainly wouldn't be gawking at Ludwig, *I'd* be yanking my gun out of its holster to prepare for the next attack!

X To incinerate Ludwig's body, Trepkos produces a vial filled with flammable liquid and makes a bonfire. He's been living in a volcano for who knows how long, and he's carrying around a bottle of gasoline?! Right. *That* seems like a sensible thing to do. (On the other hand, is it likely that a silicon-based parasite living in a volcano would have an aversion to fire? And—if it liked volcano heat in the first place—wouldn't it find the human body tepid at best?)

X As with "Ice," the volcano parasite in this episode seems to control each host a bit differently so the plot can work to maximum benefit. Tanaka runs away so we can see how the parasite is spread without our heroes being infected. Ludwig hangs close to Mulder—trying to accomplish who knows what—so Trepkos can kill him and we can learn the truth. And O'Neil handcuffs herself to Scully to ensure that the spores can spread to a new host and we can have the excitement of wondering how Scully will possibly escape. (In fact, O'Neil is the *only* one who seems interested in the propagation of the organism. Evidently she found a way to get in touch with the needs of her inner parasite.)

And while we are on the topic of propagation, how did Scully escape infection? True, she has O'Neil isolated in a room. But the chain on the handcuffs would ensure a significant crack in the door, and the spores are *airborne*. Since the spores are launched in the direction of the door with what looks like *explosive* force, wouldn't some of them make it beyond the door to be subsequently inhaled by our heroes?

Continuity and Production Problems

Just before a parasite bursts forth, the creators give us the standard horror fare of swelling bulges and neck protrusions. To create this effect, a prosthetic is attached to the skin and the edges covered with makeup. Watch carefully as Tanaka prepares to do his impression of Old Faithful. As the special-effects crew orchestrates the final bulging before the eruption, a seam comes loose, separating from Tanaka's skin on the side of his neck.

SECOND SEASON

Trivia Questions

1 What did Trepkos take for his bipolar disorder?

2 List the numbers of the three samples taken from the volcano that contained trace evidence of the organism.

Trivia Answers
1 Lithium carbonate.
2 7, 12, and 22.

Red Museum

PLOT SUMMARY

In Wisconsin, a teenager disappears—only to reappear, terrified, with the words "HE IS ONE" written on his back. It has happened before, and when Sheriff Mazeroski of Delta Glen asserts possession, Mulder decides to take a look. He and Scully discover that Mazeroski's conclusion comes from his bias against the Red Museum—a local New Age cult founded by a former medical doctor named Odin. Odin advocates bodily possession by enlightened spirits and teaches strict vegetarianism. Interestingly enough, the toxicology report on the next victim shows large amounts of scopolamine—a controlled substance available to medical professionals only.

Suspicion lurches elsewhere, however, when Mulder and Scully apprehend the town pervert, Gert Thomas. Gert readily confesses to the kidnappings, saying he wanted to expose the activities of another local physician, Jerrold Larson. Larson has been injecting the young people with alien DNA and paying Thomas's boss to inject the cattle as well. "Someone" is conducting a test, using the vegetarians of the Red Museum as a control group. Fearing disclosure, this same "someone" sends an assassin to eradicate all evidence. Though Mulder wants the man alive for questioning, Mazeroski kills the assassin as he attempts to burn down the beef processing plant. Of course, no record exists to identify the man, but Scully remembers him as Deep Throat's killer.

Plot Oversights

☒ Out There—that shadow organization ultimately dedicated to revealing the Truth—seems to work its pixies overtime during this episode. At just the right time, a retired farmer materializes to drive Mulder and Scully out to a specific ranch. Though it appears that many ranchers in the area use bovine growth hormone, this particular spread is run by a rancher who employs the town pervert—the very same man who is kidnapping the teenagers. In addition, it also seems that this particular rancher is one of only a few ranchers in the area who are being paid to inject the cattle. Does it seem reasonable that Mulder and Scully would be brought to this place by mere happenstance?

And if that weren't fortunate enough, a plane crash only hours later alerts Mulder and Scully to the mysterious dealings of the town doctor. This in turn leads our heroes back to the Kane home—site of the first abduction. While there, Mulder uncovers the activities of the town pervert because of yet another startlingly beneficial occurrence. Though the pervert usually does his peeping in the dark, "someone" leaves the light on in his hidden-video cubbyhole. A small pinprick of light emanating from this cubby draws Mulder to its existence and results in the arrest of the pervert.

☒ In a lovely bit of continuity, the assassin who executed Deep Throat at the end of "The Erlenmeyer Flask" reappears in this episode. Yet he continues to display a characteristic I find odd: He seems to make a habit of allowing anyone and everyone to get a really good look at his face.

Onscreen Locations

☒ Delta Glen, Wisconsin
☒ Graham County Sheriff's Station

Every time he drives past an individual, he turns to look at that person face-on before proceeding away. (Of course, this may be some post-hypnotic suggestion planted in the assassin's subconscious by the pixies of Out There. After all, this is what allows Scully to recognize him!)

☒ The use of scopolamine to subdue the teenagers initially causes Mulder and Scully to suspect Odin. It is a controlled substance, and Odin was a medical doctor. But events soon reveal that the town pervert is the kidnapper. What does he do for a living? He works for a rancher. So . . . how could he purchase such large doses of a controlled substance?

☒ In discussing the contents of Dr. Jerrold Larson's attaché with Mulder, Scully mentions "the broken vial." That vial looked fine to me when she pulled it out of the little bag. Did she drop it at some point?

☒ Yet more evidence of Mulder's Zen numbering system for new files. This case file for these events carries a number of "XWC060361." (See "3" for more details.)

Changed Premises

☒ The reeducation of Dana Scully seems to be proceeding in fits and starts. Enjoying some ribs at the local barbecue restaurant, Scully tells Mulder that she "got the creeps" while Mulder was interviewing Gary Kane—the first teenager to be kidnapped in Delta Glen. It's good to see she's picking up the lingo. In "Shapes," Lyle Parker used that phrase, and Scully acted like she had never heard it before. On a less positive note—even after escorting Tickle-Me-Alien out of the High Containment Facility at Fort Marlene during "The Erlenmeyer Flask"—Scully seems hesitant in this episode to acknowledge that the substance found in the container labeled "Purity Control" was in fact extraterrestrial.

Equipment Oddities

☒ The town pervert's hidden-video cubbyhole deserves a bit of scrutiny. When we first see it in action, only the center of the screen is illuminated, forming a fuzzy ring around a liberal view of Beth Kane's bra-clad torso. (Beth Kane is Gary Kane's mother.) A reverse angle then shows a close-up of Gert Thomas's peeping eye covered with a small circle of light. This would suggest that most of the mirror is opaque, with only a small opening—somewhere near the center—functioning as one-way glass. (A later view of the hidden room supports this view by showing us a videocamera whose lens would be approximately the right size to fit in this theoretical opening.) However, later in the episode, Mulder finds the room because a *pinprick* of light shows through the mirror. What happened to the opening that was big enough for Gert's eye?! Most startling, as Mulder smashes the mirror, we see its back is *completely* opaque! If that's the way it's been all along, how did Gert Thomas see through it? X-ray glasses?

Continuity and Production Problems

☒ Interestingly enough, Beth Kane has a twin sister who works for the government. Her name is Nancy Spiller, and she's a forensics instructor at the Academy. We see her in "Ghost in the Machine."

☒ Enjoying some of Delta Glen's local cuisine, Mulder notices that a group of teenagers is harassing a member of the Red Museum. Mulder walks out of the restaurant, pulls off his bib, and tosses it aside. The camera cuts to the ruffian and then back to Mulder, and he tosses the bib aside a second time. (Must be one of those yo-yo bibs. It comes back just in case you aren't through eating.)

Trivia Questions

❶ What kind of shirt does Gary Kane wear just before he is kidnapped?

❷ Where do Mulder and Scully eat in Delta Glen?

Trivia Answers
❶ A Green Bay Packers T-shirt.
❷ Clay's BBQ.

Excelsis Dei

PLOT SUMMARY

The rape of nurse Michelle Charters brings Mulder and Scully to the Excelsis Dei Convalescent Home in Worcester, Massachusetts. Charters claims that seventy-four year old resident Hal Arden—in non-corporeal form—assaulted her. At first glance, the pair can find nothing to substantiate her story. There is one odd item. Many of the residents in the home have experienced significant improvement from untreatable diseases such as Alzheimer's.

Then Hal Arden suddenly chokes to death as his roommate Stan Phillips frets nearby. When Phillips's daughter comes to remove him from the home, the old man runs away—though he supposedly has a degenerative nerve disease. And the orderly who chases after him somehow tumbles from the roof to his death.

In time, Mulder looks to the Excelsis Dei's Asian orderly for answers. His name is Gung, and he has been growing mushrooms in the basement, using his knowledge of folk medicine to create a pill to give the residents some awareness and dignity in the final days of their lives. Unfortunately, the residents have discovered Gung's stash of capsules and are overdosing on them—resulting in the death of some and leading to violent psychic manifestations in others. The confiscation of Gung's capsules returns the home to normal. Unfortunately, its residents also quickly degrade to their former, confused existence.

Onscreen Locations

🅧 Excelsis Dei Convalescent Home, Worcester, Mass.

🅧 Hotel Hartley, Worcester, Mass.

Plot Oversights

🅧 Nursing jobs must be really scarce in Massachusetts. This episode features a *registered nurse* who gives baths and makes beds. Normally this type of work is done by orderlies.

🅧 Lawyers must be scarce as well in Massachusetts. Mulder and Scully talk with Charters—a woman who has filed a lawsuit against the federal government—and for some reason her counsel forgets to come to the meeting.

🅧 Since I've already voiced a few less than complimentary comments toward Scully and her demeanor toward the recently or soon-to-be deceased, I thought I'd let a medical professional give you her opinion. Debbie Mirek of Fullerton, California, is a registered nurse and certified to teach CPR. She had the following comments about the scene where Hal Arden dies: "Where is the orderlies' CPR training? I love the way they all stand around and wring their hands. [Hal Arden] would have a better chance at the local A&P. And Scully can't do CPR. The sequencing is off. Granted, most doctors don't know CPR either but most law enforcement officials are required to be certified as part of their jobs. Guess Scully was sleeping during that part of her training."

🅧 The spirits in the convalescent home appear to have at least one unexpected skill. Mulder finds the body of another dead orderly buried in Gung's mushroom farm *behind a locked door.* So the spirits killed him, dragged him up to the door, *picked the lock,* buried him, and then locked the room on their way out?

Equipment Oddities

⌧ Attempting to discover if Stan Phillips could have made it to the fourth floor, Mulder asks the staff physician if it would be possible for Phillips to take the elevator. The physician says the elevators haven't worked in years. Okay, wait a minute: The view out Phillips's window makes it obvious that he resides on the second or third floor. On this same floor, there is at least one resident confined to a wheelchair, and supposedly—before Gung's concoction— most of the residents were barely aware of their surroundings. How in the world did this facility pass state inspections with barely ambulatory patients confined on upper floors without a working elevator?!

⌧ Somebody really, *really* needs to shut down Excelsis Dei Convalescent Home. Not only do the elevators not work, not only does it smell bad—according to Scully—but also the plumbing is atrocious. After trapping Mulder and Charters inside a bathroom, a spirit causes water to begin spraying from the faucets. In addition, nice, clean water begins shooting out

of the bathtub *drain!* Who hooked up a supply line to the bathtub drain?!

⌧ After Stan Phillips settles down, the bathroom door opens and water floods everywhere. Oddly enough, there's a reflection on the door coming from *inside* the bathroom that looks just like . . . a window! So, did Mulder attempt to break its glass and provide a drain for the water filling the bathroom, or did it have some sort of psychic force field?

Continuity and Production Problems

⌧ Just prior to being raped, Charters works to change the sheets in the room of a resident who died earlier that day. Unexpectedly, the door closes and the bed races across the floor to block the entrance to the room. Note the position of the pillow. Charters walks up and suddenly the pillow has leaped to the other end of the bed.

Trivia Questions

❶ In what rooms do Mulder and Scully stay at the Hotel Hartley?

❷ Where is Gung from?

Aubrey

PLOT SUMMARY When police detective B. J. Morrow stumbles into a field in Aubrey, Missouri, and finds herself digging up the decades-old bones of Special Agent Sam Chaney, Mulder can't resist joining the investigation. Before disappearing in 1942, Chaney was studying a trio of murders in Aubrey. All three victims were young women. Each had the word "SISTER" carved into her chest. Now the murders have begun again. Even stranger, Morrow is having nightmares that predict the attacks and reveal the murderer's face—that of Harry Cokely. Recently released from prison, Cokely was convicted of rape in 1945 after attacking Linda Thibedeaux in Edmond, Nebraska, and carving "SISTER" on her chest. Officials never made the connection to the 1942 murders in Aubrey.

Mulder and Scully's interrogation of the ex-convict proves fruitless. In an unkempt house, they find a decrepit, bitter old man—incapable of the necessary violence. Then, an interview with Mrs. Thibedeaux reveals that Cokely's assault produced a child, and a document search identifies the child as B. J. Morrow's father. Upon hearing this, Mulder concludes that a genetic compulsion is causing Morrow to reenact her grandfather's crimes. Realizing this as well, Morrow locates and kills Cokely, hoping to end the violence. It seems to work. Unfortunately, Cokely's legacy may yet survive. Morrow's compulsions began soon after she became pregnant.

Onscreen Locations

- ☒ Police Headquarters, Aubrey, Missouri
- ☒ Crime scene, Aubrey, Missouri
- ☒ Coroner's Office, Examining Room C
- ☒ Lincoln Park, Aubrey, Missouri
- ☒ Highway 377, Missouri/Nebraska border
- ☒ Memorial Hospital, Aubrey, Missouri
- ☒ Thibedeaux Residence, Edmond, Nebraska
- ☒ Shamrock Women's Prison, Psychiatric Ward, High Security

Geographical Inconsistencies

☒ Aubrey, Missouri, doesn't exist. Even funnier, *The Official Map of* The X-Files puts Aubrey about seventy miles west of Springfield, where I live. I can assure you that it's quite impossible to drive from that location to *any* town in Nebraska in one hour as this episode indicates. (Springfield is in the southwestern corner of the state, and Nebraska abuts Missouri only in Missouri's extreme northwestern corner.)

☒ In addition, there is no Highway 377. There is no Cimarron County in either Missouri or Nebraska. (There is in Oklahoma.) And Edmond, Nebraska, and Gainesville, Nebraska, don't exist.

Plot Oversights

☒ This Cokely guy, he likes to live dangerously. He's sitting next to his oxygen tank and he's *smoking*. Surprisingly enough, Mulder and Scully don't seem bothered by this! Here's a little real-life advice for you: If you are in a room with a man who uses oxygen to supplement his breathing and he decides to smoke . . . *RUN!*

At the same time I was doing a plot summary for this episode, I had hired a friend to do some painting. Her name is Lynn Wertz, and during her lunch break she joined me to watch the show. I explained the setup for the episode and the concept of nitpicking and she delighted in a bit of her own as the scenes wandered by. (Once people start nitpicking, it's hard to get them to stop!) Just after concluding that Morrow is the murderer and probably will attack Linda Thibedeaux once again, we watched our intrepid FBI agents race for their car so they could warn her. Lynn frowned. "That's what telephones are for," she observed. I couldn't agree more. Why don't Mulder and Scully *call* Thibedeaux?

After cutting short her attempt to murder Linda Thibedeaux, Morrow heads for Cokely's house. Somehow she knows that whatever is happening to her won't stop until he's dead. Sometime later, Mulder and Scully arrive at Thibedeaux's house. Hearing of the attack, Mulder heads straight for Cokely's house in Gainesville, Nebraska. At the same time, Scully takes Thibedeaux back to Aubrey, Missouri, from her home in Edmond, Nebraska. With me so far? Good. In Aubrey, police lieutenant Brian Tillman stomps around and says he doesn't believe that Morrow attacked Thibedeaux, but *eventually* he decides it must be true, and the two of them head for Gainesville as well. Meanwhile, Mulder arrives at Cokely's house and—*only minutes later*—is on the floor with his head split open. Morrow leaps onto Mulder's stomach and prepares to cut him. *Miraculously,* Scully and Tillman then appear to stop her. How did they get there so fast? Mulder only went from Edmond to Gainesville, but Scully had to go from Edmond to Aubrey to Gainesville, and Aubrey is in *Missouri!* (Yes, there *might* be a way to make it work if the road from Edmond to Gainesville is a cow trail and the roads from Edmond to Aubrey and from Aubrey to Gainesville are superhighways, but. . . .)

Equipment Oddities

Words fail any attempt to relate how impressed I am with the graphic imaging software used in this episode as Mulder and Scully try to identify the slash marks on the decades-old bones of Chaney. With some sort of three-dimensional modeling program, Scully effortlessly enlarges a rendered female rib cage to the same size as Chaney's and then asks the computer to run a comparison on the marks to see if they match. The computer accomplishes this in *four seconds*—no doubt allowing for variations in depth of cut, length of stroke, angle of inclination, etc., etc. Even more amazing, moments later we see the computer zoom in—using a split screen—on *both* rendered three-dimensional graphics, and the transitions between frames are *seamless.* (Remember, this is in late 1994.) There are two possibilities for this inspiring display of raw computational power. Either the bulging metropolis of Aubrey invested in a high-end graphics workstation and the FBI just happened to have software compatible with it, or Scully is uplinked with Quantico and she is doing all this stuff on-line. Neither explanation is really satisfactory. Why would a small police force invest *tens* of thousands of dollars for this piece of equipment? Is the police chief independently wealthy? And if Scully is on-line, what kind of modem is she using to get that type of data bandwidth on the transfers? She would need something like a digital fiber-optic line to transfer the individual frames of the zoom as fast as she does, and even then I doubt that a PC manufactured in 1994 could handle the full-screen full-motion video we see here. (I had an amusing moment during this scene. As everyone onscreen racked their brains trying to figure out what the marks on Chaney's bones could *possibly* spell—as Mulder and Scully used their supercomputer to run all the possible pattern matches—Lynn Wertz looked at me and said, " 'Brother'! It says 'Brother'!" I just grinned because . . . it did.)

Trivia Questions

1 What was the name of Chaney's partner?

2 What is the name of one of the women Cokely killed in 1942?

☒ Well, *they're . . . back!* In the review of "Blood," I noted that Scully's eyeglasses don't appear to have any prescription—nice flat, thin lenses. I suggested that my gentle readers watch the lenses as the camera pans around her head near the beginning of that episode. This episode contains a *very* similar pan as Scully makes her final field journal entry. If you compare the two you'll see that her glasses in this episode are real—the lenses have a curvature. One question: Why does she wear the other pair? Did she have her contacts in already but someone was coming by and she wanted a more austere, no-nonsense look? (As she observes near the end of "War of the Coprophages," "Smart is sexy.")

Continuity and Production Problems

☒ Near the beginning of the episode, Mulder briefs Scully on Special Agent Sam Chaney. He hands her a folder. She opens it and moments later, flips over the top page. A reverse angle of Scully shows the page flipped. Then the scene returns to the over-the-shoulder shot of Scully, and the page is no longer flipped. Then the reverse shot returns and the page is!

☒ During one of her "spells," Morrow goes to a house that Cokely rented in 1942, rushes into the basement, and rips up the floorboards. The bones of Chaney's partner are buried beneath. Keep your eyes on Scully as she descends the stairs. She trips and almost does a swan drive before she regains her balance. (I know this would happen in real life. I just expect more from a hero!)

☒ Not sure what this means, but Mulder can get dressed *incredibly* fast. Learning that Morrow is Cokely's granddaughter, Mulder concludes that Morrow has committed the murders. He leaps from a couch in a motel room and heads for the door, wearing only his shirt and tie. (Okay, okay. He's wearing pants, shoes, and socks as well—along with *whatever else* he wears for undergarments—but the point is, his *upper* body shows only a shirt and tie.) Scully grabs her coat and follows him out the door. The conversation continues as we cut to the exterior of the motel room and *instantly* Mulder wears his suit coat *and* his overcoat.

GENRES

A Listing of X-FILES Episodes by Content

Obviously not everyone enjoys every type of story. Since *The X-Files* covers such a wide variety of topics, I thought it might be helpful to have a general grouping system to identify the category of the "oddness" presented in each episode. Of course, all of this is open for debate, but since it's my book, I get to choose the headings and make the assignments! (You might also note that some episodes land in more than one category.)

Abduction

(Possibly alien, possibly not)

"Pilot"

"Conduit"

"Fallen Angel"

"Duane Barry"

"Ascension"

"One Breath"

"Fearful Symmetry"

"Nisei"

"731"

"José Chung's *From Outer Space*"

"Momento Mori"

"Tempus Fugit"

"Max"

"Demons"

Alien Involvement

(Where the involvement is direct and known)

"Space"

"Fallen Angel"

"Genderbender"

"Little Green Men"

"Colony"

"End Game"

"Paper Clip"

"War of the Coprophages"

"Piper Maru"

"Apocrypha"

"José Chung's *From Outer Space*"

"Talitha Cumi"

"Herrenvolk"

"Musings of a Cigarette-Smoking Man"

"Tunguska"

"Terma"

"Tempus Fugit"

"Max"

Body Invaders

"Ice"

"Space"

"The Host"

"Firewalker"

"F. Emasculata"

"Piper Maru"

"Apocrypha"

"Tunguska"

"Terma"

"El Mundo Gira"

Genetic Anomalies

"Squeeze"

"The Jersey Devil"

"Fire"

"Tooms"

"The Host"

"Aubrey"

"Humbug"

"D.P.O."

"2SHY"

"Home"

"Teliko"

"El Mundo Gira"

"Leonard Betts"

"Small Potatoes"

Government Conspiracy

"Pilot"

"Deep Throat"

"Conduit"

"Ghost in the Machine"

"Ice"

"Fallen Angel"

"Eve"

"Young at Heart"

"EBE"

"The Erlenmeyer Flask"

"Little Green Men"

"Blood"

"Sleepless"

"Duane Barry"

"Ascension"

"One Breath"

"Red Museum"

"Fresh Bones"

"Colony"
"End Game"
"F. Emasculata"
"Soft Light"
"Anasazi"
"The Blessing Way"
"Paper Clip"
"Nisei"
"731"
"Piper Maru"
"Apocrypha"
"José Chung's *From Outer Space*"
"Wetwired"
"Talitha Cumi"
"Herrenvolk"
"Musings of a Cigarette-Smoking Man"
"Tunguska"
"Terma"
"Momento Mori"
"Unrequited"
"Tempus Fugit"
"Max"
"Zero Sum"
"Gethsemane"

Natural Danger

"Darkness Falls"
"Død Kalm"
"Quagmire"
"El Mundo Gira"

Paranormal Phenomena

(Phenomena outside the context of a belief system)
"Shadows"
"Beyond the Sea"
"Lazarus"
"Born Again"
"Roland"

"Excelsis Dei"
"Clyde Bruckman's Final Repose"
"The Walk"
"Oubliette"
"Pusher"
"Avatar"
"Unruhe"
"The Field Where I Died"
"Paper Hearts"
"Never Again"
"Elegy"

Serial Killers

"Squeeze"
"The Jersey Devil"
"Ghost in the Machine"
"Fire"
"Beyond the Sea"
"Genderbender"
"Tooms"
"The Host"
"3"
"Aubrey"
"Irresistible"
"Humbug"
"D.P.O."
"Clyde Bruckman's Final Repose"
"2SHY"
"Syzygy"
"Grotesque"
"Pusher"
"Teliko"
"Paper Hearts"
"Unrequited"
"Elegy"

Sinister Experimentation

(Known to be done by humans)
"Eve"
"Young At Heart"

"The Erlenmeyer Flask"
"Sleepless"
"Red Museum"
"F. Emasculata"
"Soft Light"
"Nisei"
"731"
"Wetwired"
"Tunguska"
"Terma"
"Zero Sum"
"Demons"

Supernatural Phenomena

(Phenomena within the context of a belief system)
"Miracle Man"
"Shapes"
"Our Town"
"3"
"Die Hand Die Verletzt"
"Fresh Bones"
"The Calusari"
"The Blessing Way"
"The List"
"Revelations"
"Syzygy"
"Grotesque"
"Teso Dos Bichos"
"Kaddish"

Time Travel

"Synchrony"

Irresistible

Onscreen Locations

☒ Ficicello Frozen Food

☒ FBI Field Office, Minneapolis, Minnesota

☒ County Morgue, Minneapolis, Minnesota

☒ Los Cerritos Adult Education

☒ Latent Fingerprint Analysis Lab

Ruminations

Credit where credit is due. Pfaster originally sets his sights on Scully because he happens to be held in the same cellblock as a suspect whom Mulder and Scully interview. I found it odd that—in a city the size of Minneapolis— all those awaiting arraignment would be brought to the same location. (No doubt this is a holdover from Barney Miller, *which featured a set with a small holding cell!) I called the Minneapolis city police and, in fact, all prisoners are brought to a central location! Score one for the creators.*

Unanswered Questions

☒ Why do people see Pfaster as a demon in this episode? Is he possessed, or was this effect thrown in just to "creepy-up" the episode?

Plot Oversights

☒ So, Mulder, Scully, and Bocks are standing beside this grave near the beginning of the episode and it's raining and it's a crime scene and no one seems concerned about throwing a tent of some kind over the grave to preserve any forensic evidence that might exist concerning

PLOT SUMMARY In Minneapolis, Special Agent Moe Bocks requests the assistance of Mulder and Scully. There's been a series of grave excavations in which the corpses' hair has been cut off and fingernails removed. Bocks suspects alien involvement, but Mulder believes it's actually the work of a fetishist—a conclusion he reached before leaving the capital. When a troubled Scully wonders why they came to Minneapolis in the first place, Mulder flashes a pair of Vikings football tickets.

The game goes on without them. The fetishist has escalated his activities and begun harvesting his trophies from the living. After performing the first victim's autopsy, Scully reaches her emotional limit. Under the guise of escorting the body back to Washington to have it checked for fingerprints, Scully talks with a counselor, trying to sort out her feelings. The trip serves well. The lab lifts a fingerprint—identifying the suspect as Donny Pfaster—and Scully finds the strength to return to Minneapolis. Unfortunately, Pfaster has already fled by the time agents raid his apartment. In short order, he captures Scully as she drives from the airport.

Frantic hours later, Mulder leads a team of agents to a house belonging to Pfaster's dead mother. They arrive in time to save Scully's life. Afterward, Mulder takes a few moments to provide his understandably harried partner some much-needed comfort.

the identity of the desecrator. Does this seem right?

☒ I'm thinkin' Pfaster is going to be seriously disappointed with the prostitute he brings home. The guy has a fetish for nails, and I'd be willing to bet that hers are fake. If that's what the guy wants, why not go to the store and buy a box or two? (And couldn't he do the same thing with wigs?!)

☒ Speaking of this prostitute, note how she shivers on arrival. Note how she comments that it's *freezing* in Pfaster's apartment and asks about the heat. Note how Pfaster explains that the forced air unit is broken. Question: If it's "freezing" in the apartment because Pfaster doesn't have any heat, doesn't that imply that it's "freezing" outside? (This actually seems sensible. This *is* Minneapolis in mid-November.) And if it's freezing outside, why do all the prostitutes on the street look so comfortable in their skimpy outfits only moments later? Just an act?

☒ The date on this episode is unquestionable. Scully gives it as she begins the prostitute's autopsy. Unfortunately, the last date we had on an episode was also unquestionable. The end of "Firewalker" gives a date for its events of November 11 through November 13. Yet, Scully does the autopsy in this episode on November 14, a Monday, and we know she and Mulder arrived in Minneapolis on Saturday, which would be November 12. In other words, they were in two places at once. (They're *clones!* Aaaah!) In addition, Mulder and Scully were supposedly quarantined for *thirty days* at the end of "Firewalker." Then came "Red Museum," "Excelsis Dei," "Aubrey," and finally "Irresistible." It seems *unlikely* that "Irresistible" could take place on November 14!

☒ Posing as a special agent, Pfaster calls Washington, and the guy in the fingerprint lab tells him when Scully is returning to Minneapolis. The Real FBI tells me this *wouldn't* happen. They are *careful* about this type of information.

☒ Did Scully get lost as she left Minneapolis-St. Paul International Airport? One would expect her to drive straight to the FBI field office in Minneapolis. Yet, in short order, we see her driving on a desolate two-lane county road. I've flown into the Minneapolis-St. Paul airport several times. It sits right off Highway 5—a four-lane, restricted-access road just like an interstate. In addition, the FBI field office is in the very heart of the city. Unless Scully took a detour, she should have driven on four-lane, restricted highways almost all the way to the field office's doorstep. (Of course, if she did that, Pfaster wouldn't have been able to abduct her!)

☒ Several nitpickers felt that Scully should have fared better as Pfaster attempted to kidnap her. After all, Pfaster had a car. And Scully? Well, Scully had a car . . . and a *gun!* (As a trained law enforcement officer, it does seem that she would be equipped to handle this situation. Then again, maybe she was just rattled by the case.)

☒ Learning that Scully is missing, both Mulder and Bocks immediately assume that Pfaster took her. Minneapolis—sad to say—is like many other big cities in the United States. It does have more than *one* criminal! Now, I *can* understand how Mulder would jump to this conclusion—he jumps to conclusions all the time, some right, some wrong—but Bocks seems just as convinced, though the only evidence they possess is paint that could come from any one of sixty thousand cars in the area. (I suppose that Mulder *just knew* Pfaster would be a sucker for that red hair.)

☒ What is it about growing up with lots of older sisters that turns a man into a woman-hating villain? Last episode, we learned that Harry Cokely had five older sisters. In this episode, Donny Pfaster has four. Were they forced to spend too many days as young, impressionable boys playing "dress-up"? ("Guess what, Donny? We're going to play house again today, and this time you're going to be the ballerina!")

Equipment Oddities

☒ Those flat glasses have reappeared on our favorite redhead! During Scully's first field journal entry, watch as the camera pans around her head.

Continuity and Production Problems

☒ Not sure this is a nit, but at least it's fun to notice. Near the beginning of the episode, Mulder, Scully, and Bocks walk through a cemetery on the way to a desecrated grave. The camera is set so a row of tombstones sits between that camera and our heroes. The fourth of these tombstones contains the name Raymond Soames. You may or may not remember that Ray Soames was also the name of a young man who died prior to the events of "Pilot." Interestingly enough, the dates on the tombstone appear to be "1971–1989," which would be just about right for the birth year of the Ray Soames in Bellefleur, Oregon. He graduated from high school in the Class of 1989. The *death* year on the tombstone, however, is not the same as that of the young man from the pilot, since Soames was twenty when he died.

There are a few possibilities here. One, the creators might have included this tombstone as a homage to the pilot. Two, the creators might have had this tombstone manufactured *for* the pilot, but because the death year was incorrect, they didn't use it. Or three, Ray Soames of Bellefleur, Oregon, might have been only one of a group of

alien/human clones, much like Jeremiah Smith and his buddies in "Talitha Cumi."

☒ After Scully's first field journal entry, the scene dissolves to a busy street shot with cars coming and going. A bus approaches with "UBC" on the destination sign. I believe that stands of "University of British Columbia." Shouldn't that read "UBCaM" (University of British Columbia at Minneapolis)? Just joking. UBC is located in Vancouver, where *The X-Files* is filmed.

☒ After capture, Scully attempts to escape by pushing Pfaster into a bathtub filled with water. Pfaster's pants are drenched, as is the left sleeve of his shirt. Scully runs off. Pfaster follows, his shirt still wet. Yet, when we see him retrieve Scully's weapon from a dresser drawer only moments later, his shirt is dry! (No doubt, he removed it, threw it in the dryer, took it out, ironed it, and put it back on before resuming his search. That's what living with four older sisters will do for you!)

☒ At the end of the program, Mulder comments that Pfaster was the younger brother of four older sisters, and the camera shows us what we must assume is a family portrait. So . . . why are there only *three* sisters in the shot?

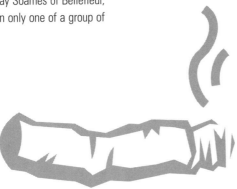

SECOND SEASON

Trivia Questions

❶ Which chapters is Pfaster supposed to read for his mythology class?

❷ With whom does Scully speak in the Employee Assistance Program?

Trivia Answers
❶ Ten and eleven.
❷ K. Kosseff, L.C.S.W.

Irresistible

Die Hand Die Verletzt

PLOT SUMMARY

In a forest near Milford Haven, New Hampshire, two teenage boys reenact a black magic ceremony—hoping to scare witless their two female companions and "get some." The next morning, one of the boys, Jerry Stevens, lies dead with his eyes and heart cut out. Unknown to the young people, several prominent members of the community are practitioners of the black arts—though in recent years they have wandered from their beliefs. Taking advantage of the teenagers' invitation, a true "dark force" has arrived to punish the faithless adults.

Seeing Stevens's body, Sheriff Oakes contacts the FBI. Mulder and Scully soon arrive. But our intrepid pair can do little more than scurry from event to event, played like marionettes, as the dark force—in the form of substitute teacher Mrs. Paddock—carries out the proscribed vengeance. Having killed Jerry Stevens, she forces a teenage girl to commit suicide. The adults recognize what's happening, and one even renounces his faith altogether. Unimpressed, Paddock sends her python for him. And when the others try to offer Mulder and Scully in a ritualistic sacrifice to regain their standing, Paddock causes them to kill themselves instead. In the end, our heroes stare helpless at a blackboard that contains Paddock's farewell message. It bids them good-bye, saying it's been nice working with them.

Onscreen Locations

- ☒ Parent Teacher Committee, Milford Haven, New Hampshire
- ☒ Milford Haven, New Hampshire
- ☒ Crowley High School Library
- ☒ Crowley High School, psychologist's office

Ruminations

The date on this episode comes from the library card that Mulder examines. The card for *Witchhunt: A History of the Occult in America* by M. R. Karshewski shows that Dave Duran checked it out on January 16, 1995. (I know it seems to read "JAN 6 1995" but examine the vertical line to the left of the "6." Doesn't it look like there's a "1" hidden against it?) Since the events of this episode occur after Duran checked out the book, the episode must carry a date on or after January 16. (But not too *much* after—see "Colony.")

Geographical Inconsistencies

☒ Milford Haven, New Hampshire, doesn't exist.

Plot Oversights

☒ At one point, Mulder gets a drink from the water fountain and notes that the water is going down the drain counterclockwise. This surprises him and he says that the Coriolis force in the Northern Hemisphere "dictates" that the water should go down the drain clockwise. Scully—who did her undergraduate work in physics—agrees that it isn't possible for water to go down the drain counterclockwise in the Northern Hemisphere. Now, I'm not a physicist, but I know people who are, and I played around a bit on the Internet and everything that I've read said that the Coriolis effect on water going down a drain is *minimal*. Water *can and does* go down a drain counterclockwise in the Northern Hemisphere because there are *plenty* of other more powerful influences on the rotation of the water—things such as basin shape, water flow pattern, and faucet placement. The Coriolis effect only ensures the rotational direction of *large* systems such as hurricanes and typhoons.

X In a dramatic moment, Mrs. Paddock opens her desk drawer to show us the eyes and heart she extracted from Jerry Stevens. She then lays a stack of papers on the body parts and closes the drawer. I guess she isn't planning to give those papers back to the students, since at least some of them will be soaked with blood. Or does she have some black magic spell to take care of the stains? (I wonder if she rents out her services. My wife has a blueberry stain on a silk shirt that's giving her fits. . . .)

X After speaking with the high school's psychologist, Mulder finds Scully "surfing the Web." She has located an article that regurgitates almost word for word the events surrounding Jerry Stevens's death. Mulder asks if Scully got it from the local paper. As Scully continues reading, the article turns to a claim that the Jews are responsible. Scully then triumphantly declares that the excerpt came from *Volkischer Beobachter*—a newspaper published in Germany in 1934; she says that the rumors are the same but the blanks have been filled in with whomever is feared or persecuted at the time.

Scully makes it sound like everything she read came from the German newspaper. In fact, a close inspection of her computer screen will reveal that this is *not* true. The text that Scully reads is displayed on the lower portion of the screen. The search parameters used to find that text are displayed in the upper portion. The pertinent line reads, "Please enter search criteria: Milford Haven, current, news." This is followed by information stating that the article comes from a news group called "Newsbytes.current.events" and is about Milford Haven, New Hampshire! In addition, the quotation marks in the article show that the excerpt from the 1934 German newspaper contains only one sentence. ("The Jew is known to remove organs and sacrifice teens in his religious ceremonies.") Shame on you, Scully, for misleading your partner!

X Without going into great detail for obvious reasons (some information is best left vague), the method of suicide employed by a young lady in this episode would not result in the instantaneous death portrayed (unless some black magic caused a more rapid response).

Equipment Oddities

X Scully must have an incredible form of surge protection on her computer. During one scene, in the middle of a ferocious lightning storm, she uses her computer to query the FBI's database and produce a work history for Mrs. Paddock. Granted, the power is off and her laptop is running from the battery pack, but one strike on a telephone line and her modem is toast!

X The black magic displayed by Mrs. Paddock in this episode is awesome indeed. Not only does she orchestrate an intricate vengeance on those she deems unworthy, she also manages to call Mulder's cell phone by dialing only seven

SECOND SEASON

Trivia Questions

1 Who intends to put on *Jesus Christ, Superstar* at Crowley High?

2 What is Mrs. Paddock's first name and middle initial?

133

Die Hand Die Verletzt

numbers! Since Mulder is based in Washington, D.C., his cell phone probably carries an area code of "202." Normally, to reach Mulder from a phone in New Hampshire, a person would have to dial *eleven* digits.

Continuity and Production Problems

☒ I wanna know who's sitting in Jim Ausbury's sink and spitting! After Ausbury's daughter claims she was forced to participate in cultic rituals, Mulder and Scully interview Ausbury and his wife. Moments later, Mulder accompanies Ausbury into the kitchen to get a glass of water. When asked if he did what the young woman claims, Ausbury crushes the glass, and water sprays upward. Then the shot changes and someone spits at Mulder and Ausbury! (Okay, okay, no one really *spits* at them. It's a bad edit, so the water leaps from the glass twice . . . but it really *looks like* someone is spitting at them. Really. For sure. Trust me.)

☒ After Shannon Ausbury's death, Mulder finds her father, Jim Ausbury, in the basement of the Ausbury home. Jim confesses to conducting occult rituals. Handcuffing Ausbury, Mulder bounds up the basement stairs to rendezvous with Scully at the high school. At the top of the stairs, the kitchen is lit. That's strange, because all the power is out in the town, and minutes later—when Mulder and Scully return—the kitchen is dark.

Fresh Bones

Onscreen Locations

- ☒ Folkstone, North Carolina
- ☒ County Road 10, Folkstone, North Carolina
- ☒ Folkstone I.N.S. Processing Center
- ☒ Temporary camp morgue
- ☒ Processing center brig
- ☒ Psychiatric infirmary
- ☒ Folkstone Municipal Cemetery

Plot Oversights

☒ A pair of guards comes down with an *extremely convenient* attack of "vocational amnesia" in this episode. Arriving at the processing center for the first time, Mulder and Scully are escorted inside—right through the interned Haitians—by two Marines. They are supposed to be taking our heroes to see Colonel Wharton. Yet, for some reason, halfway there, the Marines suddenly decide that they have better things to do and wander off! This *is* fortunate, however, because it allows a Haitian to accost Scully, thereby giving Chester Bonaparte an opportunity to save her and sell Mulder some "protection."

☒ When interviewing Bauvais, Mulder says that a shell was found buried under a dead soldier's home. Earlier, Robin McAlpin—wife of the second suicide victim, John McAlpin—said that her son Luke found the shell buried in his sandbox. So, is Luke's sandbox really *underneath* the house, or is Mulder just changing a detail to see how Bauvais will react?

☒ In discussing McAlpin's death, an official-

PLOT SUMMARY After two Marines commit suicide in only two weeks, Mulder and Scully travel to Folkstone, North Carolina. Given the ritual symbols at each site, Mulder concludes that voodoo played some role in the deaths—especially since the Marines were stationed at a nearby immigration processing center and many of the refugees confined there are Haitian.

Run by Colonel Wharton, the processing center reeks of tension. One month ago, a riot broke out, and a young boy was killed. Blamed for the incident, voodoo practitioner Pierre Bauvais has been confined to the brig. In reality, however, Wharton has caused the problems. He recently began to practice voodoo and has even ordered beatings to force the Haitians to reveal the secrets of their religion. When that tactic fails, Wharton has Bauvais killed, making it look like suicide.

With the help of a ubiquitous boy named Chester Bonaparte and a visit from Mr. X, Mulder and Scully uncover the truth. Unfortunately, their investigation brings them under voodoo attack from Wharton. Just in time, Scully is saved by a protective cachet purchased from Chester, and Mulder is rescued by a temporarily resurrected Bauvais.

Afterward, the pair search for Chester to thank him for his help. Only then do they learn that he was the boy who died in the riot.

looking medical person tells Scully that McAlpin's head was "hanging on his shoulders like a broken peony." I take this to mean that the car crash snapped McAlpin's vertebrae. Amazingly enough, we see him alive and walking later! Now, I know this episode features voodoo magic, but I've read *The Serpent and the Rainbow* by Wade Davis (the researcher whom Mulder mentions in this episode), and to the best of my remembrance, I do not recall *any* mention of the ability of zombification drugs to repair broken necks.

☒ Coming out of Wharton's office for the second time, Scully takes her place behind the wheel of the rental car and is promptly pierced by a strand of thorns wrapped around the steering column. Surprisingly enough, she tosses the thorns out the window and drives off! Hello! *Hello!?* You're in voodoo country, remember? Even if you don't believe, Dr. Scully, wouldn't it be a good idea to have those thorns tested for toxins? And when that wound *keeps* itching and gets red and inflamed, *maybe* you should think about having it checked?

☒ Robin McAlpin hands Mulder an envelope that contains a photo of Wharton and Bauvais in Haiti, taking part in a voodoo ceremony. The photograph is obviously a composite—several different pictures digitally combined. Yet, Mulder treats it as the real thing! (We *have* seen him and Scully analyzing photos before to determine if they are fake. Why not this time?)

☒ Finally clued into what's happening by the appearance of Mr. X, Mulder and Scully sneak in and search Wharton's office—the same office that's in the middle of the processing center . . . a center that's surrounded by high fences . . . and Marines. Right.

☒ No offense intended, but if I ever collapse and fall unconscious to the ground, I do *not* want Dr. Dana Scully to come anywhere near me! Colonel Wharton falls to the ground at the end of the episode. Scully runs up, flips him over, and proclaims him dead. She doesn't check a pulse. She barely has enough time to tell if he's breathing. (And obviously she doesn't even

attempt CPR.) Methinks she's a *wee bit* eager to start that autopsy!

☒ And speaking of autopsies, why was none done on any of the individuals who "died"? Answer: It's awfully hard to come back from the dead after your internal organs have been excised, weighed, and then tossed back into the body cavity. Granted, Wharton probably blocked the autopsies on Guttierez, McAlpin, and Bauvais, but who blocked the autopsy on Wharton?

☒ And speaking of Wharton, why was he buried in Folkstone Municipal Cemetery? Was he from Folkstone originally? Wouldn't *Colonel* Wharton be entitled to burial in a military cemetery? (Of course, if he was transported somewhere, he would have awakened *before* interment, and then we couldn't have the scene with him pounding on the hatch of the coffin!)

Equipment Oddities

☒ Mulder and Scully pick the oddest times to forget their flashlights. They search through Wharton's office with their flashlights blazing and then, only minutes later, they run around in a dark cemetery without them.

Continuity and Production Problems

☒ There is something exceedingly strange going on in this episode. No, not the voodoo. Not Wharton. Not Bauvais or even Bonaparte. Something even stranger still. It's Robin McAlpin. Does she look familiar? Perhaps like a slightly older version of Peggy O'Dell? You remember Peggy. In "Pilot," she had supposedly been abducted by aliens right after her high-school graduation. She was confined to a wheelchair and later "died" after running in front of a semitruck. Yet here she is again. Another clone, perhaps? (Just like Raymond

Soames? See "Irresistible.") Or is she part of some kind of abductee witness protection program? You gotta know that some sneaky lawyer somewhere is stashing away those victims whose lives have been threatened. After all, someday, somehow, sometime, those aliens are finally going to reveal themselves and then—*POW*—were talking *major* class-action lawsuit here!

🅇 Chester Bonaparte's Haitian accent leaves a bit to be desired. Perhaps he's been living too long in the processing center and he's picking up American vowel formation. On the other hand, death and resurrection are probably murder on your speech patterns!

🅇 Vancouver—the production site for *The X-Files*—strikes again. In the first cemetery scene, watch as Mulder, Scully, and the groundskeeper stroll past a tall signpost. Take a good look at the lettering. Could it possibly say, "VANCOU-VER CEMETERY"?

SECOND SEASON

Trivia Questions

❶ Whose daughter died with a bellyful of snakes?

❷ What is Mulder's room number at the motel?

Trivia Answers
❶ Clyde Jessamin.
❷ 7.

Colony

(Part 1 of 2)

PLOT SUMMARY

An anonymous E-mail—containing the obituaries of three doctors who look like identical triplets—draws Mulder and Scully into a case that will *eventually* lead Mulder to the Arctic Circle, where he will bargain with his life for answers and "the truth." Unknown to the pair at the start, "something" crashed into the arctic ice in recent days, and the pilot—misidentified by news reports as a Russian—has begun a systematic eradication of an unusual group of individuals with identical facial and body features, one of whom sent the E-mail.

Adding to the confusion of the case, Mulder is summoned to his father's home in Massachusetts, where he finds a woman who claims to be his abducted sister. She claims her memories were erased after being taken, and has only recently reclaimed them through hypnotic regression. She also reveals that her adoptive parents are actually aliens living on Earth and that a bounty hunter (the pilot) has been dispatched to eliminate them. (Among this bounty hunter's abilities, he can change appearance at will.) Meanwhile, Scully discovers the remnants of a strange lab in Germantown, Maryland. Before the bounty hunter demolished it, the lab contained large vats that served as incubators. Even more odd, Scully opens the door at her supposedly safe motel room to greet Mulder, only to have her cell phone ring with a call . . . from Mulder.

Onscreen Locations

- ☒ Research Vessel *Alta*, Beaufort Sea, Arctic Circle
- ☒ Woman's Care Family Services and Clinic, Scranton, Pennsylvania (Ya know, this clinic really needs a longer name.)

- ☒ Globe and Mail, Binghamton, N.Y.
- ☒ FBI Field Office, Syracuse, N.Y.
- ☒ 737 26th Street, Syracuse, N.Y.
- ☒ Germantown, Maryland
- ☒ Martha's Vineyard, West Tisbury, Massachusetts
- ☒ Federal Stockade, Tileston, Virginia

Ruminations

Good episode! Some really nice foreshadowing on the involvement of Mulder's father with the consortium. Mulder hurries up the front stairs of his father's house and finds him on the porch. William Mulder lights a cigarette and for a moment looks just like Cancerman.

Nice tie back to "The Erlenmeyer Flask" as well. In that episode we saw an alien/human hybrid whose body chemistry was toxic to humans, who had increased strength, and who could breathe underwater. Each of these elements plays a part in this episode and the next. I think it's safe to assume that the creators want us to believe that the aliens featured here are the alien half of the alien/human hybrids seen in "The Erlenmeyer Flask."

The date on this episode is deduced from two pieces of information. First, screen text notation tells us that the crash of the bounty hunter's ship came two weeks before the efforts to resuscitate Mulder at the beginning of the episode. Second, from "End Game," we learn that Mulder's excursion to the Arctic Circle takes place on or around February 3, 1995. Backdating two weeks leads us to the third week of January.

One final item, just in case you don't watch your television with the closed captioning turned on. There's an interesting conversation between the bounty hunter and Dr. Aaron Baker. As Agent Weiss approaches Baker's home, the closed captioning has Baker stating that there were years when "our" people got along, when "we" shared the entire planet, but the bounty hunter is unwilling to share, and Baker doesn't understand.

Geographical Inconsistencies

🅇 Given the screen text listed above, you might be interested to know that Daniel B. Case assures me Syracuse does not have numbered streets.

🅇 And—according to the list on the FBI's official Web site—the FBI doesn't have a field office in Syracuse, New York.

🅇 Scully tells Mulder that she will be staying at a motel in Germantown, Maryland, just off the "I-90." Interstate Highway 90 doesn't go through Maryland.

🅇 Tileston, Virginia, doesn't exist.

Plot Oversights

🅇 After the opening credits, we join the Research Vessel *Alta* as it works in the Arctic Circle. For twenty minutes, a UFO has hovered overhead. Suddenly the craft darts away, angling downward to crash into the ice with an explosive plume. The nitpicker in me wonders: Is this considered a *good* landing on the bounty hunter's home world? Did he fall asleep and accidently push forward on the joystick? Did his *hamster* die?! What happened here?

🅇 After the incident above, the *Alta* pulls the bounty hunter from the arctic waters. We learn

later that he walked out of the hospital where he was taken. Obviously the medical examinations showed *no* anomalies in an alien bounty hunter?

🅇 As mentioned, Mulder receives the obituaries for three doctors. Yet later we learn that no remains have been found for *any* of these doctors. *No* remains. Not a bone, not a tooth. At most, it's only been a week since these guys disappeared, and their obituaries are already listed in the paper? Wouldn't they still be listed as "missing persons"?

🅇 In addition, Mulder says he can find no evidence that the doctors ever existed prior to their death. Presumably this would include a lack of birth certificates, Social Security numbers, *medical licenses*. So how did these doctors get jobs working at abortion clinics with no documentation on their educational history? Do those places hire just *anyone*?

🅇 Mulder must have a far-reaching reputation. He calls Agent Weiss in Syracuse and introduces himself only as "Agent Mulder," yet Weiss seems to recognize the name immediately and is so familiar with Mulder that he doesn't even need to ask for a telephone number where he can contact Mulder once he locates the requested information. This is an interesting tidbit of information given that the FBI has more than *ten thousand* special agents.

🅇 I'll discuss Mulder's technoamnesia concerning Scully's cell phone below, but there's another telephone oddity in this episode as Mulder and Scully play tag with their answering machines. Mulder tries to call Scully's cell phone. She's in the shower. The next scene informs us that it's "7:05 P.M." Moments later, we see a shot of the clock in Scully's motel room and it reads "11:21." Since it's dark out, this is most likely 11:21 P.M. There's a knock at the door. Scully answers it. It's Mulder (she thinks). Her cell

Trivia Questions

🄰 Who was the first suspect in the murder of Dr. Landon Prince?

🄱 What code does Mulder use to access the responses to the ad in the *Globe and Mail*?

Trivia Answers

🄰 Reverend Calvin Sistrunk.

🄱 1236.

139

Colony

phone rings. It's Mulder (for real). Now, according to the times shown us by the creators, more than *four hours* have passed since Mulder last tried to contact his partner. Does this seem right for this situation?

Equipment Oddities

🗙 The bounty hunter doesn't seem to know how to operate his retractable ice pick at the beginning of the episode. Just before he spears Dr. Prince, note the placement of the bounty hunter's thumb. It's nowhere near the button that supposedly protracts and retracts the pick! (Yet somehow the ice pick performs admirably.) From here on out, however, the bounty hunter remembers to use the button.

🗙 I'm a bit confused how this bounty hunter does that wild and crazy shape-shifting thing. After Weiss dies, we see that the bounty hunter has deposited his stripped body in the truck of Weiss's car. Obviously the bounty hunter needed Weiss's clothes to pull off the deception. Yet we see the bounty hunter shape-shift to his normal form while wearing Weiss's clothing, and everything still seems to fit. Doesn't the bounty hunter seem noticeably *taller* than Weiss? Wouldn't that at least give the bounty hunter high-water pants? (Or was Weiss dressed in that same expand-o-magic cloth we saw during "Genderbender"?)

🗙 Scully's apartment gets a front door in this episode. After dressing down, she leaves via a door in her living room that leads straight to the main hall outside her apartment. As far as I know, all previous entrances and exits to Scully's apartment were accomplished via a small entryway attached to her kitchen. (We will, hereinafter, refer to this kitchen door as the back door). It always seemed odd to me that a person had to enter Scully's apartment through the kitchen, but sometimes builders do odd things during remodeling jobs, so I didn't say

anything about it.

Now we suddenly have a door that opens into her living room from the outside hall—a door that makes *much* more sense. Unfortunately, I don't believe we ever get a good look at this particular stretch of living room wall prior to this episode, so it's impossible to say whether the front door is *really* new or we just haven't seen it before.

Here's an interesting thought, though. At the beginning of "Ascension," Mulder rushes to Scully's apartment after hearing her pleas for help on his answering machine. We see him stride up the front steps of Scully's apartment complex. He stops and looks in her broken window from the outside. It's very evident that he's looking into her living room. This gives us the orientation of Scully's apartment to the exterior of the building. Next we see him enter Scully's apartment via the kitchen. In other words, he walked all the way down the main hall of the apartment complex, turned right, walked into the small entry area, turned right again, and began walking through Scully's kitchen so he could eventually reach her living room. If Scully's front door existed at this point in the series, why not take the shortcut? (So . . . what do you think? Is the front door new or not?)

🗙 This episode has one of the worst displays of technoamnesia of any *X-Files* episode. Mulder learns from the woman who claims to be his sister that the CIA agent he and Scully have been working with is probably an alien bounty hunter. He calls Scully's home telephone to warn her. Sometime later, he learns that Scully's life may be in danger from a message she left on his answering machine, so he calls the motel where she will be staying. But the dork at the counter forgets to give her the message. Then, *finally,* he tries her cell phone, but she's in the shower. Well, why didn't he *try her cell phone in the FIRST place?! Hours* have gone by! Did he have something *better* to do than contact his partner and ensure that she was safe?

X And while we're pondering Mulder's telephone habits, he is apparently a bit compulsive about the outgoing message on his answering machine. Evidently, while he was at his father's house, he called his machine and recorded a new outgoing message! (Too bad he didn't bother to check his *incoming* messages while he was at it.) When Scully first calls Mulder's machine, the outgoing message says, "This is Fox Mulder. Leave me a message and I'll get back to you as soon as I can." The second time, it says, "Hello, this is Fox Mulder. Leave a message, please."

Continuity and Production Problems

X The episode opens with Mulder being airlifted to a military medical facility. Scully appears to assist with his recovery. As she and the lead doctor argue over how to proceed, Mulder's heart stops. The scene cuts to a wide shot. Mulder has no oxygen mask. Then the scene cuts to a close-up and he does.

End Game

(Part 2 of 2)

PLOT SUMMARY Hearing Mulder's voice coming from her cell phone, Scully tries to apprehend the Mulder who stands nearby. She doesn't realize he is an alien bounty hunter—possessed of superhuman strength. A lesson follows in the finer points of furniture demolition with Scully as the student *and* battering ram before the bounty hunter calls Mulder to arrange a trade for Samantha. Mulder agrees, and Skinner calls the sharpshooters. (According to Samantha, a bullet to the base of the neck is the only way to kill the bounty hunter.) The exchange occurs on a bridge, and once Scully is safe, the marksmen open fire. Uninjured, the bounty hunter tumbles into the water and escapes, killing Mulder's sister in the process. Oddly enough, when divers find her body the next day, it decomposes just like the other aliens.

Then a note leads Mulder to an entire group of "Samanthas." Unfortunately, the bounty hunter follows and murders these as well. Frustrated, Mulder contacts Mr. X and manages to track the alien to the Arctic Circle. The resulting confrontation quickly proves that even Mulder is no match for the bounty hunter. However, Mulder convinces the alien to provide him with one answer before being left to die. According to the bounty hunter, Samantha lives. Then a naval search team recovers Mulder. With Scully's help, he survives the ordeal to begin his quest anew.

Onscreen Locations

- ☒ Beaufort Sea, 87 miles north of Deadhorse, Alaska
- ☒ USS *Allegiance,* cruising depth 1000 feet
- ☒ Vacation Village Motor Lodge, Germantown, Maryland
- ☒ Old Memorial Bridge, Bethesda, Maryland
- ☒ Women's Health Services Clinic, Rockville, Maryland
- ☒ Kennedy Center, Washington, D.C.

Ruminations

Quite an exciting episode, eh? Action-packed, emotionally intense. People flying, people screaming. We like it!

The date on this episode comes from the Global Position Satellite gizmo that Mulder uses to locate the submarine toward the end of the show.

And again, we have some fascinating foreshadowing in this episode once you remember that William Mulder had some part in the consortium and may have contributed to the abduction of his daughter. When Mulder tells his father that a man took Samantha in exchange for Scully, William Mulder seems not a bit surprised by the events; he merely asks, "Was this your decision?" Could it be that the senior Mulder is remembering the decision he made twenty-plus years prior and the anguish it caused his wife?

There are little things I appreciate about The X-Files. One of them is the way the creators deal with the character of Dana Scully from the aspect of cinematography. During this episode, Scully sleeps on Mulder's couch as she waits for Mr. X to appear. A camera pan first shows us the "X" in the window. Then the fish tank. Then the couch. And finally, Scully's face. In its travels, the camera barely engages a portion of her legs. Her body is obscured in shadows. *This is refreshing. Yes, we know that Scully is nicely shaped. Yes, she has lovely legs. But we, the viewers, can figure that out on our own. We don't need her figure blatantly paraded across the screen. And apparently the creators know this!*

Plot Oversights

☒ Maybe it's just because I'm a nitpicker, but whenever I see a military simulation, I always wonder how close it is to real life. This episode opens with a scene aboard the USS *Allegiance*, cruising at a depth of a thousand feet. The ship's captain is hurrying to the conning tower (i.e., the control center). Sonar has picked up some "paint." The captain reports it to Pacific Command and is ordered to engage the object. The captain brings the sub about and orders the weapons room to lock torpedoes on target. A broad-spectrum squeal erupts and disables the sub's nuclear reactor.

Well, as it turns out, there's a guy in my church who served in the submarine corps! Former electronics technician, submarine-qualified, second class petty officer Michael Eugene Trail was kind enough to let me steal a few minutes of his time and we discussed this scene. (This is *not* an exhaustive list of nitpicks concerning this scene; it's really just a start! We did this in a hurry.)

For one thing, the captain is saluted on his way to the control center. Michael says this wouldn't happen. He also said the captain's chest pins should have been reversed. And a lieutenant (two bars on the collar) would *not* be running sonar. Also, the captain of a submarine would not hesitate to engage the object. A submarine is a *military* vessel. Its crew is ready at any moment to go into battle. In addition, when the captain gives the heading change to the helmsman, the helmsman should repeat it back to the captain to indicate that he understood the order. Of course, none of this includes the standard television problem with military reen-

actments. There's simply *too much backtalking!* Military personnel do not question every order from their superiors.

☒ How does this bounty hunter imitate people so well? He's got Mulder's mannerisms almost down pat. He begins to tell Scully that he got shot once and he didn't like it. How did he know that Mulder was shot only once? Just a guess?

☒ Why only one sharpshooter at the bridge during the exchange? Mulder claims that the FBI has both sides of the bridge covered (as they should). If the sharpshooters are trying to hit the back of the bounty hunter's neck, why not station a few more sharpshooters on either end of the bridge and get a *clear* shot of the target? (I realize this would put Mulder and Scully and Samantha in the line of fire but, come on, according to Mulder these guys can hollow out a dime at two hundred yards.) Of course, the other problem seems to be that the sharpshooters don't seem to know the difference between the base of the neck and the side of the head. So much for the anatomy courses!

☒ Once pulled from icy waters, Samantha's body begins to corrode as it thaws. Later in the episode we learn that the retrovirus that killed Weiss also reacts to the cold. It goes dormant. From this, Scully appears to conclude that the melting of Samantha's body is related to the emergence of the retrovirus from its dormant state. There is an immediate and obvious problem with this theory. Evidently the retrovirus can be transmitted through the air. Twice—in this episode and in the previous one—we see the bounty hunter shot and nearby humans reacting as the retrovirus enters their systems. This is consistent with events in "The Erlenmeyer Flask." However, *if* the corroding of the "real live dead alien" bodies is the result of retrovirus activity, one would expect the virus to become airborne and affect bystanders just as it affects those nearby when an alien is shot. It doesn't.

🅇 How does Mulder beat the naval attack fleet to the submarine in the Arctic Circle?! Mr. X tells Mulder that an attack fleet left Anchorage, Alaska, "this morning." It's night when he offers Mulder this piece of news. That means the fleet has a twelve-hour head start—at least—and they are in Alaska to begin with and Mulder is in Washington, D.C. Yet Mulder beats them there!

🅇 Why doesn't Mulder have his face covered when he finds the sub? He's in the Arctic Circle. It's winter. He's just walked *ten miles*.

🅇 One also wonders why the bounty hunter didn't take off with the sub before Mulder arrived. Why is this guy still dorking around when he should be heading home? Is he scouring the ship's supply for Cheez Whiz? Stocking up on cans of *Spam,* maybe?! (No doubt they are delicacies on his planet.)

🅇 Pretty amazing that Mulder's left wrist didn't show massive bruising at the beginning of the previous episode as the camera gave us the overhead shot of Mulder in the tub. After all, it must have taken a *pummeling* after being handcuffed to the bounty hunter as he tossed Mulder around. (You may recall that the last episode began with a flash-forward to the end of this episode.)

🅇 As mentioned above, scientists discover that the retrovirus that kills Weiss is susceptible to cold. They discover that the virus goes dormant when they lower the temperature "5 degrees Fahrenheit." "Lower the temperature 5 degrees from what?" you ask. Good question! Since Mulder's basal temperature is 86 degrees Fahrenheit and he lives, we must assume that the virus goes dormant in temperatures five degrees cooler than a human's body temperature of 98.6 degrees. This raises a question. If the retrovirus goes dormant at 86 degrees Fahrenheit, how long could the retrovirus sur-

vive while airborne in temperatures much, *much* colder than that? Mulder contracts the retrovirus on board a submarine that had lost power five days earlier—a submarine that is sticking out of the ice in *the Arctic Circle!* (In winter, no less!) Wouldn't it be really, *really* cold inside that metal tube?

Equipment Oddities

🅇 Just a few equipment oddities about the USS *Allegiance* that Michael Trail was kind enough to point out. Given that the *Allegiance* is under thirty-two feet of glacial ice, it's unlikely that her captain would have satellite communications available. (The antenna array has to float on the surface of the water.) And even if the *Allegiance* did manage this miracle, Michael says that the conversation between the captain and the admiral is too instantaneous for satellite. In addition, a nuclear reactor failure and the resulting switch to battery backup would not result in the cessation of communications between the captain and the engine room, as shown in this episode. (Even *I* guessed this! I simply couldn't imagine that navy design would vest all means of communication in one power source. It made no sense that the captain wouldn't be able to communicate with his engine room during such a crisis.) On a positive note, Michael did say that the sonar screen shown during this scene is true to form!

🅇 At some point, when we weren't looking . . . Mulder *moved!* Yes, the apartment *looks* the same as it does in previous episodes, but it's several stories *higher* than it used to be! For one thing, "Little Green Men" clearly establishes that there is no door across the hall from Mulder's apartment. (See the scene where the man comes to take Mulder to see Senator Matheson.) Yet, in this episode, William Mulder comes to see his son, and there's a door across the hall labeled "43." Also, "One Breath" shows only the number "4" on Mulder's door when Melissa comes to his apartment to tell him that Scully is getting weaker. (You can see that there's no door across the hall in this scene as well.) Yet, in "End Game," Mulder's door reads "42" when Scully comes to his apartment. Why would Mulder move and not tell us? Of course, without the sudden change to the fourth floor we wouldn't have the fabulous elevator scene where Mr. X and Skinner beat each other up. (Nah! *That* couldn't be it. The creators wouldn't try to slip that one by us, would they?)

X After being pulled from the river, Samantha's body is loaded into an ambulance that carries the letters "FBI," indicating that this is some sort of official vehicle. The Real FBI tells me that they do not operate ambulances. (They can get them if they need them, of course, but they don't say "FBI.")

X I am still amazed that the bounty hunter in actuality *landed* his craft. He came screaming out of sky, and there was an explosion. Amazingly enough, the vessel is still spaceworthy! Must be that *advanced* alien technology!

X And speaking of advanced technology, these FBI computers ain't too shabby themselves. Scully comes to Mulder's apartment, turns the computer on, and it automatically retrieves E-mail from some server. Fine. No problem. Mulder has a batch file that launches the appropriate programs to log on and do the deed. But here's the really fabulous part. *Mulder's* computer in *Mulder's* apartment does not fetch *Mulder's* mail. Mulder's computer in Mulder's apartment somehow knows to fetch *Scully's* mail just because she's sitting in front of the computer. Now, I know there *are* experimental programs to recognize the user being developed at places such as the Media Lab at MIT. But how did Mulder get a copy of it for his computer, and where's the little camera that's needed to make it work? (Or does Scully know that Mulder has his computer set to periodically rifle through *her* E-mail?)

X The fish seem to be missing from Mulder's fish tank, but I suppose they are *much* easier to take care of if they don't exist!

X It's the nit that keeps on giving. Yet again, we see the bounty hunter shape-shift to a being who's larger and his clothes still fit.

Continuity and Production Problems

X Here's a strange one for you. When Scully comes to Skinner's office to plead for him to find a way to locate Mulder, note Skinner's American flag. It's upside down, isn't it? (If you want to see it hanging right side up, go to the first meeting between Skinner and Cancerman in "Paper Clip.")

X Desperate to find Mulder, Scully illuminates the "X" in her window. In time, Mr. X appears at Mulder's apartment. Startled when Scully opens the door, X decides to leave. Scully follows him out into the hall. Just as the pair reaches the elevator, she steps to his side of the hall and follows behind him. Why? It seems like an unnatural move in the midst of her questioning of X. (I suspect the camera setup was in the way.)

X After being tossed out of the submarine by the bounty hunter, Mulder lands on the ice under the fins on the sail. (According to David D. Porter of River Ridge, Louisiana, that's what the "superstructure" that comes out of the top of the submarine is called.) The fins rotate and begin to descend. Presumably this is how the submarine surfaced in the first place. The fins shoved through the ice while in their upright and locked positions. So . . . why isn't there a corresponding break in the ice?

X This episode treats us, a second time, to Mulder's mysterious reappearing oxygen mask. (See "Colony" for more details.)

Fearful Symmetry

PLOT SUMMARY

An elephant's rampage brings Mulder and Scully to Fairfield, Idaho. No one knows how the elephant got out of her cage at the Fairfield Zoo, nor do they know what rendered her invisible for a time (though she did reappear in the morning—collapsing on the pavement, dying of exhaustion). Zoo administrator Willa Ambrose can't explain it. Then a tiger disappears, reappearing later in downtown Boise before being shot. Oddly enough, Scully's autopsies reveal that both animals had recently been pregnant.

Ambrose finds that fact impossible. Besides, she has greater concerns. The zoo has lost its funding, and the Malawi government wants her to return a gorilla named Sophie whom Ambrose has tutored in sign language. When Mulder picks this inopportune moment to disclose his theory that the animals are being abducted and impregnated by aliens, Ambrose scoffs. But even Sophie claims to be pregnant, signing, "Baby go flying high." The next night, Sophie disappears as well. She reappears the following morning on a highway and is soon lethally injured by a car. As the animals of the Fairfield Zoo are dispersed to zoos across America, Mulder and Scully return to Washington—leaving Mulder to wonder if the aliens are conducting a conservation program or constructing their version of Noah's Ark.

Onscreen Locations

- ☒ Idaho Mutual Insurance Trust, Fairfield, Idaho
- ☒ Fairfield Zoo
- ☒ W.A.O. Offices
- ☒ Construction site, Highway 24
- ☒ Jojo's Copy Center
- ☒ Blake Towers construction site, downtown Boise

Ruminations

I realize that this is going to make some people mad, but at the end of the episode when Mulder was locked in the room with Sophie and she charged him and he still had his gun, I would have fired every bullet in the clip. Ever seen what a gorilla can do to a tire? Starring as the piece of luggage in a Samsonite commercial is not my idea of a good time!

Plot Oversights

☒ Early in the episode, an invisible elephant rampages through Fairfield, eventually trampling through a road construction site. Bewildered, a road worker watches until the invisible elephant knocks him flying through the air. Then the rest of the workers rush up and flop him over. Wouldn't it be better to leave him where he landed until the paramedics arrive?

☒ So . . . why do the elephant and the gorilla come back to earth some distance from their departure point but the tiger hangs around outside its cage for a bit so that it can maul the young man from the Wild Again Organization? Surely the creators wouldn't do something like that for mere plot convenience, would they? (*NO!* Say it isn't so!)

☒ I always enjoy the little spats between Mulder and Scully, but this episode has one that borders on silly. Mulder is trying to tell Scully that a videotape shows a young man thrashed around by a phantom attacker. Scully balks at this idea and launches into a description of the young man's wounds. This is when I started grousing, "Why are you two wasting time arguing about this? *Watch the tape!*"

☒ Mulder speaks of the abducted animals being returned two miles west southwest of the zoo, but the tiger winds up in Boise! The zoo is in Fairfield. That's about *eighty* miles from Boise. So . . . the tiger traveled eighty miles before it became visible again?

☒ Mulder has a little slip of the tongue when he's offering his theory of alien animal abduction to Ambrose. Attempting to explain why the animals don't return properly, he sites "astrological variance" as a potential problem. In other words, the alien teleporter operators can't figure out how to make the controls work when the moon is in the seventh house and Jupiter aligns with Mars?! (I think he meant "*astronomical* variance.")

☒ I find Mulder's attitude fascinating in this episode. With the abduction of the animals, Mulder concludes that it might be an alien conservation program because we wicked humans are eliminating so many species. (Never mind that the aliens can't get the poor creatures returned to the right coordinates and this fact directly contributes to the animals' deaths.) Yet, when *humans* are abducted, Mulder has *never* floated the theory that the aliens are merely trying to preserve the kind and gentle among the populace against the ravages of the Military/Industrial/Entertainment Complex that would seek to dominate and control their lives.

☒ Toward the end of the episode, Mulder and Scully come to the zoo one fine morning to investigate the death of Wild Again Organization member Kyle Lang. Since Lang was killed the night before, this is probably the next morning. After Scully departs to do Lang's autopsy, Mulder spots a zoo employee named Ed Meecham in the warehouse. Ed appears to be heading for a van owned by the Fairfield Zoo. Next, we see the van pulling up to another warehouse and it's suddenly dark! Minutes later we learn that this warehouse is somewhere on the road between Fairfield and Boise. My map says it's about a hundred miles from Fairfield to Boise if you travel on the main highways. These facts elicit this question: What did Mulder and Meecham *do* all day? They spent at most two hours on the road, and they started out in the morning. How can it be night when Meecham arrives at the warehouse?

☒ I *love* the verse that's on the marquee of the church in the last scene of this episode. "Man has no preeminence above a beast: for all is vanity." (Eccl. 3:19) I've spent many years looking at church marquees, and I can honestly say that I have *never* seen that verse displayed before! (Must be the Church of the Sanctified Depression. Either that or a mission run by the Sisters of Prozac.)

Equipment Oddities

☒ Called back to the zoo by Scully, Mulder drives up at night with his face illuminated from *inside* the car. No doubt driving with that map light on again. He was probably out cruising for babes and he wanted to make sure they noticed his chiseled features.

Continuity and Production Problems

☒ The episode opens with a pair of Latino Americans cleaning the floor of an office building. Does the older one look familiar? Won't we come to learn in "Apocrypha" that this man is actually "Luis Cardinal," a thug who works for Cancerman? Why is he in Fairfield? Is there more to this animal-abduction thing than we've been told? What could it mean? What *could* it mean?

Trivia Questions

❶ What is the name of the truck driver who almost runs into Ganesha?

❷ What are the visiting hours at the Fairfield Zoo?

Trivia Answers
❶ Wesley Brewer.
❷ 10:00 A.M. through 5:30 P.M.

147
Fearful Symmetry

GREAT LINES
"I'm buff."

—**Frohike** to Mulder, explaining that he's been working out and he would like Mulder to pass along that information to the love of his life, Dana Scully.

X Just a wee bit of creator trickery to give us an interesting visual. After extracting the uterus of the dead elephant, Scully examines it under a large, illuminated magnifying glass. The first camera angle shows us a close-up of the uterus. So far, so good. The next shows us a close-up of Scully's face through the magnifying glass. Specifically, it shows us a close-up of Scully's *brightly illuminated* face. How can this be? The circular fluorescent tube that the magnifying glass employs is mounted on the *underside* of the fixture that encloses the lens. Evidently the creators flipped the magnifying glass over and had Gillian Anderson plant her face directly in front of the tube so they could get this shot. You can even see the circular reflection of the fluorescent tube in the corneas of her eyes! (Besides the fact that her pupils are tightly contracted and later wide shots show far less illumination on her face than this close-up.)

TRIATHLON TRIVIA ON CITIES

MATCH THE CITY TO THE DESCRIPTION TO THE EPISODE

CITY	DESCRIPTION	EPISODE
1. Allentown, Pennsylvania	A. Krycek was "buried" there	a. "The Erlenmeyer Flask"
2. Ardis, Maryland	B. Good people, good food	b. "Lazarus"
3. Arecibo, Puerto Rico	C. Duane Barry killed a cop nearby	c. "Unruhe"
4. Barnes Corners, New York	D. Site of the Grissom Sleep Disorder Clinic	d. "Die Hand Die Verletzt"
5. Bellefleur, Oregon	E. Where Mulder took a vacation	e. "Small Potatoes"
6. Black Crow, North Dakota	F. An invisible elephant stormed its streets	f. "Aubrey"
7. Braddock Heights, Maryland	G. Special people call it home	g. "Paper Clip"
8. Browning, Montana	H. Harry Cokely lived there in 1942	h. "Genderbender"
9. Connerville, Oklahoma	I. They make lightning	i. "731"
10. Craiger, Maryland	J. Headquarters for Rat Tail Productions	j. "Our Town"
11. Crystal City, Virginia	K. Where Mary LeFonte wanted a passport photo	k. "Død Kalm"
12. Delta Glen, Wisconsin	L. Site of Scully's first X-Files case	l. "Never Again"
13. Demeter, Virginia	M. Scully watched too much television there	m. "Sleepless"
14. Dogway, West Virginia	N. Where Skinner lives	n. "E.B.E."
15. Dudley, Arkansas	O. Jack Colquitt's birthplace	o. "Ascension"
16. Easton, Washington	P. Where Scully met "Brandoguy"	p. "Humbug"
17. Fairfield, Idaho	Q. Where Carl Wade lived	q. "The Walk"
18. Forks of Cacapon, West Virginia	R. Destination of Leonard Trimble's ashes	r. "Paper Hearts"
19. Gibsonton, Florida	S. Where Max Fenig called home	s. "Tunguska"
20. Greenwich, Connecticut	T. Toads fell from the sky there	t. "Wetwired"
21. Hakkari, Turkey	U. A UFO crash site	u. "Max"
22. Jerusalem, Ohio	V. Monkey babies invade small town	v. "Duane Barry"
23. Klamath Falls, Oregon	W. Site of the first recovered, living EBE	w. "Apocrypha"
24. Martinsburg, West Virginia	X. Mulder chartered a boat there	x. "Tempus Fugit"
25. Mattawa, Washington	Y. Where Mulder had a close encounter	y. "D.P.O."
26. Memphis, Tennessee	Z. Birthplace of Warren Dupre	z. "Unrequited"

27. Mexico City, Mexico	AA. Flight 549 crashed nearby	aa. "War of the Coprophages"
28. Milford Haven, New Hampshire	BB. The Kindred lived there	bb. "Fearful Symmetry"
29. Miller's Grove, Massachusetts	CC. Proud home of Charlotte's Diner	cc. "Oubliette"
30. Northville, New York	DD. Its beef was tainted with alien DNA	dd. "Musings of a Cigarette-Smoking Man"
31. Perkey, West Virginia	EE. It's in the same area as the very first X-File	ee. "Shapes"
32. Port of Tildeskan, Norway	FF. Karen Philoponte was buried there	ff. "Red Museum"
33. Pulaski, Virginia	GG. Hosts a high-security power plant	gg. "Nisei"
34. Rixeyville, Virginia	HH. Home to a recycling plant	hh. "Little Green Men"
35. St. Petersburg, Russia	II. Where Krycek and Vassily Peskow met	ii. "Pilot"
36. Stamford, Connecticut	JJ. Headquarters for the Right Hand	jj. "Revelations"
37. Steveston, Massachusetts	KK. It was terrorized by cockroaches	kk. "Terma"
38. Tannersville, Pennsylvania	LL. Dr. Berube lived there	ll. "Eve"
39. Terrence, Nebraska	MM. Duane Barry called it home in 1985	
40. Traverse City, Michigan	NN. Where Joel Simmons died	

SCORING

(BASED ON NUMBER OF CORRECT ANSWERS)

0–10   Cancerman is pleased.

11–19   José Chung could use you as a resource.

20–29   Expect Mulder and Scully to call for advice.

30–40   You must be . . . the *Stupendous* Yappi!

CITIES ANSWER KEY: **1.** J gg **2.** LL a **3.** Y hh **4.** S u **5.** L ii **6.** A w **7.** M t **8.** EE ee **9.** I y **10.** CC g **11.** N s **12.** DD ff **13.** JJ z **14.** W dd **15.** B j **16.** Q cc **17.** F bb **18.** FF r **19.** G p **20.** NN ll **21.** U n **22.** HH jj **23.** Z b **24.** V e **25.** GG n **26.** E l **27.** O dd **28.** T d **29.** KK aa **30.** AA x **31.** P i **32.** X k **33.** MM v **34.** C o **35.** II kk **36.** D m **37.** BB h **38.** R q **39.** H f **40.** K c

Død Kalm

Onscreen Locations

☒ Norwegian Sea, 65 degrees latitude, 8 degrees east longitude

☒ Bethesda Naval Hospital, Bethesda, Maryland

☒ Port of Tildeskan, Norway

Ruminations

Obviously, the date on this episode comes from Scully's field journal entry, but the events in the show could easily stretch for a week on either side of March 12, 1995. In the first place, it takes eighteen hours for the sailors to be found. There's travel time to Norway, twelve hours by boat to the Arden, at very least thirty-two hours on board that ship, and another thirty-six hours in recovery for Scully.

This episode also contains a bit of insight on how Mulder views the working relationship between him and Scully. After recruiting her to examine the only survivor among those who fled the Arden, Mulder says, "Meet me back at my office." His office. His X-Files. His work. His nameplate on the door.

Unanswered Questions

☒ So what was this "something" that caused all the "oxidization" in this episode? The episode suggests three possible theories, but none of them adequately explains the observed phenomena. This "something" was either a wrinkle in time, some kind of oxidizing electro-magnetic energy, or "heavy" salt in the water. The wrinkle-in-time theory seems to have the

PLOT SUMMARY On the Norwegian Sea, young American sailors flee the USS *Arden*, fearing the rapid onset of old age. Even still, only one reaches Bethesda Naval Hospital alive. Intrigued, Mulder wants Scully to have a look. He suspects time acceleration—a side effect of wormhole experiments conducted by the government. Hearing Scully's description of the wrinkled survivor, he decides to investigate further.

In Norway, merchant mariner Henry Trondheim helps Mulder and Scully locate the *Arden*. But all three are stranded on board when pirates steal Trondheim's boat. In the end—though the rapid aging continues for the ship and quickly overtakes the trio as well—Mulder and Scully arrive at a theory less fantastic than time acceleration. "Something" in the sea has gotten into the desalinization tanks. Once ingested, this substance is causing rapid cellular damage. To survive, the group must drink water from the only fully recycled source available, the sewage system.

The therapy helps Scully and Trondheim but does little for Mulder. Trondheim soon begrudges Mulder's ration of "clean" water. Intent on survival, he barricades himself in the sewage processing room to hoard what's left, only to have a nearby bulkhead collapse with poetic justice—flooding the compartment and drowning Trondheim. Thankfully, the navy soon arrives to rescue our heroes. Afterward, doctors use Scully's field notes to restore Mulder's health.

slimmest support. We do see rust reappear rapidly on the ship's commissioning plaque. And Captain Barclay's nails have grown to a tremendous length in just a few days. But—as Scully points out—their hair doesn't turn gray and it doesn't fall out. More fundamentally, it doesn't seem to grow at all!

The oxidizing-electromagnetic-energy theory would explain the rust forming rapidly on the commissioning plaque, the deterioration of the ship, and the aging. But it wouldn't explain why pirates weren't affected or why the water in the sewage system kept them in health. Neither would it explain why Barclay's fingernails were so long.

Likewise "heavy" salt in the water would account for the aging, but it would have to be airborne in the fog to work on the ship. And if this heavy salt could do what it did to the ship in such minute airborne quantities, what difference would it make for our heroes to drink "clean" water? Wouldn't the same fog that corroded the ship "corrode" everyone's lungs? And besides, how could heavy salt in the water make Barclay's nails grow so fast without it affecting everyone else's nails—and hair, for that matter?

It's possible that "the truth" lies somewhere in a combination of electromagnetic energy and heavy salt. But that still wouldn't explain Barclay's nails. (Maybe he got bored waiting to die and started playing with his secret cache of artificial ones?)

Geographical Inconsistencies

X While briefing Scully at the beginning of the episode, Mulder says that on December 12, 1949 a Royal Navy battleship disappeared between Leeds and Cape Perry. Oddly enough, my map shows that Leeds, England is quite a distance inland from the coast of England yet Mulder seems to indicate that the ship departed from that city on its ill-fated voyage to Cape Perry. Do Royal Navy battleships come equipped with wheels as well as a keel?

Plot Oversights

X The screen text at the beginning of the episode reads, "Norwegian Sea, 65 degrees lat-

itude, 8 degrees east longitude." That probably should be "65 degrees *north* latitude."

X Yet again, the faire pixies of Out There seem to work overtime on Mulder and Scully's behalf. The navy has searched for the *Arden* for more than a day. They've utilized satellites and planes to comb the area but found nothing. Mulder and Scully fly to Norway, hop on a boat, and sail directly to it! Too bad Mulder was so stingy about his information on the 65th parallel north. Maybe the navy could have gotten there sooner and saved Captain Barclay's life.

X Is the "something" that affected the water providing heat as well? This is the 65th parallel north. It's March. The *Arden* has no power. Wouldn't it be really cold?

X Why are all the cupboards bare aboard the *Arden?* Wouldn't it carry a well-stocked pantry? The sailors fleeing in the lifeboat didn't appear to have much in the way of supplies with them. Wouldn't there be *something* more than a can of sardines and a few lemons left behind?

X And now the $64,000 question. How did the navy reverse the effects of aging after the end of this episode? (During "The Calusari," we enjoy Mulder and Scully at their normal radiance.) If cellular damage contributed to the onset of rapid senescence (to borrow the term from Mulder), the navy might be able to halt further damage, but the damage would be done. In essence, the navy has discovered the fountain of youth because they can take an old, wrinkled, decrepit man and turn him into Mr. GQ himself.

Equipment Oddities

X Bethesda Naval Hospital must have elevators that don't go all the way to the top floor. The building's exterior clearly shows at least sixteen floors in the building, but the indicators on the elevator from which Scully disembarks near the beginning of the episode only go up to the seventh floor.

 Interestingly enough, although there's no power, Trondheim manages to backflush the sewage system and suck the water out of the bowl of the toilets. Kind man that he is, he even sits down in the sewage processing hold and makes noises that sound *just* like some kind of pump!

Continuity and Production Problems

 When the navy rescues Mulder and Scully, the close-up of her field journal shows the pages flapping in the wind, but the wide shot has them perfectly still.

SECOND SEASON

Trivia Questions

❶ When was the USS *Arden* launched?

❷ According to a Norse legend, who eats the sun at the end of the world?

Død Kalm

Humbug

PLOT SUMMARY

When the Alligator Man dies from a gaping side wound in Gibsonton, Florida, Mulder and Scully embark on a delightful romp beyond the borders of normality. The murder fits the profile of forty-seven others over the past twenty-eight years, and Mulder wants to investigate further. The pair soon discovers that Gibsonton hosts a wide assortment of "very special people." Sheriff Hamilton was once Jim-Jim, the Dog-Faced Boy. Dr. Blockhead continually performs astounding acts of body manipulation and pain endurance. The Conundrum simply consumes everything in sight. Even the diminutive overseer of the Gulf Breeze Trailer Court—who takes umbrage at Mulder's assumption that he was once a circus performer—has an employee named Lanny who carries a deformed twin named Leonard still attached to his side.

And though Hepcat Helm—inspiration and proprietor of a "tabernacle of terror"—dies shortly after they arrive, Mulder and Scully find the motive of the killer difficult at best to understand. In the end, Scully solves the case. She identifies Leonard as the culprit after discovering that the deformed twin can detach. Brokenhearted, Lanny confesses that he knew of Leonard's escapades, but maintains they weren't meant to harm . . . only to seek out a new, more acceptable brother. Still, Leonard cannot be brought to justice. His last attempt at filial recruitment sent him racing toward the Conundrum, and the Conundrum promptly ate him!

Onscreen Locations

☒ Gibsonton, Florida
☒ Gibsonton Museum of Curiosities

Ruminations

This is a funny episode. There are so many great exchanges in it. Among my favorites: The verbal shellacking that Mulder takes from the proprietor of the Gulf Breeze Trailer Court for presupposing that he had worked in the circus simply because of his diminutive stature; the parallelism the following morning as Scully stares at Lanny's conjoined twin and Lanny stares at Scully's partially exposed breast; Dr. Blockhead sneering in derision as Mulder strikes a pose, aghast at the thought of going through life looking like the handsome FBI agent. Well done! Very well done.

On a related note, there are odd moments in the life of a nitpicker. I remember well the first time I watched this episode and Scully accepted Dr. Blockhead's offer of a live insect. Into her mouth it went, and Scully pretended to chew before walking away. Then the camera angle changed and Scully showed a confused Mulder that she actually palmed the bug. My immediate response was, "She didn't palm that bug." Because of the way her hand was placed, she didn't have any choice but to put the bug in her mouth, and I knew that without even rewinding the tape. (I just knew it!) I didn't think any more of it until I watched a "bloopers" show that Fox ran months later. They showed the rough footage of this scene and explained that, yes, indeed, Gillian Anderson did put the bug in her mouth. It's a great piece, because after she walks off-camera, you can hear her eject the thing from her mouth—after which the camera crew gives this rousing shout!

A small musical note: While all the music of

The X-Files *is well done, this episode features a precursor to one of my favorite selections. "José Chung's* From Outer Space*" has a starkly isolated, slow-walking bass motif that works fabulously well for the entire episode. I believe "Humbug" contains the genesis of that walking bass as Scully enters the Gibsonton Museum of Curiosities.*

Finally, the date on this episode comes from a rent check that the Conundrum hands to the proprietor of the Gulf Breeze Trailer Court. A close-up reveals that the date line begins with "Feb 2." It can't be February 2, 1995, because that would put the events in this episode directly on top of the events in "Colony" and "End Game." So it's likely that the date is in the range February 20–28. In other words, it comes before, *not after, "Død Kalm." (Unless of course, the Conundrum doesn't have the right date written on the check!)*

Plot Oversights

X There are two interrelated terms in the Nitpickers Guild Glossary that come into play early in this episode: cabbagism and cabbagehead. A cabbagism is dialogue that is specifically added to a scene to explain a term or device to the cabbageheads in the audience. In addition, "cabbagehead" can refer to the character who is told the information— provided the character should already *know* the information. In this episode, Mulder explains the term "ichthyosis" to *Dr.* Scully. Why? Because, although Scully probably would already know what this was, we don't. So Scully gets to play the cabbagehead.

X By the end of the episode we learn that Leonard attacks people because he's looking for another brother. This explains the identical nature of the abdominal wounds on all victims. Leonard is attempting to attach to them in the same way that he attaches to Lanny. Oddly enough, when Leonard attacks Hepcat Helm, he appears to bite him on the throat (though the

next day, Scully lifts the lower portion of Helm's shirt to examine the wound). Was Leonard really attempting to attach to Helm, or was there another motivation for the attack? (Given the similarities between Leonard and the creatures in Helm's Tabernacle of Terror, one is forced to wonder if Leonard had negotiated with Helm to do some modeling on a royalty basis and Helm had fallen behind on the payments.)

X Having visited the Gibsonton Museum of Curiosities and received a pamphlet on Jim-Jim, the Dog-Faced Boy, from the proprietor, Scully runs a background check and discovers that the once "dog-faced" boy is now Sheriff Hamilton. I find Scully's motivation to do this background check a bit suspicious. It's true that the proprietor gives her the pamphlet and hints that it might help with the case. But when Scully asks what it has to do with the murder, the proprietor launches into a pitch for a recently acquired ex-P. T. Barnum exhibit. He charges Scully five dollars to look at it, and the exhibit is nothing but an empty box. Now, I ask you, after being taken for a fool, does it seem likely that Scully would treat the pamphlet on Jim-Jim, the Dog-Faced Boy, as anything other than a red herring?

X At the beginning of the episode we learn that Leonard has killed forty-eight people in twenty-eight years. Mulder finds the steady rate unusual for a serial killer, since Leonard has not escalated the level of violence in his attacks over such a long time. Forty-eight people in twenty-eight years is approximately 1.7 victims per year. Yet, in *this* episode alone—within just a few days—Leonard kills three people and attacks a fourth. Hmmm. *That* certainly made it easier for our heroes, didn't it?

X Okay. It's cute. It's funny. It's ironic. It's poetic. But really . . . how can the Conundrum eat Leonard, and Leonard still live? Directly afterward, the Conundrum pats his stomach, and it sounds like Leonard is growling contentedly.

Trivia Questions

1 What was the Alligator Man's real name?

2 Where do Mulder and Scully eat after arriving in Gibsonton?

Trivia Answers
1 Jerald Glazebrook.
2 Phil's Diner. (A place I heartily recommend. With a name like Phil's, it *has* to be good!)

"We're
exhuming
...your
potato."

—**Mulder** to Sheriff
Hamilton after Hamilton
discovers our two heroes
digging in Hamilton's
backyard. (I especially
love the way Scully
attempts to cover her
embarrassment by launch-
ing into what sounds like
a perfectly reasonable
explanation for why they
would suspect Hamilton
in the first place, only to
have Mulder break in and
admit that they found out
he used to be Jim-Jim,
the Dog-Faced Boy.)

As the episode ends, the Conundrum lan-
guishes in the passenger seat of Dr. Blockhead's
VW Beetle. When Scully asks if he's okay, Dr.
Blockhead replies that he doesn't know what
the Conundrum's problem is. He offers that it
might be the Florida heat. Now remember, the
Conundrum runs around in a loincloth. And
Blockhead thinks that *the heat* might be affecting him? What should that tell you about Mulder
and Scully wearing *overcoats* almost the entire
show?

Equipment Oddities

Mulder and Scully sure could use their ubiquitous flashlights in the Tabernacle of Terror,
couldn't they? Too bad they seem to have forgotten them.

Continuity and
Production Problems

Here's a fun one for you. Mulder and Scully
go to arrest Dr. Blockhead. Finding him noncha-
lant and uncooperative, Scully plays the bad
cop, hoists him to his feet, and spins him around
to handcuff him. Blockhead—being the escape

artist he is—promptly removes the handcuffs,
spins, and locks Scully in her own bracelets
before bolting out the door. At least, that's
what it's *supposed* to look like. If you use frame
advance, you might notice that as Blockhead is
bolting out the door, only *one* of the cuffs is
attached to Scully's wrist. The other cuff
swings free. In a truly intriguing turn of events,
the very next time we see the lovely Agent
Scully, she is fashionably attired with *both*
handcuffs secured to her wrists, and there
does not appear to be *anyone* in the room who
could have accomplished this feat . . . except
herself! (Now . . . there are *several* additional
comments I could make at this point, but some
things are best left alone.)

The Calusari

Onscreen Locations

- ☒ Lincoln Park, Murray, Nebraska
- ☒ Dr. Charles Burks' Lab, University of Maryland, College Park
- ☒ Holvey Residence, Arlington, Virginia
- ☒ State Department, Washington, D.C.
- ☒ University of Maryland, College Park
- ☒ St. Matthew's Medical Center, Arlington, Virginia

Ruminations

It's the details that I love about The X-Files! As mentioned above, Scully initially suspects child abuse in the Holvey home—specifically Munchausen by Proxy perpetrated by Golda. To investigate the domestic situation further, Scully sets up an appointment between the Holveys and none other than Karen F. Kosseff. You might recall that Karen F. Kosseff was the social worker Scully went to see when she was having difficulty dealing with the particulars of Donny Pfaster's obsession in "Irresistible." Kudos for continuity!

On a completely unrelated note, I felt after watching this episode several times that the creators passed up a prime opportunity for humor once everything gets back to normal at the end of the show. Think about it. Given Scully's die-hard objectivism (see "Whose Truth Is Out There?" for more details), wouldn't you love to read Scully's field entry journal on this case? "After entering Golda's room, I discovered Maggie Holvey suspended five feet above the floor and I was subsequently lifted and tossed across the room by an unseen force. However,

PLOT SUMMARY Three months after Steve and Maggie Holvey's toddler wanders onto a set of train tracks and dies, Mulder sees an enhanced photo that shows "something" lured the young tot into danger. If that's not odd enough, Mulder and Scully soon learn that Maggie's Romanian mother, Golda, often calls Charlie, the toddler's older brother, a "devil-child," and medical records show frequent illness. Suspecting child abuse, Scully arranges a meeting with a social worker. When Steve tries to escort Charlie to the session, however, the garage door opener malfunctions. In short order, the father hangs dead by his neck.

Golda is killed next—soon after Maggie chases away a group of Romanian men called the Calusari, who are attempting to cleanse the house of evil. Charlie is nearby for this murder as well, but during a counseling session he screams that the real perpetrator is "Michael." Maggie gasps when she hears the name. Michael was Charlie's stillborn twin. As a believer in spirits and superstitions, Golda had always maintained that unless the souls of the two boys were separated, evil would follow. That night, Michael takes bodily form, tricking Maggie into taking him home. Scully pursues as Mulder contacts the Calusari. Freed from interference, they perform the separation ritual on Charlie, banishing Michael just in time to save Scully's life.

no evidence exists to support the theory that extra-natural forces were at work."

And what about poor old Mulder at the end of this episode? How would you like to be told right after an exorcism that the expunged evil "knows" you? (Yikes!)

Geographical Inconsistencies

☒ Murray, Nebraska, doesn't exist.

Plot Oversights

☒ Concerning the accident with Teddy—the toddler son of Steve and Maggie Holvey—Mulder comments that the conductor couldn't stop the train. The conductor?! Isn't the guy who sits in the engine compartment of the train usually called the engineer?

☒ After Steve Holvey dies, Mulder finds ash all over the garage. A University of Maryland professor named Charles Burks identifies it as "vibuti," or holy ash—the by-product of creating something from nothing. When Scully balks, Burks challenges her by asking if she has ever read the Bible before, referring to Jesus creating the loaves and the fishes. (Presumably Burks is talking about the miracle that is commonly called the feeding of the five thousand.) Scully retorts that this account was a "parable." "Parable" is a specific literary term. It refers to the stories that Jesus told to illustrate the Kingdom of God. In the four Gospels, it is fairly simple to determine what is a parable and what is not. The feeding of the five thousand *clearly* is not. It is a part of the narrative of Jesus' life. Obviously, Scully—like any other reader of biblical literature—has every right to decide whether she will choose to believe that the feeding of the five thousand actually transpired, but the passage shouldn't be misidentified to make it easier to dismiss.

☒ Ya know, you have to appreciate a woman like Scully who can be picked up by a malevolent entity, hurled halfway across a room, slammed into a wall, dragged across the floor, and who can—only moments later—get up, shake it off, and be as good as new!

Continuity and Production Problems

☒ I'm a bit surprised the Holveys didn't conclude that something spooky had entered their lives even before Michael killed Teddy the toddler. The episode begins with the Holveys at Lincoln Park—a family entertainment center. Steve Holvey approaches his family with four ice cream cones. He has two cones in each hand. The two inner cones have two scoops, and the two outer cones have one. Extending his right hand, Steve offers a cone to his youngest son. The shot changes, and both of the cones in his right hand now have only *one* scoop. This is no doubt an attempt by evil twin Michael to ensure that his despised toddler brother will have no opportunity to enjoy a cone with two scoops. Oddly enough, the Holveys don't seem to notice. Even more odd, when Steve Holvey straightens, the remaining cone in his right hand has changed back to two scoops. Then Steve extends his left hand toward Charlie. The single-scoop cone in that hand is closest to Charlie, and he does appear to grasp it, but when the camera angle switches to show us a close-up of Charlie, his cone materializes another scoop of ice cream out of thin air! (Thankfully, it isn't covered in "holy ash.")

☒ In discussing Teddy Holvey's escape from his child safety harness and subsequent death on the railroad tracks, Mulder questions how the toddler could have gotten loose in the first place. He floats the rhetorical possibility that Teddy Holvey might have been the reincarnation of Houdini and then adds, "and that would be an X-File in itself." This last phrase was obviously overdubbed later. Mulder's voice placement is completely different.

☒ Someone needs to tell social worker Karen Kosseff that her print shop made a mistake on her business card. It reads, "Karen F. Kosseff, L.C.S.W" instead of "Karen F. Kosseff, L.C.S.W."

Note that it's missing the final period. (I know. Pick, pick, pick, pick, pick.)

X Kosseff interviews Charlie in a playroom designed for this purpose. Near the door that leads to an observation room sits a "rocking fish." (It's like a rocking horse except that it's yellow and the child sits within the hollowed-out body of the fish.) In the initial camera pan around the room, we can see that the fish faces the door. As Kosseff and Charlie speak, the scene cuts to Mulder, Scully, and Maggie in the observation room. When the scene returns to Kosseff and Charlie, the fish has somehow done a 180-degree turn and now faces away from the door. (Kosseff and Charlie haven't moved.) Then Charlies gets mad, screaming that it wasn't he who did the bad deeds, kicking the toys on the far side of the room. When the shot returns to the observation room, we see that the fish has flipped again!

Trivia Questions

1 How many were in the bed at first before the little one said "Roll over"?

2 Who attempts to give Charlie a shot to help him sleep?

Trivia Answers
1 Six.
2 Nurse Castor.

F. Emasculata

PLOT SUMMARY

Unexpectedly, Skinner sends Mulder and Scully to assist U.S. marshals in their search for two escaped convicts. It's an odd assignment for the Bureau, more so because of the "moon-suited" individuals working at the prison. Staying behind, Scully discovers that a lethal contagion is spreading among the convicts. She also learns that Robert Torrence—the first prisoner to contract the disease—received a package from Pinck Pharmaceuticals just before growing ill. In fact, Pinck Pharmaceuticals is secretly using the prisoners to test the effects of the contagion and is doing it with the government's approval.

In short order, the epidemic is contained, and cleanup is thorough. Scully can save only the envelope sent to Robert Torrence as evidence of the conspiracy. Unfortunately, soon after Mulder returns from the manhunt, Scully discovers that even this envelope is worthless. Pinck Pharmaceuticals chose patient zero carefully. He had the same name as the researcher who discovered the contagion in Costa Rica. If the scandal comes to light, the company will claim a simple postal error and apologize. Mulder even suspects that he and Scully were assigned to the case so the conspirators could use their expertise and then discredit them if they went to the news media. Skinner concurs, telling Mulder to watch his back. This is just the beginning.

Onscreen Locations

☒ Guancaste Rain Forest, Costa Rica
☒ Cumberland State Correctional Facility, Dinwiddie County, Virginia
☒ Dinwiddie County Hospital

Ruminations

There's a scene in this episode that is executed very well from a sound-effects standpoint—even if the result is a bit distracting. The creators deserve kudos for doing it correctly. After capture, one of the convicts' wives is placed in a quarantine enclosure so Mulder can interview her. Every shot that originates from inside the enclosure contains the low rumble of the air-handling fans and the "muddying" of Mulder's voice. Every shot originating from outside the enclosure doesn't!

Oh, and . . . nice T-shirt.

Plot Oversights

☒ The episode begins with *Dr.* Robert Torrence collecting bugs in Costa Rica. Did this guy get his doctorate from the local hardware store?! He finds what looks like a dead wild boar (although it seems like such a creature would be hairy instead of covered with elephantlike skin). Insects are crawling all over the carcass, and it is covered in pustules. Pulsing pustules. Now, it doesn't take a rocket scientist—which Torrence obviously isn't—to figure out that pulsing pustules are probably under some kind of pressure. What does that mean, boys and girls? That means, you probably don't want to be around them while they heave to and fro! Yet, *Dr.* Torrence not only plants his face directly over one of the pustules, he also takes his hands and starts gently squeezing it like some kind a *huge zit!* Could this *be* any dumber? Of course . . . in short order, the pustule sprays him and he seems genuinely surprised. (Ding, ding.)

✗ Attempting to discover the truth, Scully makes her way to the basement of the prison, where she finds several bodies wrapped in thick, clear plastic. After donning a pair of gloves and a dinky little surgical mask, she cuts open the plastic. Obviously, I don't wish in any way to impugn the actions of the highly trained, brilliant Special Agent Dana Scully, but . . . *what is she thinking?!* What did she hope to gain by breaking the quarantine on the body bags? Granted, the plastic wasn't perfectly clear, but the pustules are very visible without breaching the barrier and exposing yourself to a deadly contagion. (By the way, fellow nitpickers, I'm sure the following factoid was *not* lost on you: Dr. Osborne died as a *direct* result of Scully's irresponsible actions.)

✗ Continuing on with Scully's bizarre behavior, we soon see that she has returned to the basement. She has her mask off. She has the plastic peeled back, and she's standing near the body—the body that has the pustules that *just* sprayed Dr. Osborne! Funny, I never pictured Scully with a death wish before.

✗ After becoming infected, Dr. Osborne decides to confide in Scully. Strangely enough—even after Scully learns the method of transmission for the contagion—Mulder comes into Skinner's office and, during a conversation with Cancerman, admits that he doesn't know how the disease is spread. Later, during a phone conversation between Mulder and Scully, it never comes up! Mulder is still trying to find the last criminal, and the guy is probably infected. Didn't Scully think that a little detail like how you catch this deadly plague might be important?

✗ And while we're on this topic, how did the contagion spread through the lockdown population? According to dialogue in the episode, the parasites are not airborne. They exist in the fluid expelled from the pustules. When that fluid contacts a new host, the parasites burrow into the skin. The prisoner Robert Torrence contracted the contagion when he received the package that contained a piece of meat that was infected with the parasite. He is designated "patient zero" in this episode. But Torrence is in solitary confinement—in lockdown. Doesn't that mean that his exposure to other prisoners and prison guards is extremely limited? For the contagion to spread, wouldn't Torrence have to spray them? This would all seem to indicate that Torrence could *not* have been the primary source of infection in the prison. Similar packages would have to be sent to all the other prisoners in lockdown. But—if so—why is Torrence designated patient zero, and why is there such fear of contagion? Seems to me like it's pretty simple to keep this thing from spreading! (And if you are wondering if the parasites can spread by both fluid *and* air, I would remind you that Scully stood nearby when Osborne received his baptism, yet she wasn't affected. Good thing, too. Big weeping pustules on the lovely Dr. Scully would *ruin* that flawless complexion!)

✗ After Dr. Osborne collapses to the floor, Scully goes to his side and positions herself so that the pustule on his neck is pointed directly at her face! Good. Really good. (Why do I get the impression that, during this episode, there is some kind of highly specialized stupefaction field that only affects people with doctoral degrees in some biological field of endeavor?)

✗ I also find it amazing that Osborne spends so much time trying to determine if Scully is infected and no one comes looking for him! Especially in light of the fact that the powers that be apparently know he has the parasite.

✗ Near the end of the episode there is some tension over how the authorities will extract an escaped convict from a Greyhound bus. I guess

SECOND SEASON

it would be too simple to tell everyone on board that the bus had a mechanical problem and ask them to disembark?

Equipment Oddities

X A short time after being sprayed by the pustules on an animal carcass in Costa Rica, Dr. Robert Torrence sits at his base camp, feeling generally lousy and trying to get in touch with his field base via radio. It's night. He has a flashlight. It's pointed at his face. I suppose we, the viewers, should be grateful for Torrence's heroic effort to give us a well-illuminated view of the gory outcome from his ineptitude, but . . . is this guy not *miserable* enough already? It is not sufficient that he's running a high temp, has neurotoxins working into his brain, and has big, ugly boils erupting on his body? Why would he want to *blind* himself as well? ("I can't see! I can't see! Everything has *gone white!*" "Well, get the flashlight out of your face, dingbat!")

X Um . . . okay, so, you have this FBI agent who's a medical doctor, right? And she's just been told that there's a flulike illness sweeping the lockdown population of the prison. Ten of the fourteen who were infected have died. This medical doctor/FBI agent wants to find out what's going on, so she takes a pair of gloves and a *dust mask* and starts snooping around although everyone else is in moon suits. Does this make sense? What good will that dinky little mask do if there's really a deadly airborne virus in the prison?

Soft Light

Onscreen Locations

☒ Hotel George Mason, Richmond, Virginia

☒ Wysnecki Residence, Richmond, Virginia

☒ Yaloff Psychiatric Hospital, Piedmont, Virginia

Ruminations

The date on this episode takes a bit of deduction. Mulder and Scully appear the day after Patrick Newirth dies. (Well . . . we don't really know that it's the next day but we will assume that it's close to the date of Newirth's death given Mulder and Scully's rapid response in previous episodes like "Born Again!") Shortly after our intrepid heros arrive in town they visit Margaret Wysnecki's home. She was the second person to disappear and Mulder finds a round-trip train ticket in her trash dated March 17. Scully identifies this date as the day Wysnecki disappeared. Then a pair of policemen die at the train station. The next day Mulder tells Scully that their suspect was at the station the night before—as well as on March 17 and March 31. Scully responds by saying that those are the dates when Margaret Wysnecki and Patrick Newirth disappeared. Since Scully has previously identified March 17 as the day Wysnecki disappeared, Newirth must have disappeared on March 31. Hence, the date listed above.

Hearing the description of the hotel room from which Newirth disappeared—door locked and chained, windows secured from the inside, no fire escape, no way in or out— Scully begins examining the heat register.

PLOT SUMMARY An acquaintance on the Richmond Police Department asks for Scully's help with a baffling case. Three people have disappeared so far, leaving behind only scorch marks on the carpet. Shortly after arriving, Mulder notices that lightbulbs at two of the crime scenes have been unscrewed. The fingerprints on the bulbs match. In addition, two of the victims had recently arrived via train at the Richmond depot and security monitors show a man with a "Polarity Magnetics" jacket sitting in the depot's main lobby. Since the first victim worked at Polarity Magnetics, Mulder and Scully head for the company next.

There, Dr. Christopher Davey quickly identifies the man at the train station as Dr. Chester Banton. He says that Banton disappeared shortly after a terrible accident that gave him a "two-billion-megawatt X ray." In fact, the energy surge somehow changed Banton's molecular structure. Now, anyone who touches Banton's shadow is reduced to ash. (Banton has been living at the train station with its soft light and diffused shadows, trying to keep those around him from harm.)

In time, Mulder and Scully locate Banton, only to have him whisked away by dark forces led by Mr. X. As the episode ends, a furious Mulder tells X they are finished. X comments that he's choosing a dangerous time to go it alone.

When police detective Kelly Ryan, the acquaintance who asked for Scully's help, questions Scully's interest in the small opening as a possible entrance—doubting that anyone could have "squeezed" in there—Mulder simply replies that you never know. This is, of course, a lovely bit of continuity, harkening back to none *other than Eugene Victor Tooms of "Squeeze" and "Tooms."*

No one can tell me that Mulder isn't a nit-picker. In this episode he takes a blurry piece of footage and reads "Polarity Magnetics" from a patch on a guy's jacket. That's a skill that's honed only by the constant dissection of video imagery! (Or someone who's really in love with his video collection.)

Unanswered Questions

X Why did Margaret Wysnecki die? The episode never establishes a connection between her and the other killings—aside from her presence at the train station. But she didn't die at the train station, she died at home, implying that Banton followed or escorted her to her house. Why would Banton follow her home?! And why are there burn marks near the *far end* of her entrance hall? Did she open the door, walk back into the wall, and *then* Banton killed her? It's almost as if Wysnecki expired *solely* for the purpose of giving Mulder and Scully the clue that sends them to the train station. (Mulder finds a train ticket in her trash.) I must say that Wysnecki was certainly noble to make the ultimate sacrifice just to provide Mulder and Scully with this lead. And I hear she won the prestigious Tuiti Award in 1995 under the category Unseen Female Character Who Contributed Most to the Solution of a Difficult Plot Problem. (The Tuiti Award derives its name—of course—from a Hollywood slang term meaning "fortuitous." I hear it's a term that's used a lot out there when referring to plot development.)

Plot Oversights

X After determining that Wysnecki was at the train depot on March 17, Mulder tells Scully to have Ryan dispatch a pair of uniformed officers to look for suspicious characters. That night, both officers die, and the local police want to know why Ryan sent them there in the first

place. (You will recall that Mulder and Scully are here at Ryan's personal request. She hasn't told her superiors that the FBI is involved.) Strangely enough, Mulder and Scully seem happy to leave Ryan twisting in the wind with her superiors. Why not just tell Ryan to tell her bosses about the train ticket found in Wysnecki's house?

X Discussing Banton's work, Dr. Christopher Davey tells Mulder and Scully that Banton was researching dark matter—quantum particles, nutrinos, gluons, mesons, quarks. Scully identifies these as subatomic particles, and Davey adds that they are, theoretically, the very building blocks of reality. Then Scully chimes in to say that no one knows if they "truly exist." This is Scully, the same person who did her undergraduate work in physics. Her statement that no one knows if quarks exist didn't seem right, so I talked with Nitpicker Central's resident solar physicist, Mitzi Adams. It is as I suspected: Saying that quarks don't exist is roughly the same as saying that atoms don't exist. True, no one knows *for sure* if they exist, but the theoretical principles do allow mathematical projections that are borne out by observation of predicted phenomena.

X Explaining the effect of his shadow, Banton says it splits molecules into component atoms; it unzips electrons from their orbits; it reduces matter into pure energy. In other words, it doesn't sound like the shadow has any preference for what it eats. It should eat *everything*. But, of course, it doesn't. It doesn't harm carpets, or walls, or doors, or furniture. It only eats people. How does it know?

X And another thing: Wanna guess what kind of explosion would be caused by converting, say, 150 pounds of a normal human body almost instantaneously into *energy*? I wondered this myself and—not being a physicist—I passed this question off to Mitzi Adams, who calculated an energy release of release of 6×10^{18} joules (given

Einstein's formula of $e = mc^2$). To compare that level of energy with the atomic bomb dropped on Hiroshima, Mitzi consulted with Dr. David Dearborn, an astrophysicist who works at Lawrence Livermore National Laboratory. Turns out that 6×10^{18} joules is equivalent to a yield of 1,500,000 kilotons! In contrast, the Hiroshima bomb was near 15 kilotons. In other words, the almost instantaneous conversion of a human body to energy would result in a release of energy *one hundred thousand* times greater. (I would love to include the notes Dr. Dearborn sent along with his E-mail, but space does not permit. Suffice it to say . . . it *wouldn't* be a beautiful day in the neighborhood.)

X Apparently—at some point in the show—Mulder drove back to Washington, D.C., and put the "X" in his window. That's the only method we've seen that he has to contact Mr. X. One question: If Mulder went back to Washington to contact X, why not have the first meeting with X *in* Washington instead of at the train station in Richmond?

X This Mr. X has the most amazing luck. Having decided to abscond with Banton, he has his forces cut the power to the psychiatric hospital that houses Banton. Then, Mr. X and two thugs head for Banton's room. As X's men attempt to restrain Banton, some kind of emergency lighting clicks on. Banton's shadow annihilates the two individuals who have raised him to his feet. Angry, Banton walks out of his room. Mr. X backs away. Banton and X stare at each other for a time. See bright light behind Banton. See bright light make shadow. See shadow touch X. See X go poof! (At least that's how it should have happened, but for some "tuiti" reason, it didn't!)

Equipment Oddities

X Wow! I am really impressed—I mean *really* impressed—with the video processing equipment that Richmond, Virginia, has in its *train*

depot! Not only do they have cameras everywhere (which was expected), they also can zoom in on paused video. They can reframe and deblur. The capabilities rival those seen in the image processing labs at FBI headquarters! All this . . . in a *train* station.

X There seems to be a casket peeking out amid the flowers at the graveside ceremony for Detective Kelly Ryan. You might recall that she was reduced to a pile of ash by Banton's shadow. One wonders why one would need a casket, given the circumstances. (All part of the prepaid funeral plan?)

Continuity and Production Problems

X Light plays a significant role in this episode and, at times, behaves as adroitly as any actor—always precisely hitting its mark no matter what the physical circumstances! For instance, the opening sequence of this episode features Banton coming to the Hotel George Mason to speak with a colleague. As Banton stands at the colleague's door, a side shot shows us the hallway. Note that all the bulbs in the hallway appear to be the same wattage. Note that the hallway lights create a circular area of illumination on the floor. All but one, that is. Conveniently, the light directly to Banton's left somehow creates a rectangular pathway of light that stretches across the hall to Room 606. (Evidently, the bulb read the script and realized that it would have to do so in order for Banton's shadow to annihilate that room's occupant, Patrick Newirth.)

X And speaking of Newirth, he hears Banton in the hallway and steals a glance through his peephole. Note that the bulb is now creating the standard circular pool of light on the floor. Then, the shot changes, and the little bulb again changes its light to allow Banton to emit his carpet-creeping shadow-o-doom.

SECOND SEASON

Trivia Questions

1 For whom did Patrick Newirth work?

2 In what year was Detective Kelly Ryan born?

2 1965.
(In case you don't remember. They make Cancerman's cigarettes.)
1 Morley Tobacco.

Trivia Answers

𝗫 And speaking of this carpet-creeping shadow-o-doom, it's apparently elastic as well! As Banton retreats from his colleague's door, his shadow doesn't run across the carpet and onto Room 606's door, as one would expect, it actually stretches *underneath* the door a foot or so!

𝗫 Yet more great acting from light in this episode! When Banton encounters two police officers outside the train station, a shot of his feet clearly shows that his shadow only extends behind him. However, once the police officer behind Banton dies, the light knows that the officer in front of Banton is next. With great aplomb, it quickly changes position so the shadow can now extend to kill this second officer as well!

𝗫 The footage near the end of the episode—showing Mulder walk across the floor of a stadium—comes from the first meeting between X and Mulder in "Sleepless."

Our Town

Onscreen Locations

- ☒ County road A7, Dudley, Arkansas
- ☒ Dudley, Arkansas
- ☒ Kearns residence
- ☒ Chaco residence
- ☒ Seth County morgue
- ☒ Seth County Court House

Ruminations

No doubt, everyone *noticed the slogan of Chaco Chicken, "Good People. Good Food." Interesting, considering the town's main avocation. But did you catch the bit with the bucket-o-chicken? With dinner in hand, Scully returns to the room that she's been using to sort through the bones found in the river. Mulder floats his latest theory that the humans represented by the various and sundry piles of bones were eaten . . . by other humans. He then suggests that they pay an unannounced visit to the birth records division of the county courthouse. As Mulder exits, Scully looks down at her newly purchased bucket-o-chicken, takes another look around the display of human bones, crinkles her upper lip, and—turning to follow Mulder—leaves her dinner on the copier. Fun stuff!*

Also—though I am hesitant to admit it—every time I see the good folks of Dudley gathering around the big stew pot near the end of the episode, that old slogan just forces itself into my mind: "Never underestimate the power of soup."

PLOT SUMMARY

Hearing they've been assigned to investigate the disappearance of a federal poultry inspector named George Kearns, Scully balks, claiming it's a waste of their time. Mulder isn't so sure. Kearns was assigned to Dudley, Arkansas, and tales of fox fire and mysterious abductions have long existed in the Ozark Mountains. Neither of these phenomena can compare to the town's real secret.

Arriving in Dudley, Mulder and Scully visit the Chaco Chicken plant where Kearns worked. Inexplicably, a woman named Paula Gray goes berserk and attacks the floor manager, only to be shot dead by the sheriff. An autopsy shows Gray had an extremely rare genetic disorder. Scully recalls that the plant physician said Kearns and Gray shared symptoms and has only one explanation. She wonders if someone dumped Kearns's body into the meat grinder—turning it into chicken feed, thereby passing the disease up the food chain.

At Mulder's request, police drag the river and find evidence of a more chilling possibility. When the net surfaces, human bones appear—all have ends *boiled* smooth. (For six months in 1944, town father Walter Chaco lived with a cannibalistic tribe in New Guinea. Returning to Arkansas, he brought back their secret of their long life.) Thankfully, Mulder digests all the evidence in time to keep Scully from becoming stew.

Geographical Inconsistencies

☒ There is no "county road A7" in Arkansas. County roads are identified solely with numbers.

X Mulder claims Creighton Jones's car was found on the "I-10" right in the middle of Dudley, Arkansas. There is no Dudley, Arkansas. But even if there were, it wouldn't be near I-10. Interstate Highway 10 runs through Louisiana.

X There is no Seth County in Arkansas.

Plot Oversights

X Dr. Robert Woolley tells me it probably would be possible to contract Creutzfeldt-Jakob disease from eating a person afflicted with it. *However,* he also added, "When CJD has been spread via preparations of human growth hormone from affected patients, symptoms took four to twenty-one years (yes, years) to develop. The fastest I can find is eighteen months in a case where the disease was spread by a corneal transplant." Amazingly enough, the people of Chaco seem to contract it in just weeks!

X Okay, so the people of this town are enjoying long life, right? I mean, Paula Gray looks like she's in her early twenties and she's really forty-seven. So what is she doing with her good looks, tight little body, and secret of immortality? She's working in a *chicken processing plant!* Not that there's anything *wrong* with cutting up chickens all day, mind you. But, I mean . . . these people are supposedly going to live . . . like . . . close to forever! Is this really what they want to do the *rest* of their lives?

X This town presents a fascinating complex of social structures. On one level you have Mr. Chaco—the head honcho of Chaco Chicken— surrounded by his employees both supervisory and common. Obviously, he has prospered more than the others. Yet, on another level, you have them all gathered at a common table to slurp down a clearly illegal concoction. Did no one ever look up from the chicken processing line and think, "Ya know, that there Mr. Chaco? He's no

better than the rest of us and we're all going to jail for life if anyone finds out what we been doing out in the field, so what say we just comes up with a new profit-sharing 'rangement?"

Equipment Oddities

X I'm confused. Early in the episode, the floor manager at Chaco Chicken tells Mulder and Scully about a grinder that chews up the leftover chicken parts and turns them into chicken feed. In the final scene of the episode, the creators *strongly* hint that Mr. Chaco was himself turned into chicken feed in the selfsame grinder. Yet a dredge of the local river produces piles of bones—apparently the remains of individuals eaten by the good citizenry of Dudley, Arkansas. So why didn't Chaco and the others put the leftover human bones into the grinder? Why throw them in the river?! (Because then there wouldn't be anything to find and Mulder wouldn't figure it out and Scully would be "mmm-mmm good"!)

X Since when do Mulder and Scully rent *two* cars during their cases? In this episode, as Scully drives to the Kearns house, Mulder heads for the home of Mr. Chaco. Just a bit later, we see Mulder drive up to the bonfire that the good townsfolk have created in a field. If Mulder walked to Chaco's house, he would have had to walk to the Kearns house before he could procure the car and, frankly, by that time Dana Scully would have been turned into . . . well, you get the idea.

X Talking with Mulder about her discoveries at the Kearns house, Scully says the power has been cut. So, um, why did the doorbell work only moments earlier? Battery-operated, maybe?

X Let's talk about the metal head harness that the kinfolk of Dudley employ before giving their victims the old Marie Antoinette treatment. We see it in use twice at the end of the episode. And—just before Scully is placed within its grasp—we get a close-up. It features a flat metal plate, mounted horizontally to form a platform for the head. The edge closest to the body is curved to allow the chest to fit tight against the metal. The other edge has a depression—evidently for the chin. A metal strap makes an arc over the plate and has several holes to account for varying head sizes.

The first time we see the harness in use, the citizens of Dudley force Chaco into the contraption. His head faces downward. His chin rests in the depression, and the metal strap wraps over his head somewhere near the top of his neck. This makes sense. Thusly secured, the victim would have very little maneuvering room. The metal plate would keep him or her from lunging forward, and the strap around the base of the skull would keep him or her from drawing back. There really is only one problem with the setup: The edge of the ax will be hitting the metal plate unless the ax handler is incredibly precise. (Given the option of going first or last to such a fate, I think I would prefer to go first. A dull ax would be no fun at all!)

Having progressed this far, let us now turn our attention to Scully's confinement in the device. The soup mavens press her to the ground and twist her head to the side before securing the metal band. This time the band runs *above* Scully's eyebrows. In this position the band is completely ineffective! Unless Scully's head is shaped fundamentally different from most humans, the circumference of the skull has already begun to decrease in this area. Scully *should* be able to withdraw her head from the metal harness with little difficulty. Yet she remains, looking helpless and scared until the valiant Mulder arrives to spare her a fate worse than salad. (I suppose her *hair* might be caught in the band, but let's see. Hmmm. Decapitation versus losing a bit of those auburn locks. Tough choice!)

Continuity and Production Problems

⌧ Some guys make the best hostages. Take Jess Harold, for instance. He's the floor manager whom Paula Gray attacks. Holding a knife to his throat with her right hand, Paula keeps a tight grip on his body with her left. Unfortunately, the close-ups show us that an intolerable situation has developed. Gray's hair is hanging down in her face. Amazingly enough, in a subsequent wide shot, we see that the hair has been brushed back into place. How? Well, Gray couldn't have done it. Both of her hands have prior engagements. Evidently, during a cutaway, Harold reached up and gave Paula's hair a quick styling. (Is he a considerate guy, or what?)

⌧ Here's a mystery: Mulder comes in as Scully does the autopsy on Paula Gray. Scully says she has discovered what was wrong with the woman. Gray had Creutzfeldt-Jakob disease. Scully knows this because she has a specimen of Gray's brain under the microscope. Yet Gray's head is intact (i.e., not cut open). So how did Scully get a brain specimen without removing Gray's skullcap? (Did she borrow a technique from her own abduction experience? The old "suck the brains out the nose" trick?)

SECOND SEASON

Trivia Questions

❶ On what date in 1961 did Creighton Jones pull off the road to take a nap?

❷ Who is the fourth person to come down with the symptoms of Creutzfeldt-Jakob disease?

Trivia Answers ❶ May 17. ❷ Clayton Walsh.

169

Our Town

Anasazi

(Part 1 of 3)

PLOT SUMMARY

Dark forces move to destroy Mulder even as other events offer incredible potential to finally unmask the truth. In New Mexico, an earthquake resurrects a buried boxcar containing the piled corpses of strange beings. In Dover, Delaware, The Thinker hacks into the Department of Defense database and downloads the original UFO intelligence files—*the* record of the government's knowledge and involvement with extraterrestrials. He quickly passes them to Mulder for safekeeping, not realizing Mulder's drinking water has already been poisoned with a psychosis-inducing drug.

Finding that the files are encrypted in Navajo "code talk," Scully searches for a translator as Mulder's condition worsens. Then Mulder's father unexpectedly calls, asking Fox to come home. Bill Mulder intends to tell his son of his own dark involvement with the conspirators, but Krycek kills him before he can confess. With Mulder out of control and threatening vengeance, Scully shoots her partner and spirits him unconscious across the country, hoping to cleanse his system of the toxin. Thirty-six hours later, he wakes in New Mexico, and Scully introduces Mulder to a Navajo "code talker" translator named Albert Hosteen, who insists he has something that Mulder must see.

Soon Mulder stands among the bodies in the unearthed boxcar. Then Cancerman arrives to thwart the discovery with a military strike, but Mulder somehow disappears. Furious, Cancerman orders the incineration of the corpses.

Onscreen Locations

- ☒ Navajo reservation, Two Grey Hills, New Mexico
- ☒ Dover, Delaware
- ☒ United Nations building, New York City
- ☒ US Botanical Garden, Washington, D.C.
- ☒ West Tisbury, Martha's Vineyard, Massachusetts
- ☒ Offices of the Navaho Nation, Washington, D.C.
- ☒ FBI Headquarters, Firearms Unit
- ☒ Navajo Nation, National Reservation

Ruminations

Great season-ender! Lots of good stuff! Nice tieback to "The Thinker," first mentioned in "One Breath." Great juxtaposition with William Mulder sitting at the same table with Cancerman. Interesting plot development to allow Scully to shoot Mulder and still have it be for his own good! And, of course, the ultimate cliff-hanger as Mulder appears to be trapped inside a burning, buried boxcar at the very end (although this last item will get some well-deserved scrutiny in the review of "The Blessing Way").

In addition, it always brings a smile to my face when the creators decide to have a little fun with the more observant of the fanpool. After receiving the digital tape from The Thinker, Mulder loads it up on his computer and is dismayed to see that it looks like gibberish. A medium shot shows us the monitor, and then the camera cuts to a close-up as the screen flips to the next page. Freeze that frame! Count down five lines. See the word "do-ray-me-faso-la-todo." Grin on cue. (No doubt this section of the file delineates a fiendishly macabre plot by the Consortium to drive aliens insane by attempting to teach them the solfège system! Either that or it's about an experiment to turn them into blathering idiots by subjecting them to continuous reruns of The Sound of Music.)

And I am certain that you noticed Chris Carter gave himself a cameo in this episode! He's the man at Scully's inquisition who asks, "Weren't you originally assigned to the X-Files to debunk his work?" Well, I guess he should know, shouldn't he? (Wink, wink.)

There's also a really nice detail added to the scene where Mulder comes to his father's house. You may remember William Mulder's first appearance, in "Colony." Fox Mulder climbs the stairs to the porch. William Mulder lights a cigarette. The two approach each other. Fox reaches out to hug his dad. Deflecting the gesture, William Mulder instead thrusts forward a stiff hand. The image is one of a son desiring his father's intimacy and being denied. Now consider the moment when William and Fox Mulder greet each other in this episode. Fox stretches out his hand. William takes it and suddenly pulls his son into a hug. The roles have reversed. Now father wants intimacy—fearing the repercussions of his imminent confession.

One last odd little detail. I believe this episode gives us the first look at the room "across the wall" from Scully's living room. It is a bedroom, and Scully escorts Mulder there so he can rest. I've seen this scene humorously cited several times as "Mulder spending time in Scully's bed." Unfortunately, this isn't Scully's bedroom, since there's another bedroom at the other end of the hall, and a bedroom scene from "War of the Coprophages" strongly suggests that that bedroom is the one she calls her own. (Sorry to disappoint you.)

Unanswered Questions

X Why is the railcar buried in New Mexico in the first place? Wouldn't it be simpler for the conspirators to burn the bodies if they wanted to keep their existence a secret? The scientists

who conducted the experiments on the beings certainly didn't dig the hole for the railcar with shovels purchased from the local five-and-dime. In other words, burying the railcar involved some sort of excavation crew and probably an industrial helicopter to airlift it to that location. If secrecy is so important, why go to all this trouble? Or . . . could it be that the railcar is buried in some kind of landslide? Well, the next episode shows us a tantalizing clip of video. Someone drops a can of cyanide gas into the enclosure. The beings scurry to and fro, attempting to escape through the tunnel they have dug. This would imply that the aliens had been kept in this location for some time. But if the conspirators wanted to create a confinement area, why not just build one? Why bury a railcar? Didn't they have anyplace else to store "the merchandise" while a holding pen was under construction?

Plot Oversights

X At the beginning of this episode, a young Navajo finds the buried boxcar and hauls one of the strange corpses back to his house. Strangely enough, as the young men of the town stare, Albert Hosteen approaches the body without hesitation—despite the fact that later events in the episode indicate Hosteen holds dear the traditions of the Navajo. On the advice of Bob Potter, I did a little research into Hosteen's behavior. I have some friends named Ben and Noreen Davis who live here in Springfield. As it turns out, they have a brother-in-law who is Navajo and lives in Dennehosto, Arizona. Don Tsosie tells me that—without performing a ritual—is it unlikely Hosteen would approach the dead body.

X It is the stuff of fun science fiction—this bit with The Thinker hacking into the Defense Department's supersecret files—but it *is* just that: science *fiction*. This *wouldn't* happen. Files as sensitive as the original UFO intelligence documents probably would be stored *only* on a network or system that was not connected via modem or data line to the outside world. In other words, you couldn't "phone home." And even if the files *were* stored on a dial-up network, there are *simple* precautions I am absolutely certain the Department of Defense *would* take to restrict access. For instance, every network I know of requires a user name *and* password to log on.

The normal scenario presented by science fiction has the heroic hacker somehow acquiring a valid user name and then assaulting the target network with the user name and a series of fictitious or randomly generated passwords. For each log-in request, the server first checks to see if the user name is valid and then does the same with the password. Eventually the hacker stumbles onto the correct password after a gajillion attempts.

Now, suppose you are writing a program to protect a system from unwanted intruders. How would you make life difficult for this hacker? Easy: If you get a user name with an invalid password, you would temporarily store the user name in memory with the time and date of the failed attempt. If you get ten or twenty failed attempts within ten minutes or so for the same user name, you kill the connection. (And if you really want to be secure, you *invalidate* the user name. In that way the hacker would have to start all over with a new user name.)

And lest you think that a hacker could stumble onto the correct password in ten tries or less, I offer you this little bit of math. The number of possibilities for an eight-character password limited to the twenty-six letters of the alphabet would be equivalent to 26 raised to the power of *8*. That's 208,827,064,576 possible combinations!

But there's even more the Department of Defense could do! They could give those with access to the super-duper-secret files more than one user name and password. Then they could require that an individual log on through three or

four levels to get to the information. At any level, if the person making the request failed to supply the correct password, *all* of that individual's user names could be invalidated!

I know that The Thinker claims he accidentally stumbled into the Defense Department files, but the chances of that are *so* remote that I'm inclined to think that The Thinker had help. Perhaps there's more than one "Deep Throat" character floating around "Out There"? (No doubt this is more of the pixies' handiwork.)

⊠ The meeting between The Thinker and Mulder produces some amusing moments. The Thinker tells Mulder that he believes he downloaded the government's secret record of its involvement with extraterrestrials. Yet later, we see that the files are all encrypted. Even the headings are encrypted! So . . . how did The Thinker know what he downloaded? Was the file named "ReallyBigSecretUFOStuff.doc"?

⊠ In addition, The Thinker tells Mulder that he has a party of ninjas "shagging his butt." They know who he is because he never expected to get in to the Department of Defense computers and didn't take any precautions. So this guy was boinking the DoD and it *never occurred* to him that even if he *didn't* get in, someone *might* be interested in why he kept knocking on their door? If he didn't take any precautions, wouldn't the DoD's computers get vital information on him *the moment* he requested a connection even if he didn't get past the security measures?

⊠ I've asked before, but we finally get another look at the basement door in this episode. It *still* reads "Fox Mulder, Special Agent." I wonder when Scully gets her name added to the area.

⊠ You have to appreciate a petite five-foot, three-inch woman like Dana Scully who cannot only shoot her partner in the shoulder using only a one-handed grip but also heft his unconscious body around afterward—especially given Mulder's

Anasazi

height of six feet and weight of 170 pounds! (No doubt she's been working out at the gym.)

Changed Premises

X Called into Skinner's office to offer an explanation for Mulder's recent behavior, Scully answers a question by stating that she began working with Mulder "a year and a half ago." According to the screen text of this episode, it's April, and previous episodes indicate that the current year is 1995. "Pilot"—the episode that details Mulder and Scully's first case together—carries a date of March 1992. So actually they've been working together for *three* years.

Equipment Oddities

X I love the moment when The Thinker gives the files to Mulder, handing over this really big manila envelope. We later see that it contains only a dinky digital cassette! Who taught this guy his "covert-information-passing techniques"? He might as well erect a neon sign that says, "Okay, I'm Giving Mulder the Information Now!"

X (This is pushing it, but a look at your tapes and see what you think.) When Scully shoots Mulder, pay close attention to her gun. It's visible for only a second after she fires, but to me, it looks like the slide has locked back. If that's true, it can mean one of two things: Either the slide is jammed because the next round didn't

load properly or . . . "Barney" had only one bullet in her gun . . . again! (See "Deep Throat.") Oddly enough, after two quick cutaways, the slide is back where it should be.

X Of course, the greatest equipment oddity of the second season of The X-Files occurs in this episode as Mulder talks on his cell phone, *inside* a refrigeration railcar that's *buried* in a *canyon* out in the middle of the *desert* in *New Mexico!*

Continuity and Production Problems

X It's nice to see that Gwen Goodensnake finally made something of her life. You might recall her from the episode "Shapes." After that episode, she disappeared. Now we finally know what happened to her. She's working in the offices of the Navajo Nation in Washington, D.C.!

X As Scully stands to leave after her meeting with Goodensnake, watch the upper left-hand picture on the wall directly behind the desk. You should see a microphone boom swing into view. (Okay, okay. I know this isn't really Goodensnake. It's *supposed* to be a character named Josephine Doane. Just a little nitwit there. Get it? nit . . . wit.)

YOU MIGHT BE AN X-PHILE . . .

(My wife, Lynette, and I sat down over lunch and came up with these. Some of them are a bit obscure. If you don't get one or two, ask a die-hard X-phile.)

. . . if you know what "X-phile" means.

. . . if you've ever called the FBI and asked to speak to the Paranormal Investigative Task Force.

. . . if you've ever put a masking tape "X" on your window just to see what would happen.

. . . if conspiracy radio has become your favorite station.

. . . if you've suddenly developed a hankering for sunflower seeds.

. . . if you've ever gone outside at night with a flashlight and tried to signal UFOs.

. . . if you're sure that Windows 95 is a hideous, brain-sucking, stupefying experiment conducted by Cancerman's minions.

. . . if you've tried to call 1-900-555-YAPP for psychic advice.

. . . if you regularly check your body for alien implant scars.

. . . if you regularly check your watch to see if it has stopped.

. . . if you regularly check your toilet for Tooms and Flukeman.

. . . if you suspect identical twins are really alien/human hybrids.

. . . if you think you've been impregnated by Luke Skywalker.

. . . if you won't talk to your friends until they activate a CSM-25 Countermeasure Filter.

. . . if you've moved to X-ville. (You'll need to visit *The X-Files'* Internet newsgroup to understand that one.)

. . . if you've made the pilgrimage to Vancouver.

. . . if you're certain the FBI labs were discredited by the Consortium because they had irrefutable evidence of the existence of extraterrestrials.

. . . if you can call Assistant Director Walter Skinner by his middle name.

. . . if you've ever stared at snow on the television with pen in hand, trying to receive binary messages.

. . . if you expect your cell phone to work every time you turn it on.

. . . if you were disappointed that your newborn baby didn't have a tail.

. . . if you suspect the bees in your backyard carry smallpox.

. . . if you can quote John 52:54.

. . . if "Fox" sounds like a sensible name for a boy.

. . . if "Deep Throat" doesn't make you think of a porno movie.

. . . if you own *anything* named Queequag.

. . . if your rallying cry is "Roswell! *Roswell!*"

. . . if you've ever said "Welcome to Earth" to a cockroach.

. . . if Fox Mulder's theories have always sounded reasonable.

. . . if you've never asked, "What does the 'X' stand for?"

You Might Be
an X-Phile . . .

THIRD
SEASON

The Blessing Way

(Part 2 of 3)

Onscreen Locations

☒ Navajo Reservation, Northwest of
   Los Alamos, New Mexico

☒ 46th Street, New York City

☒ Garden of Reflection, Parkway Cemetery,
   Boston, Massachusetts

☒ Martha's Vineyard, West Tisbury,
   Massachusetts

Ruminations

The fun continues! Excellent expansion of the conspiracy mythology with the introduction of the Consortium and the Well-Manicured Man. Great scene with Frohike coming by Scully's apartment to hold a private wake for Mulder. And what an ending! (Although, I have always wondered why people who find themselves in the proverbial "Mexican standoff" don't start blasting away immediately. If you wait until the other person fires, isn't it a little too late?)

A nitpicker notices the oddest things. In "Humbug" we see Scully attired in blue pajamas and a white robe. Guess what she wears in this episode when Frohike comes for a late-night visit? That's right: blue pajamas and a white robe! Kudos for continuity!

The date on this episode comes from a comment Scully makes during her private wake with Frohike. She points at "April 16" in a newspaper article and identifies it as the day before yesterday.

Unanswered Questions

☒ Obviously, for many nitpickers this episode's

PLOT SUMMARY

Believing Mulder is dead, Cancerman's men apprehend Scully as she leaves New Mexico. They confiscate her paper copy of the stolen documents, demanding the digital tape copy as well but Scully tells them Mulder has it. In Washington, Scully finds herself censured for insubordination. Oddly enough, when Scully returns to the headquarters building days later—entering by the front door—a metal detector locates an implant at the back of her neck. A physician later extracts the small disk.

Meanwhile, the Navajo find Mulder buried under some rocks near the burned-out boxcar. Seeing that he is barely alive, the Navajo begin a Blessing Way chant to ask the Holy People to save Mulder's life.

In Boston, Scully attends the funeral for Mulder's father, only to have a "well-manicured man" approach. He warns her that certain members of a "consortium" want her dead since they are satisfied she doesn't have the digital copy of the files. Soon, Skinner insists on meeting with her in a secure location. Scully goes with him but suspects that he's the chosen assassin. Unfortunately, Melissa Scully comes to her sister's apartment minutes later, and the real assassins fatally injure her by mistake. Even still, the episode ends with Scully and Skinner holding each other at gunpoint in Mulder's apartment—listening as something rustles the door.

big unanswered question was: How did Mulder escape from the buried boxcar? I've heard lots of interesting theories advanced—even to the extreme of postulating the existence of a *second* boxcar that was burned, leaving Mulder unharmed. (Unfortunately, this theory quickly fails with an examination of the footage.

There's a large rock near the boxcar that appears often enough to sustain the notion that the boxcar Mulder enters *is* the boxcar that receives the incendiary.)

Just for the record, here's what I think the creators would like us to believe. For some undisclosed reason in the years prior to "Anasazi," the boxcar was buried in the desert, carrying "merchandise" that was alive and moderately healthy. Awaiting their fate, the odd little beings contained within *somehow* punched a hole in the side of the refrigerated boxcar and began digging an evacuation tunnel. At some later point, the conspiracy or the consortium or whoever decided to kill all the little beings with a few well-placed cyanide canisters. (Everything thus far is supported by the odd videoclip that plays in the middle of Mulder's out-of-body experience.)

Here's where it gets twitchy: It is *possible*, then, that the mound of corpses found by Mulder was created not by an individual who entered the boxcar and piled up the beings after they died but by the frantic efforts of the beings to escape the gas filling the boxcar. (In this case they would be covering the entrance to the escape tunnel.) If you are willing to accept that, you might be willing to believe that Mulder— standing in the dark after the hatch closes at the end of "Anasazi"—could somehow *divine* the existence of this escape tunnel. Given that leap of faith, you also might be willing to imagine Mulder diving under the bodies and burrowing his way through the corpses that fill the escape tunnel even as an incendiary goes off behind him and burns up all the oxygen in the boxcar. (Then again, Mulder is a hero, and heroes can do stuff like this!)

Plot Oversights

🗙 At the beginning of the episode, military personnel accost Scully and demand the "DAT" copy of the files. Given the tape shown us in the previous episode, I believe the appropriate term

would be digital cassette. "DAT" stands for digital audiotape (which *can* be used for the storage of computer files, but in this case, it wasn't!) Then again, these are just grunts, right? What would they know!?

🗙 Maybe I'm just paranoid, but I guarantee you that if I had been Scully and I had those documents in my hot little hands, I would have found a Kinko's Copies shop very quickly and made some copies. Did it never occur to *anyone* that *somebody* might come looking for those files?

🗙 The character represented by Chris Carter's cameo in the last episode is missing when Scully is censured in this episode. Why?

🗙 During her private wake with Frohike, Scully learns that The Thinker has been killed. His body was discovered on April 16. Realizing the implications of this piece of news, Scully rushes to Skinner with the article. She wants Skinner to compare the bullet that killed The Thinker to the bullet that killed William Mulder. She tells Skinner that since The Thinker's "date of death" postdates the disappearance of her partner, a match between the two slugs would exonerate him. Wait a minute: The article doesn't fix The Thinker's "date of death" on April 16, as Scully claims. It says The Thinker's body *was discovered* on April 16. As a forensic pathologist, Scully should be the first to know that the date when a body is discovered has little to do with when the person actually died.

(Here's a ponderment on a closely related topic, although it's not a nit. What happened to the gun Mulder took from Krycek in the previous episode? If you recall, Krycek kills William Mulder. A short time later, Mulder ambushes Krycek as Krycek sneaks toward Mulder's apartment. Mulder takes Krycek's gun. Scully shoots Mulder. Krycek runs away. The gun lays beside Mulder as Scully runs up to tend to his wound. Scully *must* have that gun, and since Krycek killed William Mulder within the past day or so, aren't the chances pretty good that *that* gun is the murder weapon? As far as I know it's never tested or mentioned again.)

☒ After the discovery of the metal disk, Scully has a doctor remove it after administering a local anesthetic. Why doesn't Scully take off her coat for this procedure? It looks like her collar is in the way.

☒ Not a nit, just an observation. In the past, Scully has complained about regressive hypnotherapists asking leading questions, but I never really found anything to complain about until now. This guy Scully visits on the urging of her sister seems to have every intention of making Scully remember his version of events. He asks questions such as, "Someone must have cared for you. Do you remember who that someone was?" and "Maybe you trusted them not to hurt you. Could this be possible?" (While watching this exchange I felt like saying, "Sure, Doc. Why don't you just write up what you want her to remember and *spoon-feed* it to her?!")

Equipment Oddities

☒ I find it amazing—with all the traveling Scully has done—that she has never had trouble with metal detectors before this episode.

☒ "Ah," you say, "but the metal detectors in the FBI are *really* sensitive." Yeah? Well, let's talk about that. The disk in Scully's neck looks to be about the size of a thin slice of a pencil eraser. If the metal detector is *that* sensitive, wouldn't Scully's earrings set it off? Wouldn't metal buttons set it off? Wouldn't one coin in a pocket set it off? (Would the fillings in teeth set it off as well?) I would imagine this *really* tries the patience of the poor guard working on the metal-detector detail!

☒ Interestingly enough, after Scully turns in her weapon to the FBI, we later see her retrieve a

gun from a nightstand in her apartment that looks *identical* to the one she carried during the first season! (Guess she hadn't earned enough Brownie points to qualify for an FBI weapon yet. And—come to think of it—that's probably why Mulder let her have only one bullet in "Deep Throat!" I'm just *joking!*)

Continuity and Production Problems

☒ As usual when it comes to prosthetic boulders, the two young Native Americans who lift the fake rocks off Mulder at the beginning of the episode make a valiant attempt to pretend that the rocks are heavy but—ultimately—the effort fails. For one thing, the young men would have wedged their hands *under* the rocks if they were lifting the real thing.

☒ "Squeeze," "Beyond the Sea," and "Ascension" clearly show that the number on Scully's back door reads "35." Yet in this episode Scully opens her front door (which suddenly materialized in "Colony"), and the door across the hall reads "3." Now, I suppose there could be thirty other apartments scattered up and down the hall in this building, but that doesn't seem likely!

☒ Normally the creators do a splendid job remembering who was injured where and how long it should take to heal. (And I do make some allowance for skin abrasions on women, since a woman can cover a multitude of scratches with a bit of makeup.) In this episode, however, the creators seem to forget that the bullet from Scully's gun in the previous episode went "clean through" Mulder's shoulder. They *do* create the entry wound on Mulder's chest, but there's no exit wound on his back. And—as any pathologist will tell you—there is an easy way to determine an entry wound from an exit wound. The exit wound is *bigger!*

☒ Something very, *very* strange is going on in

THIRD SEASON

Trivia Questions

❶ Where was Kenneth J. Soona's body found?

❷ With whom does Scully engage in holotropic breathwork?

Mulder's apartment complex. Not only was the Consortium attempting to poison him with an "agonist" (to use Scully's term), they also have embarked on some kind of devious mind game by rearranging the apartments on the fourth floor of Mulder's building! When Scully accompanies Skinner to Mulder's apartment so they can talk, the door across the hall reads "45." That's odd, because in "End Game" it read "43." Not only that, as we watch Scully unlock Mulder's apartment, there is only one other apartment entrance door on the wall between Mulder's door and the elevator. Yet in "End Game" there were *two* other doors. (You can see them when Scully comes to check Mulder's computer and when Scully meets X for the first time.) In fact, the hallway itself looks five or six feet *shorter* in the "The Blessing Way"! (Insert *Twilight Zone* theme here.)

Paper Clip

(Part 3 of 3)

Onscreen Locations

- ☒ 46th Street, New York
- ☒ Rural West Virginia
- ☒ Route 320A, Craiger, Maryland
- ☒ Southeast Washington, D.C.
- ☒ Greenwich, Connecticut

Ruminations

I'm telling ya, when it comes to these alien-conspiracy/human-experimentation/"truth-truth-who's-got-the-truth" shows, ain't nobody does it better than The X-Files! *This episode completes a wonderful triad of shows and starts the ball rolling for what will be a fascinating season of poking around the edges of "the truth."*

On a completely different topic, the opening of this episode speaks of a white buffalo that was born on the same day Mulder recovered from his days in the desert. Because of the rarity of this event—and the fact that there actually was a white buffalo born in recent days here in the States—I thought I might use the birth to fix a date for this episode. Unfortunately, the real white buffalo was born in late August 1994, which is far too early. Unless there's some kind of weird time travel involved, the date of this episode would be late April 1995.

Some minor housekeeping next. When Mulder and Scully find Scully's file at the Strughold Mining Company, a piece of documentation lists her address as "3170 W. 53rd Rd., Annapolis, MD." Some have taken this to be her current address, but that's unlikely. The beginning of "Ascension" reveals that the num-

PLOT SUMMARY Hearing the standoff inside his apartment, Mulder bursts in and forces Skinner to surrender. Only then does Skinner reveal that he has the digital cassette everyone seeks. He took it for safekeeping. Satisfied, Mulder and Scully seek out Victor Klemper—a Nazi scientist given amnesty in exchange for medical knowledge gained while torturing Jews. (Mulder has found a photograph showing Klemper standing beside his father.) Though tight-lipped, Klemper does suggest they investigate the Strughold Mining Company. There Mulder and Scully discover long tunnels filled with medical records. Soon a large spaceship passes overhead and a paramilitary strike force appears. The pair barely escapes with their lives.

Meeting with Skinner, Mulder and Scully finally agree to trade the cassette for their safety before returning to question Klemper further. The Well-Manicured Man greets them instead. He claims the medical records were gathered for secret experiments and adds that Mulder's father was opposed to the project, so the Consortium took Samantha to keep him quiet.

Meanwhile, Krycek and two others attack Skinner, stealing back the digital tape. Still, Skinner tells Cancerman that a Navajo translator memorized the files and recited them to twenty others. The group will remain silent only if Mulder and Scully are left alone. Though grief-stricken, the pair then renews their commitment to find the answers they seek.

ber on the exterior of her apartment complex is "1419." (Of course, Scully could have moved since then, but . . . two apartments with the same layout?)

In the "didja notice?" category, when

184

Paper Clip

Mulder and Scully look at Scully's file, she comments that it has a recent tissue sample because of the plastic case. Samantha Mulder's file had a recent tissue sample case as well—hinting that she's still alive.

As I've said before, it's the details that I love about The X-Files. *Appearing at the Strughold Mining Company, an assault team races to the vaults. To gain entry, a member of the team punches in the access code and, yes, he punches in the same code that opened the door for Mulder and Scully! Good job.*

Unanswered Questions

X Who are the "friends" to whom "Brandoguy" refers? You might recall that after the Well-Manicured Man learns Mulder is still alive, he informs the Consortium of this development, and a guy who sounds like Marlon Brando says it's time to contact their "friends," who will handle the matter more satisfactorily.

Some background first. The Consortium is facing the threat of exposure with the theft of the secret files from the Defense Department computers. They apparently fear Mulder and Scully's involvement in the case will increase this threat. Therefore, when Brandoguy says that their "friends" will handle the matter more satisfactorily, we probably can assume that the actions of the "friends" will in some way discourage Mulder and Scully's investigation.

At the Strughold Mining Company, Mulder and Scully are visited by two groups. First, a large spacecraft appears, and a herd of little people run past Scully. Then an assault group arrives and begins spraying the building with bullets. Given that the spaceship and the little people would not diminish Mulder and Scully's interest, I think it's safe to say that they are not the "friends." But what about the assault team? Didn't the Well-Manicured Man scoff at Cancerman for believing he could fix the problem "with enough bullets"? If the members of the assault team are the friends spoken of by

Brandoguy, the Consortium seems to have voted in favor of Cancerman's solution. There are *plenty* of bullets flying around during their attack!

Also, if the spaceship and the little people are not the "friends," what were they doing at the Strughold Mining Company? Remember that they *spotlighted* the exit door for Scully! Did they come to *warn* Mulder and Scully of the danger from the assault team and give them a way out? (Could it be that the little people are, in fact, the pixies of Out There who have been helping Mulder and Scully all along?)

X *Was* Skinner bluffing when he told Cancerman that Albert Hosteen knew the entire contents of the digital tape? Probably. After all, Skinner met Hosteen only minutes before the tape was stolen in the stairwell. And if Hosteen knew the contents of the tape, why not let him tell Mulder and Scully? On the other hand, Hosteen *was* one of the men who originally translated the information into Navajo code talk. How much does he remember?

Geographical Inconsistencies

X Craiger, Maryland, doesn't exist.

Plot Oversights

X Mulder functions amazingly well in the episode for someone who was shot approximately one week earlier, then died and came back to life!

X A significant portion of this episode revolves around Cancerman's effort to get back the digital cassette and produce it for the inspection of the Consortium that meets at 46th Street. Given that Cancerman blatantly misleads them in this episode, why doesn't he complete his deception and simply make another copy of the Defense Department files? He could flash around this second digital cassette, satisfy everyone in the room, and then dispose of the original problem at his leisure.

☒ I wonder if Melissa Scully had a living will. She seemed all for the idea in "One Breath." Yet in this episode we see her sustained for days with *extreme* medical procedures.

☒ At Victor Klemper's suggestion, Mulder and Scully visit the Strughold Mining Company. Given Klemper's inquiry if the pair knew the formula for Napier's constant, Scully tells Mulder the entrance code to the vaults is probably "27828." *Amazingly* enough, the code works! Why is that amazing, you ask? Well, for one thing, I don't recall anyone saying anything about the code being only five digits long. The numbers after the decimal point in Napier's constant go on forever, with no discernible pattern! So the code might be five digits or eight or—heaven forbid—*ten million* digits long. Also, the constant begins "2.71828 . . ." not "2.7828 . . ." as Scully's code implies, so—really—she should have tried "27182"!

☒ After stealing the digital cassette from Skinner, Krycek and two other men drive to Southeast Washington, D.C. The two men get out, and Krycek realizes that the car is about to explode, so he runs. It appears that Cancerman had every intention of killing Krycek and *destroying* the digital cassette. I'm confused. I could have sworn that the Consortium told Cancerman that they wanted to *see* the digital cassette. Strangely enough, when Cancerman lies and tells them it was destroyed, all seem willing to accept his word.

Changed Premises

☒ Samantha Mulder gets a new birthday along with a new middle name in this episode. An X-File opened by Mulder himself—and viewed by Scully in the episode "Conduit"—lists "Samantha T. Mulder" with a birth date of "January 22, 1964."

The file in this episode lists "Samantha *Ann* Mulder" with a birth date of "11/21/65."

Equipment Oddities

☒ The previous episode ended with Scully and Skinner training their weapons on each other. I probably shouldn't mention this, but if Scully wants to be taken seriously, she probably should put her finger on the trigger instead of keeping it extended and resting on the side of her weapon! (In fact, she waits until *after* Skinner hands over his gun to draw her finger onto the trigger. This would not inspire confidence on Skinner's part!)

☒ I never realized that the Consortium was so hard up for *money*. In a dramatic moment, Mulder extracts his sister's file and peels back her label to reveal his name underneath. This is when I thought, "Huh?!" Do the creators expect us to believe that the Consortium had the resources to build this *huge* storage facility but they couldn't afford a *new* manila folder for Samantha's files? Why recycle Mulder's folder?! (Or is this just more evidence of the pixies of Out There at work?)

☒ Every creator, at one time or another, faces a difficult problem in his or her plot, and there's no solution except to get goofy. Unfortunately, this episode contains one such instance. Skinner tells Mulder and Scully that he can negotiate to return the digital tape and guarantee their safety. Mulder doesn't want to lose the information contained therein. Scully wants to see her fatally wounded sister. The obvious solution would be to make a copy of the tape before turning it over. (Hey, I didn't say it was honest, I just said it was *obvious*.) To ensure that Mulder and Scully cannot retain this information, the creators have Skinner say that he can't print out a hard copy and then add that The Thinker put copy protection on the digital cassette.

To summarize my reaction to Skinner's com-

THIRD SEASON

Trivia Questions

❶ What is Fox Mulder's middle name?

❷ In front of what motel does Krycek's car explode?

Trivia Answers
❶ William.
❷ The Lynwood Inn.

▌▌▌

Paper Clip

*The creators continue
to add to our information
on the Consortium in
this episode, giving us a
wonderful scene in which
the Well-Manicured Man
dresses down Cancerman.
Evidently all are not equal
in the room on 46th Street.*

ments: *THIS . . . IS . . . GOOFY!* Let's take it a piece at a time. Skinner says he can't print out a copy of the file. Well, *someone* printed out a copy of the file, because *Scully* had hard copy in "Anasazi." The Thinker didn't do it because the envelope he handed Mulder only contained the digital cassette. (And if you are wondering if Mulder removed the hard copy prior to our joining the scene, I would remind you that Mulder didn't know the files were written in Navajo code talk *until* he brought them up on the screen. If the envelope contained a printout, he would have already known this or he would have commented that the screen looked just like the papers that were in the envelope.)

In addition, if the information on the digital cassette can be displayed on a computer screen, there are *many* ways to copy it, whether the cassette is copy-protected or not! There's everything from the brute-force method of setting up a camcorder focused on a monitor to the more sophisticated methods of trapping characters at the BIOS level. Trust me, it *can* be done.

But beyond that, why would The Thinker copy-protect it in the first place?! Isn't he an anarchist? Isn't his whole motivation to get the truth out? Doesn't he understand that his life is forfeit because of his actions? Hasn't he handed

the torch to Mulder to carry on the work? It simply *makes no sense* for The Thinker to limit Mulder's ability to bring the truth to light.

For me, the only possibility that satisfies the constraints of the plot while maintaining *some* believability is to say that the files are encrypted on the tape and can *only* be viewed with an imbedded decryption program that came along during the download. Perhaps this program—which originated at the Defense Department—only allows the printing of one copy and somehow circumvents any other types of electronic access. (Of course, that *still* doesn't account for the old "camcorder pointed at the monitor" trick!)

D.P.O.

Onscreen Locations

- ☒ Lloyd P. Wharton County Building, Connerville, Oklahoma
- ☒ Forensic Lab, Johnston County Sheriff's Office
- ☒ County road A-7
- ☒ Felton Community Hospital, Felton, Oklahoma
- ☒ Johnston County Jail
- ☒ Oklahoma State Psychiatric Hospital

Ruminations

The date on this episode comes from Oswald's record on a video arcade game.

Of course, I'm sure you noticed that Oswald finally achieved his mother's measure of greatness at the very end of the episode. He was on television! (Actually, he was on television for the entire episode, wasn't he?)

And I hesitate to bring this up, but this episode *does* end with a unique sound effect! I will leave it for you to watch the show yourself and lend an ear.

Geographical Inconsistencies

- ☒ Interestingly enough—just as in "Our Town"—this episode features a county road A-7 (although in "Our Town" it didn't have the hyphen). Like Arkansas, Oklahoma doesn't have county roads that use the nomenclature "A-7." Some county roads *do* use a mixed alphanumeric designation, but the number always comes first.

PLOT SUMMARY Five lightning strikes—all targeted at young men—bring Mulder and Scully to Connerville, Oklahoma, where Scully autopsies the latest victim. Despite a few anomalies, it looks like an accident, but Mulder isn't convinced.

The investigation quickly leads to Darren Peter Oswald—the only one of the five to survive. Though evidence places him at the scene of the latest strike, he denies any knowledge of the incident. Oddly enough, Mulder's cell phone melts during the interview. That night, Oswald wanders into a field and calls down lightning. In short order, a bolt fires through him. Since his accident, he's been able to channel incredible surges of electricity. He intends to use his power to win the hand of the woman he loves—his boss's wife, Sharon Kiveat.

The next morning, Mulder and Scully find a fulgurite—a fusing of sand into glass by lightning—at the site of Oswald's latest high-voltage adventure. It contains Oswald's footprint, and Mulder soon realizes the young man's powers. By the time Oswald is finally apprehended, however, his boss is in the hospital, Sharon Kiveat has been terrorized, and the local sheriff is dead. Unfortunately, the state prosecutor doesn't known how to *begin* building a case: All tests show Oswald to be a perfectly normal teenager.

- ☒ Felton, Oklahoma, doesn't exist.

Plot Oversights

- ☒ Well, I'm torqued! I *can't believe* the creators would do this to us! Evidently Mulder and Scully have had some incredible adventures together and *we missed out on them!* This is unbelievable! Are we not loyal fans? Do we not deserve to enjoy the audacious exploits of our favorite FBI agents? Will we *ever* learn of these unseen cases?

"What is he *talking* about now?" you ask. I direct your attention to the date of this episode: *September* 12, 1995. And what was the date of the *last* episode? Sometime late in *April* 1995! That's *four and one-half months!* Okay, so maybe nothing happened. Maybe they searched for William Mulder and Melissa Scully's murderers and turned up nothing. Maybe. But to hear Scully tell it, *some* really interesting stuff transpired during that time! Near the beginning of the episode she refers to "everything" they've "just been through." "All" they have "just seen." *What* have they *just* been through?! *What* did they *just* see?! *We have to know!*

⊠ After being interviewed by Scully, Oswald's friend "Zero" goes to Oswald's house. When Oswald finally comes out to play, Zero tells him that he won't believe who came by the video arcade today. Oswald jumps into the conversation by guessing the FBI. At this, Zero seems stunned and wonders how the FBI found Oswald. Now, granted, Zero's neurons don't appear to fire at full capacity, but he was standing right *beside* Mulder when our fearless FBI agent pointed to the high scores on Oswald's favorite video arcade game and said, "Scully, look at this." (The screen is filled with "D.P.O.," which are Oswald's initials.) Zero also appears to be only a few feet away when Mulder and Scully head down the line of reasoning that leads them to Oswald. Is Zero's mind so pickled that he can't make the connection between these events?!

⊠ After giving Mr. Kiveat a heart attack, Oswald brings him back to life by delivering a shock to his chest. Later, while showing Mulder the EKG recorded during the incident, Scully explains that the spike on the strip indicates some kind of

"electrical intervention [that] started his heart." Now, you may consider this obsessively picayune nitpicking, but—according to my medical sources—it's impossible to "start" a human heart with an electrical jolt. I know you've seen it on television a million times, but that little box with the paddles isn't called a "heart-starter," it's called a "defibrillator." And it's *called* that for a reason! It uses an electric shock to knock down a heart that's "fibrillating" into a steady rhythm. In fact, the EKG that Scully holds is correct. It shows rapid, irregular contractions of Kiveat's heart. The normally precise Dr. Scully should have noted that the electrical intervention *defibrillated* his heart, since his heart obviously hadn't *stopped*. It just wasn't maintaining a steady rhythm.

⊠ Sharon Kiveat is mistaken in the testimony she gives against Oswald, but given that her husband has just had a heart attack, it's understandable. She says that the day after Jack Hammond died, Oswald told her he had "dangerous powers." But dialogue earlier in the episode indicates that Mulder and Scully arrived in Connerville the day after Hammond died, and they appear to interview Oswald on that same day after progressing quickly from the autopsy to the crime scene to Kiveat's garage. In addition, when Sharon Kiveat strides into the garage just *before* Mulder and Scully arrive for the interview, Oswald cryptically refers to "those things that I said yesterday" as he speaks with her. The proper timeline appears to be: On September 12, Oswald tells Kiveat about his powers and that evening kills Hammond. The next morning, on September 13, Mulder and Scully arrive; Oswald tries to tell Sharon Kiveat not to say anything about his powers, and Mulder and Scully interview Oswald. (Unless, of course, Mulder and Scully went fishing for an entire day after visiting the crime scene and prior to their interview of Oswald!)

GREAT MOMENTS

Great scene at the end in the confrontation between Scully and Oswald. It feels like both of them are about to explode when Sharon Kiveat steps in to sacrifice herself and call a truce.

☒ Scully has been hanging around Mulder *too* long. When the sheriff lets Oswald go because there's no hard evidence that the young man can channel electricity, Scully just stands there with the attitude, "I'm right. I just know it. And you should take my word for it." Why not tell the sheriff about the fulgurite with the shoeprint? Isn't *that* "hard" evidence?

☒ After Sharon Kiveat agrees to go with Oswald, why doesn't Scully follow them out? In fact, Scully is strangely absent until after the fireworks at the end of the episode. (Rest-room break, maybe?)

Equipment Oddities

☒ The episode begins with Jack Hammond picking a fight with Oswald over a game in a video arcade. Oswald shuts off all the lights and then activates the jukebox. Nervously, Hammond withdraws and escapes to his car. Then the radio comes on, playing the same song that plays on the jukebox. Twisting the tuning knob makes no difference, and in short order, Oswald has shorted out the car and cooked Hammond's heart. The last two displays of power seem reasonable, but the music on the radio is troublesome. Presumably Oswald is somehow transmitting the music to the car radio—which would require Oswald to emit radio waves on all frequencies simultaneously. Or he is directly manipulating the coils on the car's speakers, using the varying magnetic fields of the jukebox's speakers as a guide. Given Oswald's less-than-blinding intelligence, does this seem like something he could do?

☒ On a hunch, I strolled down to my local video arcade and started checking the high scores. As I suspected, high scores are called "high scores" for a reason. They show . . . the *scores* (or, the number of rounds won in a row in the case of ninja-kung-fu-neck-twisting-heart-rip-ping-mano-a-mano-mortal-combat-type games). Interestingly enough, the video game that Oswald plays the night he fries Hammond doesn't keep a record of high scores. It keeps a record of high *dates and times!* Why? Well, if the machine just listed the high scores, Mulder and Scully would not have discovered that Oswald was in the arcade the night that Hammond died! (No doubt the machine was programmed by the pixies of Out There.)

☒ You might recall that in "Conduit," Mulder said that sand fuses into glass at 2,500 degrees Fahrenheit. That's hot! So why doesn't the sole on Oswald's army boot melt when the fulgurite forms beneath his heel?

Continuity and Production Problems

☒ Not a nit, just an observation. This episode has just about the most blatant "boys will be boys" shot I've ever seen. (And I suppose it *is* justifiable, given that it's supposed to be from Oswald's perspective and he is, of course, a boy. Still, I would imagine that cameraman had some fun shooting this one!) As Oswald works under a car in his boss's garage, Sharon Kiveat comes stalking toward the camera. With the lens set low under the car, all we see is legs and heels heading straight in our direction. Then the camera rolls out and pans up to take the shot *straight up* her filmy skirt! (No doubt the director needed several takes on that one to get it just right! Still, I do hasten to add that the creators haven't been even remotely as exploitative with their female actors as most other shows on television, and they certainly have provided a healthy share of "for the girls" footage as well: Mulder in boxers, Mulder in Speedo, Skinner in underwear. . . .)

Clyde Bruckman's Final Repose

PLOT SUMMARY

Investigating a serial killer who preys on professional prognosticators, Mulder and Scully travel to the Twin Cities. They soon learn that The Stupendous Yappi—a "renowned" psychic—is working on the case as well. Even Mulder is unimpressed as Yappi gyrates.

That night, however, an old insurance salesman finds a body in his Dumpster, and Mulder quickly concludes that Clyde Bruckman is the real thing. Strangely enough, Bruckman's psychic gift—a gift he would love to "give" back—is almost entirely limited to the foreknowledge of how a person will die. He also can sense a vague impression or two about the killer, but little else. Even stranger, the killer knows Bruckman is receiving these impressions. After Bruckman receives a death threat from the killer, Mulder and Scully hide him at the very hotel where the killer works as a bellhop. Rushing out to the latest crime scene, Mulder and Scully even bump into him as he delivers a meal to Bruckman's room! Enthralled to meet Bruckman, the killer finally learns the reason he has committed the brutal crimes. As if it's obvious, Bruckman tells the bellhop that he kills people because he's a homicidal maniac.

Thankfully, Mulder and Scully return in time to end the killer's rampage, but Bruckman has had enough. Returning home, he commits suicide.

Onscreen Locations

- ☒ St. Paul
- ☒ North Minneapolis
- ☒ Le Damfino Hotel

Ruminations

This is a fabulous episode! The first of my three favorite episodes of the third season of The X-Files (which I personally think is the best season thus far despite its lurchings into gore). Kudos to the creators for this one. Very well done!

Others have noted the multiplicity of inside jokes in this episode. I'll only call your attention to the few additional ones that a slightly compulsive nitpicker would notice. The first occurs as Bruckman listens to the winning numbers in the lotto drawing. Putting them in numerical order, the winning numbers are 8, 12, 38, 40 and 44. From Bruckman's ticket we see he picked the numbers 9, 13, 37, 39, 41, 45! In other words, he's off by one on every number!

There's also a wonderful homage to "Beyond the Sea" in this episode as Mulder tests Bruckman's psychic ability. You may recall that near the beginning of "Beyond the Sea" Mulder tests Luther Lee Boggs's psychic ability by handing him a piece of blue cloth—purportedly from a crime victim. Boggs makes a grand show of producing "clues" to solve the case, only to have Mulder retort that he tore the cloth from his New York Knicks T-shirt that morning and it has nothing to do with the crime. Now come with me to this episode as Mulder tests Bruckman. After a time Scully arrives and calls Mulder into the hall. Bruckman is in the background with a wadded-up piece of blue cloth pressed against his forehead, doing his impression of the Amazing Karnak, when suddenly Bruckman yells that the cloth came from

Mulder's New York Knicks T-shirt. Mulder hesitates but then replies, "miss" (to indicate that Bruckman was wrong).

Plot Oversights

🗙 After the opening credits, local police discuss the case at the most recent crime scene. They begin to speak of the "help" that the lead investigator has recruited for the case. We find out later that they are talking about the Stupendous Yappi, but the dialogue is very cleverly written to make it sound like they are discussing Mulder. At one point, however, a detective comments that he heard the "help" is a bit unorthodox. While this description fits Mulder, it strains when applied to Yappi. After all, when was the last time you heard of an "orthodox *psychic*"? (No readings on Saturday, maybe?)

🗙 After police find a body floating in Glenview Lake—just as Bruckman predicted—Scully is *still* unimpressed. She muses that perhaps Bruckman is just lucky. In another city this statement might have merit, but this is the Twin Cities area. There's a reason Minnesota is known as the land of ten thousand lakes. In my handy-dandy *Rand McNally Road Atlas,* I count more than *130* named lakes in the St. Paul-Minneapolis area alone.

🗙 A few minor items. When Mulder comes to

the hotel room where Bruckman is held for safe-keeping, we see that Scully hasn't latched the door. Why not? Isn't Bruckman's life in danger? Also, when Bruckman tells Mulder of his recurring dream, he says he's lying naked in a field, and moments later, mentions bugs attacking him. But in the footage shown of this event? Not naked. No bugs. (My gratitude to the creators for the former.)

🗙 Bruckman meets the killer when the killer brings a meal to Bruckman's room as part of his employment as a bellhop. Scully realizes this a short time later and rushes back to the hotel in broad daylight. In addition, Mulder confronts the bellhop in the hotel's deserted kitchen. Let's put this together. It's during the day. There is room service, and no one's in the kitchen with Mulder. Hmmm.

Changed Premises

🗙 Upon entering a crime scene, Mulder is told by a detective that they suspect the work of Satanists because the eyes and entrails of the victim have been left behind. Mulder retorts that Satanists usually take the eyes and leave the body. Then he adds, "and not in anything but modern myths." Obviously Mulder has forgotten about the events of "Die Hand Die Verletzt." In that episode, a practitioner of the black arts named Mrs. Paddock visited Milford Haven, New Hampshire. In her first act, she killed a young man and extracted his heart and eyes. (I personally don't have any problem identifying her as a Satanist.)

Equipment Oddities

🗙 The lotto ticket that Bruckman purchases contains a few oddities. First, it's labeled "LOTTO 5." This would indicate that players pick five numbers in this particular gambling incarnation. Why then does Bruckman have *six* numbers on his ticket? Also, the ticket carries a date of

THIRD SEASON

191

Clyde Bruckman's
Final Repose

October 9, 1995. But screen text clearly identifies this episode as transpiring from September 16 to 21. Now, perhaps Bruckman could purchase a lotto ticket several weeks in advance, but how can he listen to the winning numbers for that ticket on the radio in the middle of September?!

I'd like to know where Scully got her cordless phone. Seeing an advertisement for the Stupendous Yappi as the episode concludes, Scully becomes enraged and throws her handset at the television. At the exact moment of impact, the television shuts off. Since the telephone strikes the center of the screen, it's unlikely that it hit a button on the set itself. And it doesn't seem reasonable that Scully would have enough time to grab the remote as the handset hurled across the room to hit the power during the great collision. The only reasonable explanation is that the phone has a built-in remote control. When it hit the set, the power button just happened to depress, thereby turning off the television. A phone with a remote. I kind of like that idea.

"Mr. Bruckman, there are hits and there are misses and then there are misses."

—**Scully** *to Bruckman after he tells her they will end up in bed together for his death. I love the look on Scully's face as she gently attempts to tell him that there's no chance that is going to happen. (Even though it does at the end of the episode!)*

Clyde Bruckman's Final Repose

The List

Onscreen Locations

☒ East Point State Penitentiary, Leon County, Florida

Ruminations

Well, they all can't be winners, can they? This episode has a few too many maggots crawling across rotten flesh as far as I'm concerned, but then again, I'm just the nitpicker. Unfortunately, the third season has even more graphic episodes yet to come (not to mention some of the episodes at the beginning of season four).

Plot Oversights

☒ Supposedly Neech has studied all the world's religions. In his final speech, however, he seems to imply that Muslims believe in reincarnation by quoting Allah as saying that the spirit shall rise again and be reborn into *this* life. Either Neech is in error or I missed that aspect of Islam when I studied it in Comparative Religions.

☒ In addition, Neech employs an interesting turn of phrase when he speaks of the men he will execute. Just before two thousand volts of electricity surge through his body, Neech proclaims, "These men will die *righteous* deaths." Now, *normally* if a person dies a righteous death, that's a good thing. He or she gets to go on to the happy place. I'm wondering if Neech got himself worked up into a lather and just misspoke. (Wouldn't *that* be a kicker?! Here's this guy who's *supposed* to be giving people the

PLOT SUMMARY Strapped to the electric chair in a Florida prison, Napoleon "Neech" Manley uses his final words to declare that he will return and avenge his death by killing five men. Unimpressed, the warden tells the executioner to fry Neech. Two days later, a prison guard lies dead in Neech's former cell, and Mulder decides to investigate. Given the security on death row, it seems unlikely that a prisoner could have done it. Then a second guard dies, and his decapitated body is found in the warden's office.

On a hunch, Mulder convinces the warden to give him the name of the executioner. (It's normally a secret, known only to three men at the prison.) Mulder and Scully quickly discover that whoever is murdering the men somehow learned the executioner's identity and killed him as well. For a time, suspicion falls on a prisoner guard named Parmelly. Parmelly has been carrying on an illicit affair with Neech's wife. But as Mulder and Scully arrive at the wife's home to arrest Parmelly, Neech appears and tricks the woman into shooting Parmelly—thereby sending herself to jail for murder.

Mulder and Scully head back to Washington, D.C., empty-handed. As they leave, Neech appears a final time and forces the warden to drive his car into a tree.

willies at the moment of his execution when all of a sudden this phrase "righteous deaths" pops out of his mouth. You have to wonder if his neurons weren't backpedaling *big time* when the power hit. "Wait. No! *That's not what I meant!* I meant. . . ." Bzzzzzzzzt.)

☒ Mulder's getting a little sloppy with his multimedia presentations. He usually has everything in place and ready to go before he starts his talk, but in this episode he has to load a slide in the middle of his monologue. And I would remind you that for this "X-chat," he had only . . . um . . . let's see (counting on my fingers) . . . three, *three* slides—including the one he loaded! (He couldn't put the third one in when he loaded the other two?!)

X I'm all for strong, self-directed, courageous women—women who can look danger in the face, women who aren't intimidated by their surroundings, women who don't wander willy-nilly through life sniffing at every shadow. But come on, Scully is just plain *ditzy* at one point in this episode. She's on "Q" block, *death row,* and she wanders away, *alone,* into the *showers!* Does this seem like an intelligent thing to do? Isn't this the one place you probably *do not* want to go? (Scully's blonde roots must be growing out. Sorry, sorry. *Really* sorry about that one. It was uncalled for.)

X Desperate for answers, the warden beats up a prisoner named Roque in the Q block showers. He wants to know who's on Neech Manley's list. Here's what I find strange. When the warden does this a second time, with another prisoner, the prisoners on Q block can hear the scuffle. As they should! After all, the shower room is all hard surfaces, and it sits adjacent to the cells. The sounds *would* ping around freely. So how come John Speranza—another death-row inmate—doesn't at least hint to Mulder that the

warden killed Roque? There is no question in my mind that the warden and Roque could be heard out in the cell block.

X Not a nit, just an observation. At the end of the episode, Mulder parks the car on the edge of the road, forcing Scully to walk through a patch of scruffy grass to get to the blacktop. If Florida is anything like Missouri, Scully is *not* going to be happy with Mulder in the next few hours. Her ankles are going to be covered with chigger bites!

Continuity and Production Problems

X It looks like the creators reused or rebuilt at least part of the prison set. The staircase looks just like the staircase that Mulder and Scully descend in "Eve" when they visit Eve 6.

Trivia Questions

❶ When was Neech convicted?

❷ What was the name of Neech's lawyer?

Trivia Answers
❶ 1984.
❷ Danny Charez.

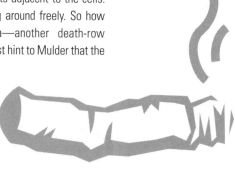

2SHY

Onscreen Locations

☒ Cleveland, Ohio
☒ Cuyahoga County Morgue
☒ Cleveland Police Department, 1st District
☒ FBI Regional Office, Computer Crime Section
☒ Cuyahoga County Jail

Ruminations

The date on this episode should be simple. After all, Scully announces it as she begins her autopsy of Lauren Mackalvey. Unfortunately, there are two items that call into question the date Scully recites. First, a date of August 29 would put this episode before the events in "D.P.O." and "Clyde Bruckman's Final Repose" according to their stated dates, and not after. Violating the air date order of the episodes wouldn't be too bad in itself, except there's another date given in this episode that contradicts the one provided by Scully. Handed the results of a DNA search of the known-offenders database, Scully opens the folder, and the memo inside carries a date of October 27, 1995. I find it hard to believe that this case stretched for two months! If so, Mulder and Scully left Cleveland for a time to pursue the cases mentioned above as well as to investigate Neech's slaughter during "The List." Personally, I vote for the latter date. Maybe Scully just had a brain glitch.

As I've said, it's the details that I love about The X-Files. In the final scene of the episode, Mulder slides a piece of paper in front of Incanto and says it contains the names of forty-seven women from five states. Mulder wants to

PLOT SUMMARY A call from the local police brings Mulder and Scully to Cleveland, Ohio. A body has been found, identified only by a driver's license as Lauren Mackalvey. It is coated in a slimy brew of viscous hydrochloric acid and pepsin—a digestive enzyme. Oddly enough, the remains are also lacking a large amount of fat. An interview with Mackalvey's roommate provides Mulder with the first solid lead. The night before, Mackalvey had a date with a man who wrote her eloquent E-mail messages that included passages from little-known Italian poetry. Working with police detective Alan Cross, Scully puts together a list of area scholars who would have access to such literature, and a manhunt begins door-to-door.

Unfortunately, Cross's portion of the list includes a translator named Virgil Incanto. Unable to produce body fat, Incanto must "harvest" it from others—often finding his victims among the "big and beautiful" lonely-hearts club. In short order, Cross is dead, and once the detective fails to report to the station, a new search commences. It eventually leads police to Incanto's apartment. Incanto's computer then yields the names of Incanto's potential victims. And at the home of Ellen Kaminsky, Mulder and Scully even manage to catch Incanto in the act—putting an end to his constant diet of fat-filled treats.

know if Incanto killed any of them. Incanto pleads guilty to all. But the really nice thing about this scene is that there are, indeed, forty-seven names on the list!

One final thought before the nitpicking begins. This episode presents a truly tragic case of missed opportunities. If Incanto had had but a small measure of human compassion, he could have lived a full and wonderful life even with his "special" condition. Indeed, he could have lived a full and wonderful life because of his special condition. After all, many old-style fast-food restaurants in small towns still use lard to fry their wares. The old grease is collected in a barrel in the back and hauled away to be recycled or worse. Incanto could have provided a valuable service to humanity by simply waiting for the lard to congeal and then sitting down to partake with a spoon. And even if he had more selfish motivations in mind, just think of the stature his condition would have garnered him in the right circles. He sucks fats, for crying out loud! Do you have any idea what the men and women of Beverly Hills pay for that service?! This guy could have surrounded himself with beautiful women all . . . day . . . long! Just a little slit, in goes his straw, slurp, slurp, out comes the straw . . . cha-ching! Three thousand dollars! Not only that, he could have read them Italian poetry as they recuperated and had them drooling on him! It's a missed opportunity, I tell you!

Geographical Inconsistencies

⌧ The episode opens with a camera pan from the sky to Mackalvey's car. The automobile is parked on a dock. There's a large body of water directly ahead and the skyscrapers of Cleveland, Ohio, in the distance. Except . . . the commercial district of Cleveland is on the banks of Lake Erie, and according to Daniel B. Case, there are no islands in Cleveland's harbor, so there's no way this car could be sitting "across the bay" from that city!

Plot Oversights

⌧ Who rolled the prostitute after she died? When Ellen Kaminsky fails to show for dinner, Incanto attempts to harvest a hooker. Another

"couple" interrupts him, and he runs away. A close-up shows us that the prostitute lies on her back. Yet, the next morning, when Scully lifts the plastic to examine the body, we see that the prostitute now lies on her stomach.

⌧ Following Mulder's suggestion, Scully assists with the compilation of a list of scholars in the Cleveland area. Incanto appears on this list. Having compiled the list of thirty-eight names, our fearless FBI agents then divvie up the names with the local police and start to canvass. Might there be a simple way to narrow this list a bit? Mulder knows that the killer was in Aberdeen, Mississippi, only a few months ago. I wonder if the Aberdeen Police Department would have been willing to prepare a similar list of scholars. If Incanto's name had appeared on both lists . . . well, it would have been a short show!

⌧ Apparently Incanto moves a lot, but his apartment is loaded with books. Are these borrowed? Or does he pack them all up when he moves to a new town to begin a new round of lipo-slurping?

⌧ Did anyone else notice that Incanto apparently didn't avail himself of the detective's less-than-ripped physique? Then again, maybe Incanto's a hetero-fat-sucker.

⌧ Okay, so let's talk about Incanto's identity. According to Mulder, he has no record at the Department of Motor Vehicles. He has no birth certificate, no Social Security number, not even a bank account. Mulder goes on to say that Incanto works as a freelance translator of Italian literature and his publisher pays him in cashier's checks. This guy must be one amazing translator for his publisher to go to all that trouble. Now, granted, payment in cashier's checks isn't that big a deal, but the publishing company has to account for those expenditures in some way. Normally the company would keep a record of the payments made to Incanto and issue a Form 1099 at the end of the year—with a copy submitted to the Internal Revenue Service. But if Incanto has no Social Security number, the company could not process the 1099! So . . . for the publisher to expense out the payments made to Incanto, its accounting department would have to bury the money someplace else. Now, why would a publishing company go to all that trouble and risk an audit by the IRS? Is there a severe shortage among translators of Italian literature? Does Incanto work really, *really* cheap? And how did Incanto explain to the publisher in the first place that he didn't *have* a Social Security number? *Everyone* who is a citizen of the United States is supposed to have an SSN. Also, what about the rental agreement? How did Incanto get a place to live without identification? Does he have fake identification, or does he just look for lonely landladies and smile a lot?

In addition, Incanto's approach with respect to his victims seems to take a very strange new direction just prior to this episode. In Aberdeen, Mississippi, Incanto stalked members of a lonely-hearts club. In this episode, he uses the Internet. But to establish an account with an Internet Service Provider (ISP) he would have to supply a name and address. (Apparently, Mulder didn't get either after contacting the ISP and inquiring about Incanto's account under the name "2SHY.") Not only that, Incanto uses one of his victims' credit cards to establish the account! Surely a man as intelligent as Incanto would realize that at *some* point *someone* would discover that the credit card was stolen! Most Internet accounts are billed monthly. After the Aberdeen victim's death, *somebody* would have either reported the cards as stolen or canceled the accounts. (It they didn't, it was *very* sloppy police work.) In short, Incanto seems to adopt tactics that make it much more difficult to keep his identity a secret just as Mulder and Scully waltz into the case. While there is a share of anonymity on the Internet, gaining access to that anonymity requires a fair amount of disclo-

sure! (My guess is Incanto had just received his 153rd free diskette from America On-Line and he finally decided to give it a try!)

🅧 At Kaminsky's apartment, Mulder kicks in the door, and he and Scully commence a search. But for some reason, Mulder walks right by the light switch panel beside the front door of the apartment, preferring instead to stumble around in the dark! (It's true that Mulder later tries the light in the bedroom and finds it doesn't work, but how did he know that the light in the living room wasn't even worth the attempt?)

🅧 In the early part of the episode we learn that Incanto's goo is composed mainly of hydrochloric acid, and it's twice as strong a stomach acid. (It does, after all, start dissolving flesh on contact.) So how come it doesn't burn Scully's fingers when she peels it away from Kaminsky's mouth?

🅧 It's a good thing that Scully's so beautiful. Otherwise Incanto would have gooped up her mouth and nose like all the other woman. Notice his approach as he has the lovely Dr. Scully down on the floor. He hovers over her face. He's obviously trying to hack up a big enough ball of goo so it will just fall into place and seal her mouth. *WHY?!* All the other times he's been in this situation, we see him lunging at his prey like a paramedic fresh out of CPR class! I can say with some assurance that if he had pounced and proceeded to slather his guck all over Scully's face, she would have been *too* distracted to even *think* about grabbing the scissors. The only thing I can figure out is the poor guy was just plain *intimidated* once he got up close and personal. No doubt he was thinking, "Wow! Look at that flawless skin and those gorgeous eyes. And that hair! I mean, it's . . . it's almost *too* red!" (*MEANWHILE* . . . I'm shouting at my television, "Come on, buddy, *kiss her!* What are you *waiting* for?!")

THIRD SEASON

Trivia Questions

🅵 What poem does Incanto want to read to Ellen Kaminsky?

🅶 Where does Ellen Kaminsky live?

2SHY

Trivia Answers
🅵 *E Cazzone.*
🅶 658 South Hudson Avenue, Apartment 23.

X And what about Incanto's consumption rate? At the very beginning of the episode, Lauren Mackalvey states that she and Incanto have been corresponding for three months. I take this to mean that Incanto came to Cleveland at about this time. (Mulder supports this theory by telling Scully that four women disappeared in Aberdeen "a couple of months" ago.) Yet there obviously hasn't been a rash of disappearances in Cleveland, because *somebody* would have mentioned it during the investigation. It appears, then, that Incanto killed four women in Aberdeen, came to Cleveland, took a three-month hiatus, and has now begun to kill again. *However,* the episode consistently presents his need as nearly *insatiable.* He kills Mackalvey—extracting more than *forty-three pounds* of fat from her—and in very short order tries to meet with Kaminsky to continue his binge. In fact, his need is so great that he commandeers a prostitute when Kaminsky doesn't appear for their date. In addition, the end of the episode shows us Incanto after only a week on a nonfat diet, and he's flaking everywhere! After only a week! Doesn't this imply that he needs a somewhat steady and generous intake? Or is he like Tooms? After he devours four generously-proportioned women, does his metabolism purr along contentedly for a bit? (And even if it does, the guy looks to be about thirty-five. The end of the episode suggests he only consumed approximately fifty women. At a rate of four every three months, that's twelve a year. That means his trail of slaughter only goes back about four years. What did he do before that? Buy fifty-gallon drums of beef tallow?)

Equipment Oddities

X The computers in this episode are very odd. On the monitors, we see features that are *distinctively* Macintosh. Note the title bar on the windows of both Incanto and Ellen Kaminsky's computers. See the little box to the left. See the horizontal lines, broken by the title in the center of the bar. *That's* Macintosh. Yet these very same computers look just like PC clones, and the mice have three buttons. I suppose that both Incanto and Kaminsky might be using bootlegged Mac clones, but that seems . . . *odd.*

X And speaking of Incanto's very odd computer, it apparently scrolls *down* in text interface mode! Every computer I've ever worked with scrolls *up* in text interface mode.

Continuity and Production Problems

X Demonstrating what Incanto's brew has done to Mackalvey's skeleton, Scully holds a small bone in a pair of forceps and crushes it. Watch the position of the forceps in the wide shot and compare it to the close-up. As the shots change, the forceps jump back and forth on the bone.

X There appears to be a bad edit in this episode. During the interview with Mackalvey's roommate, Mulder learns that Mackalvey met "2SHY"—Incanto's screen name—through the Internet. Mulder then asks to use her phone. As soon as he starts to dial, we see Scully answer. Mulder tells her that the killer from Aberdeen has apparently begun using an online service to find new victims. Scully asks how he made the connection to the murders in Aberdeen, and Mulder states that he just got off the phone with the service provider. He has learned that 2SHY's account was opened with an Aberdeen victim's credit card. Unfortunately, there is no time at which Mulder could have placed the call to the service provider in the sequence of events we are shown. Either he's lying, or a piece of the episode was cut (probably a short segment showing Mulder giving his badge number to the online service). If the episode had then proceeded to the shot of Scully's cell phone ringing, everything would make sense!

ROUGH BLUEPRINTS OF MULDER'S AND SCULLY'S APARTMENTS

Never one to miss out on a chance to look foolish, I thought it might be fun to give you my "guesstimate" on the layout of the domiciles rented by our favorite pair of FBI agents. As I reviewed the episodes for this *Guide,* I jotted down a note here and there on the various camera angles used for scenes shot in Mulder and Scully's apartments. From these I composited the following rough blueprints—and they are *rough.* The room sizes and ratios are all approximate. (Actual mileage may vary.) For your perusing pleasure, I have also included pointers on the blueprints to show the camera angles I chose and labeled each with a number. In the reference section below each drawing I have listed the episode and the scene that corresponds to that particular camera angle so you can look them up yourself and check me out!

Mulder's Apartment

42-2630 Hegal Place
Alexandria, Virginia

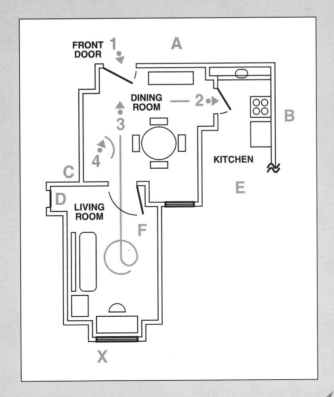

References

1 "Anasazi": The Lone Gunmen come to Mulder's apartment to tell him that the Thinker wants to meet with him.

2 "Deep Throat": Mulder cooks just before Scully calls to say she's discovered that Ellens Air Force Base is a UFO hot spot.

3 "Grotesque": Scully comes to Mulder's apartment and finds pictures of gargoyles everywhere. The camera gives us a beautiful 360-degree panorama of Mulder's living room.

4 "E.B.E.": Scully comes to Mulder's apartment moments after Mulder discovers a surveillance device in an electrical outlet. Pay close attention to the right side of your screen just before the scene cuts to Mulder's living room. Is that a bare wall stud? Did the edge of the set accidently get included in the shot?

Notes

A This is the area where the infamous "Hall Extension Zone" exists. (See "The Blessing Way" and "Herrenvolk" for more information.)

B Just before the Lone Gunmen beat on Mulder's door near the beginning of "Anasazi," there's a brief shot of Mulder standing in his kitchen. On the wall behind him there is an elongated patch of light in the shape of a window. See "E" below.

C Tooms gains entrance to Mulder's apartment in "Tooms" via a wall vent near this location.

D This door either leads to a closet or is another entrance to Mulder's apartment. In the first four seasons, it is never used. (In fact, I believe "Grotesque" is the only episode that even shows the door!)

E Most likely, Mulder's bathroom is located in this area. Given the patch of light mentioned above in "B," the back wall of this area appears to be fairly close, making the room somewhat small. There is a scene near the end of "War of the Coprophages" that shows Mulder in bed, and the woodwork in the room is very similar to the woodwork in Mulder's apartment. Could this scene take place in location "E," and does it show that Mulder has a bedroom? Well, we get only limited views of the bed and the television, so it's impossible to say for sure. And Eddie Van Blundht's statement in "Small Potatoes" seems to indicate that Mulder does *not* have a bedroom. (Looking around Mulder's apartment, Van Blundht throws up his hands in frustration and wonders where he is supposed to sleep. Evidently Mulder uses what is supposed to be his bedroom for a living room.)

F The door between Mulder's entry area and his living room disappears in "Sleepless" and never returns.

X This is the window where Mulder places the masking tape "X."

Scully's Apartment

(Location unknown. Building has the number "1419" on the front. See "Ascension.")

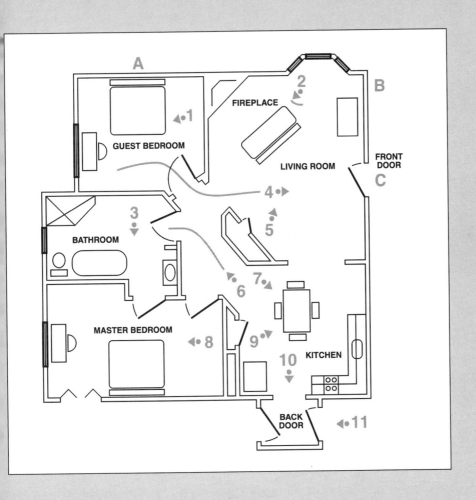

A

B

FIREPLACE

◄•1

GUEST BEDROOM

FRONT
DOOR

C

LIVING ROOM

4•►

3
•
▼

BATHROOM

5

7•◄

•►6

MASTER BEDROOM

◄•8

9•►

10
•
▼

KITCHEN

BACK
DOOR

◄•11

References

▌ "Anasazi": The morning after Mulder spends the night at Scully's apartment, he calls her from this bedroom to accuse her of betraying him.

▐ "Squeeze": Scully races from her bathroom to find her gun after realizing that Tooms is about to attack.

3   "Squeeze": Scully makes final preparations to take her bath.

4   "Anasazi": Finding Mulder at her front door, Scully helps him to her guest bedroom and makes him lie down.

5   "Beyond the Sea": William Scully taunts his daughter about leaving up her Christmas tree all year.

6   "Squeeze": Scully calls Mulder's answering machine to say that she's furious with Tom Colton.

7   "Beyond the Sea": Scully and her father banter after supper.

8   "War of the Coprophages": Scully packs a few things before joining Mulder in Miller's Grove, Massachusetts.

9   "War of the Coprophages": Scully cleans her weapon at her kitchen table.

10   "Beyond the Sea": Scully escorts her parents to the door.

11   "Beyond the Sea": Scully's parents leave her apartment.

Notes

A   This wall suddenly sprouts a window near the end of "Tempus Fugit." The creators use a camera angle very similar to number 4 above, so it's easy to compare it to the footage in "Anasazi."

B   As Scully gets up to answer the call from her mother about the death of her father near the beginning of "Beyond the Sea," the camera clearly reveals a door at this location. Since Scully didn't have a front door at this point in the series, it is likely that this door was supposed to indicate a closet. (The front door, "C," didn't appear until "Colony.")

The Walk

Onscreen Locations

▪ Army Hospital Psychiatric Ward, Ft. Evanston, Maryland

▪ Ft. Evanston officer's gym

▪ Callahan residence, Rosslyn, Virginia

Ruminations

There are some beautiful graphics in this episode as Trimble's astral projection attacks. My favorite occurs as Trimble drowns General Callahan's adjutant, Captain Draper.

Geographical Inconsistencies

▪ Fort Evanston, Maryland, doesn't exist.

Plot Oversights

▪ The medical doctor who interviews Stans at the beginning of the episode comments that Stans has attempted to kill himself three times in the past three weeks. So why isn't Stans on suicide watch"? Shortly after this meeting, he walks out of his room—traveling all the way down to the hydrotherapy room in the *subbasement*—and no one makes a move to stop him!

▪ Several times, Lieutenant Colonel Victor Stans is addressed as "Lieutenant Colonel." I believe the proper army protocol is to address him simply as "Colonel."

▪ Although the episode never confirms the reason that Trimble's associate Quinton Freely

PLOT SUMMARY The story of Lieutenant Colonel Victor Stans brings Mulder and Scully to Fort Evanston. Stans recently lost his family in a house fire. He claims a phantom attacker has destroyed his life and refuses to let him commit suicide. Mulder finds the story compelling. Scully chalks it up to post-traumatic stress syndrome. Then those closest to the base commander begin to die as well. General Callahan's adjutant dies first; next, his son, and, finally, his wife—all dead by an unseen hand.

In fact, Sergeant Leonard Trimble is behind the attacks. Trimble lost his arms and legs in the Gulf War, and though he tries to pretend his revenge isn't personal—speaking of the soldiers who died or were injured in the war—the truth is he wants someone to pay for *his* injuries. He wants all those responsible to feel what it's like to lose everything they care about. Somehow Trimble has learned the art of astral projection, and he is using this ability to murder.

Through Stans, Callahan eventually learns the identity of his tormentor. He storms into Trimble's room but can't go through with the planned execution. Enraged, Trimble sends his phantom to attack the general. Thankfully, Stans acts quickly—suffocating Trimble with a pillow to save his commanding officer's life.

takes mail from the homes of his victims, dialogue strongly suggests that Trimble needs a connection to a given location before he can project himself there. Strangely enough, General Callahan reports to Mulder and Scully that his answering machine goes wacky at his home twice *before* Freely appears to take Callahan's mail.

And speaking of Callahan's mail, either the post office did a *really* lousy job delivering the letter that Freely shows Trimble, or the episodes have suddenly begun going backward in time! (Aaaah!) The postmark on the envelope looks like July 1995. But we should be somewhere in October or November during this episode (if the air date order is the order in which the cases occurred).

Why didn't Mulder send the tape in Callahan's answering machine to the audio boys in Washington?

After interviewing Trimble, Mulder tells Scully that they need to call Callahan and make sure he stays away from his home. For some reason, Mulder and Scully wait until they leave the base and are en route somewhere in their car before doing so. In the meantime, unfortunately, Trimble kills Callahan's wife.

The end of the episode shows Stans delivering the mail at the army base. This guy is a lieutenant colonel, and he's *delivering* mail? Did Callahan strip him of his commission? Did Stans always fantasize about being the mailboy? This is simply not the kind of job that a lieutenant colonel performs!

Equipment Oddities

Mulder has the coolest gizmos. In this episode he has a pocket tape recorder that doesn't just rewind the tape when you press the rewind button, it can actually play a tape in reverse so you can check for backward masking!

Realizing that Stans wasn't fantasizing about a phantom attacker who wouldn't let him die, Callahan pulls a pistol from a drawer, snaps in the clip, and heads for the hospital. In Stans's room, he makes a show of putting the gun to his head and pulling the trigger several times. Nothing happens. From this, Callahan has con-

cluded that Trimble is preventing him from killing himself. However, moments later Callahan enters Trimble's room, and we see that the quadruple amputee is wide awake. I thought Trimble could only do his magic when he was in a trance! In addition, Callahan soon becomes incensed with Trimble's taunts and reaches up to rack the slide on the pistol.

Hold it!

I know I've mentioned "racking the slide" several times without explaining it, so let me take a moment to offer a quick tour of the standard semiautomatic pistol. Bullets are loaded into a clip that sits inside the handle. The actual firing chamber is forward from the top of the clip and resides at the very back of the barrel. The pistol is constructed so the top piece of metal can slide back and forth. This "slide" accomplishes several things when a round is fired. The expanding gases from the detonation of the charge in the shell send the slide backward, simultaneously opening the ejection port, lofting the spent shell into the air, and cocking the hammer. Then the recoil spring shoves the slide forward. The slide grabs the next round from the top of the clip and jams it into the back end of the barrel. This process continues until all the bullets in the clip are gone, at which point the slide locks back.

With this in mind, let's reexamine the scene above. General Callahan pulls out his pistol and snaps in the clip. Since he has stored the clip separate from the pistol, it is highly *unlikely* that there is a round already at the back of the barrel. After all, this is the normal, safe method for storing such a weapon. Callahan goes to Stans's room, puts the gun to his head, and pulls the trigger several times. This accomplishes nothing because *there is no bullet loaded into the barrel.* To load a round after inserting a new clip, you *have to manually pull back or "rack" the slide* ("Ah," you say, "but perhaps Callahan racked the slide when we weren't looking." If that were the case, then when Callahan racks the slide in Trimble's room, we would see the already-cham-

The Walk

bered bullet ejecting through the slot in the top of the weapon, just as we do when Mulder racks the slide on his pistol in "Little Green Men.") Without a bullet in the firing chamber, Callahan *can't possibly* commit suicide as he stands with the pistol to his head in Stans's room. All he'll do is snap the firing pin in his weapon! (And *that's* why you don't "dry-fire" a pistol.)

Continuity and Production Problems

X More clones! At the beginning of this episode, an army doctor interviews Stans. His double works for the NSA. We saw him in "Shadows."

X Sorry, I just don't buy the inclination angle on Callahan's pistol as he fires at the wall behind Trimble. I just can't see how a gun pointed down can send slugs into the wall *above* Trimble's head. (Unless of course, Callahan is using some of those famed "magic" bullets employed during the John F. Kennedy assassination!)

Trivia Questions

1 What is Trimble's room number in the hospital?

2 Where were Trimble's ashes buried?

Trivia Answers
1 G555.
2 Tannersville, Pennsylvania.

Oubliette

PLOT SUMMARY Working as an assistant to a photographer in Seattle, Washington, Carl Wade becomes infatuated with a teenager named Amy Jacobs and kidnaps her. At the same time, across town, Lucy Householder collapses at work, muttering the phrase that Wade mumbles as he spirits Amy from her home. Interestingly enough, Lucy was taken as a young girl as well and spent five years in captivity.

Mulder suspects some kind of empathic transference between Amy and Lucy, but Lucy is too emotionally scarred to assist with the case. Even worse, she quickly becomes a prime suspect when Amy's blood is found on her work uniform. Frightened by the events, Lucy runs. Somehow she finds her way to her former captor's house, the same house where Amy is being held. Unfortunately, Wade and Amy are gone, and when the FBI arrives, Lucy looks even more guilty. Still, she provides Mulder with enough clues to deduce Wade's location. Racing to a nearby river, Mulder and Scully find Wade holding his victim's head underwater—determined that no one will have her if he cannot. Mulder then shoots Wade, but neither he nor Scully can resuscitate Amy. Unexpectedly, Amy then comes back to life even as Lucy Householder drowns in the backseat of a car. Apparently Lucy gave herself so Amy could live.

Onscreen Locations

- ☒ Valley Woods High School, Seattle, Washington
- ☒ University Medical Center, Seattle, Washington
- ☒ FBI Regional Field Office, Seattle, Washington

- ☒ Bright Angel Halfway House
- ☒ Easton, Washington

Ruminations

Tracy Ellis does a fabulous job in her portrayal of Lucy Householder in this episode, giving us a woman who is at once ruthless in her apathy and yet self-sacrificial in her compassion.

Geographical Inconsistencies

☒ While looking at a map of Washington State, Mulder mentions "Interstate 12." There is no Interstate Highway 12 in the continental United States.

Plot Oversights

☒ I have to say I am *really* impressed with Larken Scholastic—the company that provides the school pictures for Valley Woods High School. The episode opens with the photographer taking class pictures as his assistant Carl Wade stares at Amy Jacobs. In the next scene, we see Wade at home with one of Amy's class pictures as he cuts it out and stands it beside one of his own. Here's what I found admirable. Halfway through the show, we learn that Amy's family never received her class pictures. (Obviously, Wade stole them.) *And,* in addition, we hear Scully tell Mulder that Wade was fired *the day after* the shoot at Valley Woods High. In other words, the Larken Scholastic photographer took the class pictures, developed the film, and made the enlargements all in one day so Wade could steal them before he got fired the next day?! Wow! (Of course, the other option would be to say that Wade broke in and stole the pictures later, but doesn't that sound like an interesting tidbit that Scully would mention as she tells Mulder about Wade being fired?)

☒ Follow the ticking stopwatch. Wade marches out to his car and starts the engine. Amy listens to him go, looks around, sees a pinhole of light, goes over to a blackened window, and rips away the paper. This takes about thirty seconds. Amy finds the basement window covered with boards. She rips away a board, tosses it to the floor, and turns back toward the window. This takes an additional five seconds or so. The episode cuts away to Mulder and Lucy. When it returns, Amy is removing the last remnants of the paper that covered the window. She pulls a second board. This takes about five seconds. She hears the car returning and begins yanking on the third board. This takes about five seconds. Wade gets out of the car and extracts several bags from the backseat. One of them bears the logo "Bilton's Photo." It appears that the creators wish to leave the impression that Wade went into town for photographic supplies.

The town must be *really* close! From the time that Wade's car pulls away until it returns, there's only about *forty-five* seconds. Not bad for a shopping spree.

☒ So, um, why doesn't Special Agent Kreski start CPR on Lucy when she flops over in the backseat of the car?

☒ Scully gives up much, *much* too quickly as Mulder attempts to revive Amy Jacobs. I'm told by those who know that Mulder and Scully *should* have continued the CPR until they were exhausted or until the paramedics arrived, especially given Amy's age and the fact that she drowned in *cold* water. In fact, an attempt lasting *forty-five minutes* under these circum-

stances would not be unreasonable. Yet Scully the medical doctor—Scully the highly trained agent—is ready to give up in fewer than *thirty seconds!* (Granted, it wouldn't be much of a show if the last forty-five minutes were spent trying to revive Amy Jacobs. But after creating a character as intelligent, compassionate, and disciplined as Scully, I do feel the creators have *some* responsibility to ensure that her behavior is not *grossly negligent.* I guess this one bothers me so much because the creators have Scully not only *not* doing her job but heckling Mulder to stop as well.)

☒ And speaking of this halfhearted attempt at CPR, it probably would have been a good idea to drain the water from Amy Jacobs's lungs before they began!

☒ There *has* to be something going on in Scully's personal life that has her extremely distracted in this episode! Not only does she give up almost immediately on resuscitating Amy Jacobs, she also hears the poor girl say that she's cold but does *nothing* about it! This is unbelievable! All these big, strong, brave, *coat-clad* FBI agents are standing around this young lady who's drenched to the bone—wearing only a nightgown—and they just march her off into the woods! Granted, some *guys* might be insensitive enough not to notice that the young lady could use a coat, but . . . *Scully?! Scully* can't figure out that the young lady should be kept warm?!

Equipment Oddities

☒ Oddness abounds with respect to the red splotch that follows Amy around the basement as Wade takes a roll of pictures. At first glance the splotch—which is circular, with a diameter of approximately two and one-half inches—looks like some kind of laser sight. But laser sights are usually small pinpricks of intense light. Not only that, the red splotch flashes just

Trivia Questions

❑ What is the name on the tow truck operators' work order?

❷ According to this episode, what highway runs through Easton, Washington?

like an indicator on a flash unit for a camera. In fact, the reverse-angle shots of Wade with the camera *do* show a flashing indicator on his flash. But, but, but . . . wouldn't the light from that indicator *diffuse* through the room? Has Wade rigged some kind of lens to focus the red light from the indicator, or is this some newfangled gizmo that I've never seen before?

Continuity and Production Problems

🅇 Sometimes the look of *The X-Files*—though *always* visually appealing—strains to make sense in real life. After Wade confines Amy to his basement, we see the darkness cut open by a small slot of light. Lit only in the meager, reflected illumination that this envelope-sized slit provides, Amy blinks at the intrusion. Then Wade's eyes appear in the slot, as if he's examining his prey. The imagery works well, but is there really any chance he could *see* Amy? Think about it. The slot provides the *only* light for the basement according to the establishing shot. Wade's head has obscured most of that. There's obviously a generous portion of light upstairs. Wade's eyes would be adjusted for that light level, not the light level in the basement. I just don't see any way that he could actually see her without cupping his hands around his eyes to force his pupils to dilate. (My guess is he was just trying to do his impersonation of Eugene Tooms. "Oooo. I'm a creepy guy. I'm a creepy guy." See "Tooms.")

🅇 Those clever creators tried to pull a fast one on us. In the scene where Wade takes pictures of Amy in the dark, freeze-frame on the third flash and you'll see that the visual-effects crew—instead of simply flashing Amy with a bright light—inserted several frames of the film's negative. (Then again, I suppose Wade could have rigged up a high-powered X-ray machine in addition to his camera equipment.

Perhaps he's not only a "creepy" guy but also has visions of being a "creepy *superman*" guy!)

🅇 Scully is practicing her sleight-of-hand technique again—this time with an umbrella. Keep your eye on it as Scully and two other agents come to arrest Lucy Householder. The agents approach the front door of Bright Angel Halfway House. Scully's umbrella is open and dutifully hovering over her head. Then the camera angle changes to give us the view from inside the halfway house: The umbrella is instantly closed and at Scully's side.

🅇 The photos of Amy found by the FBI at Wade's house are very interesting. They look like they come from the scene earlier when Amy is assaulted with brilliant flashes of light. Yet if you will freeze-frame during one of the brilliant flashes, you will see a much different image in terms of lighting than those shown in the prints. The flashes in the episode illuminate *everything*, washing both Amy and the walls an almost even white. The lighting in the prints is almost artistic. And in the case of the second picture, there's even a shadow over a portion of the young girl's face!

🅇 Looks like the bullet hole is missing from Carl Wade's jacket as he makes a grand showing of flopping in the water after Mulder shoots him.

🅇 At the end of the episode, Scully comes to see Mulder in Lucy Householder's room at the Bright Angel Halfway House. Crank up the volume and listen closely as Scully tells Mulder that the doctors want to keep Amy Jacobs for a day or two just to be sure. Here that ringing around the edges of Scully's voice? That's audio feedback! (Currently, I help run sound at my church. I am *too* familiar with that sound! Actually, it will be interesting to find out if this is a problem on the master tape of this episode or if it was something local to Springfield.)

Nisei

(Part 1 of 2)

Onscreen Locations

- ☒ Knoxville, Tennessee
- ☒ Allentown, Pennsylvania
- ☒ Substation C, Allentown, Pennsylvania
- ☒ Japanese Embassy, Washington, D.C.
- ☒ U.S. Coast Guard Headquarters, Newport News, Virginia
- ☒ Dept. of Oncology, Allentown Medical Center
- ☒ Office of Senator Richard Matheson, Washington, D.C.
- ☒ Quinnimont, West Virginia
- ☒ Edwards Terminal, Queensgate, Ohio

Ruminations

Welcome to the next round of intrigue! Now Mulder learns that Japanese war criminals are involved as well as German. And after her encounter with the congregation of women in Allentown, Scully must face the fact that something tangible and sinister happened during the months she can't recall. Though still unknown, the events of her abduction have grown beyond the merely bothersome.

Unanswered Questions

☒ Just what *was* the Japanese diplomat doing in Allentown? The episode seems to indicate that he killed Steven Zinnzser—the distributor of the alien autopsy video. But if he was sent solely as an assassin, why was he carrying top-secret intelligence information? Is this just another carrot that the conspirators are dangling in front of Mulder?

PLOT SUMMARY

A videotape advertised as an authentic alien autopsy leads Mulder and Scully to Allentown, Pennsylvania, where they find that the tape's distributor has been murdered by a high-ranking Japanese diplomat who is immune from prosecution. Riffling through the diplomat's briefcase, Mulder discovers satellite photos of a ship and a membership list for the local chapter of MUFON (Mutual UFO Network).

As Mulder returns to Washington to have the Lone Gunmen examine the pictures, Scully meets with several female members of MUFON. It's a disturbing encounter. They recognize her. They know she was taken ("Ascension"). They even know about the implant ("The Blessing Way").

Meanwhile—from Senator Matheson—Mulder learns of four Japanese scientists who died only weeks earlier. (They are the scientists on the "alien autopsy" video.) During World War II, all were part of a group known as 731—a group that conducted atrocious human experiments. Matheson hints that the experiments continue: monsters creating monsters. Eventually Mulder tracks down a mysterious boxcar and watches intently as some kind of being is loaded on board. At the same time, Mr. X suddenly appears to urge Scully to warn Mulder off the case.

Scully's call reaches Mulder as he stands on a bridge, watching the train with the boxcar pass underneath. Despite her alarm, he jumps.

Geographical Inconsistencies

☒ Queensgate, Ohio, doesn't exist.

Plot Oversights

⌧ No doubt the pixies of Out There had a hand in it, but isn't it fascinating that Zinnzser just *happens* to get killed as Mulder and Scully make their way to his house? Did someone find out that Mulder and Scully were on the way and dispatched the Japanese diplomat to take care of the situation? It seems incredible that Mulder could respond to an advertisement in a magazine, order a tape, wait for it to arrive, play it, decide to go to Allentown, and just by chance meet up with another individual who went through the same progression of steps in the same exact amount of time. For one thing, if that tape was so damaging, wouldn't the Japanese diplomat start out for Allentown only *moments* after he received a copy of the tape? Mulder waited until he talked with Scully about it.

⌧ On the other hand, I get more impressed with Mulder every day. He's on a small boat when a commando team arrives—sporting at least ten guys with machine guns—and *Mulder* escapes! He even makes what had to be a huge splash in the water, but no one hears it. (No doubt he used his Jedi mind control. "You don't need to look over the railing." "I don't need to look over the railing." "That wasn't a splash you heard." "That wasn't a splash I heard.")

⌧ Really considerate of the Japanese to load the strange little being onto the train in broad daylight, isn't it? (Wink, wink.)

⌧ Let's see. An "express" train—that usually means no stops—from Queensgate, Ohio, to Vancouver, British Columbia. I bet there's just a *ton* of people making that commute . . . in spite of the fact that it's *halfway across the United States and into Canada!*

Changed Premises

⌧ Senator Matheson suddenly has no fear that his office is bugged in this episode. He talks with Mulder freely. But in "Little Green Men," Matheson used Bach to cover his whispers. In addition, Matheson is now in a position to help Mulder again—contrary to the claims of Mr. X in "Ascension." Could the two be connected? Might Matheson show no fear that his office is bugged because the listeners already know what he is going to say?

Equipment Oddities

⌧ Did anyone else find it fascinating that this top-secret video of the procedure in the railcar would be shot to satellite *without* encryption? Or is Steven Zinnzser another anarchist like The Thinker and he was able to decode it?

⌧ A few episodes back I took the time to offer my humble understanding of the firing process for a semiautomatic pistol. This episode contains what I believe is yet another problem with a pistol. (I am not familiar with the particular weapon that Mulder uses in the scene described below. The pistol used in "The Walk" was a 9mm Baretta. *That* weapon, I know.) Discovering the Japanese diplomat fleeing from Zinnzser's house, Mulder gives chase. There is a struggle. Mulder loses his primary weapon and draws his backup from an ankle holster. He fires to get the Japanese diplomat's attention. (Remember that.) Then he makes a few demands of the diplomat. The diplomat refuses to respond. Mulder snaps back the hammer on the backup pistol to reinforce his point. Hold it! If he fired the weapon, the slide would have snapped back the hammer. (Unless he dropped the hammer on the weapon when we weren't looking, but there is no reason for him to do this!)

⌧ The conspiracy guys have all the coolest gadgets. The boxcars evidently have surveillance ameras that automatically pan to keep the primary subject in the frame! (Watch as Scully reviews Mulder's tape and recognizes the lead Japanese doctor.) Of course, even the most advanced technology has problems. We will see in the next episode that this "pan-and-scan" camera stays focused on the lead Japanese doctor as he punches in his access code for the oor. Ooops! This is probably *not* a good thing, ince the video is being bounced off satellite.

Continuity and Production Problems

◪ Curiouser and curiouser. Now Beth Kane rom "Red Museum" has moved to Allentown nd changed her name to Penny Northern. How o I know it's she? The first time she sees cully she says, "She's one." Does that sound amiliar? If you recall, Beth Kane's son was kidapped in "Red Museum." As he stumbled out f the woods in his underwear, his back read, He is one."

◪ In "The Blessing Way," the door across the all from the front door to Scully's apartment was labeled "3." In this episode, it appears that Scully's front door is labeled "5." This contradicts previous episodes ("Squeeze," "Beyond the Sea," "Ascension") that show her back door labeled "35." Did Scully move when we weren't looking, or is this just a bit of landlord humor?

Trivia Questions

❶ What is the name of the high-ranking diplomat who kicks Mulder?

❷ Where was the body of this diplomat found?

Trivia Answers
❶ Kazuo Sakurai.
❷ In the C & O Canal.

731

(Part 2 of 2)

PLOT SUMMARY
After losing contact with Mulder, Scully demands more information from Mr. X. Deferring, he suggests she examine the implant removed from her neck. Agent Pendrell discovers that it's some kind of neural processing chip. A manifest search reveals one shipment from the chip's manufacturer to a Dr. Shiro Zama in Perkey, West Virginia. There, Scully finds the remains of a massacre, though she is quickly apprehended by Brandoguy of the "Consortium." (See "The Blessing Way.") He wants to show her something that will answer her questions.

Meanwhile, Mulder finds Zama dead on the train and follows Zama's assassin into the boxcar. Unfortunately, the assassin doesn't know the exit code for the car, and there's a bomb on board. Then a call comes for Mulder on the assassin's cell phone. It's Scully, standing in an identical boxcar. She says that she remembers being in such a place. She's satisfied that Zama was merely conducting inhuman experiments and the government has been using the alien-abduction ruse as a cover story. When Zama stopped sharing his results, those sponsoring him moved against him.

Mulder isn't convinced. He has the boxcar deposited in the countryside, certain that the government will come for the creature stored in the back. Only X eventually appears—killing the assassin before carrying a wounded Mulder to safety as the boxcar detonates behind the pair.

Onscreen Locations

X Perkey, West Virginia

Ruminations

An exciting second half . . . as always!

I've harped several times about Mulder an[d] Scully dropping the clip on their weapons an[d] not racking the slide to eject any bullet tha[t] might be in the firing chamber. In this episod[e] Mulder does it precisely right! (Except, o[f] course, he dry-fires the weapon several time[s]. I've been told that's not a good thing to d[o] because there's no bullet in the chamber [to] absorb the impact.)

I find it absolutely fabulous that the bomb [in] this episode doesn't tick and doesn't beep. [It] just counts down silently—which is the way [it] should be! (Now, if the bomb designers real[ly] wanted to give someone the willies, they coul[d] remove the display for the timer as well. Th[e] timer certainly doesn't need it, and that woul[d] leave the good guys without a clue when th[e] bomb would go off. Of course, then we couldn['t] have the dramatic countdown!)

And how about that gorgeous explosion a[t] the end as the bomb in the boxcar detonates[?] Beautiful job!

The creators really do make the extra effo[rt] at the end of this episode to give it that specia[l] X-File's zing. They brought in William B. Dav[is] just to do a fifteen-second cameo for the ver[y] last scene! Kudos!

Unanswered Questions

X Who were the beings at Hansen's Diseas[e] Research Facility? Were they human/alie[n] hybrids? Or were they some kind of mutate[d] humans? They certainly *look* like aliens, and w[e] know from the existence of Dr. Secare in "The Erlenmeyer Flask" that the Consortium *is* experimenting to create a human/alien hybrid. And the four Japanese doctors at the beginning of the episode wear gas masks as they autopsy one of the beings, reminding us of the toxic nature of Secare's body chemistry. On the other hand, the soldiers who execute the beings at the beginning of the episode wear no special breathing apparatus. One would expect some protection if the beings shown here are of the same ilk as Secare. So are we dealing with *two* alien races, with *two* types of human/alien hybrids?

Or . . . were the original creatures created by these tests used to foster the entire alien mystique in the first place? Does the image of the big-headed, oval-slanted-eyed alien really come from World War II—from the concentration camps, from the horrific experimentation rooms of Unit 731? Nazi and Japanese scientists *were* being spirited to the United States at the end of World War II. The government *did* want to continue the research. Why not concoct the story of alien abductions and proliferate the image that resulted from the forbidden experiments as the model of "the grays"? Roswell occurred in 1947—only two years after the end of the war. What if it was just a hoax to cover the genesis of an entirely new set of experiments? What if true alien contact came *years*, even *decades* later? In that case, the being on the boxcar would merely be the poor victim of a monstrous process. But if that's true, how did Mulder and Mr. X escape the hemorrhagic fever released when the boxcar exploded? Wasn't Scully told that *that* was the primary threat from the creature? And wasn't she given this information by those who wanted her to believe the creature was fully human?

Geographical Inconsistencies

☒ Perkey, West Virginia, doesn't exist.

Plot Oversights

☒ The episode opens with a death squad coming to Hansen's Disease Research Facility. They round up the beings, march them out into the woods, line them up in front of a mass grave, and mow them down. Sometime later, Scully comes to the facility and is escorted out into the woods to see the corpses in the pit. Then a helicopter appears. Scully watches it approach for a time. Now, I may not measure up to the brave and valiant standards of special agents of the FBI, but I think I can say with some confidence that if I were standing near a pit gazing down on hundreds of dead bodies and heard a helicopter approaching that possibly carried the same evil men who slaughtered these innocents, I don't believe I would stand there and watch it come closer. I would get my behind in gear and high-tail it into the woods!

☒ Mulder seems to survive an awfully long time with that piano wire around his neck. But . . . then again, he's a hero, and heroes can do that!

☒ Scully tells Mulder that Zama was experimenting on lepers, the homeless, and the insane. So, in which of these three categories do the women of Allentown fall?

Changed Premises

☒ Scully seems ready and willing to accept a fully human explanation for these events, though she was the one who had "Purity Control" tested in "The Erlenmeyer Flask" and heard her colleague say that it was extraterrestrial in origin. Some people just don't want to believe! (Actually, this *is* in character. See "Whose Truth Is Out There?")

Equipment Oddities

☒ So there's this boxcar and it has this "thing" in it. Zama is so jealous of it that he's willing to

Trivia Questions

❶ What is Mulder's phone number?

❷ An anonymous phone call helped medical personnel find an injured Mulder. From where did it originate?

I love it when Mulder attempts to leave the boxcar with the code the assassin used to enter, and the assassin's cell phone suddenly starts chirping! You can almost see Mulder's heart stop. Also, his expression is absolutely wonderful when the assassin holds out the phone and says, "It's for you."

blow it up before anyone else can possess it. In addition, the boxcar that houses the creature requires an entry code *and* an exit code. One gets the impression that Zama is guarding his discovery quite carefully. Yet . . . Zama is happy to leave his briefcase, containing his research notes, in his train compartment, and he doesn't even *lock* the attaché?! Does this seem right?

🅇 Boo! *Boo!* Hiss, boo! Um . . . where to begin? After hearing from Mr. X that the chip implanted in her neck might hold the answers she needs, Scully takes it to Agent Pendrell to run a few diagnostics. Pendrell says the chip is really complex yada, yada, yada, and then floats the theory that the chip seems to be mimicking the process of memory formation in the brain. Scully compares this to a hard drive on a computer, recording what a person thinks. (Never mind that this thing was planted in Scully's *neck*. How could it be recording memory formation in the *cerebral cortex* of an individual when it was implanted in a person's neck?) Pendrell then advances this concoction of hyperbolic hypotheses one step further by suggesting that the chip also could replicate a person's thought processes! Scully chimes in with the next groundless extrapolation, that someone could know a person's every thought. This is when I started booing. I don't buy it! I don't care how advanced the Consortium is. This technology doesn't exist, and it's not going to exist for a while—a *long* while. And it's especially not going to exist in a chip *that* tiny. (If what Pendrell says is true, the technology would *have* to be extraterrestrial. We simply don't know enough about how the human brain works. If we did, artificial intelligence would already be here, and my computer would be watching these episodes as I vacationed in Fiji!)

And if that wasn't bad enough, Pendrell then says, "The chip is so delicate that I effectively destroyed it when I began working on it." So, in other words, all these mighta-coulda-woulda-bees are based on a chip that's been *shorted out?!* Does it not seem a bit unreasonable to

base *any* conclusion on the results of a test that destroyed the chip in the process?

🅇 With what did Mulder restrain the assassin? Did he use the guy's piano wire? Too bad Mulder forgot his handcuffs. They would have been a lot harder to cut through with a scalpel.

🅇 Evidently there are certain individuals in the intelligence community who have special telephone numbers. As Scully attempts to call Senator Richard Matheson, she dials eight, not seven digits.

Continuity and Production Problems

🅇 If you look closely as Mulder flips through Zama's journal, you'll see that those clever creators created only one page for Zama's journal and then copied it a bunch of times to make a book!

🅇 When Mulder finds Zama in the bathroom, the latch on the door protrudes. Mulder steps inside and turns over Zama's body. A woman screams and suddenly the latch has retracted. (Evidently it was just as startled as Mulder!)

Revelations

Onscreen Locations

▣ First Church of Redemption, Waynesburg, Pennsylvania

▣ Ridgeway Elementary School, Loveland, Ohio

▣ Linley Home for Children

▣ State Forensic Laboratory, Hamilton County, Ohio

▣ 21st Century Recycling Plant, Jerusalem, Ohio

Ruminations

I've read the complaints about this episode. I've seen the grumbling over Mulder the "believer" suddenly turning into a hardcore skeptic when the dynamic duo finally ventures into an area that Scully is willing to embrace among domains of extreme possibility. I've noted the truthful observations that Scully has always been willing to go along with Mulder's harebrained theories, and now that she has a few of her own, he responds with cynicism and mockery.

Personally, though, I happen to think that the characterization in this episode is . . . precisely right! Yes, it is true that up to this point, we see Mulder believing in "every light in the sky" (to borrow Scully's phraseology). Yes, it is true that Mulder seems completely unwilling even to admit the possibility of anything unusual at work in the events portrayed. And yes, it is true that Mulder stares dumbfounded at the bent, red-hot metal bars after Kevin is abducted from Scully's motel room—offering the lame explanation that the kidnappers must have had an acetylene torch—when he should have already

PLOT SUMMARY Tracking a string of religiously motivated murders, Mulder and Scully head for Loveland, Ohio. All eleven of the previous victims claimed to be stigmatics—individuals who spontaneously exhibit the wounds of Christ's crucifixion—and a social worker has alerted Mulder to the case of Kevin Kryder. A year ago, Kevin came to school bleeding from his hands. Authorities suspected child abuse and put him in a shelter. After questioning, Kevin's father was released, but then he barricaded himself inside the Kryder home, claiming Kevin was chosen by God and needed protection. The father was institutionalized.

Now Kevin has begun to bleed again, and—though Mulder doesn't believe anything supernatural is occurring—he fears the murderer will target the young boy because of what others have claimed. Scully, on the other hand, finds the events extraordinary. Those involved with Kevin seem to center on her when speaking of one who has come to protect the boy, and her science can't explain Kevin's wounds or his ability to be in two places at once—let alone the killer's ability to burn his victims with a touch. In time, the killer does abduct Kevin—proclaiming that his death will usher in the new age. And while Mulder stays within the normal bounds of policy and procedures, Scully acts without him to save Kevin's life.

leaped to the obvious conclusion. (Normally, Mulder would put together the fact that Owen Jarvis had fingerprints burned into his throat, the front doorknob at the Kryder home was melted off, and the bars are red-hot. Normally, Mulder would conclude that the person who is seeking Kevin can generate incredible heat through his or her hands.)

But I still contend that the characterization in this episode is . . . perfect! *The question is: Why?* Let's consider Scully's actions first. Certainly, her deep-seated religious belief rooted in Catholicism would create no conflict with her trained scientific mind. In reality, science depends *on a universe that is ordered and knowable, a universe that operates according to some persistent principles.* It's a small step for a person who holds to the existence of those principles to believe that such order and persistence have a Source. Especially a Source that "played fair" with the analytical mind.

With regard to Mulder, it is this very Source that fires his contentiousness, however. In the sidebar "Whose Truth Is Out There?" I discuss the dramatically different approaches by which Mulder and Scully arrive at "the truth." Mulder's method begins and ends . . . *with Mulder!* He creates the theory. He sets the criteria by which the theory is judged. He evaluates the evidence by the criteria he establishes to prove or disprove his theory. In short, he decides when something is true, and it really doesn't matter to him what anyone else thinks.

For Mulder to admit that the events in this episode might have some *extranatural* component, he must allow the possibility of merit in the core belief system that surrounds the events. And—aside from the fact that Mulder makes a practice of rejecting anything arising from the religious "mainstream"—entertaining, however temporarily, the concept of the transcendent Being espoused by the Judeo-Christian belief system would seriously disrupt his fundamentals.

The Judeo-Christian belief system lays claim to a Source who not only calls all things into existence but also a Being who is the final arbiter of truth; a Being whose very nature is Absolute Truth. Given Mulder's subjectivism, the notion of such a Being is abhorrent. Even approaching it turns him crotchety and "tests his patience" (to borrow Mulder's own terminology), for the existence of this Being would destroy Mulder's sovereignty over "the truth" and vest it beyond his appeal, correction, or postulation. The only remaining question would be "What does the Being say is truth?"

Doesn't it seem reasonable, then, that Mulder would make every effort to dismiss Scully's suspicions? (Not that he would admit any of this to himself, of course, because according to his truth, he always believes in everything that has merit!)

On a different topic, this episode opens with a preacher talking of miracles and supposedly demonstrating the stigmata. I have to admit that—as a nitpicker—I would have been sitting in the audience thinking, "Wait a minute: That's not right! The blood is flowing uphill, and it's too thick!

Plot Oversights

☒ So, um, if Kevin supposedly displays the wounds of Christ, why does he only bleed from his palms at first? What about the back of his hands?

☒ Man, these social services people in Ohio are tough! At school, Kevin goes to the blackboard to do a division problem. He begins to bleed. He goes to the nurse's office, and afterward Family Services sticks him in a foster home. Isn't there a possibility that he fell down outside and punctured his palms? With no evidence of wrongdoing and without a statement concerning the origin of the wounds, Family Services takes custody of the kid?! Now, *that's* frightening! (Remind me to make sure my daughter doesn't skin her knee.)

☒ After Kevin is taken into custody by Family Services, Owen Jarvis kidnaps him from the Linley Home for Children. Owen believes that God has appointed him to be Kevin's "guardian angel." In due time, Mulder and Scully appear and search Owen's home. Finding nothing, they begin to interrogate Owen. Strangely enough

"Afraid that God is speaking but that no one's listening."

—**Scully** *to a priest after he wonders why their conversation should make her afraid. He doesn't realize that his statements—like many of the things that Scully had recently experienced—seem to have some measure of supernatural inspiration.*

they decide to hold the interrogation in the *attic!* Aside from allowing Owen to make his swan dive out the attic window, is there some *sensible* reason for bringing him up there, as opposed to interrogating him in the living room?

X I'm not an authority on Roman Catholic catechism class, so I'll let Jim McCauley of Mountain View, Califorina, tell you about this next nit. "Scully gives up on the autopsy of Owen Jarvis because his body hasn't begun to decay in the normal fashion and she believes that his corpse is redolent of flowers. She pitches his condition to Mulder as one ascribed to so-called 'Incorruptibles.' (Scully cites St. Cecilia and St. Francis.) She claims to have picked up this bit of lore from her catechism. Now, if Dana Scully grew up anywhere under the purview of the Baltimore Archdiocese, her source for this would have been a little blue paperback called *The Baltimore Catechism.* (I went to Catholic schools in California and we used it way out there.) I can promise you that no such mention is made in any of the editions with which I am familiar, which cover the period from 1951 through 1958.

"There is reference to the alleged incorruptibility of St. Francis Xavier's earthly remains in *Lives of the Saints* (a work under the imprimatur of the archbishop of New York, in my edition), but to the best of my knowledge incorruption following death has been ascribed under Canon Law to only one individual: Jesus Christ. He and his mother Mary—who, according to Catholic doctrine, never died—are proclaimed to have been assumed directly into heaven, where both the location and incorruptibility of their physical persons becomes a matter of metaphysical speculation. So if the big hairless dude smells like Aunt Min's perfume fourteen hours after his demise, the Roman Catholic Church has *absolutely nothing* official to say about his condition."

X In addition, Scully makes reference to Kevin's ability to be seen in two places at once, and

likens it to St. Ignatius "in the Bible." To which I responded, "*Huh?!*" Which Bible is Scully reading? That certainly ain't in *my* Bible!

X During a second visit to Kevin's father, Scully notes that they have increased his medication. A close-up of the chart lists several drugs, including Largactil. A call to my friendly neighborhood Wal-Mart pharmacist confirmed that Largactil is not sold in the United States.

X The killer who absconds with Kevin is named Simon Gates. Near the end of the episode, he takes Kevin to a recycling plant and tells the young boy that "the sun will be turned into darkness and the moon will turn to blood"—stating that Kevin must die for "the New Age to come." Now, I recognize the "darkness-sun/blood-moon" quote from the Book of Revelations. After all, my dad has taught eschatology—the study of end-time events and prophecy—for *decades.* But I am *completely* lost when Gates claims that Kevin has to die to usher in the New Age. *What* New Age?! What religion are we talking about here?

X At the end of the episode, Scully wants to go see a priest, so she has Mulder report to the police station to make a statement about Gates's death. But . . . Mulder wasn't even there! Is he really qualified to do this? And, moments earlier, screen text informed us that this is *two days* after Gates died. The case was pretty much solved after Gates was ground to bits in the paper shredder, wasn't it? What has Scully been doing for two days that she hasn't found the time to go to the police station and make a statement? (Did she and Mulder decide to take a little extra vacation time?)

Equipment Oddities

X You have to feel sorry for Kevin Kryder. Here's this poor kid who suddenly starts bleeding for no apparent reason at school. He's hauled off to the

THIRD SEASON

Trivia Questions

1 What is Owen Jarvis's middle name?

2 Where is Simon Gates's company based?

Trivia Answers
1 Lee.
2 Atlanta, Georgia.

217

Revelations

nurse's office. It looks like Family Services is coming after him again. And, if that wasn't bad enough, the nurse jams a thermometer into his mouth that has a red bulb on the end. Red—as opposed to blue—normally signifies a *rectal* thermometer. (And that's all I'll say about *that!*)

✖ Mulder and Scully should be grateful that Owen Jarvis was a peaceable man. He greets them at the door of his house with a rifle. Mulder commands him to put it down. Owen drops the weapon to a heater that sits between him and our two FBI agents. Except . . . in the process, Mulder lets Owen point the rifle right at him—with Owen's finger *still* on the trigger! (This would be a *bad* thing when dealing with your normal criminal-type.)

✖ Near the end of the episode, Gates attempts to kill Kevin by leaping into a shredder with Kevin in his arms. Kevin wiggles free. Gates falls into the shredder. Crunch, crunch, crunch. Scully runs up. Stands beside the control panel for the shredder. Sees Kevin. Gasps. Reaches down and pulls him to safety. Me? I would have gone for the off-button on the control panel first thing, but hey, I'm not a hero, and that would make the scene less dramatic!

Continuity and Production Problems

✖ After leaving Owen Jarvis's house, Kevin Kryder heads home. Gates soon appears to abduct Kevin, and the young boy hides in his wicker clothes basket. From the inside, the wicker is loose enough to see through. From the outside, it is tightly packed. Hmm. More of Kevin's amazing powers?

✖ When Gates takes Kevin from the bathroom of Scully's motel room, Mulder kicks down the door. Two things about this moment: First, there is an odd spot of light that races across the scene just as the door opens. Second, Mulder must have some lawsuit-inhibiting kick designed just for doors, because he manages to kick open a locked door without any apparent damage! (The strike plate on the doorjamb doesn't even move!)

War of the Coprophages

Onscreen Locations

☒ Miller's Grove, Massachusetts
☒ Miller's Grove Motor Lodge
☒ Massachusetts Institute of Robotics

Ruminations

This is a fabulous episode—absolutely loaded with delightful scenes, everything from the recurring bit with Scully providing the "roach-free" explanations to the triple assault on Mulder's belief system. (The re-education of Dana Scully to the domains of "extreme possibilities" comes to a screeching halt in this episode. After handling what looked like an alien fetus and all but admitting the existence of extraterrestrial life in "The Erlenmeyer Flask," she began to dig in her objectivist heels in "Red Museum" and now taunts Mulder with the impossibility of intelligent alien life. Bambi offers the plausible insect swarm theory to explain the colored lights in the sky. Ivanov scoffs that anyone who believes in aliens with big eyes and gray skin has been brainwashed by too much science fiction.)

And all the lovely little touches: The great continuity giving us the scene with the dog Scully inherited after "Clyde Bruckman's Final Repose"; the camera shot from inside the washbasin drain; Mulder's gyrations as he wakes up, believing he has a roach crawling up his nose; the juxtaposition of Ivanov's clunky robots with the incredible sophistication of the alien cockroaches; "Die Flea Die," "Not now," "Die Bug Die," "Waste Is a Terrible Thing to Waste"; the sailor in the convenience store

PLOT SUMMARY While investigating reports of lights in the sky over Miller's Grove, Massachusetts, Mulder's weekend runs bizarre when the good citizens begin dying—apparently attacked by roaches. Though Scully provides a different, logical, "roach-free" explanation for each death, even she can't explain why an insect found at a death site would crumble to *metallic* dust when Mulder grabs it. Of interest, the government has an insect research facility across town, operated by the beautiful Dr. Bambi Berenbaum. Though Mulder is immediately smitten, Berenbaum has no answers. She does, however, advise him that Miller's Grove also hosts a computer scientist named Ivanov, whose specialty is robotic insects.

Having collected pieces of the offending insects, Mulder takes them to Ivanov. The scientist is stunned. They look robotic—the creation of a superadvanced alien race utilizing tiny robots for space exploration. Unconvinced, Scully opts for a more terrestrial explanation, wondering if the town's alternate-fuel company accidentally brought a new breed of roaches into the county via its dung imports. Mulder and Scully go there to investigate, but the head of the company, Dr. Eckerle is so panicked by events that he begins firing wildly—igniting the methane in the building and spraying manure everywhere.

All the evidence is destroyed in the blast. And soon Berenbaum departs with Ivanov. When Scully offers some disingenuous consolation, Mulder has only one response: He tells her that she smells bad.

preparing for doomsday by stocking up on chocolate and sheer stockings; Scully sampling the spilled candy after the rest of the people in the store mistook them for cockroaches; Bambi referring to the November issue of Entomology Extreme. *It just goes on and on and on. Hand-clapping, leg-slapping kudos!*

I've talked with enough people about this episode that I will take the risk of stating the obvious for some so that others will get an answer to a question they may have. Namely, why were the roaches attracted to the people who died in this episode? Answer: They weren't! And, no, it wasn't just coincidence that roaches were found at the location of the deaths. If Mulder's theory is correct (and, his theories usually are; he is a hero, after all), then the robotic cockroaches are extraterrestrial in origin and they are fueled by methane. That's how they made it to Alt-Fuels, Inc. in the first place—through the importation of blocks of manure. In addition, it makes sense that they would be attracted to the attic where the kids were cooking manure to get high on methane. (You really have to be desperate for a high to smoke manure.) Also, the cockroaches visit the medical doctor as he goes to the bathroom—a likely methane-producing activity. As to the remaining two individuals—the exterminator and the hotel guest—one could surmise that their apparent demise by roaches was merely an indication of the severity of their flatulence!

Just for the record, I happen to like Dr. Bambi!

And speaking of Bambi and speaking of Mulder and speaking of Mulder being smitten over Bambi, did you notice Mulder's wandering hands? As he asks her if she has ever heard of an instance where a cockroach attacked a human being, note the position of his cupped hands, the downward glance of his eyes, the sudden realization of how he must look, and the hasty retreat!

Unanswered Questions

☒ So who sent these robotic cockroaches? Just more off-ramp activity from the intragalactic hyperspace bypass? (See "Space.")

☒ At the beginning of the episode, Mulder mentions that a molecular biologist and an astrophysicist have expired as well. From what did they die, and what did they do to attract the roaches?

Geographical Inconsistencies

☒ Miller's Grove, Massachusetts, doesn't exist.

Plot Oversights

☒ After visiting with Ivanov, Mulder finds a cockroach in the hall of the Massachusetts Institute of Robotics. He gives it greetings from planet Earth before taking it back for Bambi to examine. She says it's not like the leg segment he had her examine earlier. This must have happened when we weren't looking, because "earlier" they were examining a robotic cockroach's abdomen.

Equipment Oddities

☒ The episode opens with an exterminator working the basement of Eckerle's home. He sprays a roach. It refuses to drop. He knocks it to the floor and stomps on it. At this point the exterminator is taken with a seizure due to anaphylactic shock. The roach wanders off. Putting this incident into the context of the rest of the episode, we might conclude that the cockroach is of the robotic variety. But if you recall, the robotic cockroaches have a tendency to crumble to metallic dust. So how did it survive the exterminator's foot?

☒ After extracting some cockroach parts from a hotel room, Mulder takes them to Bambi. They use a large illuminated magnifying glass to study the insect's genitalia. Obviously, the process is invoking a fair degree of sexual tension in the room because both Bambi and

Love the bug. Love the bug. Love the bug. LOVE THE BUG! For me, it's the greatest moment in The X-Files. (And if you have no idea what I'm talking about, watch the episode. You'll know when you hit it!)

Mulder use the magnifying glass *backwards* and neither seems to care or notice! (In fact, you can see a picture of this in *Trust No One: The Official Guide to the Third Season of* The X-Files. The circular neon bulb that is supposed to be used to illuminate the specimen being examined is, in fact, shining in Mulder and Bambi's eyes!)

🇽 It's *really* too bad no one had a camera to take a picture of the cockroach parts under the microscope so that *somebody* would have *some* piece of evidence from this excursion. Then again, Bambi is only an entomologist, so she really wouldn't have *any* need for such a piece of equipment, would she? (Wink, wink.)

🇽 The creators cheated a bit when constructing Ivanov's robots. Supposedly the robots propel themselves with six segmented legs, when in fact it's fairly obvious that they are rolling across the floor on wheels. (No doubt, a real-live working robot cockroach is *tough* to build!)

🇽 Dr. Ivanov doesn't have any prescription on his glasses, but I'm sure you've noticed that by now!

Continuity and Production Problems

🇽 After Mulder breaks into Bambi's house experiment, Mulder tells Scully that the walls are moving in the kitchen. Indeed, we see the walls rippling moments later. It's a cool effect, but in order for this to really be happening, the roaches would have to punch through the drywall!

🇽 Dr. Berube is improving his station in life. You might remember him from such episodes as "The Erlenmeyer Flask," where he supposedly committed suicide, but the Conspiracy actually spirited him away to work as a medical examiner in Los Angeles. (We see him in "3.") He's done well for himself over the past year. Now he has a contract with NASA and is building mechanical robots under the name of Ivanov! (Imagine Bambi's surprise when he gets up out of that wheelchair and starts talking without the need of his artificial voicebox.)

Trivia Questions

❶ With whom does Dr. Ivanov have his contract?

❷ What was Dr. Jeff Eckerle's official title at Alt-Fuels?

LEAST & MOST

Personal Picks for Favorites

In talking with fellow nitpickers, one question often arises. Namely, "What do you think are the best and worst shows of [Supply Name of Series Here]?" I've found that fans *love* to debate the virtues of a given episode over another. And, while I'm hesitant to pompously stamp one particular episode of *The X-Files* with the "best" or "worst" label—although "José Chung's *From Outer Space*" and "Home" would be leading candidates, respectively—I am happy to pass along my pick for my most and least favorite shows. I realize that this is *entirely* subjective and many will probably have other choices, but you might find this interesting!

Since I would rather not end this sidebar on a negative note, let's talk about my five least favorite episodes first.

5 "Musings of a Cigarette-Smoking Man." There's not really anything I find offensive about this episode. It's just not very interesting to me—especially since we don't have any way of knowing what really happened and what didn't!

4 "Grotesque." Carving up young men's faces with a box blade? Ick.

3 "The List." Just *too* many maggots! Of course, the head in the paint can and the decapitated body in the warden's office didn't help matters any.

2 "Sanguinarium." The name says it all! "Blood Ward." And what about the camera shot near the end that lingers and lingers and *lingers* as Magic-Doc peels off his face?

1 "Home." As I said in my review, I just don't get this episode. Mulder and Scully seem reckless. The Brothers Mutant are better suited for comics books than television. And as for Ma "A'm hungry" Peacock? Somebody needs to get that woman an agent! She could make a fortune on the talk-show circuit with her looks and stories of incest (especially during sweeps months).

On the other hand, there are plenty of episodes in *The X-Files* that I consider *fabulous!* Here are my six most favorite. (These are the ones I suggest that people watch if they want to get a feel for what I consider the series at its best.)

6 "Beyond the Sea." This is Scully's first lurching attempt to delve as a believer into the world of the paranormal—pressed by the ache to feel her deceased father's approval. Gillian Anderson puts in a wonderful performance.

5 "One Breath." While all the "conspiracy" shows are strong and well crafted, this particular episode touches me with Mulder's struggle, Scully's choice of life over afterlife, and, of course, Nurse Owens.

4 "Small Potatoes." David Duchovny's portrayal of Eddie Van Blundht's "Mulder doppel-gänger" immediately popped this one on the list. That, and Amanda Nelligan singing the *Star Wars* theme. (Not to mention Mulder breaking off Van Blundht, Sr.'s, tail!)

3 "Clyde Bruckman's Final Repose." Peter Boyle playing the reluctant psychic is *definitely* a keeper!

2 "War of the Coprophages." Love the bug! Love the bug! *LOVE THE BUG!*

1 "José Chung's *From Outer Space*." So many *clever* and *hilarious* juxtapositions here! And how 'bout that Alex Trebek?

Syzygy

PLOT SUMMARY
Investigating the deaths of three young men, Mulder and Scully find the town of Comity, New Hampshire, in the grip of rumor panic. Residents are certain it's the work of Satanists, and two teenage girls, Terri Roberts and Margi Kleinjan, even testify about a secret ceremony as part of the latest murder. Scully is unconvinced, given the recent nationwide studies by the FBI that failed to uncover any definitive proof of such phenomena. But even the enigmatic Agent Scully seems affected by something in the town. She is more strident and unyielding—some might even say *rancorous*. As for Mulder, his normal obsession with his work is apparently overcome by a desire to help Comity's statuesque, blonde detective discover the mystery of the "horny beast."

The local astrologist provides a possible answer. Comity lies on the convergence point for cosmic forces. Mercury, Mars, and Uranus have come into alignment. Worse, the two young women, Roberts and Kleinjan, were born on the same day in the year. In fact, Roberts and Kleinjan *are* responsible for the murders—utilizing some kind of joint telekinetic ability to carry out every whim of destruction. Eventually the force invading the town becomes so severe that Roberts and Kleinjan turn on each other. But at the stroke of midnight, the influence wafts away and Comity returns to normal.

Onscreen Locations

☒ Caryl County Sheriff's Station

Geographical Inconsistencies

☒ While Cornell County exists in New Hampshire, Caryl County does not. Also there is no Comity, New Hampshire. But if there were, given its population, it would be one of the largest cities in the state!

Ruminations

Okay, I admit it! They got me. The first time I saw this episode I started grousing halfway through because I couldn't figure out what the creators were doing with the characterizations. About the time Scully began smoking in her motel room, I was muttering a duet with her. Of course, in the end, the creators proved their genius by attributing everything to a cosmic alignment. But—for a while there—they had me going!

And while we are on the topic of cosmic alignments, this episode tells us something important about Mulder, but I'm not exactly sure what. He seems immediately taken with Angela White—Comity's statuesque, blonde detective mentioned above. Mentioned above as well, Mulder even asks her to help him discover the mystery of the horny beast. Now, if that's not a "come-on" line, I don't know what is! He even goes so far as to indulge himself in a session of hair-sniffing when he is supposed to be offering her comfort over the loss of her cat! Yet, when White finally responds—albeit aggressively—Mulder suddenly begins backing away, even to the point of frantically punching the "0" on the telephone to summon the motel's operator (which is a very cute moment). Does this mean that Mulder likes his women passive? Or have White's actions shocked him to his senses despite the cosmic fog that overhangs Comity? I have enough faith in the creators' ability to characterize Mulder correctly that it *must* mean something, but I'm just not sure what. (Well . . . actually . . . I do have a theory, but you're not going to like it. I'm thinking that at the base of everything, Mulder feels awkward around women. On the outside, he's handsome and suave and witty, but there's a residual portion of nerdy guy left over from his days in high school and college. It still haunts him. Of course, Phoebe Green of "Fire" didn't help matters any. She was probably Mulder's first great love. He fell hard, and she skewered him! I'm thinking that all this obsessiveness over UFOs is very convenient *for Special Agent Fox Mulder. It means that women will believe he's consumed with his work as opposed to being shy.)*

Plot Oversights

🅧 Roberts and Kleinjan decide that they hate a certain young basketball player because he accidently jars a table, spilling sports drink on them. They send the basketball flying to hit him in the head and then bounce it away behind the bleachers. Of course, once the young man is behind the bleachers, Roberts and Kleinjan activate the motor to retract the bleachers and crush him. Cut to commercial. Returning, the episode shows the crime scene. The police are there interviewing the young people, who are dressed as before. Mulder and White soon arrive. Scully is already there. Screen text informs us that it is "5:10 A.M." Five o'clock in the morning? The basketball team practices with the cheerleading squad cheering them on at *five o'clock* in the morning? That's dedication!

🅧 A deeper understanding of astrology probably would redress this next issue, but there's some confusion over exactly *how* the planetary alignment is affecting the populace. Dialogue in the episode indicates that young men have died over a period of three months. Madame Zirinka says her dog has been trying to mate with the gas barbecue for the past two months. In other words, the process of cosmic conniptions has been building over many weeks. This actually would make some sense because the planets are gradually moving into position. What seems very odd is the fact that all the cosmic energy routed through Roberts and Kleinjan seems to come to a dead stop at the end of the episode. Shouldn't it gradually taper off as the planets move *out of* alignment?

Equipment Oddities

🅧 The Sheriff's Department of Caryl County makes interesting use of technology. They record the testimony of Roberts and Kleinjan with reel-to-reel tape recorders! From all the cop shows on television I would have expected cassette recorders. (I know this is a nit. I just *know* it!)

🅧 On the other hand, we as viewers should write a letter of gratitude to the Caryl County police for keeping their clocks set so precisely. The wall clock in the hallway of the police station is so well maintained that it counts down the time until January 13 *to the second!* (I know it's done for dramatic effect and, yes, it was a cheap shot!)

Continuity and Production Problems

🅧 One of the really nice things about *The X-Files* is that it gives you a chance to catch up on old friends. Anyone out there remember Marilyn from "Irresistible"? She was the woman who interviewed Donny Pfaster for the job at Ficicello Frozen Foods in Minneapolis, Minnesota. No doubt she was fired for recommending that Mr. Ficicello hire the sicko. Terrified customers saw

THIRD
SEASON

❶ What is the population of Comity?

❷ What is the name of the young man crushed to death in the bleachers?

Pfaster's picture on the news. They called Ficicello Frozen Foods, outraged that the "fetishist" had been sent into their homes. Bye-bye, Marilyn.

Afterward, Marilyn probably decided to pursue her first love, astrology. But wouldn't you know it? Some wacko started killing professional prognosticators in the Twin Cities area! (See "Clyde Bruckman's Final Repose.") So she moved to Comity, New Hampshire, for a little peace and quiet and opened an astrology parlor under the name Madame Zirinka. (Now if she can just keep the good townsfolk from burning her at the stake for being a Satanist. . . .)

 The creators tried to pull a fast one on us and save themselves a camera shot. On the night of Roberts and Kleinjan's birthday, Mulder finds that his motel room television receives only one movie, no matter *what* channel he selects. Several close-ups of the television follow, and after the final one, the camera pans to show Scully puffing away on the bed in *her* motel room. Except . . . the reflection in the television is the same for every close-up—which means that every close-up was done in Scully's room, though the first three should be in Mulder's! (I was having the hardest time trying to make the reflection work correctly for Mulder's room until I realized what the creators had done! I know. Pick, pick, pick, pick, pick.)

 Not a nit, just an observation. I've mentioned "boys will be boys" shots a few times in the course of this *Guide*. This episode has the most suggestive one I've seen. At one point, Margi Kleinjan climbs out of the back of a pickup truck. The director made sure we had a tight close-up of her teenage hips as she *mounts* the side rail in a miniskirt.

 Near the end of the program, Roberts and Kleinjan wind up in the same room at the police station, and every firearm in the place goes crazy. Along one wall—encased in a gun rack—a whole row of shotguns discharge, destroying the top of their wooden enclosure. Leaping into action, Mulder grabs Kleinjan and hauls her out of the room. A cutaway shows us the gun rack a final time and—surprisingly enough—the top of the rack now looks fine! (I suppose we also should ponder the reason why all of the shotguns were stored with live ammunition in their firing chambers. In addition, the *pump* shotguns seem to be able to fire multiple rounds without being *pumped!*)

Grotesque

Onscreen Locations

☒ George Washington University, Extension Program, Washington, D.C.

☒ D.C. Correctional Complex, Lorton, Virginia

☒ 1222 South Dakota Street, Washington, D.C.

☒ George Washington University Hospital, Washington, D.C.

☒ Georgetown University

☒ FBI Sci-Crime Lab, Latent Fingerprint Section

☒ FBI Headquarters, Evidence Room L-7

Ruminations

As far as I'm concerned, this episode is the precursor to Chris Carter's second television series, Millennium. Wouldn't surprise me at all if that series actually found its genesis here!

While it was perfectly in character for Mulder to behave as he did in this episode, I couldn't help but think that he needed to listen to his own incredulity over the actions of the townsfolk of Milford Haven, New Hampshire, in "Die Hand Die Verletzt." Given a belief in a preexistent Evil, it seems presumptuous and foolhardy to call it up. You can be sure that it will not behave. (See the "Great Lines" section of that episode.)

Finally, this episode provides an interesting tidbit about the location of Scully's apartment. At the end of the program, Scully talks with Mulder. Scully is in her apartment. Mulder is in Mostow's studio—located at 1222 South Dakota Street, Washington, D.C. The conversation ends, and Patterson appears. Mulder figures out that Patterson committed the murders that occurred after Mostow's arrest. Then Scully appears. I can find no suggestion of time skips.

PLOT SUMMARY When the Investigative Support Unit of the FBI finally arrests serial killer John Mostow after three years of intense work, Agent Bill Patterson—head of the group—is certain that Mostow's heinous killing spree is over. Then another body appears, its face mutilated just like those of Mostow's other victims. Bewildered, Patterson secretly goes to Skinner to request that Mulder be assigned to the case. Patterson and Mulder have never gotten along, but he needs Mulder's expertise.

An interview confirms Mostow's claim that an evil spirit drove him to commit the murders. His obsession with gargoyles seems to corroborate this as well. Gargoyles have traditionally been used to ward off demons. Scully finds nothing supernatural about the case. To her, Mostow clearly suffers from a psychosis. Of course, Mulder takes a different approach. He immerses himself in Mostow's environment. Soon, a creature approaches late at night. Startled awake, Mulder leaps up to pursue it and is even attacked, but for some reason the thing lets him live. Then Mulder finds himself compelled to return to Mostow's apartment where he finds the mutilated body of Patterson's associate, Greg Nemhauser. As Patterson appears moments later, Mulder realizes what has happened. The head of the ISU spent so much time trying to think like Mostow that he has become Mostow.

The scene seems to proceed uninterrupted, yet it's only two minutes from the time Scully hangs up the receiver until she arrives at Mostow's studio. That means Scully must live somewhere in the Northeast section of Washington, D.C. (Unless she has some sort of James Bondian jet-assisted flying car!)

Plot Oversights

☒ During the initial visit with Mostow in prison, Scully asks Mostow why he's sitting on the floor. Looking down, Mulder answers, saying that Mostow has been busy. There is a drawing of a gargoyle on the floor nearby. Here's what's amazing: Mostow is in a straitjacket. And since he bit one of his arresting officers, it's likely that he's been in a straitjacket for some time! So . . . what did he use to create the portrait—his *nose?!*

☒ Leaving Mostow, Mulder and Scully travel to his studio. They find the walls covered with pictures of gargoyles. A cat startles Scully and then disappears into a cubbyhole in the wall, leading Mulder to suspect that something lies beyond. Our intrepid agents soon uncover a door to a roomful of sculpted-clay gargoyles—some of which encase the torsos and heads of additional murder victims. Hold it! Yes, Mulder and Scully are the heroes. Yes, they are supposed to do heroic things, such as find evidence that *no one* else can locate. But, but, but . . . *no one* in the FBI thought it might be a good idea to scour this place for evidence?! Scully locates the door to Mostow's lair quite easily once she shoves aside a few pieces of paper.

☒ There should be a date for this episode. It should come from the empty bag that Scully examines in Evidence Room L-7 at FBI National Headquarters. (The bag previously held the box blade Mostow used to kill his victims.) Rightly so, there's a place on the bag to document the date and time that the piece of evidence was checked in or checked out. In addition, a name is written directly above one such date and time area. ("W. Green"?) So why not the date and time? Wouldn't that be standard FBI procedure? Granted, Mulder and Patterson probably wouldn't document their activities, given the circumstances, but why doesn't the bag at least record when the box blade was *initially* stored at the FBI?

☒ Patterson must have studied art at some point in his educational career. He sculpts with the same skill as Mostow. Either that or Patterson had some sort of demonic enablement. (I've sculpted a bit with modeling clay. It ain't easy!)

Piper Maru

(Part 1 of 2)

Onscreen Locations

- Pacific Ocean, latitude 42° north, longitude 171° east
- San Diego Naval Hospital
- Pacific Heights, San Francisco, CA
- US Naval Station, San Diego, CA
- Miramar Naval Air Station
- 3702 Medlock Street, San Francisco, CA
- San Francisco International Airport
- Hong Kong
- Hong Kong Airport

Ruminations

We're back in the saddle! It's always fun to return to the alien "mythology" stories and learn a few more tidbits here and there.

At the risk of insulting your intelligence and making myself look silly, I beg your indulgence as I offer my opinion on certain aspects of the episode that didn't make sense to me until I watched the show for the fourth time! To recap: Gauthier somehow gets slimed while on a dive looking for a downed P-51 in the Pacific (while wearing a pressurized diving suit, but that's another topic, and I'll talk about that in the next episode). He goes back to his house and rifles through a deskful of papers, eventually finding the letter from the salvage broker, Kallenchuck. What bothered me originally about this scene was the alien seems to know everything Krycek knows after jumping into him. If that's the case, why would the alien need to rifle through Gauthier's papers? It appears the alien is attempting to discover who supplied the information that led Gauthier

PLOT SUMMARY After learning that her sister's murder case has been made inactive, Scully finds Mulder investigating the French salvage vessel *Piper Maru*. The boat recently searched the same area as the *Talapus* ("Nisei") and discovered a downed P-51 Mustang airplane before limping home with its crew dying of radiation exposure. As Mulder seeks out the only survivor—Bernard Gauthier—Scully visits an old family friend. At first reluctant, Commander Johansen eventually tells Scully that the P-51 was part of an escort for a B-29 carrying an atomic bomb during World War II. Decades earlier, Johansen served as executive officer on a submarine called the *Zeus Faber* during another salvage attempt. Those sailors began dying from radiation as well.

Meanwhile, Mulder tracks down the information broker who sold Gauthier the location of the downed P-51 and follows her to Hong Kong. He soon discovers that her source is none other than Krycek, selling secrets gleaned from the digital cassette copy of Defense Department documents ("Paper Clip"). Once caught, Krycek quickly offers to return to Washington, D.C.—where the tape is hidden—and exchange it for his freedom. Unknown to Mulder, "something" else apprehends Krycek as well—"something" that first inhabited Gauthier and then Gauthier's wife before jumping Krycek.

Meanwhile, in Washington, D.C., Skinner is shot for reviewing the evidence gathered on Melissa Scully's death.

to the P-51. Wouldn't it already know this? Next, Gauthier slimes his wife, and she plays host to the alien for a time. This really confused me. Why jump to the wife?! Was it just happenstance? Once the alien in Gauthier had found the letter from Kallenchuck, why not just head for Kallenchuck's office? Once in Gauthier's wife's body, the alien appears to follow Kallenchuck and Mulder to Hong Kong and then to Kallenchuck's office in Hong Kong, where it flashes the French dudes and eventually jumps to Krycek. There just seemed to be a lot of loose ends in this entire scenario—with characters acting merely to move the plot along. However, I had an epiphany during that fourth time through, and suddenly everyone's actions made sense—at least to me!

Kallenchuck says that she came to Hong Kong to meet with a female buyer. Let's assume for a moment that this is true. If so, why couldn't Gauthier's wife be that buyer? Suppose Gauthier's wife originally purchased the information from Kallenchuck on the P-51 in Hong Kong. Suppose Gauthier's wife originally commissioned the dive. It makes sense that Gauthier would return home and rifle her desk to discover why she sent them in the first place. Finding the letter from Kallenchuck, the alien would realize the wife was the next logical step to find the source of the information that led to the P-51. Jumping to the wife, the alien would learn that the information was originally passed in Hong Kong and would contact Kallenchuck to meet there again. In the San Francisco airport scene, Gauthier's wife is not necessarily there to follow Kallenchuck and Mulder, but traveling to Hong Kong on her own to meet with Kallenchuck. The appearance of Gauthier's wife outside Kallenchuck's Hong Kong office is then no longer fortuitous or the result of stalking; she is coming for the meeting. This still doesn't explain how the alien knows where to find Mulder and Krycek at the end of the episode or that it should jump to Krycek next, but I think it does get us a lot farther along!

Kudos to the creators for not listing "Nicholas Lea" in the opening credits. Krycek makes an unexpected return in this episode, and listing him as is normally required would have spoiled the surprise!

Plot Oversights

✗ That Hong Kong is a wild and crazy town! Mulder punches Krycek in the airport, and no one gives the pair a second glance! (Bob Potter also tells me that a bank of four empty phones would be unheard of. There are usually lines!)

✗ I realize that certain liberties are necessary to make a plot work, but Mulder's actions at the end of this episode defy explanation. He has just located Krycek again after nine months. He knows Krycek has the digital cassette copy of the Defense Department file. And he lets Krycek go into a bathroom alone. WHY?! I would have expected Mulder to stay on him like stink on a hog! (As they say here in the Ozarks.) Mulder doesn't even stand outside the actual bathroom door. He stands outside the *hallway* that leads to the bathroom door! And if that wasn't bad enough, he doesn't even check the actual bathroom to see if there is any way Krycek could escape!

Changed Premises

✗ This may or may not be a nit, depending on how you interpret Skinner's statements to Scully at the beginning of this episode. After asking to speak with her, Skinner says, "It's been five months and there have been no new leads or evidence in her murder investigation."

We know that Melissa Scully was shot and died in April 1995 from the date on "The Blessing Way." Given the date on "Syzygy," we know that "Piper Maru" occurs sometime after January 1996. That's about nine months, not five months. However, Skinner doesn't say that it's been five months since Melissa's murder, he says it's been five months and there have been no new leads. One could make the case that Skinner is saying that it has been five months since the last new lead, but then the question would be: What was that lead? The murder weapon was left at the scene. Scully says that no one saw anyone leave the building. It sounds like there weren't any prints. We will find out in the next episode that some DNA evidence was lifted from the crime scene; but that wouldn't be considered a "new" lead when the test results came back, would it?

 In rehearsing what happened aboard the *Zeus Faber*, Commander Johansen indicates that they could not surface, though the men aboard the submarine were dying of radiation poisoning, because there was a Japanese destroyer circling above them. Yet in the next episode we will see one of those same men in the final death throes, and the screen text will identify the date as "August 19, 1953." There are only two possibilities when attempting to resolve these two facts. Either a Japanese destroyer was circling above the sub *eight years* after the end of World War II, or this man who received high doses of radiation and was severely burned managed to hang on to life for *eight years*—though the prognosis for everyone else under these conditions seems to be *much* more grim.

Trivia Questions

1 What is the name of the doctor who cares for the French sailors in San Diego?

2 Who calls to tell Scully that Skinner has been shot?

Trivia Answers
1 Dr. Seizer.
2 Kim Cook from the director's office.

230

Piper Maru

Apocrypha

(Part 2 of 2)

PLOT SUMMARY

Returning to Washington, D.C., with Mulder, Krycek disappears after an aborted attempt on his life by Cancerman's forces.

Meanwhile, DNA analysis identifies Skinner's shooter as the same man who killed Melissa Scully. And when Skinner regains consciousness, he tells Scully that his would-be killer also helped Krycek steal the digital tape ("Paper Clip"). Eventually Scully apprehends the man (Louis Cardinal), but he apparently commits suicide while in custody.

At the same time, using a locker key taken from Krycek, Mulder retrieves a package. Though empty, it contains a faint impression: the phone number for the Consortium's meeting room in New York. Mulder calls and, surprisingly enough, the Well-Manicured Man agrees to meet. In exchange for information on Krycek, he confirms that the *Piper Maru* was investigating a UFO recovery site, though he admits that no one knows what killed the sailors.

Mulder knows. The alien from the craft is responsible. It has waited in the ocean all these years and uses an oil-like substance to transfer itself from person to person. In control of Krycek, it seeks out Cancerman and trades the digital tape for the opportunity to return to its vessel, which is stored in an abandoned missile silo. Cancerman is happy to oblige, though Krycek ultimately finds the deal less than satisfactory: Once the alien vacates, Krycek discovers that he's been "buried alive" with the extraterrestrial craft.

Onscreen Locations

- Navy Hospital, Pearl Habor, Hawaii, August 19, 1953
- Northeast Georgetown Medical Center, Washington, D.C.
- Dulles International Airport, Washington, D.C.
- County road 512, Maryland
- 46th Street, New York City
- Rockville, Maryland
- New York City
- Central Park
- Black Crow, North Dakota

Ruminations

The shape of the UFO in this episode harkens back quite nicely to the craft we saw on Ellens Air Base during "Deep Throat."

Great ending on this episode. I love the way it picks up the thought first voiced by Commander Johansen in the previous episode—that conscience is nothing more than the dead speaking to us from beyond the grave. The creators do a wonderful job combining this thought with Scully's observation that the dead cry out for justice and the shot that follows of Krycek crying out for redemption.

Geographical Inconsistencies

- Black Crow, North Dakota, doesn't exist.

Plot Oversights

- This body-jumping alien does us a great service so *The X-Files* can continue as a series. Throughout this and the previous episode, it shows no aversion to flashing anyone and everyone in its path. But even though Mulder splays a threatening attitude toward Krycek, it doesn't give our hero so much as a suntan! If it's *that* considerate, why did it expose all those sailors to radiation—both on the submarine and in the *Piper Maru?*

In a conversation with Agent Pendrell, Scully looks over the information gleaned from Louis Cardinal's saliva. She says it indicates that the shooter was probably a male in his forties with B-positive blood. She then grumps that they knew this already from the waitress's description. Now . . . I'm willing to concede that Washington, D.C., waitresses might be among the best in the country, but I'd be really surprised if the waitress in that café could figure out Louis Cardinal's blood type!

My appreciation for the Consortium dropped a notch during this episode. Eavesdropping on a meeting at 46th Street in New York City, we hear that the group is just learning about the *Piper Maru* and the fate of her sailors at San Diego Naval Hospital. Mulder knew about that at the beginning of the previous episode! He's been to *Hong Kong and back!* Granted, Cancerman would not have been forthcoming with this information, since it suggests that there's an information leak concerning the Defense Department files, but doesn't the Consortium have any other sources for intelligence within the United States?

Mulder gives us the only working theory in the episode for how the alien body-jumps. He believes that it uses oil as a medium. (The same oil found on the diving suit, Gauthier, and Gauthier's wife. The same oil that spews from the captain of the submarine at the beginning of the episode and Krycek at the end.) If that's true, how did the oil get into a sealed, pressurized diving suit at the beginning of the previous episode? How did it get into a submarine that was presumably heading for its destination while submerged? (And how did it keep the P-51

pilot alive for fifty years underwater?! Or was that just some kind of mirage?)

Mulder puts on another blinding display of intuitive insight in this episode. The conversation between Mulder and the Well-Manicured Man soon centers on Krycek. After Mulder mutters that the Consortium doesn't know where Krycek is either, the Well-Manicured Man says, "Mr. Mulder, anyone can be gotten to. Certainly, you've no doubt of that." Now . . . you or I would suppose that the Well-Manicured Man is saying that the Consortium *will* find Krycek eventually. That's why we're not heroes! We listen too literally. Mulder somehow immediately makes the connection that Skinner is in danger.

The job performance of the orderlies at Northeast Georgetown Medical Center is nothing less than spectacular. Scully arrives at the hospital with Mulder's warning ringing in her ears, only to learn that Skinner has just been transferred. In fact Skinner departed so recently that Scully catches up to the ambulance on foot! Obviously, *very* little time has passed. Yet, amazingly enough, Skinner's room has already been cleared and the beds remade!

It must be wonderful to live a charmed life! Scully calls to tell Mulder that Krycek is at an abandoned missile silo "somewhere" in North Dakota. Mulder tells her to meet him at Washington's Dulles International Airport with two tickets to North Dakota. Scully doesn't even ask, "To where in North Dakota?" She just knows that she can pick a city and it will be the right one! (To bad we don't all have scripts for our existence, eh?)

Changed Premises

Skinner tells Scully that the man who shot him also helped Krycek steal the digital cassette in the stairwell of the hospital. From this statement we can conclude that Skinner actually

THIRD SEASON

Trivia Questions

1 Which two agents does Scully work with on this case?

2 What is the number of the locker that Krycek claims contains the digital tape?

Trivia Answers
1 Agents Fuller and Caleca.
2 517.

233

Apocrypha

*Fabulous scene between
Scully and Cardinal as she
screams her interrogation,
trying to determine if he's
the man who shot her sis-
ter. It's easy to tell that
she really,* really *wants to
pull the trigger!*

saw Cardinal during this tussle. A review of the footage from "Paper Clip" doesn't support this conclusion. Three men attack Skinner.

The first—the man who walked by Melissa Scully's room several times—bursts from a door with a gun to knock Skinner off balance. As Skinner subdues this first opponent, Louis Cardinal comes up *from behind* and wraps a piano wire around Skinner's neck. Skinner attempts to break Cardinal's hold by shoving him backward into the wall, but Krycek appears to punch Skinner several times before taking the digital cassette and rendering Skinner unconscious with one final wallop. It doesn't look like Skinner has *any* opportunity to see Cardinal's face.

Equipment Oddities

⌧ At one point we see that Mulder has had the diving suit used at the beginning of the previous episode, "Piper Maru," flown to his basement office. I have no way to prove it, but it seems like it would be awfully difficult to get that piece of equipment into that office. Unless, of course, the walls come apart! (Wink, wink.)

Pusher

Onscreen Locations

🗵 Mt. Foodmore Supermarket, Loudoun County, Virginia

🗵 Beltway Commuter Lot, Falls Church, Virginia

🗵 Hearing Room A

🗵 Fairfax Mercy Hospital

Ruminations

Great scene at the end of this episode, even if it did have some quirks! (See below.)

I'll say it again! It's the details that I love about The X-Files. The episode opens with Modell shopping at the Mt. Foodmore Supermarket (great name!) for "carbo-boost" protein drinks—among other things. As a group of undercover police track him through the store, Modell approaches the checkout stand and picks up a tabloid newspaper. Perusing the cover, he chuckles. And who is featured on the cover? It's Flukeman from "The Host!" Fun stuff! But . . . is this just more proof that the conspirators are on an active disinformation campaign to deceive, obfuscate, and inveigle? By releasing a rag account of the story, are "they" planting doubt as to whether the events actually occurred? (Aaaaah!) By the way, although it's not visible on the screen, the tabloid paper does carry a date that is almost readable if you examine the picture of the newspaper on page 178 of Trust No One, The Official Third Season Guide To The X-Files. The date on the paper appears to be February 12, 1996 but it's hard to tell!

And while we're on the topic of lovely details, the lobby guard at FBI National

PLOT SUMMARY In Loudoun County, Virginia, the FBI arrests a man known as Pusher. Unfortunately, he escapes by talking a police officer into causing an accident. The agent in charge, Frank Burst, turns to Mulder and Scully for help, and soon the pair locates the man, only to have him attempt a second escape by coercing an agent to set himself on fire.

Though captured, Pusher—whose real name is Robert Patrick Modell—is soon released. Not only are the allegations that he can impose his will on others considered fantastic, but also Modell puts "the whammy" on the judge. Modell has a brain tumor that has given him the ability to control another person's actions. The tumor *will* kill him without an operation, but Modell chooses instead to lead Mulder and Scully in a chase that ends with all three sitting at a table. A revolver with a single bullet lies before them.

In control, Modell forces Mulder to pick up the gun. Modell takes the first pull of the trigger before compelling Mulder to place the muzzle to his forehead and take the second. When Scully's turn arrives, however, she bolts for the fire alarm, and the bell provides enough distraction for Mulder to turn the gun on Modell a second time—this time with the bullet in the chamber.

Headquarters who tells Modell the location of the computer records is the same guard who greets Scully in "The Blessing Way" after she is suspended and has to come in by the "front door." Good continuity!

Finally, the selection of Svengali to play on the television of Modell's apartment was a nice touch.

Plot Oversights

☒ The arrest of Modell at the beginning of the episode contains several ponderments. First, Frank Burst says that he wants Modell in a car with a "cage." Yet, the police car that transports Modell seems to be missing this requirement. Second, why do the law-enforcement vehicles come to a halt at a stop sign when they all have their lights flashing? Silly me, I thought those twirling lights automatically gave police the right-of-way. (Granted, Modell may be the reason that Kerber stops the car, but why do the others, and why doesn't Burst—who's riding shotgun with Modell—complain about it?) Third, Burst tells Mulder and Scully that Kerber unlocked Modell's restraints just before he died. Okay, fine. But why are all the other officers who assisted with the arrest driving *in front of* the car that holds Modell? Wouldn't it make more sense to have a few cars bring up the rear? (Of course, if the creators did that, Modell wouldn't have escaped!)

☒ Having never set fire to myself, I cannot say for certain, but doesn't it seem like the gasoline-soaked agent would have ignited long before he touched the cigarette lighter to his clothing? Supposedly he's dripping with fuel, and he holds an open flame less than a foot from his body. Wouldn't the fumes of the gasoline catch and run the flames back to his chest?

☒ After the FBI raids his apartment, Modell talks Frank Burst into killing himself with a heart attack. For dramatic effect, the creators have Scully stare dumbfounded until the commercial break, making our favorite doctor-turned-FBI-agent seem ineffectual. And if that wasn't bad enough, Scully gives up much too quickly when she finally does find the time to start CPR.

☒ As mentioned above, the Russian roulette scene with Modell, Mulder, and Scully is great fun, but it has a few problems. It's obvious that Modell is struggling to control Mulder. It's obvious as well that Scully realizes this, because she flees the room to pull the switch to ring the bell to rattle the Mulder to pull the trigger to shoot the gun to *kill the creep!* Given this realization, why didn't Scully assault Modell? Better yet, why didn't she tackle him when he flipped open the cylinder on the revolver?! Once Modell flipped the cylinder to the side, the gun was disarmed, and it's likely Modell would have lost his hold over Mulder as he and Scully tumbled to the floor. (And honestly, I don't think Modell was controlling Scully as well. It appears that Modell can control only one person at a time. That's why Skinner wasn't affected by "the whammy" when he found Modell and Holly together in the Computer Records Office.)

Changed Premises

☒ In "F. Emasculata," Mulder one-upped a U.S. marshal named Tapia by getting the last number dialed from a pay phone. This trick allowed Mulder and Tapia to heat up the trail of two escaped convicts. In this episode, however, Mulder stands and wonders out loud if a given pay phone has redial—obviously hoping for a way to find the number of the last call placed from it. Thankfully, Scully stands nearby and can do what Mulder did in "F. Emasculata." Did Mulder just feign ignorance to see if Scully could come up with the correct answer?!

Equipment Oddities

☒ When Modell calls a pay phone at a Beltway commuter lot in Falls Church, Virginia, Mulder pulls a tape recorder from his pocket to capture the conversation. Strangely enough, he holds the recorder next to the *mouthpiece* of the handset and doesn't bother to rock the *earpiece* away from his head. Won't he get only one side of the conversation?

☒ Moments after authorities break into his

partment, Modell phones home. Frank Burst
akes the call. Mulder runs into the next room
nd picks up a second handset. For a time, you
an hear an echo. Evidently the creators want us
o believe that the conversation coming from the
ext room takes enough time to reach Mulder
hat it sounds delayed when compared to what's
oming from the handset. Modell must have a
ig apartment to cause this kind of delay! In
ddition, the delay seems to disappear only
moments later.

Continuity and
Production Problems

Coming to Modell's apartment, Mulder slaps
warrant on his television. In the close-up, it's
lmost vertical. In the wide shot, it's angled.

Trivia Questions

1 When did Pusher's first ad appear in *American Ronin?*

2 What is Robert Modell's room number in the hospital?

Teso Dos Bichos

PLOT SUMMARY

The violence apparent in the disappearance of a researcher named Craig Horning brings Mulder and Scully to the Boston Museum of Natural History. Interestingly enough, Horning was cataloging bones recently taken from the Ecuadorian highlands. The local inhabitants, the Secona, claim the bones are the remains of an amaru—a female shaman—and believe that all those who come in contact with the bones will be cursed until the bones are returned to their native land. (In fact, Dr. Roosevelt, the leader of the expedition that retrieved the amaru, died shortly after its discovery.)

Then two more individuals disappear, convincing Mulder that there is an extraordinary phenomenon at work—possibly even a transmigration of the soul into an animal host. Scully has a simpler explanation. Alonzo Bilac accompanied Roosevelt on the dig and has been a vocal opponent of keeping the bones ever since. He also continues to experiment with a Secona hallucinogen called yaje. Scully thinks Bilac has committed the murders during a drug-induced frenzy. Unfortunately, Bilac soon disappears as well—apparently dragged into a network of tunnels under the museum. Mulder and Scully follow and find a cache of torn bodies. They've been mauled to death by killer kitties, who turn on Mulder and Scully next. Thankfully, the pair manages to escape. And after the bones are returned, the attacks mysteriously stop.

Onscreen Locations

- ☒ Teso Dos Bichos excavation, Ecuadorian highlands, South America
- ☒ Hall of Indigenous Peoples, Boston Museum of Natural History

Ruminations

I really can't take credit for the "killer kitties" reference in the plot summary. Gillian Anderson used it herself during an appearance on The Late Show with David Letterman shortly after filming this episode. She also revealed that she is allergic to cats so the special effects guys rigged up a stunt cat-dummy for her to wrestle with near the end of the episode. In fact, if you limber up your freeze-frame thumb, you should have absolutely no difficulty figuring out which scenes feature the stunt dummy. And . . . once you see them, the end of this episode will always bring a smile to your face! (Needless to say, Gillian Anderson seemed less-than-thrilled with having to perform with the faux-cat.)

Plot Oversights

☒ How did the bones of the amaru make it to Boston in the first place? They are uncovered by the Secona in the highlands of Ecuador. Dr. Roosevelt tells Dr. Bilac to have the pieces cleared and packed. He says, "It's going with us." This would seem to indicate that Roosevelt planned to have the amaru's remains stored at the excavation site until he left the area. This is, after all, the highlands of Ecuador. You can't exactly place a call to United Parcel Service and have them pick it up! However, once this clearing and packing are accomplished, Roosevelt is attacked and killed by some kind of wild animal. Wouldn't the amaru still be at the excavation site? Wouldn't Bilac be in charge by default? Isn't Bilac the one who thinks that the amaru's remains should stay where they were? Why don't the Secona unpack the thing and put it back in the ground *before* Bilac leaves for America?!

🗙 Evidently Scully has given up on the concept of electricity at potential crime scenes and the bad guys' hideouts. She comes to Bilac's house late one night with a flashlight, and as she walks into the entryway she doesn't even *try* the light switch. Why should she? Every other time she's come to this type of place after dark the lights haven't worked. Why should they start now?

🗙 We are not impressed with a certain officer of the Boston Police Department. After Bilac disappears from a room at the museum, Scully asks the officer if there are any other doors and windows in the room. The guy replies that he has checked and there is only one way in or out. Moments later, Mulder finds an *open* heating vent that looks about three feet wide and two feet tall! Did the officer just *miss* this huge opening in the wall, or was he only looking for doors and windows?

Equipment Oddities

🗙 I realize that in the past I have criticized the enigmatic Dr. Scully for using her cell phone when there's a land line nearby, but I think she swings a bit too far the other way in this episode. From Bilac's home she calls Mulder's cell phone. Unless I'm missing some crucial piece of information, that means Scully had to call Washington, D.C., long distance because Mulder's cell phone company is in the Washington, D.C., area. Mulder's cell phone company then figured out where he was and forwarded the call. Not that it matters because Bilac dies in this episode, but next month Bilac's estate is going to get charged for this call! (Given that Scully is investigating Bilac at the time, this scene is strangely reminiscent of the interrogation billing techniques of *Brazil*. In that

movie the state not only tortures you for information, it also charges your immediate family for services rendered by the interrogator!)

Continuity and Production Problems

🗙 More evidence of a dastardly disinformation campaign initiated by the conspirators. In the previous episode, we saw that the Military/Industrial/Entertainment Complex had printed a story about Flukeman in a tabloid it distributes at grocery stores around the country. Obviously they did this to cast doubt on the veracity of reports circulating about a worm/man found in the sewers of Newark, N.J. And now—in this episode—we learn the extent of the conspirators' power. Somehow they managed to terminate the employment of the sewage treatment plant foreman whom we met in "The Host" and run him out of town! The poor guy is in Boston, trying to eke out a living working as a security guard for the Boston Museum of Natural History! Even worse, the Military/Industrial/Entertainment Complex wiped his memory. (Aaaaah!) Mulder saved his life, but he acts like he's never met Mulder before. (Of course, Mulder doesn't remember him, either! There's something very strange going on here.) On the upside, at least the guy survived the mating ritual with Flukeman!

🗙 Does the exterior of the Boston Museum of Natural History look *really* familiar to anyone else? Maybe, *exactly* like the exterior of the Excelsis Dei Convalescent Home in Worcester, Massachusetts? (See "Excelsis Dei.") Both buildings probably just had the same architect.

🗙 Normally, I don't comment on actors. As a nitpicker, I don't deal in reality, so my response to poor acting is usually: What's an actor? Unfortunately, the performance of a particular actor in this episode is so very poor that it destroys any sense of believability in *every*

THIRD SEASON

Trivia Questions

❶ What is Dr. Roosevelt's first name?

❷ What is Mona Wustner's educational status?

Trivia Answers
❶ Carl.
❷ She's a Ph.D. candidate at Boston University.

Teso Dos Bichos

scene in which the actor appears. The actor continually looks off-camera for the next cue and even when the verbalized lines do hit their mark, they are often stiff and unnatural. I mean, come on, I've seen *dogs* do *a lot* better than *this!* Take Scully's dog, for instance. It's irritatingly cute, but it did give a *very* convincing performance during the famed bath scene from "War of the Coprophages." And what about the dog from "Ice"? Such passion! Such integrity! Such commitment to its craft!

In comparison, *this* episode has a half-rate, two-bit canine actor named Sugar who really needs to get more experience before he or she makes another attempt at big-time television. The sad fact is this, Sugar, babe, you're cute— and you've probably enjoyed a good measure of success in your modeling career already— but listen up, darling, you *really* need to learn how to do something else besides stare at your off-camera trainer during every *moment* of *every scene!*

🗶 Speaking of great animal performances, how about them *cats!?* Not only do they generate a cacophony to add to the drama at the end of the program, they also remain deadly quiet when they attack Dr. Lewton earlier in the episode to ensure that we won't suspect them as the true culprits too soon. Kudos!

TRIATHLON TRIVIA ON PLACES

MATCH THE PLACE TO THE DESCRIPTION TO THE EPISODE

PLACE	DESCRIPTION	EPISODE
1. Allegheny Catholic Hospital	A. Scully was used to trash one of its rooms	a. "Ice"
2. Arctic Ice Core Project	B. Mulder and Scully met there in secret	b. "Beyond the Sea"
3. Astadourian Lightning Observatory	C. Where Mulder met The Thinker	c. "Fallen Angel"
4. Blue Devil Brewery	D. Hepcat Helm's pride and joy	d. "Irresistible"
5. Bright Angel Halfway House	E. Site of Scully's abduction	e. "Tooms"
6. Budget-Rest Motel	F. A youthful indiscretion occurred atop it	f. "Fresh Bones"
7. Central Park	G. Where Kevin Kryder attended school	g. "The Blessing Way"
8. Charles Lindberg Terminal	H. Aliens trashed one of its rooms	h. "731"
9. Cut Bank Creek	I. Samuel Aboah was quarantined there	i. "Soft Light"
10. Druid Hill Sanitarium	J. Lauren Kyte found employment there	j. "Zero Sum"
11. Ellens Air Base	K. Site of Warren Dupre's last stickup	k. "El Mundo Gira"
12. Folkstone Municipal Cemetery	L. Where B. J. Morrow disclosed a dream	l. "The Host"
13. Fort Marlene	M. Videolinked Mulder to the Lone Gunmen	m. "Momento Mori"
14. Garden of Reflection	N. Dr. Yonechi froze to death in comfort	n. "War of the Coprophages"
15. Glenview Lake	O. Its residents were given the black cancer	o. "Pusher"
16. Hansen's Disease Research Facility	P. There's a little Nazi storm trooper nearby	p. "Tunguska"
17. Harrow Convalescent Home	Q. Where Scully found the "wellspring"	q. "Kaddish"
18. Hotel George Mason	R. Where Mulder saw a military UFO	r. "Piper Maru"
19. Hotel James Monroe	S. After fishing there, Ish saw the manitou	s. "Squeeze"
20. JFK Elementary School	T. Mulder met the Well-Manicured Man there	t. "Paper Clip"
21. Jojo's Copy Center	U. Lucy Householder's home	u. "Duane Barry"
22. La Ranchera Market	V. It's located on Route 4	v. "End Game"
23. Lake Betty Park	W. Leonard Betts worked there after he "died"	w. "Leonard Betts"
24. Lincoln Park	X. Got worms?	x. "Little Green Men"
25. Lombard Research Facility	Y. Once inside, Scully shot Lucas Henry	y. "Anasazi"
26. Maryland Marine Bank	Z. Where Max Fenig rifled Mulder's room	z. "Humbug"
27. Massachusetts Institute of Robotics	AA. Scully was kidnapped after leaving there	aa. "Ascension"

28. Monroe Mutual Insurance Co.	BB. Site of Tooms's confinement	bb. "Fire"
29. Mt. Foodmore Supermarket	CC. Where Colonel Wharton was buried	cc. "Revelations"
30. Mt. Zion Medical Center	DD. Where Scully met the Well-Manicured Man	dd. "Tempus Fugit"
31. NASA Goddard Space Flight Center	EE. Site of Dr. Zama's atrocities	ee. "Teliko"
32. Paradise Motel	FF. Patrick Newirth burned its carpet	ff. "Shadows"
33. Park Street Synagogue	GG. Its students were swarmed by bees	gg. "Lazarus"
34. Ridgeway Elementary School	HH. Gabrielle Buente worked the night shift	hh. "Aubrey"
35. San Diego Naval Hospital	II. Where Flukeman called a toilet home	ii. "Fearful Symmetry"
36. Sir Authur Conan Doyle's tombstone	JJ. It holds Scully's ova	jj. "Synchrony"
37. 66 Exeter Street	KK. Dr. Ivanov built cockroaches there	kk. "Terma"
38. Skyland Mountain	LL. Where Robert Modell is arrested	ll. "Clyde Bruckman's Final Repose"
39. Strughold Mining Company	MM. It got the Mars rock	mm. "The Erlenmeyer Flask"
40. Tabernacle of Terror	NN. A golem haunted its attic	nn. "Deep Throat"
41. Travel Time	OO. Cared for the crew of the *Piper Maru*	oo. "Shapes"
42. U.S. Botanical Garden	PP. Tooms's favorite address	pp. "Apocrypha"
43. Vacation Village Motor Lodge	QQ. Lots and lots of files	qq. "Oubliette"
44. Watergate Hotel	RR. Duane Barry stopped there for directions	rr. "D.P.O."

SCORING

(BASED ON NUMBER OF CORRECT ANSWERS)

0–10	Skinner-like.
11–19	Scully-like.
20–29	Mulder-like.
30–44	Spooky!

PLACES ANSWER KEY: **1.** W w **2.** X a **3.** V rr **4.** Y b **5.** U qq **6.** Z c **7.** T pp **8.** AA d **9.** S oo **10.** BB e **11.** R nn **12.** CC f **13.** Q mm **14.** DD g **15.** P ll **16.** EE h **17.** O kk **18.** FF i **19.** N jj **20.** GG j **21.** M ii **22.** HH k **23.** II l **24.** L hh **25.** JJ m **26.** K gg **27.** KK n **28.** J ff **29.** LL o **30.** I ee **31.** MM p **32.** H dd **33.** NN q **34.** G cc **35.** OO r **36.** F bb **37.** PP s **38.** E aa **39.** QQ t **40.** D z **41.** RR u **42.** C y **43.** A v **44.** B x

Triathlon Trivia
on Places

Hell Money

Onscreen Locations

☒ Chinatown, San Francisco

☒ Bayside Funeral Home

☒ Highland Park Cemetery

☒ Coroner's Office, Central Station

☒ San Francisco Police Department

☒ St. Francis General Hospital

☒ Organ Procurement Organization, downtown San Francisco

Ruminations

The possible date on this episode comes from Glen Chao's description of the Festival of the Hungry Ghosts—a festival he claims is just concluding. He says it occurs on the fifteenth day of the seventh moon on the Chinese calendar. According to my sources, the Chinese year begins in mid-February. The fifteenth day after the seventh moon would land sometime in August (I think). Unfortunately, if this is correct, "Hell Money" was aired far out of sequence, given a prior date of January 12, 1996, for "Syzygy" and a subsequent date of March 7, 1996, for "Avatar."

Unanswered Questions

☒ So . . . why did Johnny Lo die? Did he cross the game's proprietor, or did he draw a bad tile and refuse to pay up? Or did he die for a completely different reason? "And what about the other young men who died in similar fashion? According to Mulder, there have also been three

PLOT SUMMARY In San Francisco, Johnny Lo is burned alive inside a crematorium. Given the security guard's testimony of three ghostly beings at the scene, Mulder wonders if the murders are the work of malevolent spirits. (After all, Lo's apartment has the words "haunted house" scrawled in Chinese on the door.)

Then the same three "ghosts" visit a graveyard—burying a body that's missing a heart, cornea, and kidney. And while interviewing Shuyang Hsin—a man who installed carpet over a bloodstain in Lo's apartment the day after his death—Mulder and Scully note that Hsin has recently lost an eye as well. In fact, Hsin is part of a deadly game. Each night, those involved contribute to a pot that increases until someone wins. Each night, one man is chosen by lot to select a tile from a bowl. If the man picks well, he wins the money. Otherwise he must donate the organ indicated—harvested and sold on the black market by the game's proprietor. Fortunately, Mulder and Scully intervene in time to save Hsin's life, but everyone involved refuses to testify, so the proprietor goes free. And, several days later, the local detective who assisted on the case, Glen Chao, wakes up to find himself inside a crematorium . . . just as the flames begin.

cases of murder by cremation in Seattle, three in Los Angeles and two in Boston."

Plot Oversights

☒ Li Oi-Huan is the first man we see select a tile and attempt to win the jackpot in the game.

He lifts the jar over his head and shakes it. (Given that the jackpot tile is the last one dropped into the jug, I can guarantee you that *I* wouldn't shake it nearly as hard as these guys, but that's another story.) Then Oi-Huan lowers the container to make his selection. He lowers it, and lowers it, and lowers it. And then he looks *down!* Granted, you can't actually see what Oi-Huan sees, but it sure seems like he could look into the jar! Somehow I don't think this would be allowed.

☒ There's a touching subplot in this episode concerning Hsin and his sick daughter. Hsin is playing the game, attempting to win the jackpot so his daughter can have the necessary treatments to get well. In one scene, Hsin wins the right to draw for the jackpot. Unfortunately, he selects a tile with the symbol for "eye." That night, the game's proprietor removes Hsin's left eye. The next day, Mulder and Scully come to interview Hsin, and Mulder notices the triangular-shaped tile that Hsin drew the night before standing upright on a table. Making the intuitive leap that it must be important, Mulder steals it. We might as well ignore Mulder's pilfering. Mulder does illegal stuff all the time. (Of course, it's not really illegal in his mind, because his cause is righteous. Just remember to hide your silverware if he ever shows up at your door for an interview!)

On the other hand, Hsin's display of this tile in the first place deserves a bit of scrutiny. Is this really how the game works?! ("Thanks for the eye. Oh, by the way, here's the tile you drew. You're welcome to take it home as a keepsake.") Is this some sort of consolation prize for losers? And even if the game's proprietor has a sick enough sense of humor to give the tile to the player, why would Hsin display it prominently in his apartment? Isn't he trying to hide what he's doing from his daughter? Wouldn't she make a connection between the fact that her father just lost an eye and that same night a tile appeared bearing the symbol for "eye"?

☒ Obviously, Mulder has done something to offend the good folks at the FBI field office in San Francisco. When Chao is attacked and taken to the hospital, Mulder and Scully must abandon their stakeout of Hsin's apartment. This allows Hsin to travel to the game unnoticed. Too bad Scully couldn't sweet-talk the field office into sparing a couple of agents for a few hours.

☒ The episode begins in the same manner that it ends: A young man burns to death in a crematorium. Early in the show, Mulder and Scully go to Johnny Lo's apartment and find blood on the carpet. Later, after Chao is attacked and brought to the hospital, Mulder makes the leap that the blood on the carpet came from Chao. This *is* normal operating procedure for Mulder. What's fascinating is that Scully concurs, telling the lead detective from the San Francisco police force that the blood on the carpet "was Detective Chao's." On *what* does she base this statement? The fact that the blood on the carpet was O-negative, just like Chao's! Excuse me: Just how many *thousands* of people in San Francisco have O-negative blood?!

Equipment Oddities

☒ Joining the scene in the funeral parlor, we see a security guard playing a handheld computerized game of blackjack. He hears a noise. He pulls out his flashlight and cautiously enters the room that contains the cremation oven. Obviously this guy has watched too many episodes of *The X-Files*, because he doesn't even attempt to turn on a light.

Continuity and Production Problems

☒ Sometime after arriving at the crematorium where the young man dies at the beginning of the episode, Mulder opens the door of the oven and asks the lead detective if he has any leads.

At this point, the camera is set inside the oven and begins a gradual crawl toward Mulder, who stands at the open doorway. As the camera moves forward, there's an odd reflection at the very top of the screen. It looks like the floor of the oven, but it also looks slightly distorted around the edges, as if the image is being magnified somehow. (I have no idea what this is, but take a look.)

X Disgusted with the game, Chao goes to its location and dumps the main table. He is surprised to see that all the "donation" tiles are the same. The game is rigged to make sure Hsin would die on this night. He shouts this inequity to the room, and a riot breaks out. Accordingly, the background music swells with percussive oriental music. Then the camera cuts to Mulder and Scully, who are investigating a cache of extracted organs on the ground floor below. Fascinatingly enough, the "background" music drops in volume exactly the same amount as the boisterous voices! What can this mean? Is the background music not really background music but music instead that originates from the game

room itself?! Does the game have its own live music as well? ("You lose!" Wah-wah-wah-wah-wah.) And even if the game does have its own musicians, why would they begin playing the moment the riot broke out? Did they just happen to have the sheet music for "Meditations on Fisticuffs" nearby? (Personally, I kind of like this idea. I've always thought that we all should carry around Walkmans loaded with personal background music so we could tell when an important moment was about to transpire in our lives. "Just listen for the swell of the strings, son.")

Trivia Questions

1 What herbal medicines was Johnny Lo taking?

2 Where does Wu Chang Kuei drag the souls of doomed men after collection?

Trivia Answers
1 Skullcap root and Chinese angelica.
2 Ti Yu—the Chinese hell.

José Chung's
From Outer Space

PLOT SUMMARY

"The truth" goes for a wild ride when author José Chung comes to the Bureau. He is documenting a purported abduction of two teenagers in Klass County, Washington, and wants to include Dana Scully's version of events, since she and Mulder investigated the case. Of course, Chung has no more certainty of what actually happened in Klass County even after speaking with Scully, but here are some possibilities.

Depending on your viewpoint: Two teenagers either were or were not abducted by gray aliens—or they were abducted by a big red alien who abducted the gray aliens as well. Roky Crikenson may or may not have witnessed the abductions, but in either case he managed to pen a screenplay about a red alien named Lord Kinbote, who spoke in King James English. And the gray aliens may or may not have been aliens at all but merely air force personnel, in alien costumes, one of whom may have spoken with Mulder. On the other hand, Mulder simply may have spent that evening eating pie in a diner. Either way, at least we know that Mulder spent the following night in Scully's room, although he slept in a chair, and that may or may not have been because of a visit from the infamous Men in Black—one of whom may have looked just like Alex Trebek!

Onscreen Locations

🗙 Klass County, Washington

Ruminations

In my opinion, this is one of the greatest hours of science fiction ever penned for broadcast television. It is a fabulous marriage of writing, acting (How 'bout that Charles Nelson Reilly?), directing, special effects, and music (Love that walking bass!). Not only that, the episode actually says something about life! It contains a fascinating—and disturbing—message about the permeability of "truth" (at least from the viewpoint of The X-Files).

There are so many things that are done so well here: The homage to Star Wars at the very beginning; the clever scene transitions; the parallelism with the placement of the characters in the hypnotism scenes; the repetitive phraseology ("I know how crazy . . . ," "You're a dead man!"); Detective Manner's "bleepin'" mannerisms; Lord Kinbote's King James English; the usage of Yappi from "Clyde Bruckman's Final Repose"; UFO pilot Jack Schaeffer sculpting his potatoes à la Close Encounters of the Third Kind; the surprise appearance of Alex Trebek. It all just works!

And how about Blaine Faulkner, the sci-fi fanatic who took the footage of the "alien" autopsy? Love the little posable alien action figure in his room. Love the Space: Above and Beyond T-shirt! (Both my wife and I really miss that series. I was certain it was going to make it. Probably would have, too, if Fox hadn't buried it on Sunday night!) And did you notice the Millennium Falcon in Faulkner's bedroom? And the Enterprise-D? And the Klingon bird-of-prey? (By the way, what was that last ship hanging near Faulkner's "I Want to Believe" poster?) Also, did you notice the poster? It uses the same cture as Mulder's, but the typography has en changed. Big "I." Little "Want to." Big Believe." From a distance it reads, "I Believe"!

There are three difficulties with this isode that I should mention before going any rther. As you can imagine, it was next to npossible to pick just one great line from this stallment of The X-Files. Also, since most of e episode occurs as remembrance, a good ortion of the nitpicking that follows can easi- be explained. Finally, it would be interesting hear the creators take on the time frame for ese events. The two young people disappear r a time in Klass County. Mulder and Scully onduct an investigation. At some later date, osé Chung spends three months in Klass ounty after which he interviews Scully. Then hung writes From Outer Space. It has to be dited, typeset, and printed. (The Nitpicker's uide for X-philes took one year from the time began writing until it hit the bookstore helves, and that's considered fast in the pub- shing world.) The episode then ends with cully reading From Outer Space with her legs ropped up in the basement office. It isn't nreasonable to think that the episode easily pans eighteen months, if not two years!

Unanswered Questions

3 What actually happened to Harold and Chrissy?

Geographical Inconsistencies

3 There is no Klass County in Washington tate.

Plot Oversights

X Call me old-fashioned, but it just seems odd. We join the two young people featured in this pisode, Harold and Chrissy, as Harold drives along some backwoods road and tells Chrissy that he's crazy about her. Chrissy smiles and says that she likes him a lot but it's their first date and she thinks they need time to get to know one another. Sage advice, indeed. Here's what I find strange: They are abducted moments later, and—in time—it is revealed that they had intercourse *before* the "aliens" appeared. In other words, Harold picks her up. They jump into the backseat. They jump each other. They have sex. They get dressed. Harold begins to drive her somewhere. Harold tells her he loves her. And Chrissy responds by saying that they need time to get to know each other?! Does anyone else out there think there's something *wrong* with this scenario?

X Reading from Crikenson's screenplay *The Truth About Aliens,* Mulder learns that Crikenson approached the abduction site as Lord Kinbote flailed over the heads of two cowering gray "aliens." (Harold and Chrissy were lying uncon- scious on the ground beneath the trio.) From all indications, this moment is very close to the beginning of Crikenson's tale of aliens. Yet, when the camera cuts to Mulder holding Crikenson's script, it looks like he's about a third of the way through! What came before this? Did Crikenson open the screenplay with his childhood? (Gotta get that character development in!)

X At the end of the program, Blaine Faulkner lands Roky Crikenson's old job as a lineman for the electric company. He rises slowly to a trans- former that is mounted on a pole. Sparks begin to fly. Faulkner gives a plaintive scream. Yes, it's cute. But is it really likely that Faulkner would be hired as a lineman for the electric company, given his ineptitude? And if he was, is it likely that he would still be alive after getting cross- ways with a power transformer that large?

Equipment Oddities

X Where does Jack Schaeffer get the cigarette

Trivia Questions

1 Not including *From Outer Space,* name two books by José Chung.

2 According to its proprietor, in what café does Mulder eat piece after piece of sweet potato pie?

247

José Chung's From Outer Space

he smokes aboard Lord Kinbote's vessel? Do those naked-alien costumes have pockets?

⊠ And while we are on the topic of the aliens' costumes, it's very impressive that the eyelids work! When Scully removes the alien mask during the autopsy, the camera provides a quick view inside. There doesn't appear to be any special machinery, but—while incarcerated by Lord Kinbote—Schaeffer squints and even closes his eyelids altogether! Kudos to the military men who designed the outfits.

⊠ In the footage of Yappi's alien-autopsy video, Scully holds a skull saw and uses it to begin cutting into the real-live dead alien's head. Oddly enough, when Scully later removes the alien mask, Robert Vallee's head is intact!

⊠ I am really impressed with the amenities in the motel room that Scully rents while staying in Klass County. After the visit from the Men in Black, Scully is awakened by a telephone call. A shot of Mulder shows a telephone on the small table beside him. Across the room, Scully reaches over and grabs the handset on a second phone, beside her bed. Two phones in the *same* room of a motel.

⊠ A milestone to note. At the very end of the episode, there's a shot of Mulder in bed, watching a video of Big Foot. This *may* be the first time that we see Mulder's bedroom. Prior to this, I wondered if Mulder even *had* a bedroom. Before this episode, we *always* see him sleeping on his couch. I assumed that he rented a small one-bedroom apartment and used the bedroom for a living room instead. (Remember, at one time there *was* a door between his entry area and the living room.) Unfortunately, there's really no way to prove that the room seen at the end of the episode is really in Mulder's apartment. Maybe he got tired of sleeping on the couch and rented a motel room for the night! On the other hand, if Mulder *does* actually have a

bedroom in his apartment, it would have to b off his kitchen. His entryway only leads to h living room straight ahead and his kitchen to h left. The living room has a door hard to the righ when you first enter, but it appears to b blocked off in "Grotesque," so it's probably closet. That only leaves the "never before see on terrestrial TV" area beyond his kitchen. (W get a glimpse of Mulder's kitchen in "Dee Throat" and "E.B.E." It's really scary that I know this stuff, isn't it?)

Continuity and Production Problems

⊠ Keep your eye on José Chung after he tell Scully that she has good taste as well as brain and beauty. He walks around Mulder's desk t take a seat on the opposite side, and when h rounds the corner, he *runs into the side!* You ca hear this big *thunk* just before he sits dow (Yes, it would happen in real life, but this is tele vision, and it's always amusing when creator don't bother to reshoot a scene.)

⊠ The first scene where Harold comes t Chrissy's house deserves a bit of scrutin Chrissy looks out the window and sees an alie shadow that eventually changes into Harold shadow as he walks away from her house Except, a bit later, the scene cuts to a revers angle of the house and there's no light that coul have caused the shadow in the first place (There is a porch light off to the side, but tha would have created an angled shadow.)

⊠ Reincarnation is alive and well on *The X Files*. The tarot card reader who was killed i "Clyde Bruckman's Final Repose" reappears i this episode as a hypnotist!

⊠ It's a common problem and nearly impossibl to avoid, but Schaeffer's cigarette grows i length just as the military come to take him fron his conversation with Mulder.

Avatar

Onscreen Locations

☒ Chesapeake Lounge, Ambassador Hotel

☒ 1223 Hanover Street, Georgetown

☒ Second District Police Station

☒ D.C. Police Impound Garage

☒ FBI Sci-Crime Lab

☒ Office of Professional Conduct Hearing

Ruminations

Just one of those odd little tidbits of information that the creators of The X-Files *like to hide along the way for diligent viewers to find! Halfway through the episode, Skinner's wife comes to his new residence. She has learned that he's under suspicion for murder and wants to make an attempt to provide him some comfort even though she knows that he probably won't receive it. After she leaves, Skinner leans down and retrieves a wedding picture from a nearby box. In the cut-away, you can see the box also contains a certificate from the American Academy of Law Enforcement Professionals. Since the certificate contains Skinner's full name, we now know that his middle initial, "S" stands for "Sergei."*

Yet again, the creators show a deep commitment to their "mythology." They pay William B. Davis to make a four-second cameo just so we, the viewers, will realize that Cancerman is behind the events.

In case you missed it, Skinner's wife told him where to find Scully, the escort, and the assassin. An examination of the closed captioning would have helped. During the salient scene, Skinner visits his wife in the hospital. As he

PLOT SUMMARY

After refusing to finalize his divorce, Assistant Director Skinner heads for a bar. In time, a woman named Carina Sayles approaches and—needing a distraction—Skinner takes her to bed. Jolting awake early the next morning, Skinner finds Sayles dead beside him. Her neck has been broken. Then someone runs Skinner's wife off the road. All the evidence points to Skinner, and in desperation he confides in Mulder. During the Vietnam War, he had a near-death experience in which an old woman carried him back to life. Recently the old woman has haunted his dreams. Skinner wonders if the old woman is responsible for the violence. Mulder suggests she may be protecting him instead.

Meanwhile, Mulder and Scully determine that Cancerman's forces have orchestrated the events to disgrace Skinner. Sayles was an escort, hired by a man who subsequently tossed Sayles's madam out a window. Taking another escort into protective custody, Mulder and Scully use her to set up a meeting. Unfortunately, the killer knows it's a trap and attacks Scully and the escort instead. Only the sudden appearance of Skinner saves the day—though he refuses to tell Mulder how he knew where to find them.

As the episode ends, Skinner dons his wedding ring, determined to make a fresh start with his marriage.

leaves, he looks back and sees the old woman lying in his wife's hospital bed. By the time he returns to the room, however, his wife once again lies in the bed. "Listen to me," she says, before the closed captioning adds, "You have to go." Evidently the creators thought the second statement made it a bit too obvious.

Plot Oversights

X Somehow Scully manages to procure a detailed account of Skinner's sleep disorder from the Bethesda Sleep Disorder Center. Wouldn't this be covered under doctor/patient confidentiality and therefore be inaccessible?

X Mulder claims that there are stories from the Middle Ages concerning the "succubus"—a spirit that would take on a corporeal manifestation to engage in intercourse with men. He claims the succubus always came in the form of an old woman. In fact, succubi were *always* said to be beautiful, desirable *young* women. In other words, if Mulder wanted to claim the involvement of a succubus, he should have interviewed the escorts—especially that leggy one at the end of the episode! (And really, if you just think about it for a moment, "young and desirable" makes a whole lot more sense than "old and haggard" when it comes to seducing men, doesn't it?)

X At some point during the episode, Carina Sayles's body is autopsied—as evidenced by the stitching on her chest. Surprisingly enough, her head hasn't been cut open. I guess the medical examiner who performed the postmortem doesn't subscribe to the Dana Scully School of Autopsy Methodology. (You may recall—in the episode "Little Green Men"—Scully tells a group of students at Quantico that it is advantageous to start an autopsy with the removal of the cranium.)

Changed Premises

X Several times this episode references the "Office of Professional Conduct." In "Fallen Angel," it was called the "Office of Professional Responsibility." The Real FBI tells me that "Office of Professional Responsibility" is the correct terminology. (It's an easy mistake to make!)

Equipment Oddities

X Rushing to the site of Sayles's murder, Mulder gets a call from Scully. In the middle of the conversation, the police escort Skinner out of the building. Mulder has a few words with his superior and then questions the lead detective about what happened. Afterward, Mulder returns the receiver to his ear and asks Scully if she got all that. Scully says she caught most of it. Obviously, the cell phone has been on the entire time, with Mulder holding it at his side. The odd thing is, when Mulder draws it up to his ear, there's a boop as if he pushed a button. Was this an accident? Why would he push a button on his cell phone while it was actively connected to Scully's phone?

X Evidently Mulder exceeded his boop quotient by the flagrant use of the boop in the previous nit. Only minutes later—after interviewing Sayles's madam—Mulder gets a call on his cell phone. Sitting in his car, Mulder extracts the receiver and begins talking. It looks like he hits the power button, but there's no boop in the sound track. (That'll teach him to be more careful where he uses those boops. After all, wouldn't want to have a "boop shortage," now, would we?)

X Realizing that the FBI has left behind a crucial piece of evidence, Mulder extracts the air bag from Skinner's car after it is used to run Skinner's wife off the road. The air bag is scanned, and a three-dimensional image emerges when run through the appropriate software. The image is then printed, and Mulder shows Scully a copy. We are *not* impressed with the printout! What little we see of the monitor screen as the graphic software constructs the face seems *much* more detailed than the blocky-blurry piece of paper that Mulder carries around. And if the graphic software is building a three-dimensional model, why doesn't Mulder have front and *side* views?

Continuity and Production Problems

❌ Trying to find out what happened while at the site of Sayles's murder, Mulder questions the lead detective. Mulder asks if the detective believes that Skinner is innocent. He steps closer to the detective during this question. The detective answers. Mulder then asks if the victim has been identified. Now Mulder has suddenly moved back to his previous position, and he steps forward again. (Normally I wouldn't use this type of nit, since the camera does cut away, and there is time for Mulder to move back. But the reaction shot of the detective is over Mulder's shoulder, and it does not appear that Mulder moves.)

Trivia Questions

❶ Who lifts the latent image of a face from the air bag for Mulder?

❷ What is the name of the escort whom Skinner saves at the end of this episode?

Trivia Answers

❶ Agent Pendrell.

❷ Judy Fairly. (Somehow I expected an escort to have a more boisterous name—something like Judy Goodly or Judy Verygoodly or Judy Sogoodlythatyoubetter-call 911 . . . never mind.)

Quagmire

PLOT SUMMARY

On very short notice, Mulder whisks Scully away to the Blue Ridge Mountains of Georgia to investigate two missing-persons reports. Only later does Scully realize that Mulder has brought her to Heuvelman's Lake, hoping to prove the existence of a large sea creature named Big Blue. Though Dr. Farraday, a local frog researcher, scoffs at the idea of a real monster in the lake, the death toll begins to rise. A half-eaten body is reeled in by a fisherman. A local shopowner is dragged into the lake (while he's making fake footprints in the mud, no less). A head bobs to the surface after a young man is pulled under. And a local photographer disappears after taking a frantic series of photos during what appears to be an attack. And if those weren't bad enough, Scully's dog even falls victim.

That night, Mulder and Scully rent a boat to patrol the lake, but soon Scully runs the boat aground and it sinks. Thankfully, Farraday wanders by to help them to shore. Then Farraday himself is attacked and Mulder gives chase—eventually gunning down the monster as it rushes to attack him as well. It turns out to be an alligator. But as Mulder wanders off, dejected, something very large quietly surfaces in the lake before disappearing into the depths.

Onscreen Locations

- **X** Striker's Cove, Heuvelman's Lake, Blue Ridge Mountains, Georgia
- **X** County road 33, Rigdon, Georgia
- **X** Ecology Sciences Lab, Heuvelman's Lake

Ruminations

Lots of great lines and fun continuity in this episode. Nice to see Queequeg again ("Clyde Bruckman's Final Repose" and "War of the Coprophages"), even if the little pooch does star as alligator appetizer. And the two surviving teenagers from "War of the Coprophages" are apparently working their way to Lauderdale from Miller's Grove, Massachusetts!

I especially love the whole idea of Ansel the photographer working for fifteen years to get his prize photo of Big Blue, only to find himself fumbling with his camera when he thinks the moment has finally arrived!

Plot Oversights

X At the beginning of the episode, Dr. Farraday presents his belief that the frog depopulation at Heuvelman's Lake is the result of man's encroachment. Dr. Bailey, an employee with the U.S. Forest Service, disagrees. He observes that frog populations are declining all over the globe and they can't possibly list all of them on the endangered-species list. Farraday then retorts that Bailey would find a way if the frogs were cute, furry animals. This seems to imply that Farraday believes the endangered-species list is slanted toward the protection of mammals. Not so. It is true that the current U.S. vertebrate list—maintained by the U.S. Field and Wildlife Service, Division of Endangered Species—has only 14 amphibians listed as endangered or threatened as compared to 71 mammals. But there are also 93 birds and *110* different types of *fish!* To make his point, Farraday should have said that Bailey would find a way if the frogs were cute, *furry-feathery-scaly* creatures. (And honestly, I think I can guarantee that a furry, feathery, scaly frog would garner *a lot* of attention!)

X Ansel must have a hearing impairment. On the day of his fateful appointment with the alligator, he positions a large inner tube just off-shore, laden with steaks. He turns his back to check his cameras, and the alligator yanks on the inner tube, causing a fairly loud "thwump." This is a quiet lakeside day, and Ansel doesn't even bother to turn his head and look!

X Did anyone else find it truly bizarre that Scully could lose her grip on her dog leash *twice* in one day? Something tells me she's just not trying!

GREAT LINES

"Three in one day, Sheriff. All this driving from crime scene to crime scene is giving me highway hypnosis."

—**Mulder** *to Sheriff Lance Hindt, trying to convince the sheriff to close the lake.*

X This Heuvelman's Lake has some fascinating geological structures. Scully runs a rental boat into a rock. The boat sinks no more than ten feet from the rock. It sinks *straight down.* Mulder and Scully talk for a time as they sit on the rock and await rescue. Farraday hears them from the shore and walks out to get them. They return with him to shore, and the water barely covers their ankles! So . . . on one side of the rock there's enough water to sink a good-size boat, and on the other there's a nice, flat shelf?! That's some drop-off!

X As we saw in "Humbug," the culprit in this episode seems to greatly accelerate its attacks so that our heroes can solve the case. Prior to the arrival of our intrepid pair, there were two disappearances spaced two weeks apart. In the few days that Mulder and Scully scamper around the lake, Ted Bertram is hauled away while making fake tracks, a young man is pulled under while snorkeling, Ansel Bray is devoured while attempting to photograph Big Blue, Scully's dog is eaten, a fisherman's arm is gnawed off, Farraday's leg is mauled, and Mulder has to defend *himself* with terminal force. That's *seven* attacks!

Equipment Oddities

X Much confusion surrounds the sonar display used on the boat that Scully pilots into a rock. The display scrolls from top to bottom. Presumably this means that up is forward and the little indicator in the middle of the screen is the boat. As Mulder and Scully are sailing along, "something" enters the screen from the bottom left side. As the screen continues to scroll down—indicating that the boat is *still* traveling forward—this "something" makes a direct diagonal path to the indicator in the center of the screen and *rams* it! Accordingly, the boat begins to take on water. Strangely enough, we soon learn that the "something" is a large rock! Can someone explain to me how a rock that size could swim *toward* the boat and sink it?! Or was the "something" on the sonar display the alligator, and Scully *just happened* to hit the rock at exactly the same time? (I feel a Tuiti Award nomination coming on! See "Soft Light.")

Continuity and Production Problems

X As Mulder and Scully discuss the existence of sea monsters outside the local tourist trap, watch the handle on Mulder's umbrella. In the shots featuring Scully, it faces toward her. Then, in the shots featuring Mulder, it flips toward him.

Trivia Questions

1 What frog has Dr. Farraday studied for the past three years?

2 What boat do Mulder and Scully rent in this episode?

Wetwired

PLOT SUMMARY

An anonymous E-mail draws Mulder to a meeting with a man who will only suggest that Mulder look into a multimurder case in Braddock Heights, Maryland. For some reason, Joseph Patnik recently went berserk, killing five people, claiming they were the same man. And shortly after Mulder and Scully arrive, Heleen Riddock looks up from doing dishes to find her husband frolicking in a hammock with a young blonde. When she kills him, she realizes that it isn't her husband after all and the blonde is a dog (really . . . a *dog*-dog).

Both individuals appeared to be heavy television watchers, and in both cases Mulder observes a cable company employee at the scene. Climbing the pole outside the Riddocks' home, he retrieves an odd-shaped video trapping device. Later analysis by the Lone Gunmen reveals that the device introduces a signal into the video stream that affects the human brain and brings latent fears to the surface. In fact, even Scully has become compromised—believing that Mulder has been a part of Cancerman's forces all along. Hospital bed rest purges the effects, but by the time Mulder returns to Braddock Heights, Mr. X has already moved to destroy all the evidence and kill those involved. X had sent Mulder the original lead, hoping Mulder would expose the conspiracy before he carried out Cancerman's orders.

Onscreen Locations

- ☒ Braddock Heights, Maryland
- ☒ Frederick County Psychiatric Hospital, Braddock Heights, Maryland
- ☒ Frederick County Morgue
- ☒ Northeast Georgetown Medical Center

Ruminations

I really like the "video breakup" effects used in this episode to represent the psychosis induced by the trapping device. Cool stuff!

Unanswered Questions

☒ So what is Cancerman trying to accomplish with the video trapping device? Mr. X says that "they" won't stop at politics and commerce but he never says what will finally satisfy the vision of the conspirators. By "politics," I assume that X means the conspirators will use their research and technology to remain in power by controlling who is elected to run the country. By "commerce," I assume that the conspirators will be able to control what people will buy—and maybe even what they will sell. So, um, what's left if the conspirators aren't going to stop there? Well . . . there's religion. Does Cancerman really want to be God? He does seem to claim the mantle of surrogate-Supreme Being in the very next episode, "Talitha Cumi." Then again, there's also . . . *entertainment*. Gasp! Wait a minute: We're going to find out in "Musings of a Cigarette Smoking Man" that Cancerman is a frustrated writer. We'll also discover that Cancerman might even control the Oscar nominations? Is *that* what this is really all about?! Is this the final motivation for all the deaths, diseases, and experimentation? Cancerman can't get published so he's on a campaign to control the very thought processes of Americans —hoping that he can eventually *mandate* that someone print his work and others read it?! (Taking a deep breath). All right. I'm willing to do my part. I'm willing to suffer for the greater good.

I'm willing to slog through his books once they hit the shelves. Now, it's up to you, publishers. I'm *begging* you. Save us from this monster and his fiendish schemes. No matter how bad his writing is, please, *please* . . . SOMEBODY get this guy a contract!

Plot Oversights

X A minor discrepancy but worth noting. Mulder tells Scully that he got the case "yesterday." Scully later recalls that he said "last night."

X Having become convinced that Mulder is out to get her, Scully fires wildly at her motel room door. I count six shots. The next day, Skinner says it was four. (But, then again, who am I to argue with Assistant Director Walter Sergei Skinner?)

X Screen text tells us that Mulder arrives at the conspirators' hideout at "5:17 P.M." Moments later, a conspirator looks at his watch and claims that it's "almost seven." Sounds like the guy needs a new watch!

Equipment Oddities

X Mulder has an amazing VCR in his motel room! The tape has been ejected, waiting to be pulled from the machine, and the television is still showing the tape in fast-forward cue! How does it do that? Does it have some kind of gonzo RAM-based storage that holds a half hour of digitized video? (I'd *love* to get hold of a machine like that!)

X The Lone Gunmen tell Mulder that the video trapping device he extracted from the box near the Riddocks' home feeds extra information into the "vertical blanking interval" of the video signal. They make it sound like this is unusual. In fact, it is not! The standard North American television signal is composed of 525 horizontal lines. These lines are divided into two fields. Each field contains 262.5 lines. The

first 21 lines of each field comprise the Vertical Blanking Interval (VBI). You can actually see the VBI if you have a television that allows you to change the vertical hold. As the picture scrolls up or down, you will notice a thick black horizontal space between the images. This is the VBI.

Now, while the television set needs lines 1 through 9 of the VBI to do its job properly, lines 10 through 21 can contain any kind of data that the originator of the video signal wants to include. In fact, closed captioning has been transmitted on line 21 of the VBI for *years!* Why is closed captioning transmitted in the VBI? Because it doesn't normally show up on the screen! (Depending on your viewpoint, it's off either the bottom or the top of the picture.) In fact, Frohike demonstrates this as he explains it to Mulder. He adjusts an oscilloscope to show color bars from the video feed and then cranks the vertical positioning knob on the oscilloscope to shove the picture up so Mulder can see the information.

Question: If the psychosis-inducing images are being introduced into the VBI, and if the VBI isn't normally even *seen* on a television set, how can the images be affecting people?! (Now, if the device was somehow combining its output with the normal video output, *that* would make sense. Of course, it also would distort the picture!)

X Continuing with our theme of things that shouldn't work in this episode but do, Mulder is somehow able to talk with Scully's mom even though the antenna is down on his cell phone.

X And what about this "photic driving response"? The Lone Gunmen say that the signal is cycling at fifteen flashes per second. From the sounds of it, this is the timing necessary to induce the response. One would assume that the signal is constructed to produce this timing when the video signal is viewed at normal speed. But Scully and Mulder both were watch-

Trivia Questions

1 According to Dr. Stroman, who contacted him about the case?

2 Whom does Scully suggest to look at the video trapping device?

255

Wetwired

Realizing that Scully—in her psychotic state—is at her mother's house, Mulder hurries there to find his normally stable partner awash in the certainty that he's come to kill her; that he was responsible for her kidnapping, and that he was part of the conspiracy that murdered her sister. A powerful scene follows as Scully holds Mulder at bay with her weapon, only to have Scully's mother step between them and put herself in harm's way to keep her daughter from making a terrible mistake.

ing the tapes on fast-forward cue. In fast-foward cue, VCRs can run from seven to twenty-two times normal speed. At seven times normal speed, the signal introduced by the video trapping device would be cycling at 105 flashes a second. Granted, we don't know exactly what the conspirators are doing here. But doesn't it *seem* like this should make a difference in the effect the signal would have on the viewer? Isn't there a physical limit to how fast the human eye can respond to stimuli?

X There's a very cute moment when Mulder visits Scully in the hospital. He comes in and quickly puts his hands up, as if he's surrendering to his formerly gun-toting partner. Then he looks up, sees the television is on, and *turns it off!* Except, I don't see any power switch on the face of the set! Mulder's hand *does* rest on the television for a bit before it goes black. Maybe he's doing some kind of Vulcan mind meld?!

Continuity and
Production Problems

X After observing an outburst from Joseph Patnik at Frederick County Psychiatric Hospital, Mulder and Scully drive to his house to begin their investigation. Scully exits the car and walks around the back to join Mulder in a jaunt across the street. Just as the final triangle-shaped window on Scully's side of the car goes out of frame, you can see a reflector panel from the camera setup make a brief appearance.

Talitha Cumi

(Part 1 of 2)

Onscreen Locations

- ☒ Arlington, Virginia
- ☒ Quonochontaug, Rhode Island
- ☒ Social Security Administration, Washington, D.C.
- ☒ Providence, Rhode Island

Ruminations

Ta-dum! The plot thickens! Great episode! Really interesting discussion between Cancerman and Jeremiah Smith. Good cameos, too! Always a pleasure to see Jerry Hardin ("Deep Throat") in action. Excellent continuity as well, with the reappearance of the clones and the alien bounty hunter/assassin. (See "Colony" and "End Game.")

And while we're on the subject of Cancerman, this episode strongly suggests that Cancerman traded his own healing for Jeremiah Smith's freedom, so I suppose we'll have to refer to him now as "The Evil Dude Formerly Known as Cancerman." (Actually, I plan to keep using this name as long as he keeps smoking those cigarettes!)

By the way, Trust No One: The Official Third Season Guide to The X-Files explains the title of this episode antiseptically, saying simply that it means "Arise, maiden" in Aramaic, claiming it as the language "in which the Bible was written." On a minor note, while a small portion of the Bible was written in Aramaic, the Old Testament was primarily written in Hebrew and the New Testament was written in Greek. Of more importance, however, is the loss of imagery caused by this sterile explanation. "Talitha Cumi" isn't

PLOT SUMMARY

In Arlington, Virginia, Jeremiah Smith somehow heals four individuals of gunshot wounds before disappearing into a crowd. Even Mulder has no explanation, but in short order, Cancerman apprehends Jeremiah Smith at the Social Security Administration in Washington and escorts him, tightly bound, to a cell. There, Cancerman berates the alien for his indulgences, claiming his actions put the entire project in peril. Afterward, an alien bounty hunter ("Colony," "End Game") is dispatched to terminate Smith. He finds the cell empty. (Apparently Cancerman let him go in exchange for healing him of lung cancer. Or Smith has more powers than Cancerman realizes.)

Meanwhile, Scully discovers that there are multiple Jeremiah Smiths working for the Social Security Administration in offices around the country. And later, Smith shows up at her apartment, saying he has important information about an elaborate plan, a project, and Mulder's sister.

At the same time, Mulder is stunned to learn that his mom has had a stroke. Even stranger, she had just met with Cancerman. When Mr. X claims Cancerman wanted something from her, a search of the Mulder summer home uncovers an alien assassination device—a retractable ice pick. Mulder then rendezvouses with Scully and Smith, hoping Smith will heal his mother. Unfortunately, the alien bounty hunter soon approaches as well, intent on completing his task.

simply an "obscure name" for the season finale. In its proper setting, the title resonates with the issues raised in the episode. These are the words spoken by Christ in Mark 5:41 as he raised a young girl from the dead. The act represented by the words is an integral part of this *episode, for Jeremiah Smith raises the "dead" to life at the beginning of this episode as well. In addition, according to* Trust No One, *the aforementioned discussion between Cancerman and Smith was inspired by the Grand Inquisitor poem in* The Brothers Karamazov. *Not coincidentally, the poem speaks of God coming incarnate during the Inquisition and healing a blind man before raising a young girl to life with the words "Maiden, arise." God is then arrested by the grand inquisitor and interrogated in an exploration of freedom, conscience, comfort, and servitude.*

By the way—and this is admittedly a very obscure piece of information—all of the newer Protestant translations of Mark 5:41 actually contain the words, "Talitha koum" instead of "Talitha cumi." I asked my college buddy Gary Long about this. Gary indicated that the newer translations follow what are believed to be the more reliable manuscripts. They read "Talitha koum." So . . . if the title of this episode was lifted from the Bible (which it most certainly was)—technically—it also should probably read "Talitha koum." (Snicker, snicker.) And in case you're wondering why I contacted Gary and how he would know this stuff, he happens to hold a doctorate in Near Eastern languages from the University of Chicago and now serves as chair, Department of Semitic Languages, for Jerusalem University College in . . . Jerusalem! (And, yes, he was the smart one!)

Plot Oversights

X When Jeremiah Smith heals the shooter in the fast-food restaurant, the blood disappears and the fabric closes up. There isn't a trace of the injury. Yet after the opening credits, Scully examines a young man who was healed, and his shirt still bears the black mark left by the bullet. Why didn't Smith clean his shirt, too? Do the aliens' powers only work on 100 percent cotton?

X One wonders why Jeremiah Smith bothered

to give the police his real name. He gave them a false address and wasn't carrying a driver's license. Did he want to be found? If so, why the fake address?

X While attempting to discover what happened at the fast-food restaurant, Skinner calls Mulder to tell him that his mother has had a stroke. Mulder and Scully rush to a hospital in Rhode Island. It's night when they arrive, and screen text reveals that it is "11:21 P.M." If they drove, this makes sense. It looks to be about an eight-hour drive from Washington, D.C., to the vicinity of Quonochontaug, Rhode Island. After arranging the transfer of Mulder's mom to a hospital in Providence, Mulder returns to Washington, D.C., with Scully and we see them in the basement office looking through news footage. Screen text informs that it's "8:25 A.M." Again, this makes sense if they drove. *Then,* as Mulder heads out the door, Scully objects. According to her, he hasn't slept in almost twenty-four hours. Why? All that travel time and she couldn't convince him that the world wouldn't stop rotating if he closed his eyes for a bit?

X Not a nit, just an observation, Mulder and Scully must be *well* known to the aliens. Jeremiah Smith is released from his imprisonment, and he heads for Scully's *apartment!* Mind you, he has never spoken to Scully before, but he knows enough about her to realize that she and Mulder are his best hope for survival. And he knows where she lives.

Changed Premises

X Why is Scully coming in the front door at FBI National Headquarters? You might recall that at the beginning of this season—during "The Blessing Way"—Scully was censured, and she had to pass through the metal detectors in the main lobby. A guard quipped that "they" were making her come in the front door these days. Interestingly enough, in this episode Scully is—

once again—entering FBI National Headquarters through the main lobby. Was she censured again for some reason and the creators didn't tell us? (Gasp!) Of course . . . if she entered the building through the back door, she wouldn't have run into Jeremiah Smith! (Hmmm.)

X In "Colony" we saw a group of individuals who had identical facial characteristics, and all worked in abortion clinics. They all used different names. That seems like a sensible precaution. In this episode we also have a group of individuals who look alike, and they all work in Social Security Administration offices around the country. But this time they all carry the same name. Isn't this just *asking* for trouble?

Equipment Oddities

X I do not understand. I do not understand. I do not *understand!* In "Fallen Angel," Mulder saw that Max Fenig had equipment that could jack into cellular pathways and eavesdrop on phone calls. As recently as the previous episode ("Wetwired"), Mulder told Scully he had information he didn't want to give her until he was on a land line. But, but, but, in *this* episode, Mulder arranges to meet Scully and Jeremiah Smith at an out-of-the-way location *while talking on his cell phone!* Guess what happens after Scully and Jeremiah Smith arrive? *SURPRISE!* The alien bounty hunter/assassin shows up only

moments later! Now, I realize the poor guy hasn't had any sleep for a while and he's distraught over his mother, but . . . "Ding, ding, Mulder!"

Continuity and Production Problems

X Mulder and Scully view news footage of the incident at the fast-food restaurant, trying to determine what happened to Jeremiah Smith. Soon Mulder finds a piece of video that shows Jeremiah Smith talking to the police detective one moment and gone the next. Mulder pauses the tape to discuss the matter with Scully. Strangely enough, in the close-ups of our dynamic duo, there is light flickering over both Mulder and Scully's faces, as if the tape is still playing.

X The scene that shows Jeremiah Smith coming to FBI National Headquarters features in the upper left portion of the screen an "extra" who seems a bit slow on the uptake! Watch as the camera pans down across the American flag. The extra stands very still for a moment and then rushes forward to pick up the receiver.

Trivia Questions

❶ What is the name of the shooter in the fast-food restaurant?

❷ Name two cities where Jeremiah Smiths live.

Trivia Answers
❶ Muntz.
❷ Pick two: Chicago, Illinois; Cupertino, California; Miami, Florida; New York, New York; Seattle, Washington.

259

Talitha Cumi

SERIAL OVOTYPES

Here a Clone, There a Clone, Everywhere a Clone, Clone

As part of my normal nitpicking routine, I often note when an actor plays more than one character in a given series. I usually file the nit under "Continuity and Production Problems," since I've never met anyone in real life who looks *exactly* like someone else. On the other hand, I've never tried to be methodical about this particular aspect of my "craft." The only time I say anything is when the resemblance is *so* obvious that I consider it hard to miss. *However,* given that *The X-Files* provides an explanation for these kinds of character similarities (i.e., they are hybrids first—seen in "Colony"), I thought it would be fun to approach the problem with a bit more diligence.

Starting with the credits for each episode of *The X-Files,* I reduced the information to what is called a "comma separated values" file so I could manipulate it and sort it by actor. Then it was a simple matter to strip out the actors who had played only one part. The results astonished me! I had no idea the list would be so long. I have reproduced it below. For your perusal, I have begun each entry with the name of the actor followed by parts he or she has played. (I did abbreviate certain episode titles to save space, but I think you'll be able to figure out which ones I'm referring to.)

If you happen to be a *die-hard* X-phile, here's a little game you can play with this list: For each actor, try to create a mental picture of the characters listed. Then compare them and confirm that the actor did, in fact, play all those parts! Though I wasn't always successful, I had a lot of fun doing this as I was putting together this sidebar. (And, yes, I realize that it doesn't take much to amuse me!)

Abrahams, Doug	Agent 2, "Genderbender"; Paul Vitaris, "Die Hand die Verletzt"; Lieutenant Neary, "Hell Money"; Harbaugh, "The Field"
Airlie, Andrew	Rob, "The Jersey Devil"; attorney, "Sanguinarium"
Allford, Roger	Garrett Lore, "3"; the harbormaster, "Nisei"
Anderson, Mar	Halverson, "Død Kalm"; Jack Hammond, "D.P.O."
Bacic, Steve	The second officer, "Soft Light"; Agent Collins, "Pusher"
Bain, Susan	Agent Sheherlis, "Grotesque"; the county coroner, "El Mundo Gira"
Banks, Linden	The Reverend Sistrunk, "Colony"; Joseph Patnik, "Wetwired"
Barber, Gillian	Agent Nancy Spiller, "Ghost in the Machine"; Beth Kane, "Red Museum"; Penny Northern, "Nisei" and "Momento Mori"
Batten, Paul	Brother Wilton, "Genderbender"; Dr. Seizer, "Piper Maru"
Baur, Marc	Man in suit, "Ghost in the Machine"; Agent Brisentine, "The Host"; Matlock, "Musings"
Beiser, Brendan	Agent Comox, "Nisei"; Agent Pendrell, "Apocrypha" et al.; Dr. Rick Newton, "Avatar"
Beley, Lisa Ann	Beatrice Salinger, "Miracle Man"; the student, "Little Green Men"

Serial
Ovotypes

Hetherington, Gary	Kennedy, "Squeeze"; Lewin, "Little Green Men"
Humphreys, Alf	Second controller, "Space"; Dr. Pomerantz, "Blessing Way"
Hurtubise, Dave	Barrington, "Roland"; the pathologist, "Leonard Betts"
Johnson, P. Lynn	Dr. Sheila Braun, "Born Again"; Deborah Brown, "Die Hand Die Verletzt"; Health Department doctor, "Small Potatoes"
Johnston, Andrew	Colonel Robert Budahas, "Deep Throat"; Agent Weiss, "Colony" and "End Game"; medical examiner, "Demons"
Kanagawa, Hiro	Peter Tanaka, "Firewalker"; Dr. Yonechi, "Synchrony"
Kaye, David	Reporter, "Firewalker"; the doctor, "Apocrypha"
Kelamis, Peter	O'Dell, "Lazarus"; Lieutenant Foyle, "Fresh Bones"
Konoval, Karin	Zelma, "Clyde Bruckman"; the peacock mother, "Home"
Kosterman, Mitch	Detective Horton, "Sleepless"; Fornier, "The List"
Kramer, Ken	Dr. Berube, "The Erlenmeyer Flask"; Dr. Browning, "3"; Dr. Inanov, "War of the Coprophages"
Lacroix, Peter	Ranheim/Druse, "E.B.E."; Dwight, "Ascension"; Nathaniel Teager, "Unrequited"
Lane, Campbell	Margaret's father, "Miracle Man"; Calusari 3, "The Calusari"; committee chairman, "Tunguska" and "Terma"
Lea, Nicholas	Michael, "Genderbender"; Alex Krycek, "Sleepless" et al.
Lewis, David	Young officer, "The Jersey Devil"; Vosberg, "Firewalker"
Lewis, Robert	The officer, "Eve"; the officer, "Duane Barry"; the ER doctor, "Paper Clip"
Loree, Brad	The fireman, "3"; security guard, "Leonard Betts";
Lysell, Allan	Chief Rivers, "E.B.E."; Able Gardner, "End Game"
MacDonald, William	Dr. Oppenheim, "Fallen Angel"; federal marshal, "The Host"; Agent Kazanjian, "2SHY"; Officer Trott, "Unruhe"
Mackay, Don	Warden Joseph Cash, "Beyond the Sea"; Charlie, "The Host"; Oates, "The List"; the judge, "Pusher"
Makaj, Steve	The patrolman, "Ascension"; Frank Kiveat, "D.P.O."; Ostelhoff, "Gethsemane"
Marsh, Walter	The judge, "Miracle Man"; the druggist, "Unruhe"
Mathew, Sue	Lisa Dole, "Roland"; Agent Caleca, "Apocrypha"
Mathews, Hrothgar	Jack, "The Jersey Devil"; the mental patient, "Our Town"; Galen, "Talitha Cumi"; man on phone, "The Host"
Mattia, Jan Bailey	Ms. Hadden, "Never Again"; the hooker, "2SHY"
McBeath, Tom	Detective Munson, "3"; Dr. Lewton, "Teso dos Bichos"
McFee, Dwight	David Gates, "Shapes"; the commander, "Little Green Men"; the suspect, "Irresistible"; Havez, "Clyde Bruckman"
McLean, Paul	Dr. Josephs, "Shapes"; Agent Kautz, "Anasazi" and "Zero Sum"; the coast guard officer, "Nisei"
McNulty, Kevin	Fuller, "Squeeze"; Dr. Davey, "Soft Light"; Agent Fuller, "Apocrypha"
Michael, Ryan	Overcoat man, "One Breath"; Agent Cameron Hill, "Unrequited"
Miller, Gabrielle	Paula Gray, "Our Town"; Brenda J. Summerfield, "Syzygy"
Moloney, Robert	The worker, "Our Town"; Bruce Bearfeld, "Tempus Fugit" and "Max"
Morgan, Darin	Flukeman, "The Host"; EdDie Van Blundht, "Small Potatoes" (although no one would recognize him as Flukeman!)
Morris, Janie Woods	Ms. Lange, "Shadows"; Lorraine Kelleher, "Avatar"

Morriseau, Renae	Gwen Goodensnake, "Shapes"; Josephine Doane, "Anasazi"
Mossley, Robin	Dr. Joe Ridley, "Young at Heart"; Dr. Randolph, "Our Town"; Dr. Kingsley Looker, "Tunguska" and "Terma"
Musser, Larry	Sheriff John Oakes, "Die Hand Die Verletzt"; Detective Manners, "José Chung"; Denny Markham, "Unrequited"
Palmer, Joel	Kevin Morris, "Conduit"; Charlie/Michael Holvey, "The Calusari"
Panych, Morris	Dr. Simon Auerbach, "F. Emasculata"; the gray-haired man, "Piper Maru" et al.
Payne, John	The guard, "The Erlenmeyer Flask"; Jerald Glazebrook, "Humbug"
Puttonen, Michael	Motel manager, "Deep Throat"; Dr. Pilsson, "Sleepless"; the conductor, "731"; Martin Alpert, "Elegy"
Raskin, Paul	Ullrich, "The List"; Dr. Prabu Amanpour, "Sanguinarium"
Rennie, Callum Keith	Tommy, "Lazarus"; the groundskeeper, "Fresh Bones"
Rhodes, Donnelly	Jim Parker, "Shapes"; General Francis, "Musings"
Roberts, Ken	The proprietor, "Colony"; the clerk, "Clyde Bruckman"
Robertson, Alan	Gray-haired man, "Fire"; Roosevelt, "Teso dos Bichos"
Rogers, Michael	Lieutenant Griffin, "Fallen Angel"; the first crewman, "Colony"
Rose, Gabrielle	Mrs. Anita Budahas, "Deep Throat"; Dr. Zenzola, "The Host"
Sanders, Alvin	Deputy Wright, "Fallen Angel"; the bus driver, "F. Emasculata"
Sandomirsky, Kerry	Tracy, "Roland"; Joanne, "2SHY"
Saunders, Mark	Doctor 2, "Lazarus"; Agent Busch, "Irresistible"
Sauve, Ron	The foreman, "The Host"; Mr. Decker, "Teso dos Bichos"
Simms, Tasha	Ellen Reardon, "Eve"; Laura Kelly, "Excelsius Dei"; Jay Cassal, "Avatar"
Sparks, Carrie Cain	The maid, "Our Town"; the train station clerk, "Nisei"; duty nurse, "Small Potatoes"
Stewart, Bobby L.	The deputy, "Ascension"; resident 2, "War of the Coprophages"
Stewart, Malcolm	Commander Carver, "3"; Agent Bonnecaze, "Avatar"; Dr. Sacks, "Tunguska" and "Terma"
Thompson, Brian	The pilot, "Colony" and "End Game"; the bounty hunter, "Herrenvolk"
Thompson, Don	Holtzman, "Conduit"; Henry Willig, "Sleepless"; Lieutenant Col. Stans, "The Walk"
Thurston, Robert	Jackson Toews, "Irresistible"; Dr. Larry Steen, "El Mundo Gira"
Tipple, Gordon	The detective, "Eve"; Joe Crandall, "Young at Heart"
Touliatos, George	Dr. Katz, "Eve"; Larry Winter, "Blood"
Tremblett, Ken	Dyer, "Darkness Falls"; uniformed officer, "Elegy"
Turner, Frank C.	Dr. Collins, "Tooms"; Dr. Hakkie, "Duane Barry"
Twa, Kate	Marty (female), "Genderbender"; Detective Ryan, "Soft Light"
Unger, Kimberly	Karen Koretz, "Fallen Angel"; Joan Gauthier, "Piper Maru"
Vacco, Angelo	Angelo Garza, "F. Emasculata"; the doorman, "Talitha Cumi"
Walker, Matthew	Dr. Surnow, "Roland"; Arlinski, "Gethsemane"
Webber, Timothy	Detective Talbot, "Tooms"; Jess Harold, "Our Town"; Dr. Farraday, "Quagmire"
Wick, Norma	The reporter, "Space"; the reporter, "War of the Coprophages"
Wilde, Bob	Rand, "Little Green Men"; the limo driver, "Nisei"
Williams, Denalda	Marilyn, "Irresistible"; Zirinka, "Syzygy"
Woodward, Meredith Bain	Defense attorney Brent, "Pusher"; Dr. Ruth Slaughter, "Ascension"
Zachary, Jude	Winston, "F. Emasculata"; Jones, "Musings"
Zeilinger, Beatrice	The paramedic, "End Game"; the burly nurse, "The Walk"

FOURTH SEASON

Herrenvolk

(Part 2 of 2)

Onscreen Locations

☒ Bond Mill Road, rural Maryland

☒ Providence, Rhode Island

☒ United Nations building, New York City

Ruminations

I must admit that when I saw this episode the first time, I was disappointed. "Talitha Cumi" held such promise for advancing our information on the "project" or the "plan" or whatever you want to call it. After waiting over the long summer months, I wasn't prepared to learn that Jeremiah Smith was nothing more that a file clerk who didn't know anything and was evidently hoping that if he showed Mulder what little he knew, Mulder could make the intuitive leap to the rest.

But in retrospect—after watching the episode four more times—it does have much of The X-Files flair. Of course, we're at a season boundary, so someone has to die. This time it's Mr. X. Thankfully, he has a good replacement! We like Marita Covarrubias! What a great start for the character: "Not everything dies, Mr. Mulder." (As an aside, there's a story going around that Chris Carter was originally looking for a blonde, leggy type to play Scully. I wonder if the Marita Covarrubias character is a reincarnation of that initial sketch. Imagining her as Scully is an interesting exercise!)

Unanswered Questions

☒ In one scene, Brandoguy of the Consortium gives Cancerman one of the pictures that Mr. X

PLOT SUMMARY After plunging his ice pick into the alien bounty hunter's neck, Mulder flees in a boat with Jeremiah Smith. He wants Smith to heal his mother. Smith counters that going to the hospital will only mean death for him so the larger plan can continue—a plan he describes as "hegemony, a new origin of species." Smith then offers to take Mulder to a place where he can see the work in progress and his sister as well.

Meanwhile, Scully returns to Washington and learns that the other Jeremiah Smiths have disappeared. For some unknown reason, their workstations contain an immense database, apparently cataloging every human inoculated for the smallpox virus.

In Alberta, Canada, Mulder and Smith visit a farm where young clones tend a nonterrestrial plant. They have no parents and no speech. They are merely workers, and all the girls look like Samantha. Before Mulder can learn more, the bounty hunter kills Smith. And if that wasn't bad enough, one of Cancerman's assassins soon executes Mr. X. *All* is not lost, however. X's final scrawl in his own blood leads Mulder to a new contact at the United Nations named Marita Covarrubias. And Cancerman arranges for the alien bounty hunter to heal Mulder's mother—explaining that the most dangerous man is the one with nothing to lose.

took of him and Mulder's mom. How did Brandoguy get this picture? X gave it to Mulder, who showed it to Skinner and Scully. Does the Consortium have agents in every one-hour photo shop around the nation? (Aaaah!)

Plot Oversights

✗ There's a line missing from this episode as the bounty hunter approaches Mulder and Jeremiah Smith at the beginning. At the end of "Talitha Cumi," Smith told Mulder, "He's here to kill me."

✗ Hearing that the Consortium might kill Mrs. Mulder, X comes to Mulder's apartment and warns Scully. This guy really has come a long way. Up to this point, he hasn't shown any great concern for human life. This is the same guy we've seen slaughter people in cold blood, and he almost shot *Mulder* in the previous episode! And it's the same guy who knew why Scully was taken but did nothing to stop it. Yet when it comes to Mulder's mother, he is willing to risk exposure to make sure she's okay. (And, of course, he dies because of it.)

✗ I am astounded by Mulder's patience in this episode. He travels from Washington, D.C., to Alberta, Canada, with Jeremiah Smith and apparently is content to wait for countless hours before Smith gives him *any* information about "the plan." *Finally,* after arriving at the farm and seeing all the identical children, Mulder demands that Smith explain it to him. (And, of course, Smith can't, because he doesn't know! I would get *really* tired of this bait-and-switch game if I were Mulder.)

✗ In regard to the database file that is found on the Smiths' computers, Agent Pendrell claims that one of the fields has an infinite number of variations. Well . . . no. If it's a finite field, it has a finite number of variations! (I have yet to see an infinite field in a database record because that would require an infinite amount of memory just for that one record.) In this particular case, the field is composed of three letters followed by twelve numbers. Just for the sake of argument, let's say the letters have to be "A" through "Z" in the standard English-language

alphabet. The number of possibilities for this field would be equivalent to 26 times 26 times 26 times 1,000,000,000,000, or 17.576 quadrillion. Certainly, that's a large number, but it ain't infinite.

✗ By the way, pouring gasoline all over yourself *will* keep the bees away. Mulder does it in this episode as he and Jeremiah Smith race into an apiary filled with toxic, nonterrestrial bees. They are attempting to hide from the bounty hunter. On the other hand, I'm not sure I'd recommend this course of action when being chased by a thug with murderous intent. Seems like one well-placed match would remove the main obstacle in the bounty hunter's quest to complete his mission!

✗ Attempting to learn the purpose of the database file, Scully takes a biopsy from her smallpox inoculation scar and one from Pendrell's. She puts them through some fancy-shmancy staining process, takes pictures, and determines that they are different. From *two* samples she constructs a theory that the smallpox vaccinations were used to tag and catalog humans. Does this seem like a reasonable scientific approach? A controversial theory from *two* samples?!

✗ Returning to the States from the farm in Canada, Mulder tells Scully to meet him at the hospital that cares for his mother. He's bringing Jeremiah Smith there to heal her. In the subsequent scene, we see the hallway that leads to Mrs. Mulder's room guarded by a large team of agents. In time, Mulder wanders onto the floor alone, and everyone is surprised. In other words, Skinner never bothered to set up a perimeter defense around the building?! Why wasn't Mulder surrounded the *moment* he set foot on the property?

✗ Okay, I'm confused. A professional assassin comes to kill Mr. X in Mulder's hallway. He shoots X. It must be the guy's first day on the job, because he shoots him twice in the chest! Now, if you're trying to *kill* somebody, it probably makes more sense to shoot the guy in the chest and then shoot him in the *head* (as X himself does in "One Breath"). That way, he doesn't crawl down the hall and he doesn't scrawl a final message in his own blood because . . . he's *dead*. (Of course, then Mulder would never meet Marita Covarrubias.)

Equipment Oddities

X The episode opens with a telephone repair man climbing a pole in Alberta, Canada, using ankle-mounted spikes and a heavy-duty pole strap. A bee stings him, and he begins to convulse. Then his strap breaks and he make a belly flop onto the road. His strap breaks?! Aren't those things supposed to be really strong? I could see him losing his balance and sliding down the pole, but, of course, that wouldn't be as dramatic. (And it might even look comical!)

X Mulder calls Scully on his cell phone and says he needs her to cover his tracks because there's going to be a record of him going through customs as he entered Canada. All fine and good, but won't there also be a record of the cell tower that is relaying his call? And won't that give the dark forces an idea where he is?

X These Jeremiah Smith guys had some incredible hardware to work with at the branch offices of the Social Security Administration. Among the six of them, they had *seventy gigabytes* of *extra* storage on their machines. That's more than eleven *gigabytes* apiece! (When I first heard this, I thought, "Wow, wow, wow, wow, *wow!*" And remember—when you're reading this in the year 2005 and personal computers come standard with 100-petabyte drives—this episode supposedly occurred in 1996!)

X The database file found in the Smiths' computers deserves a bit of scrutiny. Each record appears to contain three fields. The first is always "SEP." The second is a twenty-letter code. The third is a fifteen-character alphanumeric code. According to Pendrell, there's "roughly a billion" such records in the database file. Either the Consortium could care less about optimizing their data, or they need a better database programmer. If every record contains "SEP" as its first field, the field is redundant. Three bytes over "roughly" a billion records works out to the useless allocation of *roughly* three gigabytes!

X And where's the rest of the database file? Database files exist to establish correlations between or among data. For instance, a record in the name and address file for the Nitpickers Guild not only lists the member's name and address but also his or her card number, the identifier for the first postal letter he or she sent, the date he or she became a member of the Guild, and more. The data file that Pendrell displays on his screen doesn't have any way to map its data onto "real life." All it does is establish a correlation between a twenty-letter code (which Scully later labels an identifier for cowpox virus) and a unique ID. Presumably the Consortium would want this information linked to real people— probably the Social Security numbers of the individuals listed if they are American citizens. In that way the Consortium would know that a given "tag" had been applied to a given person. Given a Social Security number, a simple search of the Social Security database would quickly yield other pertinent information, such as name and address. (Otherwise the data seems fairly useless to me.) Unfortunately, because of the way the file is constructed, the only way to make the data valuable would be to create *another* multiple gigabyte file, which listed the unique ID and the Social Security number for the person in question. So where's *that* file being stored?

X Once their car runs out of gas, Mulder and Smith set out on foot for the farm. In time they discover the telephone repairman who kissed

Trivia Questions

1 In what boat do Mulder and Smith make their getaway?

2 What does Marita Covarrubias claim was being grown at the farm?

Trivia Answers
1 The *Silver Streak*.
2 Ginseng. (By the way, Murray Leeder of Calgary, Alberta, says this really is a ginseng farm, in Kamloops, British Columbia. Of course, Murray is probably a member of the Consortium engaging in a despicable disinformation campaign designed to obscure the facts of this case!)

the pavement the hard way. Smith grabs a pair of binoculars from the poor guy's van, and the two continue their trek. Excuse me: Why don't they hop in the telephone van and *drive* the rest of the way to the farm?! (The bounty hunter uses it later, so we know it has gas and it works!)

Continuity and Production Problems

🅇 Speaking of the flightless telephone repairman at the beginning of the episode, the guy lands facedown on the paved road and then rolls over without any injuries showing on his face.

🅇 Here's some "X" fun for you. Wanting to discover the meaning of the "SEP" database file, Scully goes to Mulder's apartment and makes an "X" in the window. Take a close look at it just before the camera moves away. Now compare it to the close-up of the "X" shown moments later. They're different. Evidently Scully didn't like the look of the first "X" she had made, so she ripped it off and made another!

🅇 Then Mr. X shows up, and in a subsequent wide shot we see that the "X" in the window has changed again. The previous close-up showed us an "X" that was wider than it was tall. The wide shot shows an "X" that is taller than it is wide.

🅇 After figuring out at least part of the database file, Scully goes to see Agent Pendrell. As she enters his work area, he quickly tightens his tie. (As he should. He is, after all, starstruck by the lovely Dana Scully.) Scully asks him to bring up the file. Pendrell obliges. A close-up shows Scully's finger pointing to the string of "SEP" characters. The scene cuts back to Pendrell, and suddenly his tie is loose again. (Yes, there is time for him to loosen it, but why would he?)

🅇 Pendrell claims that he checked the file and each of the identifiers in the last field of the database records is unique. (He says they are all

different, which is the same thing.) In fact, they are not unique, and they are not all different! The visual-effects guys create only *ten* different identifiers to scroll across the screen. So when you see the identifiers fill the screen, freeze any frame you like and you should be able to find at least two identifiers that are the same! (In addition, the visual-effects crew created only two variations for the twenty-letter code that precedes the "unique" ID. Pendrell tells Scully that there are thirty variations of this code. However, we see only a small portion of the file, so perhaps the other twenty-eight are elsewhere. Yeah, that's the ticket!)

🅇 I have bad news. Remember the "X" that Scully put in the window, the one that had three different incarnations? Um . . . as it turns out, the "X" that lures Mr. X to his death is the second in the series. It was Scully's "X" that caused Mr. X's death! Evidently she didn't bother to take it down after she left the apartment.

🅇 Please return your tray tables to their upright and locked positions. We are about to enter . . . *The Hall Extension Zone!* (Double aaah!) In "The Blessing Way" I noted that the hallway outside Mulder's apartment suddenly shrinks five or six feet. Instead of three doors on each side of the hall that leads to the elevator, there are only two. Guess what? The extra doors . . . *are back!* When Mr. X attempts a retreat from Mulder's apartment at the end of the episode, the hallway once again has three doors on each side! (I think the creators are playing with our minds.)

🅇 After being shot, Mr. X crawls back to Mulder's apartment and writes "SRSG" in his own blood. The problem is that the scene features a close-up of X's hand moments before he writes this postscript. It has *some* blood on it. But it doesn't seem like there's *nearly* enough to make the thick, solid letters seen at the end of the episode. (It looks like the letters were painted on the floor with a brush.)

Home

Onscreen Locations

☒ Home, Pennsylvania
☒ Sheriff Taylor's residence, 3 Sweetgum Lane

Ruminations

Even after multiple viewings, I must confess that this episode is a complete bewilderment to me. I have a hard time getting my brain around the fact that the same team that has given us so many highly inventive episodes could produce this. If I wanted to watch a B-grade adolescent horror flick—if I wanted to see club-wielding mutants terrorizing a small town—I could go to my local video store and grab something out of the twenty-five-cent bin! At least "Grotesque" had a paranormal element to it. Honestly—in my mind, at least—"Home" treads the edge of being laughably absurd.

Two possible explanations for this episode. Both are related to Millennium. You may recall that this episode aired only weeks before Chris Carter's second television series debuted. As a general rule, creative people abhor boundaries. The official guides to The X-Files mention more than one disagreement between the creators and Fox's standards and practices department. Given the subject matter and approach of Millennium, Fox Broadcasting apparently decided to give Carter almost free reign with regard to content. I suspect that this "freedom" spilled over to The X-Files and the producers decided to make full use of it. Thankfully, as the fourth season progressed, someone, somewhere restored some measure of balance.

It is also possible that Carter and company

PLOT SUMMARY Traveling to Home, Pennsylvania, Mulder and Scully invesigate the death of a badly deformed baby—exhumed from a shallow grave. When the pair notes the proximity of an old home to the crime scene, local sheriff Andy Taylor fidgets. The house belongs to the Peacock family. It has no electricity or plumbing. The Peacocks grow their own food and raise their own stock—both human and animal, inbreeding as necessary. The townsfolk believe only three brothers remain. Mr. and Mrs. Peacock were severely injured in a car wreck ten years ago, but the boys took the bodies, so no one knows for sure if they survived.

Scully concludes the Peacocks are attempting to reproduce, utilizing one or more kidnapped females as breeders. Visiting the Peacock house, Mulder and Scully find it empty. Even still, they discover enough evidence to allow Taylor to swear out a warrant for the brothers. Unknown to our heroes, Mrs. Peacock lies under a nearby bed, listening to every word. That night she sends her boys to bludgeon Taylor and his wife to death. Mulder, Scully, and Taylor's deputy then attempt to arrest the brothers, but by the time the episode ends, the deputy and two of the brothers are dead and the final brother has escaped with Mrs. Peacock to start a new family.

realized Millennium was far beyond what most viewers would abide. Perhaps they decided to create a few gore-laden X-Files episodes to get the public ready for the new series.

Having said that, I wouldn't be doing my job if I didn't ramble a bit about the actual content of the episode. I believe this installment of The X-Files marks the first time an episode title has ever been displayed. If you watch the screen text shown after the opening commercial break, you'll notice that "Home" comes up first and then there's a pause before "Pennsylvania" appears as well. Now you know why!

Unfortunately—while it is in character—this episode also ratchets Mulder's "jerkitude" quotient to a previously unseen notch after the opening commercial break. A baby has been found in a hastily dug grave. He and Scully have been called to the case. However, since it doesn't involve the paranormal, Mulder couldn't care less. He stands by as Scully gathers evidence—happily oblivious as he relives the glory days of his childhood. Hey, it's not aliens. What should he care that a baby has just been buried alive?

Finally, this episode begins a series of appearances by the cast of the canceled Space: Above and Beyond. Tucker Smallwood—Sheriff Andy Taylor in this episode—played Commodore Glen Van Ross in the short-lived but excellent television series.

Plot Oversights

X Not to be unkind, but nitpicking this episode requires all the finesse of fishing with dynamite. Nevertheless, it's what you pay me to do, so . . . here goes! In the first place, why do the Peacock brothers bury the baby *outside* their property? Did they get lost in the rain? Was all the space around the house already filled with buried infants? There's only one reason I can see for the Peacocks to traipse beyond their fence to make the grave. If they didn't, the baby wouldn't be found, and Mulder and Scully wouldn't be called on to the case. (Who said the Peacocks were illiterate? They obviously read the script!)

X And why are they burying this baby *at all?!* It's *alive!* Granted, it has severe deformities but those seem to run in the family. Hard to imagine that this baby didn't measure up to the

Peacocks' standards. These guys couldn't even make the cover of *Mutant Monthly!*

X Mulder makes another of his intuitive leaps at just the right time so we can have an *X-Files* moment just before a commercial break. Believing the Peacocks had a hand in the death of the baby, Mulder and Scully visit the Peacock home. They find evidence of a recent birth, but the house appears deserted. Mulder then observes that if the mother is alive, the Peacock brothers probably took her with them.

This is a fascinating statement, since Sheriff Taylor told our intrepid pair that the brothers hauled both mother and father away after the accident ten years prior. Mulder has no reason to suspect that one survived and the other didn't. And only moments earlier, he was certain the mother was dead. Also, toward the end of the program he will be certain again that the mother is dead (until they find her, of course). So why does Mulder think that she might be the only surviving parent at this point in the episode?

It's a storytelling technique that the creators of *The X-Files* use often. Right after Mulder makes his observation that the brothers probably took the mother with them, the camera zooms in on a pair of eyes—the *mother's* eyes. In other words, the statement was included to foreshadow the revelation of her continued existence.

X Sheriff Taylor's initial comments about the Peacocks seem to indicate that the Peacocks keep to themselves. In fact, Taylor makes it sound like the Peacocks rarely set foot off their farm. Yet as soon as it becomes necessary to the plot, the Peacocks not only know how to drive a car, they also know where Taylor lives. If that's not bad enough, they apparently know the exact location of the sheriff's bedroom!

X Mulder and Scully's behavior near the end of the episode is very questionable. They sneak into the Peacock home when they could apprehend the Peacock brothers outside, in the light, with guns drawn. (At this point, neither Mulder nor Scully suspects that they are dealing with *super*mutants who can take *nine* bullets at point-blank range and still keep fighting!) Then, after discovering that no threat exists to any kidnap victim, they remain *in* the house when the sensible course of action would be to retreat and call for backup.

☒ Even stranger, Scully concludes that the oldest brother is the father of the other two brothers despite the fact Sheriff Taylor gave their ages as forty-two, thirty, and twenty-six. In addition, Sheriff Taylor said that Dad Peacock was still alive as of ten years ago. Why does it make more sense for a boy of *twelve* to father a child than for his *father* to father another child?

☒ Scully claims that she has contacted the state police and the highway patrol to cordon off the area. Jen Grady tells me that Pennsylvania doesn't have a highway patrol!

Changed Premises

☒ After examining the deformed corpse of the Peacock baby, Mulder and Scully discuss their genetic backgrounds. Mulder claims that—aside from the need for glasses and the propensity to get abducted by aliens—his family passes genetic muster. Obviously he has forgotten that he's red/green color-blind, as revealed in "Wetwired."

Equipment Oddities

☒ During the first visit to the Peacock home, Scully finds a bloody shoeprint. It looks like it comes from a somewhat-new pair of boots. Just where do the Peacocks purchase their attire? Say Less Shoes? Mutant Couturiers? The Hairless and Ugly Shop?

☒ In discussing the cars in the Peacock's yard, Taylor says people abandon their cars in the area all the time. In fact, Taylor's deputy discovers that the car driven by the Peacocks was abandoned by a woman who ran out of gas. Except . . . the car is a *vintage* Cadillac. Who in the world abandons a vintage Cadillac beside the road just because he or she *ran out of gas?!*

☒ I'm certainly impressed with the electronic communications equipment available in Home, Pennsylvania. Just before taking on the Peacocks, Sheriff Taylor's deputy supplies Mulder and Scully with headset walkie-talkies. There're three of these keeno-neato devices . . . even though the police force has only two people on it!

Continuity and Production Problems

☒ And speaking of the bloody shoeprint, Scully determines it's a match to those found in the field where the baby was born by comparing it to a picture she carries. I happen to have two copies of the episode and two VCRs and two TVs in my basement office. I freeze-framed the photo and the bloody print side-by-side. All I can say is: It's a good thing *I'm* not an FBI agent. I *never* would have come to the same—and apparently correct—conclusion as Scully because the photo and the print certainly *don't* look like a match to me!

FOURTH SEASON

Trivia Questions

❶ What are the first names of the two pregnant women who live in Home?

❷ What is the headline on the copy of *The Home Crier* that Mulder shows Scully?

Trivia Answers
❶ Mary Ellen and Nancy.
❷ "Elvis Presley Dead at 42."

Teliko

PLOT SUMMARY

When the Bureau assigns Scully to a missing-persons case involving four young African-American men in Philadelphia, Mulder tags along. Authorities have found only one body—that of Owen Sanders, a young man who has somehow lost all pigment from his skin. As Scully performs the autopsy, Mulder goes to New York to ask Marita Covarrubias about a West African seed found on Sanders's body. Covarrubias discloses that a body similar to Sanders's was found on a plane from Burkina Faso three months ago. Someone demanded the return of the body, thereby halting the investigation.

Immigration records lead Mulder and Scully to Samuel Aboah—a nimble man with no pituitary gland. Wanting more, Mulder forces a meeting with the man who suspended the original investigation and learns an African folk tale about the Teliko, spirits who prey on men. Surprisingly enough, Mulder leans toward a more mundane explanation. He wonders if Aboah is part of a lost tribe in Africa—born without pituitary glands—who have learned to survive by harvesting hormones from others.

By the time Mulder returns to Philadelphia, Aboah has escaped from the hospital, but he is eventually recaptured and charged with murder. Scully doubts he'll make it to trial. Without the benefits of his predatory lifestyle, Aboah has quickly begun to deteriorate.

Onscreen Locations

- ☒ FBI Pathology Lab
- ☒ United Nations building, New York, New York
- ☒ INS office, Philadelphia, PA
- ☒ Samuel Aboah's residence, 500 Demott Ave.
- ☒ Mt. Zion Medical Center, Philadelphia, PA
- ☒ Burkina Faso embassy, Washington, D.C.

Ruminations

The date on this episode is derived from two pieces of information. The original attack on the airplane carries a date of May 16, 1996. In addition, episode dialogue establishes that Mulder and Scully's involvement with the case occurs three months later.

Plot Oversights

☒ The episode begins with Aboah's attack on the man who died during the flight from Burkina Faso. The man goes to the lavatory, where Aboah pounces from the ceiling. Interestingly enough, though the man screams, no one on the plane hears him. Normally, airplane lavatories are not known for their thick, soundproof walls. (On the other hand, perhaps we should chalk this up to presumed gastronomic discomfort as well. See "Shapes." If Scully could think that Lyle Parker was howling from the effects of hospital food, suppose the other passengers on the flight might be certain that the man was simply screaming from the effects of airplane cuisine!)

☒ Throughout the rest of the episode, we see Aboah subdue his victims by tagging them with a seed dipped in some kind of cortical depressant. It seems to work very quickly by all appearances. So why didn't Aboah use his trusty blowgun on the man in the airplane lavatory,

Because then our "scream count" would show a deficit for this episode!)

☒ I was highly dubious over the proposition that removing the pituitary gland from an African-American male would turn him into an albino within a matter of hours. (Aboah attacks his first victim on a flight from Burkina Faso to New York City, and by the time the plane prepares for landing, the body has already turned a light shade of gray.) I asked Dr. Robert Woolley about this, and he concurred. Though there is no known natural process that can instantaneously shut off pigment production—and therefore there is no example in nature that would definitively prove that skin lightening *wouldn't* occur this fast—Robert thought that days or even *weeks* would be a more realistic time frame.

☒ Even more amazing on the medical front is a comment that Scully makes during Sanders's autopsy. She tells Mulder that Sanders's pituitary gland "was necretized," but she doesn't know how. Yet we see Sanders's head during this conversation and it seems to be intact. How does Scully know his pituitary gland was "necretized" if she hasn't removed his cranium? And, more importantly, *why* hasn't she removed his cranium (with a lateral cut one inch above his eyebrows, as she described in "Little Green Men")? For a good portion of the rest of the episode, Scully continues to contend that there is some type of pathogen at work. But if Scully had just cracked open Sanders's skull, she would have seen that his pituitary gland had been *dug out* with a barbed stick! Wouldn't that conclusively determine that there *wasn't* a pathogen at work?

☒ Aboah escapes from the hospital by hiding in a food cart. Specifically, a food cart with several trays on it that was left inside Aboah's quarantined room. Does this make sense? Why didn't the orderly bring Aboah's tray into the room, as opposed to wheeling in the entire cart and then *abandoning* it where there is a possibility of contagion?

☒ So, Aboah attacks four guys in three months. Then he attacks another one and appears to have plenty of time to harvest whatever he needs from the guy. Then he attacks his immigration officer only days later because Aboah is starting to turn white again. Hmmm. Four guys, three months. That's about one guy every three weeks. Yet, within the few days that Mulder and Scully are on the case, he attacks two different guys. Hmmm. That seems convenient to make the episode more suspenseful.

☒ Did Mulder really *just happen* to drive past a building that was being demolished and *just happen* to think it was a good idea to check inside and it *just happened* to be the building where Aboah brought his victims? Double hmmm.

Equipment Oddities

☒ On his way to New York, Mulder calls Scully on a pay phone. Is his *cell phone* in the shop, or did he suddenly have a pang of fiscal conscience over his liberal use of that wonderful little device?

Continuity and Production Problems

☒ Once Mulder learns of the death on the flight from Burkina Faso, an immigration officer named Marcus Duff supplies Aboah's name and address. The subsequent scene has screen text that reads, "Samuel Aboah's residence, 500 Demott Ave." When Aboah arrives home from work, however, Mulder glances at a piece of paper that has a copy of Aboah's identification card and—near the bottom of the screen—a solitary line of text seems to read, "2222 Demott Ave." So . . . does Aboah live at 500 Demott Avenue or 2222 Demott Avenue?

Trivia Questions

❶ What is Aboah's apartment number?

❷ What is the name of the fifth victim?

After Aboah shoots Mulder with one of his sleepy-time seeds, Scully comes to the rescue. Finding her partner in an air-conditioning duct, Scully knocks out a nearby vent cover and surveys the room below. Her flashlight travels across two bodies—one lies prone, the other leans up against the wall. Remember that last guy and note the position of his hands. The fingers of his right hand are curled, resting beside his body. His left hand is doing a passable Michael Jackson impersonation. (It's in his crotch. Sorry, sorry. Had to one-up Mulder and get a Michael Jackson joke in here *somewhere*.) Then Scully climbs down into the room and pulls Mulder out of the vent. As she lowers him to the floor, take another look at the dead guy beside him. Now the fingers on the guy's right hand are extended. Scully calls 911 and gives her badge number. A cutaway shows that the dead dude's *left* hand has now moved halfway to his belt. Aboah attacks. Scully shoots. The final overhead shot shows the man's right hand curled, once again. His left hand now rests on his waist.

Unruhe

Onscreen Locations

☒ Traverse City, Michigan
☒ Long Lake Road, northern Michigan
☒ FBI Special Photographic Unit,
   Washington, D.C.

Ruminations

The date on this episode comes from a close-up of Scully's computer screen during her final log entry.

And speaking of that log entry, it just might contain a bit of foreshadowing by the creators with regards to the episode "Paper Hearts." Scully writes that her captivity forced her to understand and empathize with Gerry Schnauz because her survival depended on it. She goes on to write that she now sees the value of this kind of insight—that to pursue monsters, law enforcement officers must understand them and, to understand them, law enforcement officers must venture into their minds. The creators then give us a typically thought-provoking X-Filean moment when they have Scully wonder about the reciprocal—wonder if in venturing into the minds of monsters, law enforcement officers risk letting the monsters venture into their own minds. And this, of course, is what apparently happens between Mulder and John Lee Roche just six episodes later in "Paper Hearts."

Plot Oversights

☒ I *suppose* it's in character for Mulder to send Scully to the car after the drugstore is robbed, but I was shaking my head the moment she walked

PLOT SUMMARY A kidnapping brings Mulder and Scully to Traverse City, Michigan. The abductee, Mary LeFonte, had a passport photograph taken moments before her disappearance. Instead of a pleasant expression, it shows her terrified. In addition, Mulder finds a camera at LeFonte's home filled with pictures of LeFonte surrounded by screaming, white faces. Mulder believes the kidnapper can influence undeveloped film with his mind and urges an analysis of the photos. Scully prefers more traditional methods of investigation—especially after LeFonte reappears, aimlessly wandering down a highway, the victim of a crude lobotomy.

Then a second woman is kidnapped. Certain the psychic photos contain valuable information, Mulder makes a quick round-trip to Washington. In his absence, Scully apprehends the assailant—a construction foreman named Gerald Schnauz. Schnauz explains that the second woman is safe from "the howlers," just like the first, and even tells them where to find her body.

Unfortunately, as Mulder and Scully go to the location, Schnauz escapes from custody and in short order captures Scully. He intends to end her unrest ("unruhe")—just like the others—by inserting an icepicklike device into the corner of her eye and killing the howlers that live in her skull. Thankfully, Mulder gathers enough clues from Schnauz's latest psychic photo to arrive just in time to preserve Scully's best asset.

out the door the *first* time I saw this episode. After all, the *wacko* is on the loose. He's already made overtures to Scully. ("You look troubled.") I felt like shouting, "Mulder . . . *Mulder!* Stay with her until you catch the crazy man." Of course, then the episode wouldn't have the exciting ending it does. So I suppose we should chalk this up to suspense-essential stupidity.

☒ Speaking of Scully's abduction scene, she walks up to a rented Ford Explorer, and Schnauz injects her foot with Twilight Sleep. In *four* seconds she's on the ground, preparing to pass out. Compare that to LeFonte at the beginning of the episode, who gets injected in the shoulder and fumbles around for almost thirty seconds before she hits the asphalt. Of course, if Scully had remained ambulatory for thirty seconds, she would have *shot* Schnauz. (Scully must be one of those people who are really sensitive to drugs.)

Equipment Oddities

☒ I'm confused. I get the general concept of psychic photography, but I don't understand the mechanism in this episode. A drugstore proprietor takes a passport photo of Mary LeFonte. When he peels away the paper, he sees her terrified face, but there is no hint of the image that he actually shot. Later, Mulder finds a camera in LeFonte's home. He holds his hand over the lens and takes several pictures. After developing, they show LeFonte haunted by howlers. The *latter* situation makes sense. Mulder makes sure that no light reaches the emulsion. In that way, *only* Schnauz's mental emanations can influence it. But what about the passport photo? Didn't the proprietor take the picture of LeFonte *before* Schnauz appeared? If Schnauz is influencing the film as well, why isn't there a double exposure? Can Schnauz really restore the original state of the emulsion prior to exposure and then alter it as he desires? (Wow!)

☒ The FBI has the *coolest* software! Believing that the psychic photos are crucial to the case, Mulder takes them back to the Special Photographic Unit (which really does exist, by the way). At one point, he asks the operator of a graphics software package to flip the picture so an indicated portion is on the bottom. Mulder's

hand makes a clockwise motion as he says this. Oddly enough, the picture rotates *counterclockwise* instead—putting the indicated portion on the *top* instead of the bottom! Is this a malfunction of the software or its operator? Of course not! The software must have known that Mulder was looking at a hidden shadow. If the software had followed Mulder's instruction, the shadow would have been on its head. With great consideration, the software evidently *decided* to orient the shadow right-side up!

☒ Apparently Schnauz's abilities affect not only film emulsion but CCD chips as well! It looks to me like the camera that takes his mug shot in the police station is digital. Yet Schnauz is able to project his will on it as well! (Not necessarily a nit, just a strange but true fact.)

☒ Has Mulder quit carrying his cell phone? He didn't use it in the previous episode. And, in this episode, he simply sprints after the vehicle as Schnauz absconds with Scully. Why not whip out the old cell phone and get the local police on the roads? Possibly they could block Schnauz's escape.

Continuity and Production Problems

☒ The episode opens with Mary LeFonte visiting a drugstore to purchase a passport photo. There's a moderate rain as she gets out of the car and heads inside. After taking the picture, the proprietor comments that it's clearing up and might be a nice day after all. A change in the lighting on his face even seems to support his statements. But seconds later, a cutaway shows us the front of the store, and now it's *pouring* rain! The weather must change quickly in Traverse City.

☒ After the opening commercial break, Mulder and Scully interview the drugstore proprietor. Every movement he makes is accompanied by the squeaking of his leg brace. So why didn't his leg brace squeak *before* the opening commercial break? (Prior to ripping the paper from LeFonte's picture, he takes a step to the side and all is quiet.) Is the leg brace something new? Or does he only wear it on certain days?

X After being abducted, Scully wakes to find her wrists duct-taped to a dental chair and another long strap of duct tape over her ankles. It sure looks like she could just pull her feet loose from that long strap. (Maybe Schnauz is using some of that newfangled *superadhesive* duct tape?!)

X Someone must have been playing musical headstones when Schnauz's father was buried. Take a good look at the picture of the cemetery that Mulder finds in Schnauz's wallet.

Specifically, note the amount of space between the tombstones that flank the father's grave. Now compare that to the amount of space between those same tombstones when Mulder arrives at the cemetery. Isn't there *a lot* more space in the picture?

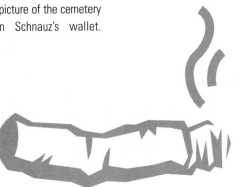

Trivia Questions

1 What is Mary LeFonte's middle name?

2 What educational distinction had Charles Selchik earned?

Trivia Answers
1 Louise.
2 He was a certified public accountant.

279

Unruhe

The Field Where I Died

PLOT SUMMARY

The episode begins with a raid on Vernon Ephesian's Temple of the Seven Stars compound in Apison, Tennessee. From an informant named Sydney, the FBI has had reports of child abuse and a large cache of weapons. Skinner has assigned Mulder and Scully to the case because of Ephesian's reported paranormal abilities.

The raid produces no tangible evidence and Sydney is nowhere to be found. While gazing across a nearby field, however, Mulder becomes trance-like. He wanders out of the buildings and straight to a hidden bunker, where he stops Ephesian from committing suicide with his wives. All are arrested. Unfortunately, without Sydney's testimony, police can hold them only for a day.

Mulder and Scully interrogate Ephesian but learn nothing new. Then they attempt to question one of Ephesian's wives, Melissa. Without warning, Melissa becomes Sydney. Scully thinks it's multiple personality. Mulder thinks it's a past life. Either way, they take Melissa to the compound to see if she will locate the weapons for them. In the field outside, Melissa suddenly narrates a battle scene from the Civil War, claiming to be a nurse in love with a Confederate soldier who died there. She identifies Mulder as that soldier. Certain that it's true, Mulder abandons the case to undergo hypnotic regression and confirm Melissa's story. Meanwhile, the twenty-four hours pass. Ephesian and his flock return to their compound. He doles out spiked Kool-Aid. Everyone dies.

Onscreen Locations

- ☒ Temple of the Seven Stars, Apison, Tennessee
- ☒ Federal Command Center, Chattanooga, Tennessee
- ☒ Hamilton County Hall of Records

Ruminations

The poetry that opens and closes this episode is really very beautiful. It's so nice to hear something so well written on television.

This episode marks the second appearance of a cast member from Space: Above and Beyond. *Kristen Cloke—who plays Melissa Reidel Ephesian in this episode—starred as Shane Vansen in that canceled series.*

Plot Oversights

☒ Vernon Ephesian claims that he has known for nine centuries that the authorities were coming for him. He says it was written in the Revelation of Jesus Christ. He also says that he heard the message of the Apocalypse when it was first given. Since the "Revelation of Jesus Christ" and the "message of the Apocalypse" probably mean the same thing, Ephesian is claiming that he knew about the Revelation of Jesus Christ shortly after it was written and that he learned the authorities were coming *from* the Revelation of Jesus Christ. If that's true, he's known about it for *nineteen* centuries, not *nine*.

☒ In the same conversation, Ephesian says that he was present to "hear Apostle John Mark deliver his message of the Apocalypse." The "Apostle John Mark" didn't pen the Revelation of Jesus Christ. The Apostle John (also called John the Beloved) did. John Mark accompanied Saul (also know as Paul) and Barnabas for a portion of their first missionary journey.

Convinced that he can learn more about Melissa's past life, Mulder talks Skinner into letting him take her back to Ephesian's compound. Strangely enough, there are no other federal officers anywhere in sight when Mulder and Scully escort Melissa through the house and nearby field. I thought the feds were looking for Ephesian's weapons. When did they give up on that activity?

Under hypnosis, Melissa claims that Ephesian beat a mother and her child. Would this be enough to get Tennessee Family Services involved? (If they are anything like the social services workers in Ohio, the kids in that compound would be *gone!* See "Revelations.")

Under hypnosis, Melissa also tells Mulder and Scully that Ephesian's weapons are hidden in some Civil War bunkers. Yet, apparently, *hours* go by before Scully passes on this piece of information to Skinner. I'd believe this kind of behavior from Mulder, but *Scully?!* If she had just passed it along, Skinner could have gotten the troops out in that field with metal detectors and possibly found the weapons in time to charge Ephesian and keep him interred.

There are timeline discrepancies with the past lives as purported by Melissa and Mulder. Since Mulder accepts all of Melissa's personalities as past lives, we probably should do the same. He is, after all, the hero, and heroes are supposedly right most of the time.

According to Mulder's hypnosis section, Melissa lives as a Jewish man in Poland after the invasion by Nazi Germany during World War II. According to Melissa, "Sydney" lives during the McCarthy era, and Truman is president. Germany didn't invade Poland until 1939, and Truman was president only until 1953. If Melissa died as a Jewish man in 1939, the maximum age for Sydney during Truman's presidency would be *fourteen!* Sydney *definitely* doesn't sound *fourteen!*

In addition, Mulder claims that Cancerman was present in Poland under German rule as a Gestapo officer. Remember that the earliest possible date for this would be 1939. However, a flashback in "Apocrypha" shows us Cancerman as a young man at a naval hospital in Pearl Harbor on August 19, 1953. For Cancerman to share a soul with the Gestapo officer, the Gestapo officer would have had to die in 1939, followed by Cancerman's birth in 1939 or some later year. But even if if Cancerman was born in 1939, he would be only *fourteen* in the scene from "Apocrypha." I think I can safely say that he's a bit older than that. (And, yes, even though a name isn't given in "Apocrypha," it *definitely* is Cancerman. The creators even had William B. Davis overdub the actor's voice to make sure we would make the connection!)

Now, granted, none of this would make any difference to Mulder because he "feels" that reincarnation is true and therefore it is true no matter what the numbers say. But one wonders why Scully didn't do the math with respect to Melissa and her supposed past lives.

Was anyone else amazed at how quickly Scully located the photographs of Sarah Kavanaugh and Sullivan Biddle? She's in the Hall of Records. She picks two names out of a register. She wanders over to a drawer labeled "Photographs—People, Civil War" and within twenty seconds has located both pictures. My wife enjoys genealogical research. She would *love* to have that kind of luck!

After learning that the two Civil War individuals he mentioned under hypnosis actually existed, Mulder tells Melissa about Sarah Kavanaugh and Sullivan Biddle. Interestingly enough, during this conversation he calls Melissa "Sarah." Are we supposed to start calling him "Sullivan" Mulder now?

FOURTH

Trivia Questions

1 What is Vernon Ephesian's real name?

2 In what year was Sullivan Biddle's picture taken?

Trivia Answers
1 Vernon Warren.
2 1862.

280

The Field
Where I Died

Changed Premses

❎ What a difference just a few seasons make! In "Born Again," Scully argued against transmigration of the soul simply because Michelle Bishop could have had access to information about her soul mate Charlie Morris. Specifically, Scully points to a picture of Morris in the station house and wonders if Michelle didn't see it when she walked through the room. Yet, in this episode, Mulder mentions two Civil War-era names. Scully looks them up and—finding them—suddenly seems convinced that transmigration of the soul is possible. What about all the Civil War documentaries? Isn't it remotely possible that Mulder heard these two names during one of those PBS specials? Or has Scully finally given up on trying to convince Mulder that he's wrong?

Continuity and Production Problems

❎ Watch closely as Scully finds the picture of Sullivan Biddle. She picks it up and turns it over. There's a label on the back. She flips it right side up to look at the picture, and the close-up shows that the picture has suddenly lost its label!

Sanguinarium

Onscreen Locations

☒ Aesthetic Surgery Unit, Greenwood Memorial Hospital, Chicago, IL

☒ Greenwood Memorial Hospital

☒ 1953 Gardner Street, Winnetka, IL

Ruminations

The "Millennium Effect" continues! (See my ruminations concerning "Home.") At least this episode has some connection to the paranormal, but there are moments in it when I just feel like holding up my hands and saying, "Enough already! We get the idea! Let's move it along here."

On an unrelated topic, Mulder apparently has a thing for women in medicine. Walking down the hall after entering the hospital for the first time, he seems to take every opportunity to notice every pretty woman in his path. And, upon hearing Scully say that Dr. Lloyd went through nineteen one-hundred-tablet refills of Sominil in the past five years, Mulder has only a one-word response. Staring at a very attractive young woman in scrubs, he simply says, "Wow!" (He hasn't been this distracted since Dr. Bambi caught him in her cockroach house during "War of the Coprophages.")

Plot Oversights

☒ Beyond the black magic pinging through the halls, many things about the Aesthetic Surgery Unit of Greenwood Memorial Hospital seem very strange. In the teaser, we see a well-proportioned woman prepped for liposuction. Nurse

PLOT SUMMARY After a doctor stabs a patient to death during a routine liposuction at the Aesthetic Surgery Unit of Greenwood Memorial Hospital, Mulder is intrigued by the doctor's claim of spirit possession. Then another surgeon uses a laser scalpel to burn a hole through a patient's head. Like the first, this doctor doesn't know what would compel him to do such a thing. While Scully notes that both were taking the same sleeping pill prescription, Mulder observes that both crime scenes included pentagrams—one on the floor, another on a patient's belly. Strangely enough, the pentagram—according to Mulder—is a sign of protection.

Of course, the rest of the surgical staff appears bewildered by the murders, although Dr. Jack Franklin admits that a decade ago something similar occurred. He says that one of the nurses, Rebecca Waite, was present for those deaths as well as the recent ones. That evening, Waite attacks Franklin in his home—leaping from a Jacuzzi filled with blood to cut him with a knife. Franklin eventually overpowers Waite but once she is in custody she begins coughing up straight pins and dies. After a bit of research, Mulder concludes that Waite was attempting to stop Franklin from offering blood sacrifices to make himself younger and more beautiful. Without her interference, Franklin quickly completes his latest ritual and escapes—after transforming himself into Dr. "Hartford."

Waite enters the woman's operating room. Apparently the woman was left there *alone* while *under anesthesia!* Evidently this hospital has some *fabulous* malpractice insurance (as well as a "protection arrangement" with the local police, as we shall see a bit later).

X More strangeness at the ASU. Upon seeing Dr. Ilaqua working on her patient, Dr. Shannon attempts to enter the operating room. She finds the door locked. Door locks on an OR?! Or is this just more of Franklin's black magic?

X In discussing the deaths in the ASU with Mulder and Scully, Dr. Franklin says that—like the deaths ten years prior—they were ruled accidental. *Accidental?!* Wouldn't an autopsy on the first victim show that Dr. Lloyd *stabbed* the guy to death? Wouldn't an autopsy on the second victim show that Dr. Ilaqua burned a hole clean through the woman's skull? How can these deaths be ruled accidental? This is *manslaughter,* at the very least! (Unless, of course, the ASU gives free cosmetic surgery to the police chief, the medical examiner, and the district attorney.)

X Okay, here's the situation. Warlock Franklin comes home. He finds some kind of incantation written on the wall. His Jacuzzi is filled with blood. Then Waite leaps out with a knife. They struggle. Waite disappears. And what does Warlock Franklin do? He runs downstairs and tries to call 911 to report the assault! Is he recharging his warlock batteries, or did he misplace his favorite amulet? Why doesn't he use one of those fancy spells that he uses only moments later to make Waite cough up straight pins? (And, yes, this *is* an all-around, generally *unpleasant* episode!)

X To offer the required blood sacrifices, Franklin must kill four people—each born on a "witches' Sabbath." After the deaths of three patients, the only witches' Sabbath left is October 31. One would think that Mulder and Scully would conclude that the final victim has a birthday of October 31. Yet, no dialogue indicates that Mulder and Scully have ordered a record search for patients with that birthday. Of course, if Mulder and Scully had made this request, Dr. Shannon—who seems to be their liaison at this

point—would have said, "Oh, that's my birthday," and then Mulder and Scully wouldn't have let her wander around the hospital by herself, and the entire ending of the episode would have had to have been *rewritten!*

X Near the end of the episode, Franklin uses his magic to put a handful of surgical instruments inside Dr. Shannon. As she is rushed into surgery, Mulder tells Scully to keep them from operating until he gives the word. *WHY?* As long as *Franklin* didn't perform the surgery, it would certainly save her life. Saving her life would mean that Franklin couldn't complete his ritual. Why *not* try to save Shannon's life? Is Mulder just trying to ensure that he can observe Franklin's black magic up close and personal?

X Franklin goes to all the trouble of carving the names of his victims into the stone tile at his home. Then, when Shannon doesn't die, he just kills someone else. I *love* this stuff! In other words, he didn't *have* to carve all the names on the stone tile for the spell to work?! So why did he carve them in the first place? Did he have some extra time on his hands? Did he want to leave behind a bit of incriminating evidence so everyone would know he was the one who actually killed the patients? Or is this yet another example of a posthypnotic suggestion by the faire pixies of Out There to assist our fearless agents? (Mulder and Scully learn that Shannon is the next target by reading her name scratched in the stone.)

X Great confusion surrounds the end of this episode. Evidently Franklin establishes an entirely new identity as a cosmetic surgeon and takes a job at a hospital in Los Angeles. There has to be black magic involved here because there's too much documentation required to practice medicine otherwise!

Changed Premses

X In discussing the witches' Sabbaths with Scully, Mulder refers to a book he found at Rebecca Waite's house as an information source. That's funny; I could have sworn that—in "Pilot"—Scully said Mulder wrote a monograph on serial killers and the occult. Shouldn't he already know about witches' Sabbaths?

Equipment Oddities

X Okay, *that's it!* I've decided. I am *heading* for Chicago! I am going to *steal* a couple of VCRs! (And I just might make a side trip to Braddock Heights, Maryland, while I'm at it. See "Wetwired.") At one point, Mulder shows Scully a videotape of Dr. Lloyd doing his Zorro impersonation on the first guy who dies. Mulder appears to be using the VCR in his Chicago hotel room. Stunned by the spectacle, Scully asks him to pause the tape. Mulder obliges, and we see the tape go to freeze-frame. Pause your tape as well and take a good look at the picture. Notice how the doctor's knees are at the *bottom* of the screen. Mulder and Scully talk about it for a moment and then Mulder points at the screen. A reverse angle shows us that the tape is *still* paused. But *now* . . . the lighting has changed at the bottom of the screen and the doctor's feet are showing! The only thing I can figure is that the VCR has some sort of three-dimensional rotation control that can actually change the perspective of the camera! *This is COOL!* I . . . want . . . one! (Think about it: You could pause the tape and rotate it around to see who was on the set that day!)

X And speaking of the laser that burns a hole through a patient's head, I suppose I should mention again that you can't see the beam emitted by any laser unless there is some type of scattering particle in the air. (See "Fallen Angel" for more details.)

X During one of the many bloodfest scenes in this episode, Waite goes after Franklin with some kind of ceremonial knife. Personally, I agree with Jason Liu of Libertyville, Illinois: I would have opted for the ceremonial Uzi!

X Technoamnesia lives on! After discovering that patients born on the witches' Sabbath are being killed, Scully—while en route to the hospital—learns that there's a patient in preop born on a witches' Sabbath. She learns this somewhat crucial piece of information from talking on her cell phone. She hangs up. She tells Mulder. They make all haste to get to the hospital. Is there some reason why Scully doesn't turn on her phone, hit redial, and tell the ASU to delay the patient's procedure until they arrive?!

X I used to think I was a diligent programmer until I started watching *The X-Files*. (I'm not programming any longer, but I did feed my family with it for almost a decade.) I used to think I was fairly thorough in the capabilities I created for the software I wrote. Unfortunately, the guys who programmed the cosmetic surgery software shown in this episode put me to shame! As Dr. Shannon works with the software package, Mulder asks her to widen the eyes on a photograph of Dr. Clifford Cox and strengthen his forehead. Shannon responds that those alterations are beyond the current surgical capabilities. Mulder asks her to do it anyway, and four clicks later, *she does!* So even though it wasn't possible to do in the real world, the programmers built a simple user interface to accomplish this task? To quote Mulder, "Wow!" (Normally, programmers have *plenty* of things to cram into a program without wasting time building features that aren't going to get used. This isn't a video morphing program after all!)

X Too bad no one saw Dr. Franklin peeling off his face, on the little monitor outside the OR. Maybe someone would have sounded an alarm. Or did Franklin use some-o-dat ol' black magic to

Trivia Questions

1 What was Dr. Clifford Cox's stated birthday?

2 Who interviews Dr. Hartford for his new surgical position?

Sanguinarium

obscure the video feed to those little monitors above *every* OR entrance?

Continuity and Production Problems

X Granted, I don't know much about pentagrams. I have no idea how you're supposed to know which way they are oriented when they reside on a floor. But Mulder claims the pentagram in Franklin's house is upside down. That's odd, because it looks like if you're walking in the front door, you'd see it right-side up! So . . . does that mean if you walk in the front door you're protected, but if you walk in the back door you'll be possessed by the "goat of lust"?

X The doctor who saves Shannon's life doesn't seem to have any prescription on his glasses.

X-SILLINESS

The Top Ten Oddities of the First Four Seasons of THE X-FILES

1 *Mulder's perseverance as an FBI special agent.* I know Fox Mulder supposedly has higher powers looking out for him, but I'm continually amazed that this guy can remain an employee of the Justice Department with his flagrant disregard for protocol and regulations; his single-minded focus on only those issues that concern him; even his clearly dangerous behavior. (He did, after all, arrange for the release of a serial child-killer in "Paper Hearts," and his actions directly lead to a young girl being traumatized.)

2 *Scully's educational history.* From all indications, Dana Scully earned her doctorate in medicine, then taught at the Academy at Quantico for two years before becoming a special agent working with Fox Mulder. The Real FBI reaction to this scenario? "Far-fetched. Wouldn't happen."

3 *CPR ineptitude.* As highly trained law enforcement officials, Mulder and Scully display a persistent lack of knowledge about basic CPR techniques—as do most of the characters on the show!

4 *The favors of criminals.* Mulder and Scully lead charmed lives—often receiving unsolicited help from those they pursue. As just one example, perpetrators seem to sense when the intrepid pair is on the case and increase the frequency of attacks to allow for their capture. In "Humbug," deformed twin Leonard averages 1.7 victims a year for twenty-eight years. Then Mulder and Scully arrive and he attacks four people in a matter of days. In "2SHY," Virgil Incanto goes three months without chewing anyone's fat. Then he binges just after our heroes take the case. In "Quagmire," the alligator kills two people in two weeks but racks up an amazing *seven* attacks during the episode. And before the events of "Teliko," Samuel Aboah kills four men in three months. During "Teliko" he attacks two more in a matter of days.

5 *Technoamnesia.* Mulder and Scully consistently discuss sensitive information over their cell phones even though they know conspirators can eavesdrop. Worse, in episodes such as "Shadows," "Duane Barry," "Aubrey," "Colony," and "Sanguinarium," our heroes seem to forget that they carry the marvelous devices, and they delay making phone calls that could save lives.

6 *That illuminated magnifying glass.* There's a large arm-mounted magnifying glass that makes several appearances on *The X-Files*. In at least three episodes—"Blood," "Fearful Symmetry," and "War of the Coprophages"—we see cast members using the glass backward. This causes the circular fluorescent fixture mounted underneath to shine in their eyes!

7 *Set wars.* Between "Pilot," "Fire," and "Beyond the Sea," Mulder's basement office gets bigger and adds a few doors. Between "End Game," "The Blessing Way," and "Herrenvolk," the hall outside Mulder's apartment shrinks five or six feet and then grows back. And between "Anasazi" and "Tempus Fugit," a window switches walls in Scully's second bedroom.

8 *Video games.* The X-Files features a whole line of fascinating video effects. An apparition magically appears on a videotape after rewinding during "Shadows." "Soft Light" features a *train depot* with equipment that can take a paused video image and zoom, reframe, and deblur. And how about that VCR in "Wetwired" that can continue to play a tape even after it's been ejected? Or the VCR in "Sanguinarium" that can change the perspective of a paused video image?

9 *A bit of privacy . . . please!* If I were Scully, I think I'd move. Seems like anybody and everybody can find her apartment. Tooms does in "Squeeze." Both John Barnett and Dr. Joe Ridley do in "Young at Heart." Duane Barry does in "Duane Barry." Alex Krycek and Louis Cardinal do in "The Blessing Way." Jeremiah Smith does as well in "Talitha Cumi."

10 *TOAL.* It's fun to watch the struggles the creators go through in *X-Files* episodes to ensure that Mulder and Scully will get stuck in the dark and have to use their handy-dandy flashlights. For instance, "Eve": Eve 6 can't stand bright illumination in her cell. "Shapes": No power at the Parker home. ("Happens all the time.") "Born Again": Charlie Morris's psychic energy pulls the plug. "Little Green Men": No power at the Arecibo Observatory, even though the equipment indicator lights are on. "3": A vampire watchman breaks all the lightbulbs. "Firewalker": Parasite-carriers shut off the power at a volcano observatory. "Die Hand Die Verletzt": Black magic leaves the town of Milford Haven, New Hampshire without electricity (etc., etc.). Even still, there are plenty of instances when our heroes walk right by wall-mounted switches and start exploring dark and dangerous places. This is when I yell, "Turn on a light!"

Musings of a Cigarette-Smoking Man

Onscreen Locations

☒ Center for Special Warfare, Ft. Bragg, North Carolina, October 30, 1962

☒ Dallas, Texas, November 22, 1963

☒ Westbrook Drive, Irving, Texas

☒ Texas School book Depository

☒ Trinity River Overflow Outlet

☒ Oswald's boarding house room

☒ Tenth & Patton

☒ Texas Theatre

☒ Memphis, Tennessee, April 3, 1966

☒ Rooming house, 418 S. Main, April 4, 1966

☒ Directly across from Lorraine Motel Room 306

☒ Washington, D.C., December 24, 1991

☒ Dogway, West Virginia, December 24, 1991

☒ Washington, D.C., March 6, 1992

Ruminations

I have to be honest and admit that I am inescapably prejudiced against this episode. Why? Well . . . there's a sad story in Trekdom. It concerns the originator of Star Trek, Gene Roddenberry. As the story goes, by the time of the second Star Trek movie, Roddenberry had been relegated to a figurehead position of "executive consultant." He wrote memos and everyone ignored him. It seems that the movie he wanted to make as the second Star Trek movie concerned the Enterprise crew traveling back in time to the assassination of John F. Kennedy. They would, of course, be unable to do anything to change history and therefore fail in the end. If the stories are true, Roddenberry pitched the same idea for Star Trek III, Star Trek IV, and Star Trek V! Ever since reading this anec-

PLOT SUMMARY

At the offices of the Lone Gunmen, Mulder and Scully listen as Frohike tells the tale of a mysterious man: a man who assassinated President Kennedy and Martin Luther King, Jr.; a man who heads a supersecret committee that has overseen everything from the Rodney King trial to the Oscar nominations; a man who met with Deep Throat on the night of December 24, 1991, following the recovery of a UFO and watched as Deep Throat executed the alien pilot; a man who even helped select Scully as Mulder's partner.

Frohike gathered the information from a serialized novel in the soft-porn magazine *Roman à Clef*. Cancerman wrote the novel under the pen name Raul Bloodworth and was ready to resign from the intelligence community after finally selling his first story following years of creative frustration. Unfortunately, an editor changed the ending—and an embittered Cancerman returned to his vile occupation.

In time, Frohike leaves the offices of the Lone Gunmen to find verification that the story is indeed a fictionalized account of Cancerman's life. He doesn't realize that Cancerman has been eavesdropping on the conversation. Nor does he realize that Cancerman has him in the crosshairs of a rifle. The hammer draws back. Cancerman mumbles that he can kill Frohike any time he wants. Then the hammer eases down and Cancerman adds, " . . . but not today."

dote, I have felt that using the assassination of JFK as part of the main plot of any fiction story is the certified indicator that you've run out of ideas! So, as you can imagine, I wasn't thrilled when "Dealey Plaza" came up on the screen during an X-Files episode. (Especially since I had just agreed to do an X-phile Guide!)

All that aside, however, I still don't think I would have particularly enjoyed this episode. I feel it strains credulity to vest so much in one man, no matter how "extraordinary." (Cancerman is the guy who keeps the Buffalo Bills from winning a Super Bowl?! Got it. This is a joke, right?) For me, the episode really doesn't start to get interesting until Part III, when Deep Throat kills the EBE. (Always good to see Jerry Hardin again!) My personal feeling is the episode would have been a lot stronger if we had seen more scenes like this that filled in a bit of the alien abduction mythology. But then, I'm just the nitpicker!

This episode makes the third appearance of a cast member from Space: Above and Beyond. Morgan Weisser plays Lee Harvey Oswald in this episode. He starred in Space: Above and Beyond as Nathan West.

The date on this episode comes from Walden Roth's comments to Cancerman that the issue of Roman à Clef that features his story will appear on newsstands on November twelfth.

Finally, I'll say it because many of you are thinking it! This episode shows us that Cancerman has a picture of Mrs. Mulder holding Fox as a child. In addition, during "Talitha Cumi," Cancerman tells Mulder that he knew his mother since before Mulder was born. "Talitha Cumi" also strongly hints that Mrs. Mulder and Cancerman had an affair. Not only that, right after Cancerman tells his cronies in the Christmas 1991 flashback that he has to see some "uh, family," the scene cuts to the basement of the FBI Headquarters building where Cancerman pauses by the door to Mulder's basement office. And if those hints aren't sufficient for you, how about "Demons?" Perhaps

Mulder's memories in that episode are nothing more than drug-induced psychosis. But when Mulder charges to his mother's house, claiming that there were things she hid from him and interrogating her with questions like "Who is my father?," she certainly does nothing to ease poor Fox's mind concerning his lineage. Mrs. Mulder simply gets irate, protesting that she will not tolerate any more of his questions. Shall we all say it together, dear friends and fellow nitpickers? "(labored breathing) Luke . . . Luke, I am your father." (That's a Star Wars reference in case you haven't seen the trilogy. And, yes, I know that Darth Vader doesn't say "Luke" in the actual movie but no one would recognize the quote without it!) Are the creators hinting that Cancerman sired Mulder? Is that why he has protected him? (Actually, this would explain a lot. I have no trouble believing that all the junk Cancerman has been spouting like, "you know how important Mulder is to the equation" and "we can't risk turning one man's religion into a crusade" is nothing more than a pack of lies to protect his own son.)

Unanswered Questions

☒ Are the flashbacks *actually* autobiographical with respect to Cancerman's life? Obviously, the answer to this question will greatly affect the nitpicking of this episode. If the flashbacks are merely the ramblings of Cancerman, then this episode tells us nothing, and discrepancies between the information contained herein and information presented in other episodes are to be *expected!* After all, would Cancerman really risk such exposure by revealing himself as the true assassin of both JFK and Martin Luther King, Jr.? Indeed, Frohike begins his rehearsal of the story in *Roman à Clef* by saying that it might reveal the background of Cancerman, who he is and who he *wants* to be. Perhaps Cancerman is twisted enough to imagine that murdering two such important people would have added to his self-worth if he had only had the chance.

On the other hand, if these events actually occurred, we learn some fascinating things about the alien conspiracy mythology from this episode. To wit, Deep Throat didn't kill an EBE in Vietnam, as he told Mulder at the end of "E.B.E." The first living EBE was not recovered until 1991. The Roswell Incident was a fake cover story. (Yes, Deep Throat tells Mulder and Scully this in "The Erlenmeyer Flask," but we didn't know if he was lying.) And, as of 1991, William Mulder—Fox Mulder's father—was *still* involved with a "project" concerning extraterrestrials.

Unfortunately, there are indications that the flashbacks are nothing more than fiction penned by Cancerman. Frohike reveals that—according to the story in *Roman à Clef*—Cancerman's birth date is August 20, 1940. This *can't* be right. The beginning of "Apocrypha" shows us Cancerman as a young man. (And, yes, it *is* he. Listen to the voice.) Screen text identifies the date as August 19, 1953. If the birth date in *Roman à Clef* is correct, Cancerman was only one day short of *thirteen* when he interviewed the sailor! And what about those cigarettes? The flashbacks strongly suggest that Cancerman didn't begin to smoke until after the Kennedy assassination. The same footage mentioned above from "Apocrypha" shows Cancerman smoking in 1953!

Plot Oversights

 Here all this time I thought the Lone Gunmen were paranoid. At the beginning of this episode we see that their headquarters has a *sign* on the door.

 During the Kennedy flashback, a general tells the young Cancerman that communism is the most heinous personification of evil the world has ever known. I wonder how he feels about fascism?

 I can honestly say that I have never seen a rejection letter as harsh as the one Cancerman

garners from Montgomery and Glick Publishing. His novel must be *atrocious!* (Of course, Cancerman's "box-o-chocolates" speech *is* pretty pathetic!) On the other hand, one phrase of the rejection letter seems strangely familiar. "Burn it!" the editor suggests, just as Cancerman did at the end of "Anazasi."

 With giddy anticipation, Cancerman rushes to the newsstand the day his novel appears in *Roman à Clef*. He is surprised to discover that it's a porn magazine. Okay. Wait a minute: The guy who knows everything about everything and controls all sentient life on the planet didn't press a button to find out the particulars on *Roman à Clef* before he signed a contract?!

 In addition, Cancerman flips to his story in the magazine and finds that the editor changed his ending. But, but, but . . . the editor said the story would be *serialized*. Doesn't that mean the novel would be published a piece at a time? Wouldn't the first issue hold only the first chapter or two?

Changed Premises

 Mulder introduces Scully to our three favorite conspiracy-theorists in "E.B.E." Briefing Scully on the trio, Mulder states that the trio publishes a magazine called *The Lone Gunman*. Alas, alack, *The Lone Gunman* has apparently bitten the dust. The sign on the door in this episode informs us that the Lone Gunmen publish a *newsletter* called *The Magic Bullet*. (Or is that just decoy information?)

Equipment Oddities

 In my review of "One Breath," I mentioned that Mulder's basement office has moved since "Pilot." In "Pilot," the office is the final turn at the dead end of a hallway. In "One Breath," however, we can see light streaming into the basement, indicating a stairwell. Strangely

FOURTH SEASON

Trivia Questions

1 What is the title of the first Jack Colquitt adventure?

2 What is the name of the editor who serializes Cancerman's novel?

291

Musing of a Cigarette-Smoking Man

enough, in "Musings of a Cigarette-Smoking Man," Cancerman strolls by Mulder's office and we can see the staircase whose existence we only presumed in "One Breath." But the scene in question is a flashback to 1991. That means Mulder had one spot in the basement, he moved for "Pilot," and then he moved back by the time of "One Breath"!

X Deep Throat dons a fascinating gas mask just before killing the alien. As Cancerman watches, Deep Throat presses it to his face. Then the camera angle changes and suddenly the straps have wrapped themselves around Deep Throat's head! (Yet more of that amazing Consortium technology?)

Continuity and Production Problems

X Just before Cancerman assassinates Martin Luther King, Jr., there's a medium-wide shot of an upper-story walkway outside a pair of motel rooms. The exterior wall is flat. However, after King is shot, the picture shown clearly indicates that the wall jutted out in the vicinity of King's room.

Tunguska

(Part 1 of 2)

Onscreen Locations

☒ Senate Select Subcommitee on Intelligence and Terrorism, Washington, D.C.

☒ Honolulu Airport, U.S. Customs, ten days earlier

☒ Flushing, Queens, New York City

☒ Dulles International Airport, Herdon, Virginia

☒ Crystal City, Virginia

☒ NASA Goddard Space Flight Center, Greenbelt, Maryland

☒ Upper West Side, New York City

☒ JFK International Airport, New York City

☒ Charlottesville, Virginia

☒ Tunguska, Siberian forest, Russia

☒ Senate Executive Office Building

Ruminations

So nice to get back to the alien conspiracy stuff!

I gotta tell ya. After that last episode—when Cancerman showed up in this one—I couldn't help but think, "Oh, look, it's the dweeby, 'mint-filled-crap-box-o-chocolates,' 'please, please, please, let me be a writer' guy!"

The date on this episode comes from a close-up of Mulder's watch while he's in Marita Covarrubias's apartment.

And speaking of this midnight rendezvous, it's fascinating to note the extraordinary lengths to which the creators go in this episode to ensure that we don't assume anything physical happened between Mulder and Covarrubias. We see him look at his watch. A close-up tells us it's "3:12." Back from the commercial break, Mulder returns to his car, starts it, and a close-

PLOT SUMMARY An anonymous tip sends Mulder and Scully on a raid that brings them face-to-face with an old enemy, Alex Krycek. Immediately, Krycek claims to be the informant who helped with the bust and says he knows of more terrorist bombs in the making.

At Dulles International Airport, Krycek fingers a courier who carries a diplomatic pouch. Strangely enough, the pouch contains no explosives, only a rock—possibly from Mars. Even more odd, the rock encases a black, oily substance that can form into wormlike creatures that burrow under skin and immobilize their victims.

Mulder then contacts Marita Covarrubias and learns that the rock came from Tunguska, Russia—the site of a violent, explosive impact in 1908. Very quickly, Covarrubias arranges cover credentials so Mulder and Krycek can travel there to investigate further. Once they leave, Senator Albert Sorenson unexpectedly summons Scully and Skinner to his office and demands to know Mulder's whereabouts. (Apparently the Well-Manicured Man wants Mulder kept *out* of this matter.) But by this time, Mulder and Krycek have already been captured in Tunguska. And as the episode ends, the Russians make Mulder part of their experiments. They strap him to an iron cot—using chicken wire to immobilize him—before pouring the black, oily substance onto his face.

up of the car's clock informs us that it's "3:15." I felt like the creators were standing over in the corner shouting, "Hint! Hint! That was a hint!"

Unanswered Questions

☒ How does the alien guck seen in this episode relate to the alien goo seen in "Piper Maru" and "Apocrypha"? In those episodes, the goo seemed to be intelligent. In this episode, it just paralyzes people.

Plot Oversights

X This episode opens with Scully testifying before the U.S. Senate Select Subcommittee on Intelligence and Terrorism. (The rest of the episode is told in flashback.) Interrupting Scully's prepared statement, the committee chairman refers to Scully as "Ms. Scully." Shouldn't that be "Dr. Scully?"

X I realize that I may not live up to the brave and valiant standards of customs officials, but I can guarantee you that if I had dropped a canister of sludge on the floor and it started moving, I *certainly* would *not* stand there and stare at it—tapping my foot like I was part of Uncle Beuford's ragtime band (as a customs official does in this episode)! I would be *out* the door, and if the door was locked, I would make a *new* door!

X We are missing almost fifteen hours in this episode. According to screen text, Mulder and Scully apprehend Krycek shortly after "3:07 A.M." in New York City. They interview him and decide to keep him around for a while. He leads them to the courier arriving at Dulles International Airport at 6:45 P.M. What did they do the rest of the day?

X At Dulles, Mulder and Scully attempt to question a man carrying a diplomatic pouch. The guy runs. Mulder and Scully pursue. Eventually the guy gives them the slip but leaves the supersecret pouch behind. Why? It doesn't look that heavy.

X Mulder picks the oddest times to leave out crucial pieces of information. At one point he briefs Scully on a courier who tried to enter the States via Honolulu, carrying what he describes as a "toxic soil sample." "Toxic?" Scully parrots. "Yes," Mulder replies before

spinning off on his latest intuitively derived theory—apparently forgetting or *not caring* that one person, perhaps two, are catatonic from exposure to the "soil sample." (I know that we don't know *for sure* that there are two catatonic individuals in Hawaii, but throughout this episode and the next, exposure to the black oil always results in the "exposee" blankly staring into oblivion. The Honolulu customs official—mentioned above—had already succumbed to this fate when we left the teaser, and the screaming courier seemed destined for nirvana as well.)

If Mulder had passed along this vital piece of information to Scully, Scully probably would have passed it along to the scientist at the Goddard Space Flight Center—the same scientist whom we see in the very next scene cutting into the rock and getting sprayed with the black, ucky wigglies. (Granted, the scientist did suit up for the procedure so he had already taken some precautions, but at least the guy should have been warned that he was dealing with a high-health-risk item.)

X Ya know, you have to appreciate a woman like Marita Covarrubias. Out of the blue, Mulder knocks on her apartment at "12:36 A.M." (according to screen text) and—though she is clothed in a white robe and pajamas—she looks gorgeous! (Almost like she was expecting him. Hmmm. More treachery from the Consortium?)

X There's an entry in *The Nitpickers Guild Glossary* (nominated by Travis McCord and harkening back to an old Monty Python catch-phrase) called BIMOL. It stands for "But it's my only line" and refers to the process of including every actor possible in an episode, even if their presence is a bit silly. Take this episode, for instance. After a scientist at Goddard Space Flight Center succumbs to the black guck, Scully investigates. With whom does she work during this investigation? The lovable Agent *Pendrell!* I guess Goddard was fresh out of *scientists* who could assist! (Surprisingly enough, one miraculously appears in the next episode.)

Changed Premises

 Although Krycek claims that he was rescued by extremists from the missile silo (see "Apocrypha"), the next episode will indicate this wasn't the case. I'll reserve my comments on Krycek's "resurrection" for the "Changed Premises" of "Terma."

Continuity and Production Problems

 You may have already noticed that "Subcommitee" is misspelled in the "Onscreen Locations" section above. That *is* the way it is spelled on the screen! ("Subcommittee" is the proper spelling.)

 Skinner chose a *fascinating* location for his new apartment. Remember the woman he bedded in "Avatar"? Remember that he didn't know she was a prostitute? Remember that the woman's matron worked out of a glass-and-steel high-rise? Now compare her residence to Skinner's new residence. Looks familiar, doesn't it? Oh, sure, I know the creators tried to call the building something different and gave it a different number, but if you watch the episodes side-by-side, I think you'll agree that it's *the same building!* In addition, I realize that the matron of the escort service was killed in "Avatar," but I would remind you that these "industries" tend to continue—especially when they have a well-established clientele. I leave it for you, gentle readers, to decide what "features" Skinner finds most enjoyable about his new location! (On a sadder note, it appears that Skinner couldn't reconcile his differences with his wife.)

 It's amazing what the creators think they can slip by us. After three and a half years . . . they *changed* the "I Want to Believe" poster in Mulder's office! Did they think we wouldn't *notice?!* (Snicker, snicker.) You can see the new poster over Mulder's shoulder just before he tells Scully about the courier in Honolulu. (If you want to compare it to the old poster, there's an excellent close-up just after the opening credits of "José Chung's *From Outer Space.*" And while you're at it, watch that episode again. It's fabulous!)

 The closed captioning in this episode has an interesting addition that never made it to audio. When Mulder finds a cockroach in his gruel, the closed captioning reads, "Bambi?" (Obviously harkening back to "War of the Coprophages.")

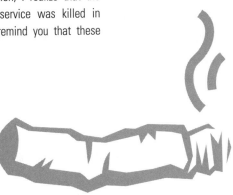

Trivia Questions

❶ What is Skinner's new address?

❷ What is the Russian port of entry for the diplomatic pouch?

295

Tunguska

Terma

(Part 2 of 2)

PLOT SUMMARY In Tunguska, Mulder struggles to wake up after being subjected to the "black cancer." (Krycek—who is really a Russian agent—recommended Mulder for "the test.") Shortly afterward, Mulder escapes, knocking Krycek into the back of a truck before leaping into the driver's seat to race away. Refusing capture, Krycek leaps from the truck just before Mulder careens over the side of a hill. Thankfully, the owner of the truck opts to protect Mulder and smuggle him to freedom. Krycek, on the other hand, is found by a group of men who want to insure that he won't be subjected to "the test." They cut off his left arm. (And, no, I'm not sure why but it has something to so with the smallpox vaccination scar!)

Meanwhile, a Russian named Vassily Peskov arrives in the United States and starts assassinating all those who had direct involvement with the black vermiform organism. He also destroys the rock itself by incinerating it in an oil-well fire. Hearing of Peskov's activities, the Well-Manicured Man wonders how the Russians could have possibly learned of the Consortium's attempt to find a cure for the black cancer.

Back in Washington, Mulder finds Scully in contempt of Congress because she has refused to disclose his whereabouts. After the charges are dropped, Mulder concludes that "someone" used him and Scully to expose the Consortium's activities. He doesn't realize it was Krycek. As the episode ends, Comrade Krycek congratulates Peskov on a job well done.

Onscreen Locations

⌧ Harrow Convalescent Home, Boca Raton, Florida

⌧ St. Petersburg, Russia

⌧ NASA Goddard Space Flight Center, Greenbelt, Maryland

⌧ Richmond, Virginia

⌧ Senate Select Subcommittee on Intelligence and Terrorism, Washington, D.C.

⌧ Federal Correctional Facility, New York City

⌧ Border crossing, Alberta, Canada

Ruminations

You have to feel for Krycek just a bit. He leaps from the truck and injures his right arm. Then, he meets some peasants who try to help him escape "the test" by cutting off his left arm. Bummer.

Unanswered Questions

⌧ Who is Comrade Arntzen? Near the beginning of the episode, the man who recruits Vassily Peskov claims that "Comrade Arntzen" wants him to know that the Cold War is not over. Later we learn that Krycek went by the name of Arntzen while he worked with the right-wing militia guys. But at the end of the episode Peskov calls Krycek "Comrade Krycek." So is "Arntzen" Krycek's real first name, or was he borrowing the name Arntzen when he worked with the militia? And if he was borrowing the name, who is the real Arntzen?

Plot Oversights

⌧ I wish I knew where Scully lived. I'd like to rent the apartment across the hall. There's no telling *what* sort of fascinating things a person

:ould learn just by listening at the door. In this episode, for instance, Skinner finally locates Scully just as she is about to enter her apartment. Instead of going inside Scully's apartment to discuss his reason for needing to speak with her, Skinner remains *in the hall,* debriefing Scully on her activities before telling her about the death of a virologist named Charne-Sayre.

X Dialogue in this episode and the last seems to indicate that the Well-Manicured Man initiated the Senate hearings shortly after Mulder disappeared. In fact, *the* question that Senator Sorenson requires Scully to answer is: Where is Agent Mulder? Here's what seems strange. The Well-Manicured Man already knew where Mulder was heading *before* the hearings began! Cancerman tells him that a man fitting Mulder's description boarded a plane to the Russian province of Krasnoyarsk. Why is Sorenson asking about Mulder's whereabouts if the Well-Manicured Man already knows that? Is the good senator acting alone?

X After Mulder escapes from the Russian gulag in a stolen truck, three guards pursue him on horseback. They fire off a few shots and then turn and gallop back to the compound. In time, the compound commander and a larger group of guards locate the overturned truck. Everyone is riding horses. This is when I frowned. If everyone was going to ride horses in the first place, why didn't the three guards remain in hot pursuit? What was gained by *all three* returning to the compound? (When I first saw the three *amigos* turn around, I thought, "Oh, they're going back for a car or motorcycles or something." But . . . then they didn't!)

X For being so buddy-buddy with the gulag's commander, Krycek certainly isn't in a hurry to return to the prison compound. He jumps off Mulder's stolen truck and promptly wanders into the woods. Why not follow the road back to the camp? Or is there a reason why Krycek

didn't want to return there?

X I'm confused. Mulder steals a truck to escape the gulag. Mulder crashes the truck. The truck driver finds him. The truck driver is angry. The truck driver takes Mulder to his house, and the truck driver's wife explains that her husband is scared because the truck afforded them some protection. Because the truck driver made deliveries, the officials at the gulag didn't recruit the man and his wife for "the test."

First, the truck driver seems extremely magnanimous to bring Mulder to his home under the circumstances. Second, moments after we hear of the great protection the truck affords, the truck driver's wife calls to a boy who appears to be her son and we see that the boy has his arm cut off—obviously to spare him from "the test." Did the truck only provide protection for Mom and Dad?!

X At one point we see Vassily Peskov kill the exobiologist who succumbed to the black cancer in the previous episode. The exobiologist is in a quarantine suit, inside a quarantine chamber inside the "Department of Exobiology" at NASA's Goddard Space Flight Center. For his part, Peskov wears no badge and appears to waltz through the area with *no difficulty at all!* Just how did Peskov pull off this bit of magic? Mitzi Adams informs me that security *does* exist at the Goddard Space Flight Center. It would be unusual indeed for a man to just wander through unannounced and unnoticed.

X One wonders why Mulder or Scully didn't scoop up the black guck that had crawled out of the eyes and noses of the old people at the convalescent home after Peskov killed them. No doubt, our heroes had a reason not to gather *this* evidence.

FOURTH SEASON

Trivia Questions

1 What is the name of the Russian truck driver's son?

2 From what occupation did Vassily Peskov retire?

Terma

Changed Premises

☒ How did Krycek get out of the missile silo? For those of you who do not recall, "Piper Maru" and "Apocrypha" feature an oily, body-hopping alien who eventually commandeers Krycek's body and returns to the States to cut a deal with Cancerman. In exchange for the digital casette of the files stolen by The Thinker in "Anasazi," Cancerman escorts the alien—still in Krycek's body—to a missile silo in North Dakota that is currently being used to store the alien's spaceship. Following a truly touching scene in which Krycek hacks and spits oil out of every orifice on his face, the alien leaves Krycek's body and reenters its craft. (Don't ask me *why* the alien wants to be reunited with its craft, especially since it's still locked in a missile silo. But, moving right along . . .) The final scene of "Apocrypha" then has Krycek pounding on the metal door that leads to a hallway outside the missile silo as the camera does a dramatic pull back—leaving Krycek screaming in terror. (Not only that, just prior to this scene, the creators precisely construct dialogue between Mulder and Scully to leave us with the final statement, "Maybe we bury the dead alive." To me at least, it seems obviously that the creators want us to conclude that Krycek has pulled his last double-cross.)

Yet, at some point, between "Apocrypha" and "Tunguska," Krycek evidently experienced a resurrection of sorts: he made it past that locked metal door to rejoin the land of the living. How?! Did I mention this silo contains an . . . *alien space craft.* I have a hard time believing Cancerman would leave it entirely without any sort of patrols so that Krycek's buddies could come to his rescue. And if I recall correctly—without water—Krycek would only last a few days. Surely, Cancerman didn't have an attack of consciousness and let him out, did he? (Or . . . gasp! . . . is Cancerman actually working for the *Russians!* Aaaaah! Or . . . double gasp! . . . did Cancerman open the silo and release the alien?

Is Cancerman actually working for the "oilies?" Double aaaaah!)

Equipment Oddities

☒ Here all this time, I thought the map light in a vehicle was for reading maps! Given the opening of this episode, I may have to retract my statements about the oddity of Mulder and Scully sitting in their car at night with the lights on. In the teaser, we see a van pull up to the Harrow Convalescent Home, Boca Raton, Florida. A Kavork-anoid suicide doctor drives. A young woman sits in the passenger seat. Their faces are illuminated from below—as if the glove compartment is open. I guess it's all the rage!

☒ Apparently the officials in the gulag cannot perform the test on individuals who do not have a smallpox vaccination scar. (You will recall that Scully identified the scar as some sort of individualized marker in "Herrenvolk.") Because of this, the Russians who find Krycek in the woods decide to cut off his arm to protect him. The knife is heated in a fire. A man approaches with the red-hot blade as his companions hold Krycek on the ground. Krycek begins to scream as the man with the knife saws away. It's not really a nit, but I couldn't help but wonder just how *long* that guy was going to be sawing with that knife, because it didn't have a serrated blade! (And it certainly wasn't a Ginsu knife!)

Continuity and Production Problems

☒ The preview for this episode contains a shot of a young woman with the black wigglies on her face. The shot obviously comes from the teaser, but it never occurs in the actual episode. The only reason I noticed it was the woman looks something like Scully, and the first time I watched the episode I was expecting Scully to get smeared with the black guck, just like Mulder.

Not a nit necessarily, just one of those quirky things to listen for. Just before we see Mulder trudging along in the mud of the Russian gulag, the camera pans across the roof of a building and then down to a column of prisoners. For some reason, the creators added the word "prisoner" to the audio at this point in the episode.

There be strange things afoot in the Russian forest. Discovering that the stolen truck doesn't have brakes, Mulder sends it careening off the side of a steep hill. In one of the sequences that make up the crash, the creators provide us with a very nice camera angle that features the driver's side of the vehicle. Surprisingly enough—for the actual crash—Mulder somehow replaced himself with a stunt dummy! (No wonder he could walk away from the crash.)

During the replay of Scully's initial appearance before the Senate Subcommittee in this episode, listen to the echo in her voice. In the shots featuring Scully, the creators pull back on the reverberation as an aural clue that we are seated near her. Later in the episode, however—during Scully's second appearance before the committee—the creators use echo on her voice continuously. Well, almost continuously. After Skinner appears to whisper in her ear, Scully turns to speak to the committee and during the words "Assistant Director Skinner," her voice suddenly loses *all* reverberation.

Continuing on with strange sound effects, does anyone else have a high-pitched squeal on his or her tape just as Mulder and Scully finish their hug?

Paper Hearts

PLOT SUMMARY

Led by a dream to the remains of a young girl, Mulder instinctively knows she is John Lee Roche's fourteenth victim. Years ago, Mulder's profile helped catch Roche, who subsequently confessed to killing thirteen girls. Mulder always wondered if there were more. The dream also helps Mulder locate Roche's previously hidden collection of cloth hearts—each cut from a victim's nightgown. A count shows sixteen—three more victims than was previously known.

At first, Roche won't talk about the last two victims. Then Mulder dreams of Samantha's abduction—not by aliens but by Roche. Back at the prison, Roche agrees to identify the fifteenth victim, Karen Ann Philoponte. But before telling Mulder about Samantha, he wants to go back to the house where he took her—to relive the moment and watch Mulder's anguished expressions.

Working alone, Mulder frees Roche from prison, taking him to Martha's Vineyard to listen to Roche's detailed account. There's only one problem. Roche doesn't know Mulder purposefully brought him to the wrong house. Somehow a tenuous mental link has formed between Roche and Mulder. Unfortunately, Mulder realizes this too late. That evening, Roche escapes to kidnap another little girl. A manhunt ensues, and Mulder *does* find Roche in time. But to save the little girl's life, Mulder must kill Roche—silencing the last possibility to identify the sixteenth victim and prove it *wasn't* Samantha.

Onscreen Locations

- ☒ Bosher's Run Park, Manassas, Virginia
- ☒ Norristown, Pennsylvania
- ☒ Hollyville, Delaware
- ☒ Greenwich, Connecticut
- ☒ Forks of Cacapon, West Virginia
- ☒ Seaboard Air Flight #1650, Washington to Boston
- ☒ New Friends Daycare, Swampscott, Massachusetts

Ruminations

The date on this episode comes from an evidence bag that Mulder and Scully give to the father of Addie Sparks.

Oh, and if you're wondering how Mulder could abandon everything he's believed about his sister's abduction for the past twenty-three years with nary more than a blink— especially after all he's seen—you need to read the sidebar "Whose Truth Is Out There?" It might explain a few things!

Unanswered Questions

☒ Did John Lee Roche kidnap and kill Samantha Mulder? Probably not. Besides the fact that Mulder saw a dozen versions of her in "Herrenvolk"—obviously the products of some kind of cloning by the conspiratorial forces of the Consortium—the nightgown Samantha wears in Mulder's dream of the abduction doesn't seem to match the final cloth heart. Normally Roche cut the cloth heart from the area on the nightgown that rested over the physical heart—near the left breast. Samantha Mulder's nightgown has a horizontal strip of lace that runs right through this area. The last cloth heart has none.

Plot Oversights

X Mulder shows amazing restraint at the beginning of this episode. He dreams of Addie Sparks's grave. He rushes to the site. He parts the leaves and then he calls for a forensic excavation team to remove the dirt to see if there's a body buried there. Mr. "I Just Know It"—Mr. Impatience himself—*waiting* for a forensic team to arrive? Isn't this the same guy who dug into Greg Randall's grave in "Conduit" without a second thought?

X Bringing Scully up to speed on the case, Mulder tells her that "VICAP" code-named the case "Paper Hearts." I don't suppose VICAP would care one way or the other, but is there some reason it wasn't called "*Cloth* Hearts"?

X Hoping a man named Frank Sparks can identify Roche's fourteenth victim, Mulder and Scully hand him an evidence bag that contains a piece of cloth. Near the top of the bag a date reads, "NOV 29/96." If this date is correct, Mulder has had a busy week! According to his watch in "Tunguska," Mulder set out for the Russian province of Krasnoyarsk on November 25, 1996. I suppose it's *possible* that he flew halfway around the world; was captured; was infected with the black cancer; escaped; talked a Russian couple into booking him safe passage to St. Petersburg; flew back to the States; appeared before a Senate subcommittee; flew to Canada; failed to retrieve the Tunguska rock and flew back to Washington, D.C., *all in a matter of four days* but . . . doesn't that seem a little rushed?

X After speaking with Frank Sparks, Mulder is sufficiently reenergized to search for Roche's cloth hearts. He tells Scully that Roche probably kept them in the car that Roche used on his trips as a vacuum-cleaner salesman. Mulder decides to track down the vehicle and search it. So . . . our favorite obsessed special agent didn't do this when Roche *originally* confessed and his

car was impounded? Why? Mulder admits that he has "always" wanted to find those hearts and count them.

X Is it *really* believable that no one in the FBI can conduct a search as thoroughly as Mulder? Mulder finds the cloth hearts in a copy of *Alice in Wonderland*. The book is hidden in the lining of a camper shell for an El Camino—Roche's old El Camino. *No one* thought to feel around in this camper shell?!

X Mulder finds the book with the cloth hearts. He begins flipping through the pages. He counts sixteen hearts and then stops. Note in the medium close-up that there are pages remaining in the book, yet neither Mulder nor Scully bothers to look through them! It's almost as if they already *knew* that Roche killed only sixteen girls. (Hmmm. Read the script, maybe?)

X Early in the episode, Mulder says that Roach confessed to killing thirteen girls, and a lie detector test confirmed that he was telling the truth. Too bad someone didn't think to ask Roche whether there were *more* than thirteen victims. (Or did Roche fool the lie detector somehow?)

X At one point Scully tells Skinner that Roche did make a sales trip to Martha's Vineyard in October 1973. Evidently she checked with Electrovac—the company for whom Roche worked—to confirm this. If Electrovac has records of Roche's sales trips back to 1973, doesn't it seem likely that they would have copies of his sales receipts as well? And wouldn't those be worth checking to determine if Roche actually *sold* the vacuum cleaner that Mulder found in his mom's basement? (Worth checking for Scully and Skinner's sake, that is. By the time of this meeting with Skinner, Mulder has already decided on the "truth" for this incident.)

X Why doesn't Mulder *drive* Roche to Martha's

Trivia Questions

❶ When was Addie Sparks abducted from her home?

❷ Which of Roche's victims lived in East Amherst, New York?

3️⃣0️⃣1️⃣

Paper Hearts

Vineyard? I realize it's a long trip, but hasn't Mulder made it before? (Mulder doesn't seem to mind long drives in "Talitha Cumi.") And why not start back for Washington, D.C., the *instant* Mulder is satisfied that Roche was a liar? (Answers: Mulder needs to fly so Roche can meet the little girl he later kidnaps. Also, flying back to Washington, D.C., in the morning means that Mulder will get a motel room and Roche will have an opportunity to escape.)

X After Roche escapes, Mulder realizes that the murderer will pursue the small child he met on the plane ride to Boston. Mulder calls the airline and asks for a passenger manifest for the flight. It's difficult to hear what the supervisor says over the phone, but it sounds like she responds that an Agent Mulder called ten minutes ago and requested the same information. Mulder repeats this to Scully and Skinner and then *hangs up the receiver.* Wait a minute: Doesn't he want to stay on the line to find out what the supervisor *told* Roche?!

Equipment Oddities

X Scully seems to have an extremely high opinion of the Internet. When Roche spins his tale of the night he abducted Samantha, Scully claims that the child-killer spent the previous day in the prison library. She suggests that since he logged onto the Net the day before, he could have found out "practically anything" about Mulder. Either Scully's been watching way too much science fiction, or she realizes how many sites out there are dedicated to *The X-Files.* If Roche logged on to one of those, he really *could* find out "practically anything" about Mulder . . . including a raft of comments by the female members of the viewing audience on how Mulder looks in a red Speedo!

Continuity and Production Problems

X *If* this episode occurs sometime near November 29 and *if* "Terma" precedes it, shouldn't Mulder still have the forehead wound he sustained when he crashed the truck?

X Not that I'm campaigning for gore, but I'm amazed that Mulder can shoot Roche in the forehead at point-blank range near the end of this episode and there's *no* sign of a bullet hole!

El Mundo Gira

Onscreen Locations

X Migrant workers camp, San Joaquin Valley, CA

X I.N.S. Service Processing Center, Fresno, CA

X Fresno County Morgue

X Mycology Lab, California State University, Fresno

X Meadowview Estates, upper Fresno County

X Highway 99, Fresno County

X La Ranchera Market, downtown Fresno

Ruminations

There are odd little bits of information that collect in a nitpicker's brain. In "Born Again," Detective Sharon Lazard interrupts Scully at the start of her autopsy of a man named Barbala. When Scully seems hesitant to talk with her, Lazard says, "Yeah, uh, I don't think he's going anywhere." In this episode, Scully interrupts the medical examiner in the middle of an autopsy, and when the examiner hesitates to provide any cooperation, Scully retorts, "I don't think he's going anywhere." A coincidence? You be the judge!

Plot Oversights

X The migrant workers break into English at the oddest times in this episode. For instance, they seem to prefer English when telling their stories—all except for Eladio, that is. Both the mother superior in the migrant worker village and

PLOT SUMMARY The death of Maria Dorontes brings Mulder and Scully to the San Joaquin Valley. Just prior to the discovery of Dorontes's body, migrant workers reported a flash in the sky followed by yellow rain. While Mulder suspects an extraterrestrial event, Scully hears something else in the workers' testimony. Dorontes was loved by a pair of brothers—Soledad and Eladio Buentes—and was last seen with Eladio. Scully suspects that she and Mulder have walked into the middle of a Mexican soap opera.

Later, however, Scully finds that Dorontes's body has been overrun by a common fungus. And the driver of the van that transports Eladio Buentes to an immigration hearing suddenly succumbs to a full-body attack of athlete's foot. As the deaths continue, a scientist at Fresno's California State University isolates an accelerating enzyme from the samples. Somehow Eladio has become a carrier for this enzyme after exposure to the bright flash and the yellow rain. The migrant workers believe he has become *El Chupacabra*—an evil, goat-sucking creature who brings death.

In time, Soledad attempts to kill Eladio for what he did to Dorontes, but he loves his brother too much. Instead, he becomes infected with the enzyme as well—disappearing into the night with Eladio, leaving Mulder and Scully to guess at their eventual destination.

Gabrielle Buentes tell the tale of the Buentes brothers to their Spanish-speaking audience in a language other than their native tongue. Does this give the story more credibility?

304

El Mundo Gira

☒ It seems very fortunate for the migrant workers that—out of all the yellow rain that fell after the "Fortean event"—only a small portion, in a concentrated area, contained the fungi-accelerant. Everyone escapes infection except Maria Dorontes and Eladio Buentes!

☒ You can say one thing for Maria Dorontes—the deceased Queen of the Fungi—she has *nice* teeth for a migrant worker. Good thing, too, because they go on display after aspergillus eats away her lips.

☒ I realize that I may not measure up to the brave and valiant standards of special agents for the FBI, but I do not understand the protocols that Mulder and Scully use when encountering pathogens. Finding the van that was transporting Eladio Buentes abandoned, Mulder and Scully approach and open the passenger-side door. Inside, the driver is covered in the athlete's foot fungus. (What a way to go, eh?) Although the close-up of the man clearly shows that the cab of the van is *filled* with airborne particulates, our two heroes stand by the open doorway and stare dumbfounded. Me? I think I'd be backing up just in case there was something in the air that was bad for my health! (Even Scully later agrees with this approach when she tells Mulder that he must not touch the enzyme Eladio carries and he must not inhale it.) Actually, truth be told, I probably wouldn't even open the door of the van until I was wearing a mask. (But then, my life wouldn't make a dramatic series, would it?)

☒ Near the end of the episode, Immigration and Naturalization Service Agent Lozano actually encourages Soledad to kill his brother Eladio. I find this unlikely behavior for a representative of the government of the United States of America!

☒ The episode ends with Mulder commenting that the Buentes brothers can't be found because "nobody cares." Given the deadly nature of enzymes they carry, one would think that *somebody* would care.

Equipment Oddities

☒ During this episode, we see fungi quickly sprouting on almost everything that Eladio touches. The one exception seems to be the handset on a pay telephone that Eladio uses to speak with his cousin. No doubt this is due to the diligence of Fresno's elite band of telephone sanitizers (with apologies to Douglas Adams). Of course, the doors aren't affected either, but everyone knows that they are immune to every disease known to man! (This does bring up an interesting thought. If the enzyme is airborne, as Scully seems to suggest by telling Mulder not to inhale it, wouldn't the Buentes brothers be fairly easy to track? Fungi are *everywhere*. Couldn't the authorities just follow the fuzzy, black trail?)

Continuity and Production Problems

☒ Granted, I had only one year of Spanish in high school, but even I know that Gabrielle Buentes's accent is terrible. She is splaying her vowels all over the place. Something tells me that she's *not* an immigrant!

Leonard Betts

Onscreen Locations

ꭓ Pittsburgh, PA

ꭓ Monongahela Medical Center, Pittsburgh, PA

ꭓ Dr. Charles Burks' lab, University of
   Maryland, College Park

ꭓ Allegheny Catholic Hospital, Pittsburgh, PA

ꭓ Elaine Tanner's residence

Ruminations

According to the production numbers, this episode was originally slated to air after "Kaddish" and "Never Again." Moving it to this slot was an excellent decision by the creators. Without ever explicitly stating that Scully has cancer, the last few moments of this episode provide the perfect motivation for the episode that follows. Faced with the possibility of a terminal disease, it is only natural for Scully to turn introspective and sling out of balance for a time in "Never Again."

Plot Oversights

ꭓ So . . . when Betts walked out of the hospital without his head, had he regrown some eyes by that point, or does he have another way to see? (Evidently he had enough visual capability to knock the morgue attendant unconscious and then take his own head to the medical waste disposal container.)

ꭓ Not to be insensitive, but has Betts been bald all his life? The guy can regrow an entire body but not hair?!

PLOT SUMMARY

When the headless body of Emergency Medical Technician Leonard Betts disappears from a morgue in Pittsburgh, Pennsylvania, Mulder concludes that something strange is afoot. At first Scully believes it's body snatching for profit. Then she attempts an examination of Betts's head and experiences an "unusual degree of postmortem galvanic response." In laymen's terms, the head *moves!* Even more odd, further tests show that Betts's head is completely filled with cancer, an impossible condition for a man who was alive mere hours before. Meanwhile, Betts's former partner, EMT Michele Wilkes, overhears Betts giving advice on her ambulance's radio and—incredulous that he still lives—tracks him down. Saddened by her discovery, Betts kills her to keep his true nature a secret.

Mulder soon arrives at his explanation for the events. Betts is the next great leap in human evolution—a creature composed entirely of cancer who can regenerate his entire body at will; a creature who feasts on cancerous tumors as a form of nourishment. Unfortunately, without EMT access to area hospitals' waste disposal, Betts begins harvesting his sustenance from the general populace—first from a drunk; then, his mother; and finally, approaching Scully, apologetically informing her that *she* has something he needs.

Though Scully kills him in the scuffle, she later wakes with a nosebleed—confused and frightened over the implications of Betts's statement.

ꭓ Scully seems ready to jump to a conclusion that may or may not be warranted with regard to Leonard Betts. After dipping Betts's head in epoxy, a large slice is taken and held up to the camera for inspection. A medical person says that they will *start* with an anterior slice of Betts, one that favors the frontal lobe. He picks up a standard microscope slide and inserts it in his microscope. (By the way, the slide looks empty, but we'll assume that there's a sample on it somewhere and we just can't see it!) The guy looks in the microscope and expresses surprise. He displays the slide on a nearby monitor. Scully said that Betts's *entire* brain looks like one giant glioma. She says every cell in the sample is riddled with cancer and then adds that "essentially" every cell in his head and his entire brain is cancerous. Now, that's an amazing conclusion to draw, given that she's seen only *one* sample!

☒ The truly horrifying aspect of this episode is the truth it reveals about emergency medical technicians. Leonard Betts is decapitated. He regrows his head. He wanders over to another hospital and only *days* later he has another job as an EMT under an assumed name! Don't EMTs have to have some kind of documentation to get a job? Can anyone just bluff his or her way through a few questions and immediately be assigned to another ambulance? Yikes!

☒ When Michele Wilkes discovers that Betts is still alive, he *kills* her! Doesn't this seem a bit extreme? This is the guy who let two boys beat him up as a child. This is the guy who reads to patients on the cancer ward. This is the guy who is very apologetic about his needs. Couldn't he think of *some* other recourse besides terminating this innocent young woman? (If Betts is this ruthless, why work as an EMT in the first place? Why not take a part-time job as an orderly working the night shift on a cancer ward? He would have access to the medical waste and he wouldn't have to be bothered *helping* people.)

☒ And speaking of Betts murdering Wilkes, Dr. Robert Woolley had a few comments. "Betts kills Wilkes by stabbing her in the back with a syringeful of what is later identified as potassium chloride (KCl). It is true that KCl can be rapidly

lethal (it stops the heart; in fact, it is the last of three substances infused for execution by lethal injection), but it must be given intravenously in order to do so. Now maybe, just maybe, he got really lucky and stabbed the needle into the woman's vena cava, but that would be quite a trick to do blindly, through her clothed back. Otherwise, it would be an intramuscular injection and the rate of subsequent absorption into the blood would be unpredictable—possibly not reaching lethal concentrations and, even if it did, taking at least several minutes. He might have stabbed it directly into her heart, though again, doing this from behind would be difficult and would require a much longer needle than he seemed to have."

☒ After murdering Wilkes, Betts takes an even worse turn. He begins harvesting cancers from the living. This seems needless. Why can't he sneak into a hospital at night wearing his EMT uniform and raid the medical waste? I have a hard time believing that he couldn't fake his way through an emergency room, given his training. (Of course, if he didn't start harvesting cancer from live subjects, then we wouldn't have the "You've got something I need" speech he gives to Scully near the end of the episode!)

Changed Premises

☒ After seeing Burks's "amazing" aura photography demonstration (see below), Mulder and Scully discuss the regenerative powers of animals. When Mulder comments that a salamander can regrow a limb, Scully retorts that no mammal possesses "that kind" of regenerative power. Obviously she's forgotten about John Barnett ("Young at Heart"). Granted, he did have help from Dr. Joe Ridley, but Barnett *did* regrow a hand!

☒ Looks like the creators gave Scully a nose job when we weren't looking. In "The List," Scully pulls back a sheet on a maggot-infested body in a prison infirmary. The warden grimaces at the smell. Mulder screws up his face. Scully just stares. Yet, in this episode, after a coffin is opened, Scully immediately puts her hand to her face even though Mulder seems only slightly affected. Did she participate in some kind of highly experimental olfactory transplant between these two shows? Or was she just showing off in front of the warden during "The List"?

Equipment Oddities

☒ In my review of "Ascension," I mentioned an attempt to take a picture of Scully's broken cell phone by holding the camera mere inches away. After the opening credits in this episode, we once again see a photographer hold the camera extremely close to a blood stained piece of cloth. Since the camera's twin-focusing laser dots don't appear to be working, one wonders how this picture will turn out!

☒ I really cannot *believe* that Scully let Mulder get away with the Charles Burks's sleight of hand in his lab while giving his "aura photography" demonstration in this episode. Isn't this the same Scully who deftly palmed the insect in "Humbug"—the same Scully whose uncle was a magician? Burks pulls the oldest trick in the book and Scully acts like it's the real thing! (Of course, we also should wonder why Mulder put Burks up to this deception in the *first* place, but probing Mulder's motivations can be a frightening proposition indeed!)

Keep your eyes on the magical film. Mulder brings a slice of Betts's head to Charles Burks. (You might remember him from an episode such as "The Calusari." Nice bit of continuity, by the way!) Burks slaps the head slice on a piece of film and exposes the film to high-frequency energy. Burks takes the film and puts it in a tub of developer. Burks waits a few seconds. Then he reaches in, lifts up the film he just put in the tub, and pulls *another* (already doctored) piece of film

from *beneath* it. Presto chango! Yet another *amazing* example of "aura photography"!

☒ Just how much amperage is Scully running through the defibrillator she uses to kill Leonard Betts near the end of the episode?! Betts is practically lying on top of her. She slaps the paddles on his head and the electrical jolt flips him *head over heels,* sending him *flying* through the closed doors of the ambulance! Granted, it *looks* fabulous, but come on, even if the shock is powerful enough to violently contract every muscle in Betts's body, it's not going to launch him like a reject from a Peter Pan audition! (He should just seize up and flop dead on top of Scully.)

Continuity and Production Problems

☒ During one scene, Scully examines Betts's discarded head. She weighs it and then carries it to an examination table. Subsequent close-ups show the head moving—opening and closing its eyes and mouth. The creators make a valiant attempt to match the look of the fake head that Scully carries to the real head of the actor as it lies on the table, but the coloring is too different to be convincing. (Not to mention the line of blood on the left side of the fake head's chin that disappears when the scene cuts to the close-ups using the actor's head!)

Trivia Questions

❶ Under what alias did Betts work for Allegheny Catholic Hospital?

❷ What is the street address for Elaine Tanner's home?

OMNIUM-GATHERUM TOTE BOARD

1. Number of episodes in which Mulder eats sunflower seeds: eighteen
2. Number of episodes in which Scully drives a car: fourteen
3. Number of times Skinner is mistaken for the enemy: four
4. Number of times Cancerman laughs: one
5. Number of times "Danny" helps out: nine
6. Number of people who call Mulder "Fox": twelve
7. Number of times Mulder gets guck on his fingers: seven
8. Number of times Scully makes the intuitive leap to peg the right suspect: four
9. Number of episodes that feature men in black: four
10. Number of references to *Star Trek:* four
11. Number of references to *Star Wars:* three
12. Number of episodes that feature a masking tape "X" in Mulder's window: six
13. Numbers of times the time is 11:21: seven

References

1. "Pilot," "Squeeze," "Space," "Eve," "Genderbender," "E.B.E.," "Miracle Man," "The Host," "Aubrey," "Colony," "Clyde Bruckman's Final Repose," "The Walk," "Hell Money," "Wetwired," "Home," "Teliko," "El Mundo Gira," and "Zero Sum." (Some of these are disputable. You can't always see what Mulder is putting in his mouth. I'm *assuming* it's a sunflower seed.)

2. "E.B.E.," "Shapes," "Fresh Bones," "Colony," "Our Town," "The Blessing Way," "Clyde Bruckman's Final Repose," "Syzygy," "Herrenvolk," "Unruhe," "El Mundo Gira," "Kaddish," "Demons," and "Gethsemane."

3. Mulder thinks Skinner could be the alien bounty hunter in "End Game." Scully thinks Skinner has come to kill her in "The Blessing Way." Holly believes Skinner assaulted her in "Pusher." After seeing a surveillance photo, Mulder deduces that Skinner's been working with Cancerman all along in "Zero Sum."

4   After hearing that an editor likes his story in "Musings of a Cigarette-Smoking Man."

5   He analyzes Kevin Morris's scribblings in "Conduit." "Runs a plate" in "The Erlenmeyer Flask." Converts a phone number into an address in "The Erlenmeyer Flask." Runs a background check on Richard Odin in "Red Museum." Researches adoption records in "Aubrey." (By the way, this episode establishes that his last name is Valadayo, but a fax in "Conduit" appears to read "Daniel Bernstein." Different Danny?) Runs a check for missing people in "Our Town." Tries to identify a man in a picture in "Avatar." Converts a phone number into an address in "Wetwired." Runs a set of fingerprints in "Leonard Betts."

6   Ish in "Shapes," Scully (for the first time) in "Tooms," Skinner in "Tooms," Samantha Mulder in "Little Green Men," Margaret Scully in "One Breath," Melissa Scully in "One Breath," Mrs. Mulder (for the first time) in "Colony," hybrid Samantha in "Colony," William Mulder (for the first time) in "End Game," Dr. Bambi Berenbaum in "War of the Coprophages," Cancerman in "Talitha Cumi," and Eddie Van Blundht in "Small Potatoes" (sort of . . . he says it to himself).

7   Tooms's bile goop in "Squeeze," the burned paint from the top of Darlene Morris's camper in "Conduit," the Kindred's slop in "Genderbender," the filmy insects in "Darkness Falls," the oil from the alien in "Piper Maru," the blood that dripped from the tree in "Teso dos Bichos," and Betts's iodine in "Leonard Betts."

8   She first realizes that Leonard is the killer in "Humbug." She intuits that the bellhop is responsible for the deaths in "Clyde Bruckman's Final Repose." She pegs Simon Gates as the man who's after Kevin in "Revelations." And we *might* say that she had a hunch Nurse Innes was the true culprit *before* Innes attacked her in "Elegy."

9   "Miracle Man" (Leonard Vance), "The Calusari" (The Calusari), "José Chung's *From Outer Space*" (The Men in Black—one of whom looks like Alex Trebek!), and *maybe* "Revelations" (the children at the Linley Home for Children describe Owen as "all dressed in black" when they tell the authorities about Kevin's kidnapping).

10   Frohike says, "Beam me up, Scotty!" in "Fearful Symmetry." Blaine Faulkner has *Star Trek* models in his room in "José Chung's *From Outer Space*." Mike Millar refers to "Dr. Spock's phaser" in "Tempus Fugit" and a tractor beam in "Max." (Also, there may be a numerical reference to *Trek* in "Synchrony." See that episode for more details.)

11   Mulder tells Deep Throat to cut the Obi Wan Kenobe crap in "The Erlenmeyer Flask." Blaine

Faulkner has a model of the *Millennium Falcon* in his room in "José Chung's *From Outer Space.*" Amanda Nelligan believes Luke Skywalker impregnated her and even sings the *Star Wars* theme in "Small Potatoes."

12 "One Breath" (Mulder is trying to find out what happened to Scully), "End Game" (Mulder evidently placed the "X" in his window prior to his meeting with Mr. X at the Kennedy Center, and Scully uses it later in the episode to try to learn where Mulder has gone), "Anasazi" (Mulder wants to learn if the stolen documents from the Defense Department are legitimate), "731" (Scully is floundering to find a way to get Mulder out of the boxcar), "Wetwired" (Mulder is desperate to learn Scully's whereabouts after she runs away), and "Herrenvolk" (Scully wants to learn the meaning of the data entries in the Social Security records).

13 Just before a phone call to Scully from Mulder near the end of "Pilot." At the start of the autopsy Scully performs in "Miracle Man." Just before a phone call to Scully from Mulder near the end of "The Erlenmeyer Flask." As Scully wakes from a nightmare in "Irresistible." When the alien bounty hunter—posing as Mulder—comes to Scully's motel room near the end of "Colony." When Mulder arrives at the hospital after hearing his mother has had a stroke in "Talitha Cumi." As Scully finds that there are multiple Jeremiah Smiths working at Social Security Administration offices around the country in "Talitha Cumi." (For those of you who don't know, November 21—"11:21"—is the birthday of Chris Carter's wife. There are other number games in *The X-Files:* for one, "1013"—Chris Carter's birthday—as well as a preponderance of 47s. Hmmm. A homage to *Star Trek?*)

Omnium-Gatherum
Tote Board

Never Again

Onscreen Locations

☒ Philadelphia, Pennsylvania

☒ Vietnam Veterans Memorial, Constitution Gardens, Washington, D.C.

☒ Adams Inn, Philadelphia, Pennsylvania

☒ Memphis, Tennessee

Ruminations

I do have to confess that the creators had me worried when I saw the previews of this episode! (Along with the print campaign that featured Dana Scully, her hip slung to the side, her thumb stuck in her pants, her shirt unbuttoned to show her navel . . .) I thought the boys had finally succumbed to temptation and decided to do a bunny show. Luckily, that proved not to be the case. Indeed, with the shuffling of "Leonard Betts" to an airdate prior to this episode, the creators gave us a kind of trilogy on Scully's cancer with the three episodes "Leonard Betts," "Never Again," and "Momento Mori."

I believe this episode marks the fourth appearance of a cast member from Space: Above and Beyond. Rodney Rowland—who played Edward Jerse in this episode—also played Cooper Hawkes. In addition, you might remember that Hard Eight Pictures, Inc., was the production company for Space: Above and Beyond. "Never Again" features the Hard Eight Lounge.

And speaking of media tie-ins, I'm sure you noticed that the symbol Scully chooses for her tattoo is no less than the symbol used by Chris Carter's second television series, Millennium.

PLOT SUMMARY Forced to take a vacation, Mulder asks Scully to do a background check on a group of Russian immigrants who claim to have documents on an alien spacecraft. At first, Scully refuses. She feels like she's lost herself in "the work." But after Mulder leaves, she grudgingly heads for Philadelphia and quickly establishes that the immigrants are frauds.

During her surveillance, however, she meets Edward Jerse. In recent days, Jerse was fired from his job and—after getting drunk at the Hard Eight Lounge—impulsively had himself tattooed with the image of a woman and the words "Never Again" underneath. Unbeknownst to Scully, the tattoo speaks to Jerse and has even compelled him to murder his downstairs neighbor. Feeling blue, Scully asks Jerse to take her to the Hard Eight Lounge. Then the pair wanders across the street so Scully can get her own tattoo. (Only later does Scully discover that the red dye used by the tattoo artist is contaminated with ergot—a parasite that can cause hallucinations.) The next morning, Jerse attacks, and Scully barely manages to fight him off.

After Scully returns to work, Mulder is confused by what she's done—wondering out loud if it's because he wouldn't get her a desk. When Scully responds that not everything is about him, Mulder starts to object before letting the room fall silent.

The serpent devouring its tail (known as the "ouroborus"—which, not surprisingly, transliterates to "devouring its tail") has a long rich history of usage in many cultures. Its certainly seems plausible that Doctor Scully would recognize the symbol and resonate with its cyclical representation of destruction and rebirth but . . .

um . . . I just can't help but find a bit of humor in all of this. After all, the creators—in essence—branded their female lead with an advertisement for another TV show! One wonders what's next. "Okay, Mulder. Your name's Mulder, right? We need you to drop your drawers and bend over because, well, the folks at 1013 Productions have a new movie coming out and we need someplace to put the logo." (Sorry, sorry. Just a little joke.)

The date on this episode comes from the file that Mulder opened on Pudovkin. The date is admittedly very difficult to see because Mulder slaps down a piece of paper on top of the information, but limber up your freeze-frame thumb and you should be able to find it.

And speaking of fun things to find, did you notice the oddity among the list of names that Mulder puts on top of Pudovkin's file? The fourth name down reads, "Yakov Smirnoff"—the name of the "What a country!" Russian comedian (who now performs forty miles south of me in Branson, by the way). I suspect that the creators are having a little fun with us!

One other tidbit of information from the file Mulder opens on Pudovkin: Ever wonder where the X-Files fall on the organizational chart for the FBI? According to the file, Special Agent Fox Mulder works for the Violent Crimes Division. (Which does make sense. Just thought you'd like to know!)

Great ending on this episode, by the way!

Equipment Oddities

X At the beginning of this episode, Scully—taking stock of her life—finally asks Mulder why she doesn't have a desk. It's an interesting question, given that Scully has at least *two* work areas in the front part of the basement office that she could call her own. There is a six-foot folding table near the door that usually holds a pile of files. (Lest you think that a table isn't good enough for a work area, *I* work on a folding table in *my* basement office, and it

serves with *distinction!*) In addition, there is the small desk with the computer a few feet away from Mulder's desk. Scully even appears to claim it as her own in "Beyond the Sea" by depositing her briefcase there. (See that episode for more details.)

Beyond wondering about her desk, however, I am forced to ask again: When is Scully going to get her *name* on the door? In this episode, we see—yet again—that the door *still* reads, "Fox Mulder, Special Agent." It is rapidly approaching *five* years since Scully was assigned to the X-Files!

X Mulder must have reorganized his office when we weren't looking. In "Paper Hearts," Mulder retrieves Roche's case from a file drawer labeled "Case Files, R–S." In this episode Mulder retrieves some files from the same drawer, including a file on Vsevlod Pudovkin. *Pudovkin* with a "P." In addition, the drawer has ample space available, while the same drawer in "Paper Hearts" was packed tight.

X The doors in Jerse's apartment seem to have a mind of their own. After Jerse forces himself into Schilling's apartment, he storms toward her. We hear her screaming. The camera pulls back. The door shuts even though the two people who are in the apartment are on the other side of the room. Likewise, when Jerse and Scully kiss, the camera wanders away, and the door to Jerse's apartment closes without human intervention. (If this were *Star Trek,* I would wonder if the doors had read the script!)

X Shortly after leaving for vacation, Mulder calls FBI Headquarters to check on Scully. The phone on Mulder's desk rings, there's a beep, and immediately Mulder starts to leave a message. Mr. "I'm going to change my outgoing message in the middle of the episode" doesn't have an outgoing message on his voice mail? (See "Colony" for more information.)

X Whatever Ed Jerse is using for a laptop and a connection to the World Wide Web, *I want it!* Researching the compound found in Jerse's blood, Scully hits a button on Jerse's computer, the modem dials, the computer beeps, and—*bam!*—Scully is on-line.

Continuity and Production Problems

X I know it's done for effect, but honestly, when Jerse murders Schilling it looks like the cameraman gets *lost!* The camera retreats from Schilling's door. Then it aimlessly wanders down some stairs and sits in the basement. At this point in the episode I usually start waving my hands and shouting, *"Hey!* Buddy! *Wake up!* Hello? Helloooo?! We're *missing* the action here. Would it be *too* much trouble for you to concentrate on your job and show us what's *going on?!"*

X Continuing with this theme, the camera decides to take the scenic route as Jerse drags Shilling's body into the furnace room. Jerse has placed her in a big cardboard box, but once he opens the furnace door, the cameraman gets distracted by the fire ("Oooooh, *flames!*"), and then the camera does a 360-degree pan of the room before we finally return to Jerse!

1 What is Scully's seat assignment on Flight 51 to Philadelphia?

2 What is Ms. Schilling's first name?

Momento Mori

PLOT SUMMARY When tests reveal an inoperable tumor near Scully's brain, she and Mulder head for Allentown. During "Nisei," members of a local MUFON chapter said they recognized Scully from their abduction experiences and even predicted she would develop cancer. Unfortunately, MUFON member Kurt Crawford tells the pair that Peggy Northern is the only abductee still alive.

Visiting Northern in the hospital, Scully learns that a "Dr. Scanlon" has been working on a cure, and she subsequently admits herself for treatment. Meanwhile, Mulder discovers that many of the deceased women visited a nearby infertility clinic. Among its computer files is a directory listing for a mainframe at the Lombard Research Facility. The listing contains Scully's name. At the facility, Mulder comes face-to-face with clones of Kurt Crawford. They have been working against the "project" to save the lives of their "mothers." (Along with Scully, the women in Allentown were subjected to a high-amplification radiation procedure that caused superovulation. The ova were then harvested for hybrid reproduction.) Most disturbing, Mulder learns that Dr. Scanlon, in fact, works for the facility. He has been killing the women of the MUFON group with his "treatment."

The information reaches Scully just in time, but as the episode ends we see Skinner participating in an early-morning meeting with Cancerman. He has decided to trade himself for Scully's cure.

Onscreen Locations

X Holy Cross Memorial Hospital, Washington, D.C.
X Allentown, Pennsylvania

X Allentown-Bethlehem Medical Center
X Center for Reproductive Medicine, Lehigh Furnace, Pennsylvania

Ruminations

Good episode! Very touching moment between Mulder and Scully and yet more details on "the conspiracy." (Insert dark, brooding music here.)

I especially like the fact that Mulder seems to grow up in this episode. At the end, he holds hard evidence that links Scully's abduction to the hybrid clones. Yet he doesn't wave it in her face and wait for her to apologize for her refusal to believe, he keeps it to himself until she's ready to hear it! That's an improvement, especially after his performance last episode!

Unanswered Questions

X Okay . . . women are abducted for their ova, so . . . men like Max Fenig are abducted . . . ?

Plot Oversights

X This episode features an assassin who scurries around in the background, stealing files, killing Kurt Crawford clones. When Scully decides to admit herself to the hospital, Mulder leaves Betsy Hagopian's house to bring Scully her bag from the trunk of their rental car. As Mulder's car pulls away from the curb, suspenseful music plays, and another car pulls forward about fifteen feet before the assassin dude gets out. In other words, this guy wouldn't *walk* fifteen feet before killing the Kurt Crawford clone?! He just *had* to park beside the house?

☒ Finding the Kurt Crawford clones working inside the Lombard Research Facility, Mulder accuses them of using him and Scully. They deny this, saying that Mulder and Scully's arrival was only coincidental. I find this hard to believe. Betsy Hagopian dies, two and a half weeks go by. Mulder and Scully arrive. And Kurt Crawford *just happens* to be downloading Hagopian's files at that particular moment?! And what about the Crawford clone who showed up at the Center for Reproductive Medicine in Lehigh Furnace, Pennsylvania? He claims to be trying to get access to its computer system. If Mulder's arrival was coincidental, one would assume that the information gathered from the reproductive center would be information the clones needed. Yet Mulder comes away from the encounter with a file directory for the Lombard Research Facility. But, but, but . . . the clones *work* at the facility, don't they? Wouldn't they already *have* this information? (The directory is just a list of names. If nothing else, couldn't the clones simply write down the names on the drawers in the ova storage room?) All evidence seems to indicate that this is just another instance of the pixies of Out There at work! (Or the Consortium feeding stuff to Mulder.)

Equipment Oddities

☒ The creators fudged when assembling the visual effects used during the assault on the Lombard Research Facility by Mulder and the Lone Gunmen. Using a laptop, Langly assists Mulder's "funky poaching" by patching into the security cameras. As Mulder and Byers approach the building, the scene shows Langly working away, and the camera cuts to a close-up of his screen. Then Mulder and Byers enter the building and again the camera shows us a close-up of Langly's screen as they slip inside. Except . . . the same video plays on Langly's screen *both* times. So Mulder and Byers went in,

and then went out, and then went in again?!

☒ There's a suspenseful scene at the Lombard Research Facility as the assassin closes in on Mulder, his gun eating away at the bulletproof barrier that stands between them. Throughout the scene Mulder cringes and screams for Langly and Frohike to open a nearby door. No doubt there's a really good reason why Mulder either forgot his gun or has decided against using it to defend himself.

☒ And speaking of this scene, the assassin seems to have ten bullets in his first clip, seven in the next, and six or seven in the one that follows next. To begin with, I have never heard of a semiautomatic pistol clip that holds fewer than nine bullets, and if the first clip held ten, it seems reasonable to assume that the subsequent clips would hold ten as well. Why didn't the assassin have them fully loaded?

Continuity and Production Problems

☒ Just informational. During this episode, Scully has three monologues as she writes in her journal. The last two have significant differences between the version we hear on the audio and what appears on closed captioning. The second monologue is shorter in closed captioning. It speaks of cancer never leaving a calling card, describing its arrival as a dark, sleepless stranger who comes "not with a bid or a summons but with a haunting promise and a declaration of imminent domain."

Likewise, in the closed captioning of the third monologue, Scully starts by saying that she hasn't written in the past twenty-four hours out of optimism. (The audio version says it's because of weakness.) It also describes Dr. Scanlon's treatment, as opposed to speaking of the respect that Scully had for Northern. Finally, the closed captioning of the third monologue has Scully hoping that Mulder will recognize the

315

Momento Mori

futility of pursuing his current path any farther. (The audio version says she is grateful for his pursuit.)

Of course, the little nitpicker in me wonders how and when the two versions came about. At first I thought the closed captioning reflected the original script and the audio version was a *late* rewrite (overdubbed after the filming was complete in "postproduction"). But when Mulder picks up Scully's journal, the close-up shows the *audio* version of the third monologue, not the closed-captioned version. And later, Mulder tells Scully he knows how much Northern meant to her—knowledge that would have come only from the audio version of the third monologue. That would seem to indicate that the audio version of the third monologue existed during the production phase (i.e., the filming phase) of the episode! So why wasn't the closed captioning updated so it would be the same as the audio? Or . . . did the creators have to reshoot footage in postproduction to account for the late rewrites of the third monologue?

Momento Mori

Kaddish

Onscreen Locations

- Ben Zion Cemetery, Brooklyn, New York
- Weiss residence, Williamsburg, New York
- Brunjes Copy Shop, 1525 Avenue J
- Park Street Synagogue
- Twenty-first Precinct holding area
- Judaica Archives, Upper East Side, Manhattan

Plot Oversights

The police seem noticeably absent in this episode. Early on, Scully shows Mulder a video-tape of Luria's murder. The three teenagers involved wear no masks, their faces are exposed for easy identification. Yet—while Scully admits that the teenagers are suspects—not one line of dialogue indicates the police are *actively* searching for these kids to arrest them. Maybe they figure it's easier to let the golem do the work for them?!

This golem certainly has a flare for the dramatic! As the two teenagers desecrate Luria's grave, the golem sneaks up and kills *one* of them. Then the golem sneaks away. Why not kill them both while it had the opportunity? Is there some kind of one-death-a-day rule that golems have to follow? (Of course, if the golem killed them both, then the last teenager wouldn't have been found hanging in the synagogue, and we will soon see that it was *important* for *that* to happen!)

After finding Jacob Weiss's book on Jewish mysticism in Luria's grave, Mulder and Scully return to his home to speak with him. Ariel

PLOT SUMMARY In New York City, Isaac Luria is murdered by three racist teenagers. Oddly enough, a short time later, one of the teenagers dies by strangulation . . . and police find Luria's fingerprints on the young man's neck. Mulder and Scully are assigned to the case to discover how the killer created the deception.

The pair arrives in New York City and seeks permission to exhume Luria's body from Ariel—the woman to whom Luria was betrothed. (The couple's formal marriage ceremony was to occur in only days.) Unfortunately, that evening, the two surviving teenagers decide to conduct their own investigation—digging up Luria's coffin, hoping to prove that the man is really dead. Though Luria's body is still interred, both teenagers soon die by strangulation as well.

All accusations turn to Jacob Weiss—Ariel's father and a former terrorist. Indeed, Weiss even confesses to the murders. But Mulder suspects a less-human killer. A book on Jewish mysticism was buried with Luria. The ancient text contains instructions for creating a golem—a creature of form but no spirit. In fact, Ariel has conjured the golem—a look-alike for Luria—never believing the ceremony would work or that the golem would run amok. The creature does give her the opportunity to wed her beloved, however, and say good-bye before she returns it to the dust from which it came.

answers the door. Mulder and Scully tell her of the most recent murder of a teenager. Ariel wants to know why they want to speak with her father and Scully says that Weiss expressed strong feelings toward the latest victim and evidence was found placing him at the crime scene. In the midst of a defense of her father,

Ariel starts telling Mulder and Scully how much her marriage to Isaac meant to her father. She even launches into an explanation of the communal wedding ring that they were to use during their vows. She says that it was made in a little village in Poland. Her father was an apprentice to the man who designed the ring and it was used for every wedding ceremony in the village until nine thousand Jews were massacred in the Spring of 1943. She says that her father hid the ring for *fifty* years believing it was a "dead relic from a forgotten place"—bringing it out *only* after learning that his daughter was getting married.

Now, don't get me wrong. It's a beautiful story but every time I watch this scene I think, "Why is she telling them this?" After all, Mulder and Scully have just expressed their suspicions that her father is a murderer. Why would Ariel launch into an explanation that would surely be used by the pair as an even more complete motive for murder? Doesn't this story absolutely confirm how deeply Jacob Weiss was anticipating the marriage of his daughter just prior to the senseless murder of Isaac Luria? Of course, this *is* the only spot that the creators have in the episode to introduce us to the communal wedding ring and, without the ring, the end of the episode wouldn't be nearly as touching.

X And speaking of the communal wedding ring, Ariel says her father hid it until the day she told him she was getting married. I couldn't locate a source to confirm this, but I find it highly *unlikely* that Ariel—being raised in an Orthodox Hasidic Jewish community, preparing to wed an Orthodox Hasidic Jewish man—would *tell* her father that she was getting married. I believe Isaac Luria would be expected to request Ariel's hand in marriage from her father *first*. (I'm almost certain that Ariel traipsing in and telling her father that she was getting married would be considered disrespectful.)

X Okay, Ariel makes a golem. The golem kills a

kid by choking him to death. The golem kill another kid by choking him to death. The golem kills a third kid by hanging him in the attic of a synagogue. The golem kills a racist by choking him to death. The golem tries to hang Weiss The golem tries to choke Mulder.

Given the golem's propensity for choking people to death, why hang anybody? Doesn't this seem a little "out of character" for a barely thinking mud man? I'm having some difficulty imagining the golem holding onto its victim with one hand as it throws the rope over the rafter with the other and then hoisting the victim into the air. Why go to all that trouble? Just *choke* him! Granted, the golem could render its victim unconscious first, but what good does it do to hang someone who's unconscious? (I'm thinking that the creators *really* didn't want to kill Ariel's father at the end of the episode and then needed to come up with some way for him to survive the golem's attack. So they added the hanging thing. Weiss could just swing by the neck for a time until Mulder and Scully arrived. *And* that also might explain why the golem didn't kill both teenagers at the cemetery. One of them needed to be hung so it wouldn't look *really* out of place for the golem to hang Weiss.)

X Amazingly enough, when visiting the Weiss residence for the third time in the episode, Mulder and Scully find the door unlocked . . . in New York City . . . in a section known for its racial tensions . . . Ariel left the door unlocked. Right.

Equipment Oddities

X The copy shop proprietor in this episode has a very cool video surveillance system. Not only can the camera pan left and right, it also can move up and down! Three times, the episode treats us to a close-up of the surveillance monitor: as Mulder and Scully speak with the proprietor, after they leave the copy shop, and as the golem comes to kill the proprietor. In each case, note the amount of floor shown on the monitor.

You can barely see any flooring during the scene with Mulder and Scully, a bit more in the close-up with the golem, and a *lot* more when the camera shows the copy shop empty. And it's not just zoom; the camera is also physically higher and pointing down!

Continuity and Production Problems

☒ Luria's grave seems shallow. Look at the edges of the grave when Mulder and Scully hop inside. As Scully stands on the coffin, the top of the grave barely reaches her waist. According to *The Truth Is Out There: The Official Guide to* The X-Files, Scully is five feet, three inches tall. Even accounting for the cute little pumps she *contin-ues* to wear on her X-Filean adventures, there is only three feet from ground level to the top of the coffin.

☒ It goes by quickly but the shot of the teenager hanging by the neck in the attic of the synagogue doesn't look right. The kid's body is hanging at an angle—as if the rope isn't actually holding him by the neck but attached to his back via a harness of some kind. Hmmm.

Trivia Questions

❶ Where was the communal wedding ring made?

❷ Of what Jewish military underground was Weiss a member?

Trivia Answers
❶ In the village of Kolin, near Prague.
❷ Irgun.

Unrequited

PLOT SUMMARY

When a general is shot at point-blank range in a chauffeured limousine, only Mulder finds the driver's story compelling. The driver, Private Burkholder, claims that he saw no one near the general after swerving to a stop. (Forensics *has* established that the general did not commit suicide. Nor has Burkholder recently fired a gun.) Skinner suspects an accomplice. Given Burkholder's connections to a paramilitary group called the Right Hand, Skinner sends Mulder and Scully to arrest Right Hand leader Denny Markham.

Markham denies any involvement in the death but claims to know the killer: Nathaniel Teager, a former Green Beret in Vietnam who was left to die; rescued from a POW camp only recently by the Right Hand. Strangely enough, Teager can hide himself from human sight.

After a second general dies—in the Pentagon, of all places—Mulder turns to Marita Covarrubias for help. She tells Mulder that the military wants Teager to succeed in his mission of vengeance. The deaths of the generals will spare the military any embarrassment over certain decisions made concerning the Vietnam War. According to her, Teager has only one target left: General Benjamin Bloch. Quick thinking by Mulder spares Bloch's life, but after Teager is shot and killed, the military claims it wasn't Teager at all—steadfastly maintaining that no POWs remain in Vietnam.

Onscreen Locations

- ☒ U.S. Capitol Mall, near the Vietnam War Memorial, Washington, D.C.
- ☒ Fort Evanston, Maryland
- ☒ Demeter, Virginia
- ☒ Army Central Identification Lab
- ☒ Army Detention Center, Fort Evanston, Maryland

Ruminations

The date on this episode places it in the same time frame as "Musings of a Cigarette-Smoking Man." In fact, it's interesting to note that Teager is probably killing people at the same time Cancerman is sitting on a bench somewhere else in Washington, D.C., giving his "mint-filled crap/box-o-chocolates" speech!

Was Teager working alone? Or was he part of an elaborate conspiracy to murder the three generals and discredit Skinner, Mulder, and Scully? I almost added these questions to an Unanswered Questions section for this episode, but I think that the events of the episode clearly answer them. It is true that Teager seems to carry out his vengeance without outside help. (Who needs help when you're invisible?) But there are elements of this episode that make sense only if "someone" is guiding the events. For instance, Mulder and Scully learn of Teager's existence from Denny Markham—the leader of the Right Hand. And why do they investigate the Right Hand in the first place? Because Private Burkholder just happens to be a member of the Right Hand, an organization that just happens to have liberated Teager from a POW camp. Markham has only two thousand people on his mailing list. (In comparison, the Nitpickers Guild has more than six thousand at the time of this writing.) How many other paramilitary organizations like the Right Hand are there in the United

States? How many military personnel have memberships in them? What are the chances that the private who was selected to drive General MacDougal would also be a member of the same organization that rescued Teager? In my book, pretty slim! And what about Markham? This guy is supposedly advocating armed resistance against the government, yet at the end of the episode he rolls! He backs up the cover story that Teager wasn't Teager but a vet with a history of mental illness! Yeah, I'd say there's someone pulling the strings here, wouldn't you?

Finally—in the "Didja notice?" category—there's a truly X-Filean moment as Mulder and Scully attempt to gain entrance to the Right Hand's compound. Scully looks over her shoulder. The camera pans the side of the road. It passes a man standing near a tree. The camera pulls back. The man is gone! (Ta-dum!)

Plot Oversights

❎ The Vietnam Veteran's Memorial seems strangely vacant when Teager approaches "Mrs. Davenport." It's been my pleasure to visit the Wall twice, and there *always* were people around.

❎ And speaking of "Mrs. Davenport," Teager informs her that her husband, Gary Davenport, is still being held as a POW in Vietnam. File this fact away: Davenport is the name of her soldier-husband. Later, Mulder and Scully interview the woman, and Mulder calls her "Mrs. Davenport." But by this time we have learned that the woman has tried to "get on" with her life, that she has remarried. Why, then, does Mulder refer to her as "Mrs. Davenport"? If she's trying to get on with her life, why wouldn't she revert to her maiden name or take her new husband's last name? (And yes, Mulder would know if she had. He and Scully are *interviewing* her. Surely they asked her name for their report! I *suppose* that the woman's maiden name might be Davenport, or she liked the last

name so much that she married *another* guy named Davenport, but . . . .)

❎ And speaking of "Mrs. Davenport," during the interview with Mulder and Scully, the woman starts bleeding from her eye. Scully identifies her condition as a "simple subconjuctival hemorrhage." Dr. Robert Woolley tells me that this condition *is* common, but—as the name indicates—it occurs *under* the outer layer of the eye. Robert assures me that Scully as a medical doctor would not use this diagnosis for an actively bleeding eye!

❎ After General Steffen dies, Mulder bends over the body and picks up the "death card" left behind by Teager to mark the kill. Picks it up . . . without wearing plastic gloves. Isn't it possible that Teager's prints might be on that card? Wouldn't that be an excellent piece of verification, demonstrating that Teager is still alive? After the commercial break, Mulder continues to hold the card, but now he has it in a little Baggie. A little *late,* aren't we?!

❎ Most of this episode is told in flashback. It begins with General Bloch giving his speech and Mulder faced with the uncomfortable prospect of an invisible assassin walking straight toward him. (A *suspenseful* opening, by the way!) After the opening credits, the episode reverts twelve hours, and eventually we return to Bloch's speech. Oddly enough, there's a large chunk missing! At the end of the episode, Bloch greets the dignitaries and begins by saying that there is probably no other audience who better understand that freedom is not free. Yet, at the beginning of the episode, Bloch says that many Vietnam vets came home to hostility, something he can never forget or forgive. He then talks for a time about the men and women who were lost in that war, and only afterward launches into his statements on freedom. (Some kind of weird alternate reality thing happening here?)

Trivia Questions

❶ Special Agents Beckwith and Fontana are dispatched to what city?

❷ What is Gary Davenport's blood type?

Equipment Oddities

☒ Markham has an interesting call box in his Right Hand compound. Mulder walks up to it, pushes the button, and the box buzzes. Getting no response, Mulder pushes the same button a second time and starts talking. This time, no buzz. Smart box.

☒ Evidently Mulder has decided not to wear an ankle holster any longer. In "Nisei," Mulder pulls a gun from the holster and informs his assailant that he had grown tired of losing his primary weapon. As recently as "Paper Hearts," we see him take off the ankle holster when visiting Roche in prison. Yet in this episode, he walks through a metal detector after removing only his primary weapon, and the metal detector remains silent.

☒ After General Steffen dies, Skinner shows Mulder and Scully a videotape of Teager entering the building. Okay, so now the FBI knows that the assassin guy can be seen on video. Couldn't the boys in the FBI's Whiz-Bang-Toy Department come up with some type of headset to exploit this weakness in Teager's invisibility act? How about a small videocamera combined with a viewscreen from a camcorder, all mounted so it would cover one eye? The agent could scan the crowd looking for anyone who showed up on the viewscreen but was otherwise invisible. And what about infrared? Teager's body is still warm, isn't it?

Continuity and Production Problems

☒ Once greeted inside the Right Hand compound by a trio of dogs, Mulder and Scully take off running for the front gate. At this point the main part of the front gate is closed with only the personnel entrance swung open. The scene shows the dogs racing forward and then cuts back to Mulder and Scully. Now the main part of the gate is open and their car has disappeared! (You'll need to use freeze frame to find the latter nit.) Thankfully, reality restores itself a moment later.

☒ The exterior of the Army Central Identification Lab in this episode bears a *striking* resemblance to the Fort Marlene High Containment Facility of "The Erlenmeyer Flask." No doubt they have the same architect!

☒ Just after Major General Bloch marches out to give his speech, he berates Skinner and tells him to do his job. Keep your eyes on Skinner. The assistant director of the FBI puts his hand to his forehead. The shot changes. Suddenly his hand is elsewhere.

Tempus Fugit

(Part 1 of 2)

Onscreen Locations

- ☒ Somewhere over upstate New York
- ☒ Northville, New York
- ☒ Flight 549 crash site
- ☒ Fulton County Airport
- ☒ Paradise Motel, Northville, New York
- ☒ Von Drehle Air Force Reserve Installation
- ☒ Great Sacandaga Lake

Plot Oversights

☒ Not a nit, but just for housekeeping. The lead investigator at the crash site taunts Mulder at one point, saying that if any of his people find "Dr. Spock's phaser" they will let him know. I believe that should be "*Mr.* Spock's phaser." Dr. Spock is the pediatrician. (It's not a nit because people make this mistake all the time!)

☒ Locating one of their own among the crash victims, the conspirators use some kind of acid spray to dissolve his fingerprints and face. One wonders if they are going to pull his teeth as well. After all, aren't dental records often used to identify remains? (Of course, it *would* be *extremely* tough to pull the dead guy's teeth without *someone* noticing! On the other hand, I suppose they could always "Leonard-Betts" him—i.e., take his head!)

☒ Returning to the control tower at the Von Drehle Air Force Reserve Installation, Frish finds his coworker dead. Specifically, he finds the man seated in a chair, holding a pistol in his lap with a bullet wound in his forehead. There are several oddities in this particular scene.

PLOT SUMMARY Celebrating Scully's birthday at a local bar, Mulder and Scully are approached by a woman claiming to be Max Fenig's sister ("Fallen Angel"). Fenig was traveling to Washington, D.C., on Flight 549—a flight that crashed two hours ago. Joining the investigative team at the crash site, the pair finds watches that read 8:01, though the official reports say the plane went down at 7:52.

Searching for the missing nine minutes, Mulder and Scully interview Sergeant Louis Frish, a military air traffic controller who tracked the flight. Frish parrots the sanctioned version of events until a strike team tries to kill him. Then he confesses to Mulder and Scully that he was ordered to relay coordinates on Flight 549. Soon afterward, a second plane appeared; there was an explosion and—in horror—he watched Flight 549 fall from the sky. With no evidence of an explosion among the debris, Mulder speculates that the military engaged a UFO in the vicinity of 549 and that encounter led to the crash.

After dispatching Scully and Frish to Washington, D.C., for safekeeping, Mulder dives to the bottom of nearby Great Sacandaga Lake. As expected, he soon finds UFO wreckage. Meanwhile, the conspirators send an assassin to kill Frish. Unfortunately, Agent Pendrell accidentally steps into the line of fire and is fatally wounded.

First, Frish approaches the man from behind, and the man's head is upright, as if he's working. I realize the creators did this for dramatic effect so we wouldn't know the guy was dead until Frish spun him around, but . . . how is the guy's head staying upright? Wouldn't the muscles in the neck relax after death and allow the head to slump forward? (Or did someone stand there and hold up the guy's head until rigor mortis set in?!)

Second, why didn't the conspirators go to a bit more trouble to make it look like a suicide? The guy is obviously posed. Aside from the fact that his head would be snapped back if he shot himself in the forehead, I have a hard time believing that his gun hand would have fallen—oh, so properly—palm down into his lap. Even a 9mm handgun has a significant amount of recoil that will throw the weapon and the guy's hand out and away from the body.

🄳 Ya know, if I were Scully, I would get sick and tired of anybody and *everybody* finding me at a moment's notice. After escaping a strike team at the control tower, Frish somehow appears outside Scully's motel room. How did he know where she and Mulder were staying?

Changed Premises

🄳 After being serenaded with a chorus of "Happy Birthday" at the bar, Scully quickly identifies Mulder as the person who put them up to it. She comments to Mulder that he hasn't remembered her birthday in the *four* years that she's known him. "Lazarus" states that Scully shares the same birthday with Jack Willis: February 23. From all indications during this season, the year *has* to be 1997. "Pilot"—the episode where Scully and Mulder first meet—carries a date of March 7, 1992. Wouldn't that mean Scully has known Mulder for almost *five* years? Or is Scully only counting birthdays?

Equipment Oddities

🄳 As Mulder and Scully return to the motel room they rented for "Max's sister," watch the street in the background. See the electric trolley bus that goes by? This is supposed to be Northville, New York. According to my 1997 Rand McNally *Road Atlas*, Northville has a pop-

ulation of 1,180 ("Saaaalute!"). A small town with an electric trolley bus system? Hmmmm. (Surprisingly enough—according to Steve Brandon of Pincourt, Quebec—the vehicle looks just like a City of Vancouver electric bus. Imagine that!)

🄳 Why does Scully let Frish make a phone call from her apartment? Can't she imagine that the conspirators have Frish's girlfriend's phone tapped and will trace the call?

Continuity and Production Problems

🄳 As "Max's sister" rifles through Max's correspondence in a motel room, "something" approaches with a thunderous rumble. Everything in the room begins to shake. If you watch closely, you might notice that the bed begins to shake *before* the rumble starts. (No doubt the approach of the UFO triggered the bed's "Magic Fingers" massage unit!)

🄳 After identifying the remains of Max Fenig, Mulder zips his body bag shut. Then a wide shot shows a portion of the body bag still open.

🄳 Not sure *what* this is, but it's worth noting, and maybe someone out there can explain it. Believing that a UFO crashed in Great Sacandaga Lake, Mulder bids good-bye to Scully and Frish before backing away from their small airplane. Two dots appear in the lower right-hand portion of the screen and hover for a few seconds before disappearing. It looks like the dots are floating above the scene. Some kind of problem with the camera, maybe?

🄳 You only thought you knew suspense when Nitpickydom Productions gave you *The Hall Extension Zone* in "Herrenvolk." Now, a new terror lurks in *The X-Files*—a terror so constructive, so painfully obvious that it will shatter all your illusions of set design. Chris Carter

...nd company proudly present: *The Window Shifters!* (Aaaaah!)

Note the scene where the inimitable Dr. Scully—FBI agent extraordinare—brings one Louis Frish back to her apartment, feel the horror as she walks into a bedroom to "get some things." See the window that now appears on the wall opposite the door—a wall that previously was solid, whole, and untorn: now ripped open, now devoured to make room for the *devious* triple window. Will Scully notice the intruder? Will she flee, screaming, into the night to stay its plans to have her as its next victim?

Nope! She putters around the room like the window has *always* been there. (No doubt the window emits some type of hypnotic field. "I've always been here. . . . I've always *been* here. . . .") In fact, it has *not!* "Anasazi" contains a camera pan that is almost identical to the one shown here as Scully helps Mulder into her spare bedroom. If you check your tape for that episode, you'll see that *there is no window* on the wall opposite the door. And a later scene seems to indicate the room's window actually resides on the wall *adjacent to* the door.

Strangely enough, a scene from "War of the Coprophages" has Scully wandering around in a room that is very similar to the one shown here in "Tempus Fugit." Given the footage in "Anazasi" and the quick tour of Scully's apartment that we get in "Squeeze," I always assumed that the scene in "War of the Coprophages" was set in Scully's bedroom at the other end of her hall. But "Tempus Fugit" seems to contradict that. It's almost like Scully's apartment isn't an apartment at all but just a bunch of walls that people can move around any way they want. (Gasp!)

Trivia Questions

1 How old is Dana Scully?

2 What is the name of the man who sits in seat 13D on Flight 549?

Trivia Answers
1 Scully was born in 1964, making her thirty-three at the time of this episode.
2 Larold Rebhum.

325

Tempus Fugit

Max

(Part 2 of 2)

PLOT SUMMARY After finding UFO wreckage at the bottom of Great Sacandaga Lake, Mulder is apprehended by the military. At the same time, Skinner overrides Scully's request to provide a safe haven for Louis Frish. The military claims Frish is responsible for the crash of Flight 549—having put an F-15 on a collision course with the plane.

Mulder doesn't believe it. He thinks a UFO intercepted Flight 549—seizing it with some kind of tractor beam to retrieve whatever Max Fenig was carrying. When a fighter shot down the UFO, the plane plummeted to the ground. The woman who claimed to be Max's sister seems to substantiate Mulder's theory. Her real name is Sharon Graffia, and she is an unemployed aeronautical engineer who has spent time in and out of mental institutions. She finally admits that she stole a device of three interlocking parts from a military contractor named Cummins Aerospace. Max claimed it was alien technology and was bringing one of the parts to Washington, D.C., on Flight 549 to give to Mulder. She also says that a second part was taken from her during an abduction.

Eventually Mulder locates the final part, but when he attempts to bring it back to Washington, "something" intercepts his plane as well. When the flight lands, the part is gone, and Mulder's watch is missing nine minutes.

Onscreen Locations

- ☒ Von Drehle Air Force Reserve Installation
- ☒ Barnes Corners, New York
- ☒ Northeast Georgetown Mental Health Center
- ☒ Syracuse Hancock International Airport
- ☒ Washington National Airport, Washington, D.C.

Ruminations

I had an odd thought during this episode as Skinner forced Scully to abandon Frish and go to the hospital. Is this the price that Cancerman demanded of Skinner to supply a cure for Scully's cancer? Must Skinner now cooperate with the goals of the conspirators?

Concerning Pendrell's death, I have only one comment for the creators: Aaaargh!

Did anyone else get the impression that the conspirators were simply following Mulder around—knowing that he would eventually find what they were looking for? At the end of the last episode, Mulder finds the crashed UFO (though others have been searching for it as well and apparently hadn't found it yet). Following his release from Von Drehle Air Force Reserve Installation, Mulder takes Scully to search Max's apartment. As Mulder and Scully watch a home video by Max, the conspirators take advantage of Mulder's discovery in Great Sacandaga Lake and locate the device for which they were searching. Then Mulder and Scully leave Max's trailer and "someone" ransacks it. Then Mulder finds the third part of the "device" and, again, the conspirators are right there waiting for him.

The date on this episode comes from Mulder's watch. If it's actually working and is set correctly (and it may or may not be—see below), the episode ends sometime around March 8, 1997. A close-up of his watch gives us *a date of "8." Since the previous episode carried a date of February 23, it seems likely that the month would be March.)*

Plot Oversights

X I must say that I am very impressed with the response time of the police and the paramedics when shots ring out in the Washington, DC., bar at the beginning of the episode. It takes less than a minute for the cops to arrive and hear Scully say that she needs an EMT. Thirty seconds later, the paramedics show up!

X I know I mentioned this in the previous episode, but the nit comes back a second time here. After the shooting in the bar, Scully asks if Frish told his girlfriend that he was in Washington, D.C. He says no. Scully then concludes that the conspirators have somebody on the inside. Well . . . maybe, Dr. Scully. Or *maybe* they traced the call back to your house!

X Trying to determine what Max carried on Flight 549, Mulder and Scully visit his trailer. Seeing Fenig's spartan life once again, Scully comments that he and Mulder were kindred spirits in some "deep, strange way." What's so deep and strange about it? They both were dedicated to proving the existence of extraterrestrials! Is Mulder more like Fenig than Scully wants to admit?

X The assassin guy in this episode really needs to take a bit of time for himself and go *shopping!* He's in Washington, D.C. He gets shot in the leg. He drags himself away and later shows up at the UFO crash site. Presumably *someone* doctored his leg, yet he's still wearing the pair of pants with the bloodstained bullet hole in them. Stranger still, that night he boards a plane and he's *still* wearing the pants. I guess this guy isn't too concerned about drawing attention to himself!

X While in college, Nitpickers Guild member

Daniel B. Case of Woodmere, Ohio, flew between Syracuse, New York, and Washington, D.C., quite often. He wrote to observe that jets aren't allowed to land at National Airport after 10:00 P.M. because of noise control, but Mulder's plane somehow manages to pull into the terminal just minutes before 10:56!

Changed Premises

X The alternate realities are waltzing again! At the end of the previous episode, "Tempus Fugit," Scully fires once at the assassin and then drops to the floor to tend to an injured Pendrell, saying, "You're going to keep breathing, Pendrell, do you hear me?" At the beginning of this episode, Scully fires *twice* at the assassin, then turns to Frish to tell him to get down and stay down before telling Pendrell, "You're going to keep breathing, do you hear me?" It is possible that the two shots from Scully are meant to be a video effect, but what about Scully's extra words to Frish and the fact that she doesn't say Pendrell's name?

X Let's talk about watches. *The* driving factor in the previous episode was the missing nine minutes on Flight 549, from 7:52 till 8:01 P.M. Mulder and Scully know about this missing time because the official report says that Flight 549 went down at 7:52, but the watches that Mulder and Scully find in the wreckage read 8:01. According to Mulder, these nine minutes are the nine minutes when Flight 549 was in the grip of the UFO's tractor beam. (And, of course, Mulder *must* be right about this. After all, he's the *hero!*)

Yet, in this episode, Mulder knows that a UFO is about to commandeer his flight because his watch has stopped! Well . . . if the approaching UFO makes watches *stop*, why did the watches keep going on board Flight 549? (As I said in "Pilot," Timex, maybe?)

Equipment Oddities

X The Nitpickers Guild has members with many

Trivia Questions

1 What is the number on the baggage claim ticket found by Mulder?

2 What flight does Mulder board from Syracuse, New York, to Washington National Airport?

327

Max

different occupations. One of our pilots, Jenifer Gordon of Westlake Village, California, noted that the stewardess in the back of Flight 549 was missing her oxygen mask during its rapid descent. (Then again, this did happen in Mulder's mind only. Maybe he didn't know the flight crew needed oxygen masks as well?)

🅇 Did Mulder forget his handcuffs? Is that why he left the assassin to his own devices in the airplane bathroom?

🅇 Mulder believes his flight was commandeered by aliens because his watch reads nine minutes slower than Scully and Skinner's watches. The sad fact is: Mulder needs a new watch! Or a new battery. Or *something!* As Mulder compares his watch with those of his coworkers, a close-up shows us that his watch carries a time of 10:47:39. The scene shows it ticking to 10:47:40 before cutting to a reaction shot of Scully. Then a second close-up shows us the watch, *once again,* going from 10:47:39 to 10:47:40! The second hand on his watch is twitching back and forth. *No wonder* it's nine minutes slow! (This also might explain why it stopped during the flight!)

Continuity and Production Problems

🅇 The assassin who shoots Pendrell spends the rest of the episode in a pair of pants that have a bloody bullet hole. It's there because Scully shot the guy in the leg. Here's what's odd. After the shooting, Scully rushes through the bar and finds that the assassin has made his escape. The camera shows us a puddle of blood, followed by another and another connected by a rivulet leading to the door. There is a significant amount of fluid on the floor. Question: How did all that blood make it out of the assassin's leg and through the fabric of his pants, leaving only a golfball-sized stain behind?

🅇 Joseph Pintar of New Hartford, New York, tells me that the Syracuse airport must have undergone a major renovation since he visited it because he doesn't remember it looking anything like the airport shown during this episode. (Wink, wink.)

TALES OF THE CONSORTIUM

These are the Episodes of Cancerman and his Associates!

If you're new to *The X-Files*, you may or may not have heard of the "Mythology" or the "Myth Arc" (as it is called among some X-philes). The Mythology is a set of episodes that gives hints, facts, and insinuations about what "they" are doing— "they" being defined as Cancerman and the Consortium that meets in a room on Forty-sixth Street in New York City and whose members include the Well-Manicured Man and Brandoguy. What follows is a list of the episodes that are *probably* part of the Mythology, along with a *brief* list of information that each episode *might* supply. Given the open-ended storytelling technique employed by the creators of *The X-Files*, sometimes it's difficult to fit together the pieces! (Note: It is not my intention here to fully detail the events of the episode. For that, you'll have to watch them yourself!)

"Pilot": "Someone" is experimenting on young people. A metal implant is found in the nose of Ray Soames. Cancerman takes the implant and stores it at the Pentagon.

"Deep Throat": The military has UFO-like craft that can hover and dart away. According to Deep Throat, aliens have been on Earth for a long time.

"Fallen Angel": The military has a UFO retrieval team.

"E.B.E.": According to Deep Throat, there was an ultrasecret conference among the major countries of the world after Roswell in 1947. All agreed that any recovered living extraterrestrial biological entity would be exterminated immediately. Deep Throat says that he killed such an EBE in Vietnam.

"The Erlenmeyer Flask": According to Deep Throat, Dr. Berube created the first viable human/alien hybrid—a hybrid who had toxic body fluids, increased strength, and the ability to breathe underwater. The military has at least one fetus that looks alien.

"Duane Barry" (Part 1 of 2): A metal fragment is found implanted in Duane Barry. It causes a grocery scanner to go haywire.

"Ascension" (Part 2 of 2): Scully is abducted.

"One Breath": Scully is returned, barely alive. According to the Lone Gunmen, she has protein chains in her blood that are the by-products of "branched DNA."

"Colony" (Part 1 of 2): An alien bounty hunter comes to Earth to kill a group of clones who are apparently alien/human hybrids. (After all, they *melt* when they die.) The female version of the clones looks like an adult version of Samantha Mulder. The bounty hunter can change his appearance at will.

"End Game" (Part 2 of 2): After killing the hybrids, the bounty hunter returns to his ship, but he tells Mulder that Samantha is alive.

"Anasazi" (Part 1 of 3): A boxcar filled with alienlike corpses is found in New Mexico. The corpses have smallpox inoculations. Mulder's father was involved with Cancerman. The term "the merchandise" is important.

"The Blessing Way" (Part 2 of 3): Scully finds a metal disk in her neck. The Well-Manicured Man tells Scully that the Consortium predicts the future by inventing it.

"Paper Clip" (Part 3 of 3): The Consortium is involved with the Nazi scientists who were given immunity from the experiments they conducted on humans during World War II. The "abandoned" Strughold Mining Company contains row upon row of filing cabinets with records on everyone who received a smallpox inoculation since the 1950s. Each record contains a tissue sample. Scully's sample was taken recently—as was Samantha's.

"Nisei" (Part 1 of 2): The Consortium is involved with Japanese scientists who were given immunity from the experiments they conducted on humans during World War II. Scully meets a group of female abductees in Allentown, Pennsylvania, who remember her from their abductions. All of them had metal implants removed from their necks as well.

"731" (Part 2 of 2): Japanese scientist Zama has either created an alien/human hybrid or a human with no susceptibility to disease. According to Pendrell, the metal disk found in Scully's neck mimics memory formation in the brain.

"Piper Maru" (Part 1 of 2): A body-hopping alien eventually overtakes Krycek. The alien can generate surges of radiation that severely damage anyone nearby.

"Apocrypha" (Part 2 of 2): When Cancerman moves a UFO to a missile silo in North Dakota, members of the Consortium wonder why he didn't bring it to Nevada like the others. Cancerman escorts an alien-possessed Krycek to the missile silo so the alien can be reunited with its vessel. The Well-Manicured Man calls the craft a "foo fighter."

"Talitha Cumi" (Part 1 of 2): A person named Jeremiah Smith—most likely a hybrid—can heal and change his appearance. Mulder intuits that colonization approaches for Earth.

"Herrenvolk" (Part 2 of 2): The Consortium maintains at least one farm in Canada that is tended by young clones without language ability or the need for parents. Humans have no immunity to the bees that are also part of the project. A computer file containing a billion records has something to do with the Smallpox Eradication Program. Scully hypothesizes that the program might have been a way for the Consortium to tag and identify humans.

"Musings of a Cigarette-Smoking Man": If the events in this episode are true, the first living EBE was recovered at the end of 1991 and Deep Throat killed it.

"Tunguska" (Part 1 of 2): The Russians have discovered an alien life-form in the rocks of Tunguska. It is called the black cancer and can immobilize its victims.

"Terma" (Part 2 of 2): The Consortium attempts to find a cure for the black cancer, but Russians destroy the stolen samples.

"Momento Mori": According to a hybrid, Scully and the other women of Allentown were subjected to a high-amplification radiation procedure that caused superovulation during their abductions. Their ova were harvested and are being used to create more hybrids.

"Tempus Fugit" (Part 1 of 2): (I included this episode and the next in this list because they share so many elements with the Mythology. But it is possible that they do not belong here. Neither Cancerman nor the Consortium appears in these episodes, and neither episode advances any information about the main conspiracy.)

"Max" (Part 2 of 2): (See above.)

"Zero Sum": The Consortium has developed a strain of highly aggressive bees whose sting carries a virulent strain of the smallpox virus.

"Gethsemane" (Part 1 of ?): (Like "Tempus Fugit" and "Max," this episode shares many elements with the Mythology. But neither Cancerman nor the Consortium makes an appearance.) According to a man named Michael Kritschgau, aliens have never visited Earth. It's all a hoax perpetrated by the military-industrial complex to cover its activities. In addition, Mulder himself is a construct of these same conspirators. Supposedly they planted memories of Samantha Mulder's abduction and even gave Scully cancer so Mulder would believe.

Synchrony

PLOT SUMMARY At the Massachusetts Institute of Technology, an old man frantically approaches to warn post-doctoral fellow Lucas Menand that he will be killed by a bus in only minutes. Given the old man's agitated state, a campus patrolman hauls him away. Menand's academic adviser Jason Nichols, then watches in horror as Menand does indeed die just as predicted. Arrested for causing the accident, Nichols tries to tell the authorities what really happened, but the old man has disappeared, leaving the patrolman frozen solid. Needless to say, Mulder and Scully soon arrive to investigate. They discover that Nichols has been conducting research in the field of cryobiology, studying the effects of freezing temperatures on biological systems. However, the compound used to freeze the patrolman hasn't been invented yet. Indeed, the compound won't be invented for many years.

The old man is Jason Nichols himself, come back from forty years in the future to stop the research that will allow Nichols's girlfriend, Lisa Ianelli, to make a fundamental leap in the discovery of time travel. According to the elder Nichols, time travel has created a world without history or hope. He is determined to thwart its discovery and eventually attacks Ianelli before killing himself and his younger self. His efforts ultimately fail, however, for as the episode ends, we see a recovered Ianelli re-creating her dead boyfriend's research.

Onscreen Locations

🅧 Massachusetts Institute of Technology
🅧 Boston Medical Examiner's Office
🅧 6th Precinct
🅧 Hotel James Monroe
🅧 Bio-medical Research Facility

Ruminations

There are two interesting numbers in this episode, and their proximity seems too deliberate to be coincidental. The elder Nichols stays in room 47 at the Lighthouse Resident Hotel, and in his room Scully finds Yonechi's flight information: Pan Oceanic Flight 1701. Trekkers will immediately recognize the latter as the registry number for the USS Enterprise, *and some will even be aware that the number 47 is very popular among the creative staff at the* Star Trek *production offices. In addition, time-travel stories have been a common theme in* Trek. *Could the numbers be a homage to the most successful sci-fi television series of all time?*

Plot Oversights

🅧 Well—given the fondness that sci-fi fans have for time travel—I suppose the creators of *The X-Files* had to try it sooner or later. The problem is: Time travel is tough to write without plot oversights. It simply gives characters *too many* ways to solve problems while introducing *too many* complications that the characters will have to avoid to be successful. In other words, for the writer, time travel is a densely populated minefield. We'll take the problems one at a time as they crop up in this episode, but—for starters—why does the elder Nichols have to come running up to Lucas Menand and his younger self at the beginning of the episode?

He's a *time traveler!* Couldn't he afford another five minutes on his time-travel card so he could arrive at the rendezvous *early*?! (Or did he oversleep in his hotel room and almost miss the most important meeting of his life?)

🅇 Early in the episode, Mulder and Scully examine the frozen patrolman at the "Boston Medical Examiner's Office." The medical examiner tells Scully that he hasn't been able to determine the cause of death. He says there's been some internal disagreement over how to proceed—mainly whether "to cut or to saw." On the advice of Pauline J. Alama of Rochester, New York, I spoke with Mark Fairbank of the Office of the Chief Medical Examiner of Massachusetts about this scene. As a minor aside, autopsies in Massachusetts are performed by a state-regulated agency, so there is no "Boston Medical Examiner's Office." More importantly, however, medical examiners in Massachusetts are not allowed to freeze corpses. Because of this, autopsy facilities are not equipped to handle frozen bodies. In the case of a frozen corpse being presented for an autopsy, a Massachusetts medical examiner would let the body thaw before proceeding. In other words, the decision would be "to cut." Period. (It's amazing the little pieces of information one acquires when doing one of these *Guides!* I love this stuff!)

🅇 The Hotel James Monroe must pay its bellmen a very respectable wage. The elder Nichols—still on his crusade to destroy time travel—intercepts a Dr. Yonechi in the lobby and accompanies him to the room where he will stay. A bellman tags along. After depositing Yonechi's bags, the bellman hands Yonechi the room keys and marches out with nary a pause for a tip. Does anyone else find this unusual?

🅇 According to the episode, the elder Nichols is attempting to thwart the discovery of time travel. To do so, he comes back to 1997 and begins flash-freezing people, apparently with a compound that doesn't exist yet but will be vital to the initial discovery of time travel. Why use this compound? Isn't this self-defeating? Can't the elder Nichols imagine that depositing this compound in a time frame prior to its invention *might* cause it to be created sooner than it should? Wouldn't it be better to poison the intended victims with something that was indigenous to 1997?

🅇 Hearing that Yonechi was only recently frozen, Ianelli offers that he might not be dead. But *no one* even mentions the possibility of attempting to revive the patrolman. The implication is that if you have only been flash-frozen for a day, you can be revived, but if you've been flash-frozen for more than a day, you're dead. I fail to see how an extra day as a Popsicle® is going to make the difference. Isn't the whole point of cryonics to preserve living tissue until a later date? Granted, the patrolman will *eventually* "go bad" like a slab of old meat in the freezer, but will twenty-four hours really make that much difference?

🅇 For some reason, Mulder and Scully seem oblivious to a simple conclusion in this episode. Finding Yonechi frozen solid in a hotel room, Scully tells Mulder that he has a pinprick on his palm just like the patrolman's and that she found an odd substance in the wound. Mulder speculates that it might be a lethal injection of some kind. Later, Ianelli tells Mulder and Scully that the elder Nichols threatened her with a medical instrument. In discussing the incident, Scully postulates that the "old man" is protecting Jason. "With a medical instrument?" Mulder scoffs, at which point Scully agrees that it's an *unlikely* choice as a murder weapon. Wait a minute: Doesn't it seem like Mulder and Scully should realize the possibility that the "medical instrument" is the device that the old man is using to kill people by lethal injection?

FOURTH SEASON

Trivia Questions

🄸 What is Dr. Yonechi's room number in the Hotel James Monroe?

🄸 Where is the Lighthouse Resident Hotel located?

Trivia Answers
🄸 312.
🄸 McKinney Street.

🅃🅃🅃

Synchrony

☒ Twice in this episode, the medical staff at MIT revive a person who has been flash-frozen—first Yonechi and then Ianelli. In both cases, the medical staff first give them an inter-cardial injection of epinephrine to start their hearts fluttering and then attempt to knock the flutter down into a stable rhythm by using a defibrillator. (Granted, according to the "flat line" monitors, *neither* heart is actually fluttering, but *maybe* the equipment was calibrated wrong and there was a little bit of flutter that didn't show up!) In Yonechi's case, he is pulled bare-chested from a frostbite tub and given the injection. The creators evidently intend for us to believe that Ianelli also lies bare-chested on the examination table because they are careful to show us very little of Ianelli's upper body. They are *so* careful, in fact, that the injection of epinephrine is given in the wrong place! With the camera holding a close-up on Ianelli's face, we see the needle inserted in the center of Ianelli's chest near her collarbone. This is supposed to be an intercardial injection. The needle is supposed to go *into* her heart! (By the way, for all the creators' efforts to give the impression that Ianelli is bare-chested, the actress evidently had other inclinations. If you use freeze-frame as they put her into the tub you might notice that she is indeed wearing some type of strapless undergarment.)

☒ How does Ianelli stabilize at the end of the episode? What happened to the compound that was used to freeze her? Was it extracted from her body somehow? (I was really expecting the ambulance that takes her to the hospital to burst into flames, but the creators had other plans.)

☒ Okay, let's conclude this section with a few words on the whole time-travel "thang." First, some important background. As far as I can tell, there are two basic types of settings in which people discuss time-travel: universe and multi-verse. The "universe" setting says that there's only one time stream. If you could ever time-travel you would be traveling in your past or your future, and what you did would affect that past or that future. This is the classic time-travel scenario. Often, stories on time travel involve a hero or heroine displeased with some current event who decides to go back in time to keep that event from occurring. In this context, time travel becomes a form of redemption and—since we as humans seem to have an innate yearning for some type of redemption to make our lives better—this concept is very appealing to the reader or viewer of the time-travel story. Some aspects of this episode fall into this category. The elder Nichols is attempting to thwart the development of time travel to make his world better: to return it to a place of history and hope.

Unfortunately, the "universe" setting for a time-travel story has some inherent pitfalls, the most commonly known of which is the "grandfather paradox": What would happen if you went back and killed your own grandfather? Since time travels in a single stream in the universe setting, logically you would never be born, so you could never travel back and kill your grandfather in the first place! This type of paradox can take many, many forms—all of which will give you a headache if you think about them too long. Science fiction writers have become very inventive over the past several decades trying to get around these types of paradoxes, but—in the final analysis—*if* time moves forward in a single stream and *if* changes can be made in that stream that will eventually negate the potential for the change in the first place . . . you are *going to* have a paradox. (The only solution I've ever read that is *remotely* satisfying to me is the assertion that the universe will somehow bring all its energies to bear to make sure such paradoxes do not occur once time travel is invented, but . . . that seems contrived.)

The multiverse setting neatly solves the paradox problem of time travel. It postulates the existence of an infinite number of parallel universes, all contentedly trundling along. Anything that *can* happen eventually *does* happen in at least one of these universes. The multiverse setting goes on to speculate that time travel might be possible, but only to universes that are not your own. So . . . you could go back and kill your grandfather, but he really wouldn't be *your* grandfather, so you would still be born and there is no paradox.

Having said all that, let us now turn our attention to this episode. What do you think? Are the creators using a universe or a multiverse setting? Well, the elder Nichols has a picture of Yonechi, Ianelli, and the younger Nichols celebrating a discovery. Yet Yonechi dies in this episode, and therefore the celebration never occurred. If the events are all taking place in the same stream, time would move past the point when the celebration *would have* occurred. There would be no picture and therefore Nichols could not have brought the picture back with him . . . but he did! In addition, since Nichols *kills* himself in this episode, there is no one to grow up to *be* the elder Nichols, so the elder Nichols could never have come back in the first place . . . in a universe setting.

It seems pretty clear, then, that the creators have chosen a multiverse setting for their story. The elder Nichols is actually from a parallel universe. He can come and wreak havoc on our timeline and it won't affect him in the slightest. Unfortunately, the multiverse setting gives writers problems when it comes to character motivations. For instance, the elder Nichols says that he has seen a world without history and hope, and that is the reason he traveled back in time. But . . . *surely* with the advent of time travel in the multiverse setting, those who embark on it will understand that they are not traveling to their own universe but to another. In other words, the elder Nichols can't fix *his* world. He's just over here mucking around in *ours!* Why?! Let's say for a moment that he really is this altruistic—that he's so obsessed and guilt-ridden over what he has done to his own world that he wants to save another world from such a fate. How can he ensure that time travel was invented

in the same way in our world as it was in his world? And even if he could, how can he ensure that we won't figure out another way to time-travel even after his killing spree? In short, he can never be sure that his actions will stop time travel from developing in our world. And besides, who asked *him* to "fix" our problems, and why doesn't he keep his nose out of our *business?!* (At ease, Phil, at ease.)

Oddly enough, the elder Nichols—from his dialogue—seems to believe that he *can* actually affect his own world. Throughout the episode he speaks authoritatively on how our future will unfold. Even odder, he claims that his world is a world where "anyone can know anything that will ever happen." But if Nichols can actually affect his own world's history, others could affect it as well. History would change every day, maybe every hour, maybe every second. (This is what I think he means when he says that his is a world without history.) But, but, but . . . how in a "world without history" could someone know "anything that will ever happen" in the midst of that kind of temporal chaos? (Anyone have a headache yet?)

And what about Mulder? Near the end of the episode, he makes statements that are internally inconsistent. Mulder first quotes Scully as saying that even in the multiverse setting, each universe can only have one outcome. Mulder says he takes that to mean that Scully believes the future cannot be altered. From this he concludes that time travel will be invented because the elder Nichols demonstrated time travel. Hold it! *If* the elder Nichols came from *our* future, then he *did* change our future by his actions. That *cannot* be disputed because Yonechi and the younger Nichols are *dead*, so Mulder *cannot* claim that the future cannot be altered. But if the elder Nichols came from *another* future, then Mulder has no basis from which to claim that *we* will eventually invent time travel because the elder Nichols didn't come from our future. (Then again, Mulder isn't exactly the most logical person in the world. It would have been nice, however, for Scully to point out the flaws in his statements!)

X Of course, none of this addresses one of those pesky little plot oversights concerning time travel: If time travel is possible, why aren't we being deluged with visitors from the future? I absolutely do not believe that the elder Nichols was the *only* person in his world who thought he could make life better by coming back to 1997. If "anybody" can know "anything that will ever happen," it implies that *anybody* can time-travel, and we should see *millions* of people tromping around trying to "fix" us. (Oh, *joy!* Something to look forward to.)

Equipment Oddities

X The very end of the episode shows us Ianelli at work in Nichols's lab. Interestingly enough, her glasses don't seem to have any prescription, just nice, *flat* lenses.

Continuity and Production Problems

X The frozen corpse of the campus patrolman doesn't seem very dead. Watch carefully just before a doctor pulls back the plastic so Mulder and Scully can have a look. See the plastic moving? And later—when Scully calls Mulder to tell him that Nichols's fingerprints were found on the patrolman's uniform—watch the "frozen" guy's elbow as the camera focuses on Scully. It starts going up and down, just as if the guy is *breathing!*

Small Potatoes

Onscreen Locations

- [X] Tablers Community Hospital, Martinsburg, West Virginia
- [X] Eastern Appalachian Regional Heath Department
- [X] Office of Dr. Alton Pugh, OB-GYN
- [X] Seventeen Prospect Parkway
- [X] Cumberland Reformatory

Ruminations

This was fun! Most of the fourth season has been dark and foreboding. It's nice to see the creators relax and "live a little." (To paraphrase Van Blundht, I know I would if I were in their shoes!) Kudos to the writers and to David Duchovny, who did a great job on this episode!

In my review of "War of the Coprophages," I noted that the final Mulder scene in that episode may give us our first glimpse of Mulder's bedroom. I also qualified that statement by saying that we have no way of proving that the room shown really is part of Mulder's apartment. This episode seems to indicate that it is not! Coming to Mulder's apartment for the first time, Van Blundht throws up his hands in disgust and wonders where he sleeps. I take this to mean that Mulder does, in fact, sleep on his couch and there's nothing beyond his kitchen but his bathroom. (See "War of the Coprophages" for more details.)

Plot Oversights

- [X] There is a *funny* scene in this episode as Mulder accidently breaks off the tail of the pre-

PLOT SUMMARY After five babies are born with tails in the small town of Martinsburg, West Virginia, Mulder and Scully come to investigate. Mulder is particularly intrigued by the single mother of the latest baby, Amanda Nelligan. She claims the father is from another planet. (The other four women were married.) Nelligan proves to be a disappointment, however, when she informs Mulder and Scully that Luke Skywalker impregnated her!

Scully then orders some genetic testing and discovers that all five babies had the same unknown father. And soon afterward, Mulder locates a janitor named Eddie Van Blundht, who has a scar where surgeons removed his tail as a child. The children *are* Van Blundht's, but he claims they are the result of consensual sex. Given Van Blundht's appearance—short, rotund, balding—Scully finds this hard to believe. She has him held over for questioning.

Unfortunately, Van Blundht soon escapes due to other unique physical traits. Utilizing a layer of extra muscle beneath his skin, he can mimic anyone else's appearance. In fact, the married women of Martinsburg thought they were making love to their husbands, and Nelligan *did* have intercourse with Luke Skywalker! Even Scully almost falls prey to Van Blundht's charm after he assumes Mulder's identity. Thankfully, Mulder makes it back to Washington, D.C., in time to rescue Scully from the doppelgänger's advances.

served corpse of Eddie Van Blundht, Sr.—right after Scully has said how wonderful it is that the specimen is so well preserved and intact. Interestingly enough, Mulder expends very little effort in snapping off the tail, yet the corpse previously survived a three-foot drop without apparent damage. Hmmmm.

Back at FBI Headquarters, we see Mulder and Scully presenting their report on the case to Skinner. Skinner notes that Mulder—who is really Van Blundht—misspelled Federal Bureau of Investigation *twice*. "Mulder" shrugs. Two ponderments: Doesn't Scully read these reports before Mulder hands them in, or does she do her own report? And where did Van Blundht write this report? Later events indicate he hasn't been to Mulder's office *or* his home yet.

This is a really cute episode, and I wouldn't change a thing, but Van Blundht's capabilities seem too awe-inspiring to be merely terrestrial in origin. I know the creators attempt to explain some of it with a layer of subdermal muscle and strange hair follicles. But . . . what about the change in height? And how does he get *thinner*? And where did Van Blundht learn to manage voices so well? And when did he study the four married women's husbands *in the nude*? Think about it: Wouldn't he have to reproduce moles, birthmarks, and level of muscular development as well as other . . . ahem . . . physical attributes? (Or did he make sure the wives were drunk and drugged so they wouldn't remember the encounter?) And why hasn't he taken more advantage of these abilities? Doesn't he realize the fame and fortune he could attain as a performer in Las Vegas with these capabilities? (It's another sad, heart-wrenching, *missed* opportunity, I tell you!)

The Nitpickers Guild Glossary contains the term "BIMD." It stands for "Because It's More Dramatic" (nominated by Mike Ballway of Evanston, Illinois). It answers the obvious questions that arise near the end of this episode: Why didn't Mulder *call* Scully as soon as he escaped from the basement in the Martinsville hospital and tell her that the Mulder who traveled back to Washington, D.C., wasn't the real McCoy? Why did he charge all the way back to Washington and break her door down? BIMD! (And I wouldn't change this for the world!)

Continuity and Production Problems

And speaking of the scene where Mulder snaps off Eddie Van Blundht, Sr.'s, tail, listen closely and you might hear an indication that the creators redid a few of Scully's lines to give the scene more comedic impact. After revealing that Van Blundht, Sr., had an extra layer of voluntary muscle under his skin, Scully notes that this is not normal. As she admits that the man's body is a unique scientific specimen and notes it is pre-served and intact, the reverb on her voice changes. Scully delivers this line just before Mulder snaps the tail. The closed captioning probably contains the original line for these moments. It reads, "I mean, my knowledge of anatomy tells me that that doesn't just happen." This, of course, isn't *nearly* as funny because it doesn't hit the fact that Scully thinks the corpse is valuable in part because it's intact.

Follow the changing tie. During this episode, the real Mulder wears a tie that features an oval shape in a semidiagonal pattern. Each oval is separated by two dots. On the other hand, Van Blundht—while posing as Mulder—wears a tie that has straight diagonal rows of paisley pat-terns interspersed with straight diagonal rows of smaller dots. For the most part, the creators do an excellent job of remembering which "Mulder" wears which tie. They do make *one*

mistake, however: After assuming Mulder's identity, Van Blundht goes to visit Nelligan in the hospital. Note the diagonal paisleys on his tie. Leaving Nelligan's room, Van Blundht spots the real Mulder and ducks into another room. As Mulder approaches Nelligan's room, take a good, long look at his tie. See the perfectly straight diagonal lines of paisleys and smaller dots? This is supposed to be the real Mulder. He *should* be wearing a tie with ovals, separated by two dots in a semidiagonal pattern. Thankfully, as soon as Mulder enters Nelligan's room, the tie corrects itself!

🅧 Apparently Fox Mulder has *three* different signatures! In "One Breath," I mentioned that Mulder's signature on his resignation letter doesn't look anything like the signature on his badge in the opening credits. In this episode, Van Blundht offers us a close-up of Mulder's driver's license. Guess what? *That* signature doesn't look like either of the other two!

🅧 Matthew Chase Maxwell of San Francisco—a self-proclaimed aquarist—tells me that he doesn't believe Van Blundht actually fed Mulder's fish, though Van Blundht goes through the motions after coming to Mulder's apartment. Quite correctly, Matthew notes that the fish do not swim to the top of the water to feed, nor do they begin lunging at the food that should be drifting down.

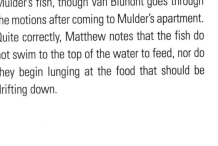

FOURTH SEASON

Trivia Questions

❶ What is Amanda Nelligan's Social Security number?

❷ What pet name does Fred Nieman use for his wife?

Trivia Answers
❶ 545-02-0809.
❷ Baboo or Honey Bear.

339

Small Potatoes

Zero Sum

PLOT SUMMARY

After a postal employee named Jane Brody dies under mysterious circumstances in Desmond, Virginia, Cancerman has Skinner sanitize the site and incinerate Brody's body. (Cancerman has promised a cure for Scully's cancer if Skinner will cooperate with the conspirators.) Unfortunately, when a Desmond police detective stops and questions Skinner, Cancerman's forces quickly kill the detective to ensure his silence.

The death shocks Skinner, but more soon follows. Too late he discovers that highly aggressive bees killed Brody after escaping from a shipment of packages to Payson, South Carolina. The bees carry a virulent strain of the smallpox virus, and the Consortium intends to use them to conduct a "trial run." Skinner quickly travels to Payson to investigate further, but by the time he arrives, the bees have already swarmed an elementary school, and children are dying.

Furious, Skinner confronts Cancerman, shoving a pistol in his face with murderous intent. Unfazed, Cancerman taunts that his death will mean Scully's death as well. Skinner fires anyway . . . into a nearby wall. Their deal is over. Skinner no longer believes that Cancerman *has* a cure.

The episode ends with a phone call between Cancerman and Marita Covarrubias. Cryptically, Cancerman instructs her to tell Mulder what he wants to hear if he asks what Skinner knows about the project.

Onscreen Locations

- ☒ Transcontinental Express Routing Center, Desmond, Virginia
- ☒ Audrey County Morgue
- ☒ Police Forensic Lab, Desmond, Virginia
- ☒ Elsinore, Maryland
- ☒ FBI Special Photography Unit
- ☒ 46th Street, New York City
- ☒ J.F.K. Elementary School, Payson, South Carolina
- ☒ Payson Community Hospital
- ☒ Crystal City, Virginia

Plot Oversights

Lots of great continuity here! Nice to finally have Scully's cancer mentioned again. Great tie back to Skinner's deal with Cancerman in "Momento Mori." (Although it might have been nice to grind it along for more than one episode. For me, there is something supremely unnerving about a character slowly drowning in his or her good intentions.) And did you notice the "Choco Droppings" in the candy vending machine? You might remember them from "War of the Coprophages"! (Remember the convenience store scene? "Roooooaches!")

And an interesting tidbit of information that the virulent strain of smallpox in this episode is a variola virus. Would this be the result of research by the late Dr. Bonita Charne-Sayre? In "Terma," Scully indicated that Charne-Sayre was an expert in variola viruses. Scully also said that Charne-Sayre was a vocal proponent of eliminating the last known strains of smallpox. Perhaps Charne-Sayre wanted the last known strains destroyed so it would be more difficult to fight the more virulent strain that she had developed for the Consortium? (As far as I am concerned, if she's willing to expose the residents of a convalescent home to the black cancer, she's as bad as Dr. Kevin "The Scum-Sucking Mug Slug" Scanlon. See "Momento Mori.")

Unanswered Questions

☒ Are the bees in this episode related to the bees in "Herrenvolk"? At first blush, the answer would seem to be "Yes"! At first blush, the bees of "Zero Sum" even shed light on the purpose of the Canadian farm in "Herrenvolk." After all, the telephone worker in "Herrenvolk" dies after a single sting, and fewer than twenty-four hours later his face is covered in pox marks and blisters (similar but not identical to those shown in "Zero Sum"). And Smith does say that Mulder has no immunity to the bees in "Herrenvolk," much like victims have no immunity to the smallpox-carrying bees of "Zero Sum." Was the farm in "Herrenvolk" a "bee factory" to prepare an army of "injectors" that would infect great masses of the populace with a highly virulent form of smallpox and prepare the world for invasion?

Unfortunately, after a closer inspection of "Herrenvolk" and "Zero Sum," the answer to our unanswered question turns out to be a resounding, "Um . . . well . . . maybe?!" It is true that Smith says in "Herrenvolk" that the farm was used to produce pollen, but he and Mulder prepare to leave before the young Samantha clone leads them to the apiary. If the bees were the important product of the farm, why doesn't Smith show them to Mulder initially? And as far as raising these bees goes, they certainly don't seem to need any help in "Zero Sum"! (As we shall see in a moment.) Also, the behavior of the bees is very different between "Herrenvolk" and "Zero Sum." The "Zero Sum" bees are extremely aggressive, yet in "Herrenvolk," Mulder runs through the plants after seeing the Samantha clone, and the bees don't seem to mind! (There's plenty of buzzing in the background, so they are around.) The only time the bees actually swarm in

"Herrenvolk" is after Mulder buries the alien assassin under a large chunk of their hive. In "Zero Sum" all you have to do is give them a glance and they come after you! ("Are you looking at me? Are you looking at . . .")

Plot Oversights

☒ The episode opens with Brody sneaking a smoke in the ladies' rest room at work. As she sits on a toilet and reads a magazine, the room fills with bees. Surprisingly enough, Brody doesn't hear them! The bees had to come from somewhere. I have a hard time believing that they all tiptoed out of the sink and made sure they were really, really quiet as they spread across the floor. These same bees "buzz" when they fly toward Brody to swarm her; why don't they "buzz" when they fly around the room? And if they do "buzz" around the room, why doesn't Brody react sooner? (I can tell you this: When I hear that distinctive sound, I start looking immediately!)

☒ Apparently not only do the bees sneak up on their prey, they also know enough to run away and hide as soon as they kill somebody! After Brody is attacked, fellow worker and friend Misty Nagata comes to find her, since she hasn't reported back to work. Nagata enters the ladies' rest room and finds Brody dead in a stall. From all appearances, there are no bees anywhere. This is mere minutes after the attack and they are all gone! (In case you doubt this, Skinner scrubbed the bathroom, yet later was surprised that bees were involved, when he discovered the hive. Also, the Desmond police detective doesn't seem to know that bees were involved in Brody's death.) I might (and it's a big "might") be able to believe that the bees ran away right after Brody dies. ("Someone's coming! Everybody hide!") But do the creators really expect us to believe that Brody didn't kill even one of her attackers in all the thrashing she did before she succumbed?

Trivia Questions

❶ What is Marita Covarrubias's work phone number?

❷ Where does Mulder get the footage of Skinner speaking with Detective Thomas?

341

Zero Sum

X Consider this sequence of events: Finding a large honeycomb in the wall of the rest room where Brody died, Skinner takes a small jarful of the stuff to an entomologist. Back at FBI Headquarters, Mulder tells Skinner he has grainy pictures of the person who killed the police detective and is taking them to the Special Photography Unit to see if they can sharpen them for identification. Skinner calls Marita Covarrubias. The entomologist is attacked and killed by a swarm of bees. Mulder calls Skinner to the morgue to see the body and says that the boys in Special Photo have pulled an all-nighter on the photos.

From all indications, there is a fairly short amount of time between the delivery of the honeycomb to the entomologist and the entomologist's death by a swarm of *hundreds* of bees. And by "fairly short," I mean twenty-four hours or less. Would someone please explain to me how a swarm of *hundreds* of bees hatches out of a chunk of honeycomb that's only about *three inches square* in *twenty-four hours* or less?!

X Not to be snide, but when Marita Covarrubias tried to put the screws to Skinner by telling him that her office has to answer to the secretary general of the United Nations, I couldn't help but think, "Oooo, we're all *quaking* in our boots now!" (Sorry, sorry.)

X I must admit some confusion over the "trial run" staged by the Consortium. No doubt these events will be contextualized by later shows and everything will make sense . . . *eventually*. But I'm having difficulty figuring out what the Consortium is trying to accomplish by freeing the bees to terrorize a small town (or worse, specifically setting them to attack the schoolchildren). Here are my presuppositions: The bees have been created to spread a virulent strain of smallpox. The bees will be used to destroy a portion—possibly a significant portion—of the populace for some agenda (probably as a precursor to alien colonization). It seems

to me that if you have this really bad bug (both bee and virus), you probably want to keep it confined until you are ready to *use* it. I mean *really* use it. To me, it seems like releasing it for a "trial run" simply increases the chance that someone will find a cure. Unless, of course, no one will ever find out about the trial run. But keeping this event under wraps seems like an extremely difficult task. Aside from the formidable task of covering up the deaths of *dozens* of children, how can the Consortium hope to contain the spread of the bees? Skinner had a *dinky* piece of honeycomb, and it produced *hundreds* of bees. The bees in the damaged package at Transcontinental Express built a huge honeycomb inside the wall of the rest room. Apparently these little buggers breed like rabbits and can build a home out of *nothing!* It seems to me that the only time you want to let these things loose is when you're ready for colonization. (Gasp! Does that mean . . . ? Aaaaaaah!)

Equipment Oddities

X A pair of equipment oddities makes Skinner's life easier as he eradicates the evidence of Brody's death for Cancerman. Near the end of the teaser, we see Skinner deleting the E-mail that was sent to Mulder. It contains pictures of Brody as taken by the Desmond Police Department. First, doesn't Mulder have password protection on his computer in the basement office? He had password protection on his home computer during "Little Green Men." Why not at the office as well? (Skinner doesn't impress me as a technologically savvy nerd-o-crat, so I have a hard time believing that he hacked Mulder's system.)

Second, Mulder apparently doesn't have an undelete function on his computer. Skinner doesn't seem to take any precautions against such a utility—he shuts off the computer very quickly after instructing some program to delete the death pictures of Brody. (Normally, to absolutely ensure that a file has been blitzed, you have to overwrite it with zeros. Usually, "deleting" a file frees up the appropriate sector for reuse but doesn't actually change the contents of those sectors until the space is needed on the hard drive.)

🗶 After hearing from Mulder that the Desmond police detective was killed with a Sig-Sauer P228, Skinner hurries to a desk drawer to discover that his weapon has been stolen. (The Real FBI tells me that special agents *do* carry this brand of semiautomatic pistol.) Given the make and model of the murder weapon, Mulder tells Skinner that he is having "comps" run on all weapons registered to federal agents and local officers. Presumably this is done with some kind of computerized process, much like automatic fingerprint analysis. (Skinner indicates that the FBI has such a computerized process in "The Blessing Way" when Scully brings him the article on the death of Kenneth Soona. He refers to an FBI "drugfire ballistics database.") So why doesn't Skinner's name pop up very quickly in the search that was initiated by Mulder? *Was* it Skinner's gun that killed the police detective? Or did Cancerman's forces plant the murder weapon in Skinner's apartment later and Skinner only thought it was his weapon?

Continuity and Production Problems

🗶 Not a nit, just an observation. I've mentioned "boys will be boys" shots before. This episode has a "for the girls" shot of Skinner in his underwear. (Just trying to be fair!)

🗶 Pay close attention to the little kid with the glasses near the end of the episode when the elementary-school kids get swarmed on the school playground. (You'll need to use freeze-frame or slow motion for this.) A wide shot shows him running up to the swing set and dodging around a swing. The camera cuts to a closer shot, and the kid runs up to the swing set a second time!

Elegy

PLOT SUMMARY

In Washington, D.C., a bowling alley proprietor sees an apparition of a murdered young woman. When police discover her body in the street nearby, Mulder and Scully are quick to arrive. The young woman is the third murder victim in as many weeks. In each case, witnesses reported visions of the dead. Mulder believes that Harold Spuller—a mentally challenged employee at the bowling alley—is the key to understanding the phenomenon, but Scully's cancer soon disrupts the investigation as her nose begins to bleed. Worse, Scully herself sees an apparition of the next victim while she washes up. Rattled, she withdraws from the case under the guise of a medical checkup.

In time, Mulder determines that those who saw the apparitions had one thing in common: They were all dying. Since Spuller has seen them as well, Mulder believes he is dying also and wants Scully to examine him. In fact, Spuller is very ill. His nurse has been stealing his medication. Addled by the drugs, *she* murdered the young women because they befriended Spuller at the bowling alley.

With the nurse apprehended, Scully finally —hesitantly—admits her apparition experience to Mulder. Her concealment of "the truth" only frustrates him. Embarrassed, Scully hurries to her car, where she sees yet another death vision . . . this time of Spuller.

Onscreen Locations

ⓧ Angie's Midnight Bowl, Washington, D.C.
ⓧ New Horizon Psychiatric Center

Ruminations

It's the details I love about The X-Files! During his first visit to Angie's Midnight Bowl, Mulder picks up a ball and throws a strike. Now . . . if you've ever bowled, you know that you don't just pick up a ball and toss it in the middle of someone else's game, but the creators were detail-oriented enough to orchestrate the extras in the background so they finish their game just as Scully dons her bowling shoes. By the time Mulder and Scully finish examining the pinsetter, the extras have cleared out and Mulder has a free lane.

Scully apparently never told Mulder about the vision she had of her father in "Beyond the Sea." That event is strikingly similar to the events in this episode: Those seen were dying or had just died; those seen were trying to communicate. Yet, although there are many opportunities for Scully and Mulder to mention the vision that Scully had of her father during this episode, it never comes up!

At the risk of insulting your intelligence, let me offer a quick explanation for Nurse Innes's behavior. Scully postulates that the wacko nurse was trying to kill Harold's happiness—trying to destroy something that she would never have again. I think that's partially correct, but I also think the creators dropped enough hints along the way that we can put together a more comprehensive picture. Innes was recently divorced—as evidenced by the pale indentation on the right finger of her left hand. Her husband had an affair with a younger woman. (When asked by Scully if she has children, Innes comments, "Just the one my husband ran off with.")

It's easy to imagine Innes becoming more and more disturbed over her husband's unfaithfulness; feeling her sanity slipping away; watching Spuller moon over the pictures of the young women he met at the bowling alley; directing her anger at Spuller; taking his medication to calm herself, only to have her rage erupt at the same type of young woman who stole her husband. Perhaps the message that appears with the apparitions, "She is me," is a message from the deceased meant to identify Mr. Innes's young lover as the true object of the murderer's wrath.

One last item in this episode. The creators once again show their considerable ability to craft believable, complex lead characters. The actions are simple to recount: Scully sees a ghost; Scully doesn't like seeing a ghost; Scully withdraws; Mulder brings her back into the case; Scully solves the case; Scully confesses that she saw the ghost; Mulder is irritated that she didn't say something sooner; Scully leaves, upset. The question is: Why, why do these characters do what they do in this episode? At first blush it would be simple to say that Scully doesn't want to acknowledge the vision because it indicates that she is dying and so she does everything she can to prove it didn't happen. Mulder himself seems to favor this interpretation near the end of the episode when he says that he knows what she's afraid of, that he's afraid of the same thing—that "thing" being her death by cancer.

But this explanation doesn't quite fit the events. Scully is flummoxed by the vision before she learns that only the dying have had them. And Mulder is not conciliatory in his tone with her at the end of the episode for someone who supposedly understands what she is afraid of. He's obviously unhappy with her. He feels slighted and betrayed that she didn't tell him sooner. Why? I didn't have this episode available when I wrote the sidebar "Whose Truth Is Out There?" so indulge me as I brag on the creators. Scully is an objectivist. Nothing rattles her more than a phenomenon that exists outside her science. How do you investigate a ghost? How do you estimate its mass or properties? By definition, it is "spirit," and spirit exists beyond the domain of the natural world. Scully simply doesn't want her neat, understandable view of the universe disrupted by such untidy elements. Note that in her counseling session, Scully is willing to offer two possible explanations for the apparition, and both are grounded in the natural. For Scully, the phenomenon simply can't be supernatural.

As for Mulder, his anger at Scully's reticence stems from his subjectivism—from his belief that his view of the events in this episode is the "truth." He even says this to Scully when he derides that she can "believe" whatever she wants but she can't "hide the truth" from him or she's working against him. In Mulder's mind, there's only one explanation for the phenomenon: It was a death omen. Period. It was a death omen because he believes it was a death omen (though it might have been manufactured by Scully's mind), and Scully has committed a crime against the core of his being because she didn't validate his belief with her experience.

Plot Oversights

X As Mulder brings Scully up to speed on a murder victim at the beginning of "Humbug," the creators cast Scully in the role of the cabbage head so that we, the viewing audience, will have an important piece of information. (For more information see "Humbug.") In this episode, the creators give Mulder his turn. At one point, Scully explains the obsessive/compulsive disorder "ego-dystonia" to Mulder. Ego-dystonia is a *psychological* disorder. Isn't Mulder an *Oxford-educated psychologist?* Wouldn't he know what ego-dystonia is? Or did he miss class that day because the previous night he was atop Sir Arthur Conan Doyle's tombstone with Phoebe Green?

X My admiration for Scully grows with each

Trivia Questions

1 In what lane did Angie Pintero see the apparition of Penny Timmons?

2 What was Michelle Chamberlain's shoe size?

Trivia Answers
1 Lane 6.
2 6 1/2.

345

Elegy

episode. Not only is she an intelligent, disciplined, strong, beautiful woman, she also has Insta-Seal Veins®! (Insta-Seal Veins is a registered trademark of Vascular Alternatives, Inc. Used by permission.) Withdrawing from the case, Scully goes for a medical checkup. A medical person draws a vial of blood. Scully bends her arm to apply pressure to the vein so it will seal. Five seconds later, she puts on her coat!

🅇 When reciting the scores for each frame of a game bowled by Penny Timmons, Spuller says eleven numbers in a row. Must be some kind of newfangled game of bowling, because I've always thought there were *ten* frames to a game! (Even stranger, Spuller recites nine numbers for Risa Shapiro and seven for Michelle Chamberlain.)

🅇 And speaking of bowling in Washington, D.C., if you're ever in the area and have a chance to enjoy a game with Craig Graham, *don't let him keep score!* Spuller recites his frame scores as: 17, 42, 67, 88, 107, 122, 131, 166, 178, 201. Hearing this list, Mulder notes that the guy bowled a "200" game. Well, *I* could bowl a "200" game with this kind of scorekeeping! Graham somehow scored *thirty-five* pins in frame eight. First . . . as far as I know, the maximum for any particular frame is *thirty*. Second, if you check the close-up of Graham's scorecard, you'll see that the guy didn't even get a strike in the eighth frame! He knocked down only *nine* pins!

Changed Premises

🅇 Okay, I'm confused. When it happened in "Tempus Fugit," I thought it was just a mistake, but it happens in this episode as well, and now I'm not sure what to think. Near the beginning of the episode—when Mulder asks Scully about a certain look she gives Pintero—Scully replies that after four years, Mulder should know what that look means. Four years? Shouldn't that be *five* years? Granted, this episode doesn't have a

date, but "Zero Sum" carries a date of March 27, 1997. And "Pilot" carries dates of March 7–22, *1992.* (Am I missing something obvious here?)

Equipment Oddities

🅇 The bowling proprietor's name is Angie Pintero. He doesn't appear to have any prescription in his glasses.

🅇 Near the start of this episode we learn that a disembodied spirit has broken a pinsetter by lying on top of it. Does this seem odd to anyone else—that a ghost could break something because of its weight? (I didn't think disembodied spirits weighed that much. Someone should tell the fitness industry. There's a market here they aren't exploiting. "Worried about Uncle Bob going through the afterlife hopelessly rotund? Call today and ask about our wraith reduction program!")

Continuity and Production Problems

🅇 There be strange things at work at Angie's Midnight Bowl. The episode begins with Pintero closing up for the night. Keep your eyes on lane two and lane four (numbering from the left). As Pintero collects empty soda cups, lane two has only a few pins, and lane four has a full set. Then the shot changes, and suddenly lane two has a full set and lane four has only a few!

🅇 After visiting the bowling alley, Mulder and Scully attend a police briefing on the killings, hosted by Detective Hudak. Standing in front of a projection screen, Hudak speaks of the victims as he gradually walks forward. Once the camera angle changes, Hudak leaps back to stand near the screen again.

🅇 In this same briefing, Hudak and Mulder exchange words. Listen to the sound of Hudak's voice as he says, "You mean Penny Timmons's last words." Hear the difference in equalization and reverberation? That's because the line was "looped." The actor came in after the footage was shot and overdubbed the sentence. The same thing happens to a lesser degree when Hudak says that Penny Timmons didn't have any dying words because her larynx was severed.

🗶 Examining crime scene photos, Scully shows Mulder that the third victim's ring was switched from her left hand to her right hand. A close-up of the photo shows the left hand pulled in next to the body. However, at the beginning of the episode, when Pintero sees Penny Timmons's body—and she *is* the third victim—her left arm is outstretched. Since the police are already on site when Pintero arrives, one wonders: Who moved Penny Timmons's hand?

🗶 Spuller has an interesting lawyer in this episode. She's either an alien/human hybrid, or she changes professions *a lot!* She was a doctor in "Shadows." Then she was a nurse in "One Breath." Now she's an attorney!

Demons

PLOT SUMMARY

In Providence, Rhode Island, Mulder awakes in a motel room, disoriented and covered in blood. Charging to his rescue, Scully discovers that Mulder's gun has been fired twice. There's also blood on a car parked outside the motel room. The car belongs to David and Amy Cassandra, and Mulder and Scully soon find the couple's bodies at a cottage in Chepatchet, Rhode Island.

Of course, police initially suspect Mulder, but the blood spatter on his shirt indicates he was not the shooter. An exam also reveals the presence of the hallucinogenic "ketamine" in his system. In fact, Mulder went to Providence to interview alien abductee Amy Cassandra. The methods used by psychologist Dr. Goldstien to recover Cassandra's memories so intrigued Mulder that he submitted himself to Goldstien's unorthodox treatment—a treatment that included not only ketamine but also direct electrical stimulation of the brain. For some reason—after Mulder underwent the treatment—the Cassandras decided to execute a murder-suicide pact using Mulder's weapon.

Indeed, the "treatment" has almost the same devastating consequences for Mulder, for though it seems to reawaken memories of Samantha's abduction and an affair between Cancerman and Mulder's mom, it also drives Mulder into a psychotic state in which he nearly murders Scully before she can arrange the medical attention he desperately needs.

Onscreen Locations

- ☒ Providence, Rhode Island
- ☒ Cassandra residence, Providence, Rhode Island

Demons

- ☒ Warwick, Rhode Island
- ☒ Quonochontaug, Rhode Island

Unanswered Questions

☒ How reliable are Mulder's memory flashbacks in this episode? It's impossible to tell, but there is one very intriguing piece of information. The young Cancerman and Bill Mulder look identical to the young Cancerman and Bill Mulder from "Musings of a Cigarette-Smoking Man." Does that mean that the events in "Musings of a Cigarette-Smoking Man" actually occurred? How could Mulder remember the physical characteristics of two men who were birthed only from Cancerman's imagination?

Plot Oversights

☒ According to the clock on Scully's nightstand near the beginning of the episode, Mulder calls Scully at her apartment in Washington, D.C., at 4:50 in the morning. According to onscreen text, Scully races up to a motel in Providence at 6:15 a.m. That's an hour and twenty-five minutes. Washington, D.C., to Providence, Rhode Island. Does this seem a tad rushed?

☒ Scully identifies the day as Sunday when she speaks with Mulder in his motel room, but moments earlier the screen text says, "April 12." The only question is: What year is it supposed to be? If the events in this episode occur on Sunday, April 12, the year would have to be *1998!* Under normal circumstances, I would guess the year of this episode to be 1997 since the creators have traditionally stayed close to the airdate schedule for *The X-Files* timeline. Indeed, the registration on the Cassandras' car carries a date of March 1997. But April 12, 1997, is a Saturday! So either Scully is confused, or this episode is a "flash-forward" to the end of the fifth season!

X Okay, I admit that this is needlessly obsessive picayune nitpicking even before I start, but when Mulder hears that the cottage where Amy Cassandra grew up is in Chepatchet, he responds that it's about twenty miles from Providence on Route 8. Seeing Scully's puzzled look, Mulder explains that his parents had a summer house "out there" when he was a kid. Later, Mulder tells a police detective that his parents had a house in Quonochontaug. This would seem to be the same house that Mulder referred to earlier as being "out there" near Chepatchet. But, but, but . . . to get to Chepatchet from Providence you go northwest. To get to Quonochontaug, you go *south,* really *south.* In fact, Quonochontaug is on the southern edge of Rhode Island. Chepatchet, on the other hand, is fewer than ten miles from the northern border. Granted, Rhode Island isn't that big to begin with, but Mulder makes it sounds like the two towns are in the same vicinity.

X Does anyone find it odd that Mulder has a seizure outside the cottage where Amy Cassandra grew up and then Scully lets him wander upstairs by himself? What if he had another seizure at the top of the stairs?

X With all this wondering over Mulder shooting the Cassandras, why doesn't someone order a gunpowder test on Mulder's hands? Wouldn't that show whether he recently fired a weapon? And what about gunpowder tests on the Cassandras? If it was really a murder-suicide pact, wouldn't the tests show that one of them was the shooter? (Speaking of which, *both* of them were shot in the heart. Doesn't this seem

like a needlessly agonizingly way to kill yourself? Why not put the bullet in your brain and make death instantaneous?)

X Even stranger, why doesn't Scully ever check to see if Mulder has a hole in his head? Scully knows that both Amy Cassandra and Mulder have been injected with ketamine. During Amy Cassandra's autopsy, Scully finds a hole in the woman's head. Shortly after Scully returns from Cassandra's autopsy, a police officer kills himself, and Scully finds a corresponding hole in his head. Scully then tells a police detective about the holes, but *apparently* no one ever checks to see if Mulder has such a hole. Given that Scully believes the people with these holes have committed suicide, wouldn't she be a wee bit interested to know if Mulder had endured a drill session as well?

X And *what is with* the psychologist in this episode?! Does Goldstien work for Cancerman or something? This guy is an *idiot!* First, he says that he doesn't know Mulder, even though he's already treated Mulder. Then he claims a "very good ethical and professional reputation." Yeah, right. If he has such a good reputation, what's he worried about? Why does he lie about treating Mulder? Is he concerned that Amy Cassandra died because of his treatment? Certainly he should be *very* concerned once he hears that another one of his patients has just committed suicide as well. Yet, when Mulder returns to Goldstien's office alone, the *dingbat* gives Mulder *another* treatment!

X In the previous three episodes, the creators have tried to fake us out twice with main characters shooting other main characters. Anybody else think it's time for a new gimmick?

Changed Premises

X This happens elsewhere, but I might as well mention it here. In "Tooms," when Scully calls

FOURTH SEASON

Trivia Questions

1 What is the street address of Hansen's Motel?

2 What is Dr. Goldstien's first name?

Trivia Answers
1 3106 Quilchena Avenue.
2 Charles.

Demons

Mulder "Fox" for the first time, Mulder retorts that while he was growing up he even made his parents call him "Mulder." Yet, in this episode, Mrs. Mulder calls him "Fox" (as she does in many other episodes—as his father does as well).

Equipment Oddities

X Shortly after arriving at Mulder's motel room, Scully drops the clip on his pistol and sees that two bullets are missing. She tells Mulder that two rounds have been fired. Actually . . . it would be more appropriate for her to say that there are two bullets missing from the clip because—without racking the slide to see if a round is chambered—Scully is only guessing on how many bullets were actually fired.

Consider this scenario: Mulder loads his clip. It appears to take fifteen bullets. At some point, someone racks the slide. The slide takes the top bullet from the clip and shoves it into the firing chamber. Someone pulls the trigger. The slide bangs back, ejects the shell, and—as it snaps forward—it grabs the next bullet from the clip. At this point there are two bullets missing from the clip, but only *one* has been fired.

I could run through the other scenarios, but that would just chew up space (especially if we consider that the gun may have been reloaded or bullets may have been manually removed from the clip). Suffice it to say that—in the simplest view—if there is no bullet in the chamber, either two or three shots were fired. And if there is a bullet in the chamber, one or two shots were fired. (Maybe Scully is playing the odds?)

X After visiting Goldstien's office, Mulder demands the car keys from Scully. Scully refuses to give them to him and drives him to his mother's house instead. After arguing with his mother, Scully is shocked to see Mulder taking off in her rental car. Question: When did she give him the keys? Or did Mulder hot-wire the car? (Yet another talent of our beleaguered hero?)

X Here's the deal: Mulder goes for a second treatment with the infamous Dr. Goldstien. Goldstien gives Mulder a shot, puts headphones and sunglasses on him, and then secures Mulder's arms to the chair. Then—as Mulder twitches—Goldstien gets out a little drill and ominously lowers it toward Mulder's head. This is when I started laughing. Mulder's head is jerking back and forth, so it's obviously not strapped down. I don't care how badly Mulder wants to remember what happened to Samantha, when that drill hits him, he's going to jerk and tear a big gash in his head. This is ridiculous! No one but a certified wacko is going to try to drill a hole in a patient's head without making sure the head can't move!

Continuity and Production Problems

X Determining that Mulder drove a certain car to his motel, Scully checks its registration. The address on the document reads, "3106 Quilchena Avenue, Providence, R.I., 02901-99." I guess Rhode Island decided that they were so small they didn't *need* the "plus four" portion of the Zip code and could get by with only "plus two"!

X The medical examiner in this episode bears a striking resemblance to Special Agent Weiss of "Colony." Oddly enough, Weiss *died* in "Colony." A case of life after death? Another alien/human hybrid? (A check of the "Serial Ovotypes" sidebar under "Johnston, Andrew" will show that Colonel Robert Budahas of "Deep Throat" *also* bears a striking resemblance to these other two men. Hmmm. Alien/human hybrids flying top-secret military planes? Hmmm.)

X Not sure what this is, but check it out and decide for yourself! Investigating the suicide of a police officer, Scully and a police detective inspect his belongings. Scully finds a magazine with Amy Cassandra's picture on the front. As the camera returns to a medium-wide shot of Scully, watch the wall behind her. There's a shadow that appears and then moves away, but neither actor moves! (I'm guessing someone on the production crew was in the wrong place at the wrong time!)

◪ Wow! The pollution in Warwick, Rhode Island, must be atrocious! Finding Mulder's car, Scully wipes a thick layer of dust from the back windshield. She comments that it's been there for a "few days." This is most likely Monday, so the car has been parked in Warwick for about *three* days. The side of the car looks clean and polished. We can assume that the rest of the car looked that way when Mulder parked it. That means a heavy layer of particulates accumulated on this car in just seventy-two hours! (Either that or the friendly neighborhood entrepreneur wandered by with a dust spewer and coupons for Zippy-Clean Car Care Specialists.)

Gethsemane

(Part 1 of ?)

PLOT SUMMARY At the FBI, Scully tells a group that the research done by Mulder on the X-Files is illegitimate and states her belief that Mulder was the victim of the biggest of all lies.

Continuing with her report, Scully tells of a man named Arlinski who recently contacted Mulder, asking for help in recovering a frozen alien body from St. Elias Mountains in Canada. With her cancer worsening, Scully stayed behind to test the authenticity of ice core samples taken from the site. *Preliminary* analysis of the body did seem to confirm its extraterrestrial origin. However, when Scully apprehended a man named Kritschgau after he stole the ice core samples, a different picture emerged. Somehow, Kritschgau knew of the corpse—claiming that it was a fake just like all the other "evidence" designed to purport the existence of aliens as a cover for the heinous activities of the military-industrial complex. Worse, Kritschgau claimed that Mulder himself had been "invented"; that Samantha's abduction had been faked; that lies were fed to Mulder's father; and that Scully had been infected with cancer to ensure that Mulder would believe and eventually publicly state his convictions.

According to Scully, the information was too much for Mulder to bear. The next morning police called her to Mulder's apartment, where she identified his body, dead from a gunshot wound to the head (*snort . . . yeah, right*).

Onscreen Locations

- ☒ NASA Symposium, Boston University, November 20, 1972
- ☒ St. Elias Mountains, Yukon Territory, Canada
- ☒ Smithsonian Institution, Washington, D.C.
- ☒ Paleoclimatology Lab, American University
- ☒ Southeast Washington, D.C.
- ☒ FBI Sci-Crime Lab, Washington, D.C.
- ☒ Department of Defense, Research Division, Sethsburg, Virginia

Ruminations

Obviously, I'm at a bit of a disadvantage with this episode. By the time you read this, the fifth season of The X-Files *will be well under way, and many of the questions raised by this episode probably will already be resolved! At the time of this writing, the season finale for the fourth season of* The X-Files *aired only two days ago.*

I suppose I should say something about Mulder's "death." After viewing this episode I suppose there were X-philes out there who actually worried that Mulder shot himself in the head, but my first thought was "Been there. Done that." (After all, Mulder "died" at the end of the second season as well!)

As for the opening credit statement "Believe the Lie," it is my fervent hope that the creators mean for this to apply only to this episode and possibly the next but not the rest of the episodes in the fifth season. For me, "Believe the Lie" comes dangerously close to nihilism—everything is senseless, nothing can be known. . . . "Vanity, vanity, all is vanity." (Although most of the fourth season has headed in this direction.) There comes a point in this style of writing when there are so many half-truths and open-ended stories being tossed around on the screen that it's simply impossible for the viewer to ever figure out how it all fits together. It becomes an existential narrative where all that matters is the present moment, and even that moment can never be believed. While that may be an interesting exercise for the creators, it produces nihilistic responses in the viewers, to little benefit. In fact, nihilism tends to engender only rancorous mockery and pervasive apathy. And both of those emotions—boys and girls—are bad things when it comes to TV land.

It probably would behoove me to conclude this section by predicting how Mulder will come back to life for the fifth season. I might float the possibility that Scully is lying to Blevins and that the body she identified wasn't really Mulder's. Or I could wonder if Mulder is simply going to grow another head, like Leonard Betts. I might even suggest that it wasn't Mulder who died in Mulder's apartment but rather a sad-sack, shapeshifting hybrid who had come to pour his heart out to Mulder after the Consortium pushed back the date for colonization an entire year. (Perhaps the hybrid had invested his life savings in the local alien ice pick franchise, thinking its value would soar once the bounty-hunter dudes showed up to take over the Earth. Obviously, without an invasion, the poor hybrid guy was busted! When Mulder made a run for Chinese food, the hybrid shape-shifted to look like Mulder and killed himself. Of course, he didn't dissolve, because the back of his neck wasn't pierced, and Mulder didn't dispose of the body because he really wanted to get back to Graceland for another visit, and since he was dead he thought it was the perfect opportunity!) Yeah, I certainly could propose some scenarios like those, but I think I'll just let the creators work it out in the fall.

Here's hoping Mulder's resurrection isn't goofy!

Unanswered Questions

X Was Kritschgau factual in his statements? As Deep Throat told Mulder in "E.B.E.," a lie is most convincing hidden between two truths. It seems likely then that some portion of Kritschgau's story is true. It would serve us well, therefore, to break apart the allegations—to consider them piece by piece.

First, how reliable is Kritschgau as a witness? There are elements to his appearance that seem contrived. At other times when "they" sent someone to "clean up" evidence, the chosen person has been untraceable (e.g., in "Red Museum"). Kritschgau—alternatively—is *easily* identified and found. Scully seems to put a high degree of faith in Kritschgau's testimony because he knows the details of Mulder and Scully's activities. But . . . wouldn't "they" have these details to begin with? Also, isn't it perfectly reasonable that if the corpse was faked, Kritschgau would *know* the details of this particular deception (if nothing else to convince Mulder and Scully of the truth of the larger allegation)? So, from my perspective at least, I find nothing that would indicate that everything Kritschgau says is the final "truth." (Scully's belief in the man can easily be attributed to her fear. She's just found out her cancer is spreading. Her life is upside down, and she is floundering for any way to make it all make sense. And, as an objectivist, the best way for it to make sense is if the "truth" is fully terrestrial and subject to the observations and predictions of science. (See "Whose Truth Is Out There?" for more details.) Beyond that, on a subconscious level—as is normal for human beings—Scully needs someone to blame. And when we as humans look for someone to blame, we often pick someone closest to us who should have done *something* different to make sure the bad thing never happened. Kritschgau's explanation conveniently provides Mulder as Scully's scapegoat.)

Second, was the corpse a fake, and was it designed to encourage Mulder to go public? There seems to be no question that the corpse is a fake. Unknown to Mulder and Scully, excavation of the corpse revealed the pour hole that Kritschgau described as part of the mechanism

1 What is the name of the police detective who asks Scully to identify the body in Mulder's apartment?

2 According to FBI records, where does Michael Kritschgau live?

to create the hoax. (It was supposedly used to gradually add water to the enclosure that housed the corpse over the course of a year so the corpse would appear to be buried in "old ice.") Also, this episode makes us privy to a conversation between Arlinski's assistant and the assassin. It seems to confirm that the corpse is a fake. Does that necessarily mean, however, that the corpse was designed to make Mulder "go public"? Possibly . . . but—if so—the conspirators don't know Mulder very well. Throughout this episode, Mulder is pushing for definitive proof. If Kritschgau is telling the truth, the conspirators had decided to tantalize Mulder with the corpse and then take it away before it could be exposed as a hoax. This would leave Mulder in the position in which he has remained for five years—believing without any proof. Why would the conspirators conclude that Mulder would make a public statement after the corpse disappeared? Isn't this the same situation Mulder faced at the end of "731"? If Mulder had been inclined to take such a bold step without hard evidence, wouldn't he have done so already, with all that he has seen? So . . . is there *another* purpose the conspirators might have for devising such an elaborate hoax? Could it be that "they" wanted to stage something so convincing that when they sent Kritschgau to reveal that it wasn't real, they hoped to demoralize Mulder and Scully into believing that *none* of what they have seen over the past five years was real?

Moving outward to the next topic of discussion: Was Mulder "invented" to perpetuate the "lie" that there are extraterrestrials on Earth? Was his father fed lies to this end? In the context of Kritschgau's statement, the "lies" fed to William Mulder would have to be that there were extraterrestrials on Earth. If that's so, it seems likely that William Mulder was about to tell his son these "lies" in "Anasazi" just before Krycek killed him. So why did Krycek kill him?! If "they" wanted Mulder to believe, wouldn't the testimony of his own father carry great weight?

And what about the fake frozen corpse? Does this mean that *all* the "grays" are merely constructs of the military-industrial complex? (By "grays" I am referring to what we normally think of when we talk of extraterrestrial aliens: gray skin; big, slanted eyes; big head; small body. . . .) Surprisingly enough, you'd be hard-pressed to find anything in the first four seasons of *The X-Files* that definitively proves the "grays" are extraterrestrial. There is one *possibility*, however. *Something* happened to Flight 549 in "Tempus Fugit." Sergeant Frish reported that he tracked Flight 549; that he saw another plane enter his radar screen; that there was an explosion; and that Flight 549 went down. Mike Millar—the man in charge of investigating the crash of Flight 549—said that Flight 549 showed no signs of an explosion. It seems reasonable, then, that "something else" exploded and that "something else" was directly or indirectly responsible for the crash of Flight 549. Indeed, Mulder *and* the military locate the "something else" at the bottom of Great Sacandaga Lake: a craft populated by "grays." Now, if the "grays" are really just humans dressed up in monkey suits, why did the military shoot them down? Just a little "oopsie"?

Finally—and most importantly—was Kritschgau correct in saying that there has never been extraterrestrial intelligent life on Earth (at least according to *The X-Files* mythology)? Well, if the creators of *The X-Files* want to float the proposition that Earth has *never* been visited, they have a bit of explaining to do! There are simply too many scenes that are shot from an objective third-person viewpoint that contain elements wholly unexplainable from a terrestrial context. In "Space," a ghostly entity that looks like the face on Mars forces Marcus Belt to sabotage the space shuttle. In "Fallen Angel," a military retrieval team battles with an invisible entity. In "The Erlenmeyer Flask," a hybrid human named Secare has toxic body fluids, superhuman strength, and the ability to breathe underwater. In addition, an associate tells Scully at material found in Berube's lab "would have to be, by nature, extraterrestrial." In "Colony," a shape-shifting bounty hunter crashes his craft into the arctic ice and proceeds to annihilate a group of hybrids with identical physical characteristics—hybrids with toxic body chemicals, hybrids who *dissolve* when the base of their skull is pierced. In "Piper Maru" and "Apocrypha" an oil-based entity body-jumps from person to person—exposing its pursuers to high doses of radiation without harming its host. Also in "Apocrypha," Brandoguy tells the members of the Consortium at 46th Street in New York City that a French salvage vessel has come into San Diego—its last given position being "the site where we recovered the UFO." In a later meeting in the same episode, Cancerman is grilled over moving the "salvaged UFO" and asked why he didn't bring it to Nevada "like the others."

Changed Premises

🗶 Once more with feeling. Section Chief Blevins assigned Scully to the X-Files in "Pilot." "Pilot" has a date that appears *on the screen*. It is not inferred. It appears *on the screen!* It reads, "March 7, 1992." "Gethsemane" occurs sometime in the spring of 1997. If you subtract seven from two, you get five, right? So Scully was assigned to work with Mulder *five* years ago. Yet . . . during her testimony before the group at the beginning of this episode, Scully reports that Blevins assigned her to work with the X-Files *four* years ago. Am I missing something simple here? (I suppose we could say that this episode actually occurs at the end of the *third* season, but that would mean Mulder didn't die. Of course, we already *know* that!)

Continuity and Production Problems

🗶 As Mulder and Arlinski travel to the St. Elias Mountains, an assassin kills the members of the Canadian geodetic survey team who found the body frozen in the ice. The first time the assassin fires, the camera shows us the inside surface of a tent moments before it is ripped apart by a shotgun blast. If you look closely, you might notice there are four little disks obviously attached to the exterior side of the tent. And you might even conclude that these little disks have wires running between them. Might the disks be the small explosives used to simulate the shotgun blast tearing through the tent?

🗶 Pursuing Kritschgau after he steals the ice core samples, Scully tracks him into a stairwell, where he pushes her down a flight of stairs. Scully bounces down the stairs on her left side. Yet later, her blouse has blood spots across both shoulder blades. Why?

🗶 When fingerprints identify Kritschgau as Scully's assailant, a computer displays Kritschgau's home address and gives it a Zip code of "20001-99." Shouldn't there be two more digits in the "plus four" section of the Zip code? (Oddly enough, "99" is the same zip code "plus four" extension as was used for the Cassandras' car registration in the previous episode, "Demons." Is this some secret message from the creators of *The X-Files* to the agents of the Consortium all over the world? Aaaah!)

THE ANSWER

"I've heard the truth, Mulder. Now what I want are the answers." (Special Agent Dana Scully, "Paper Clip")

I'm short on time. I've spent six months on this *Guide* and "it" finally happened. Three hundred plu[s] hours watching *The X-Files* and *suddenly,* inexorably, inexplicably, inextricably, insistently, instinctivel[y] . . . it *all snapped into place!* I *knew* . . . I knew "The Answer"—that answer to all my ponderous ques- tions, to all my confusion. Like a well-earned but still spontaneous smile from Special Agent Dan[a] Scully, it was the final statement to tie every loose end and make *everything* make sense.

But do "they" know I know?

The Answer is so primal, so mind-expanding that it threatens to undo *all* that is in *The X-Files*[.] Would "they" allow the telling? Would they dare to risk it all? Would they dare to lose their edge, thei[r] hook, their power? No. "They" would do *anything* to stop the spread of this kind of information.

The stakes are too high. We need . . . *protection.*

(Fiddling with a CSM-8000 Countermeasure Filter.)

TThheerree, txhxaxtx'xsx retteb. II kxnxoxwx siht iiss hxaxrxdx ot rreeaadd. IX ezigolopa[WWheenn yxoxux raeh wwhhaatt IX evah ttoo sxaxyx, Il'ouy uunnddeerrssttaanndd mxyx aionarap[TThhee AXnxsxwxexrx si ssoo pxrxoxfxoxuxnxdx esuaceb iitt exxxpxlxaxixnxsx gnihtyreve: WWhhy[axrxex ereht ssoo mxaxnxyx tnereffid kkiinnddss oxfx sneila iinn *TXhxex seliF-X?* WWhhyy dxoxexxs[eht ssttoorryy Mxuxlxdxexrx sllet ooff hxixsx s'retsis aabbdduuccttiioonn vxaxrxyx os wwiiddeelly[bxexxtxwxexexnx eht ffiirrsstt axnxdx dnoces sseeaassoonn? (Sxexex "elttiL GGrreeeenn Mxexnx."[woH ccaann Mxuxlxdxexrx dna SSccuullllyy bxex ni ttwwoo pxlxaxcxexsx ta oonnccee—axsx yeh[sseeeemm txox eb aacccccoorrddiinngg txox eht ddaatteess oxnx "reklaweriF" aanndd["lxrxrxexsxixsxtxixbxlxex"? yhW ddooeess DXoxcxtxoxrx SSccuullllyy kxnxoxwx os lliittttllee axbxox[t uxtx cisab ffiirrsstt axixdx? yhW wweerree txhxex sesproc bbuurriieedd ixnx eht bbooxxcxaxrx r[NNeeww Mxexxxixcxox? woH ddiidd txhxex desab-lio aalliieenn oxfx "repiP MMaarruu" axnxd["ahpyrcopA" ppeenneettrraattee axixrx-txixgxhxtx serusolcne? OOnn axnxdx no tthhee qxuxexsxtx[ixoxnxsx ruop aanndd TXhxex rewsnA aannsswweerrss txhxexmx lla! Iltt'ss sxox elpmis wxhxexnx uo[tthhiinnkk axbxoxuxtx ti . . . .

Gasp . . .

Someone's in the basement!

They're breaking down the door!

No! Can't let them . . . Others have to know. Must tell . . .

(Gunfire erupts. The computer monitor shatters. Circuits within spit and snap as blood shorts out connections. Papers dance like dust devils. Books shudder against an unfinished wall. A body thumps to the ground. Footsteps race away.)
Wheezing quiet.
Groaning.

(An unsteady hand rises from the floor. It struggles toward the keyboard. An index finger presses the caps lock as others find their places.)

I . . . R . . . (pause, finding one last ounce of strength) . . . I . . . O . . . T . . .
(The hand flops to the ground.)
Silence.

Onscreen Locations Index

The Least Painful Method for Finding an Episode Title

As I noted in the Introduction to this *Guide*, the creators of *The X-Files* decided not to list titles on the actual episodes themselves. This normally sends X-philes scampering for television listings and Web sites, trying to figure out what to call "that episode where Mulder and Scully . . . ." Since *Nitpicker's Guides* are often used as reference books, I thought it would be good to have an easier method for identifying an episode, and—given that all the episodes have some type of onscreen text—I thought I would include a section called "Onscreen Locations" in each review. In that way a nitpicker could confirm that he or she was, in fact, reading about the episode that he or she *thought* he or she was watching! *And,* by compiling all the onscreen locations in an index, I could give my nitpickers a place to look first when attempting to figure out what episode just began on their television screens.

Here's the drill: Watch for onscreen text. Try to remember the name of the place or the location—*exactly as it is formatted on the screen*—and then look it up in this index. The episode title will follow the entry, and then the page number will follow for that episode's review.

For instance, given the episode "Pilot," you could look up any of the following: Collum National Forest; Northwest Oregon; Coastal Northwest Oregon; Raymond County State Psychiatric Hospital; Rural Hwy. 133; or Bellefleur, Oregon. (By the way, "Washington, D.C.," doesn't appear in this list, to conserve space. Neither does "FBI Headquarters" when it appeared alone. In addition, there are a few locations that occur more that once. There's nothing I can do about that, but at least I've narrowed the possibilities for you! And I have abbreviated a few of the episode titles to save space. I don't think you will have any trouble figuring out which one I'm referring to.)

NUMBERS

6th Precinct, "Synchrony," 332–336
14th Precinct House, "Born Again," 76–78
21st Century Recycling Plant, "Revelations," 215–218
46th Street, New York, "Paper Clip," 183–186
46th Street, New York City, "Apocrypha," 232–234; "The Blessing Way," 179–182; "Zero Sum," 340–343
66 Exeter St., "Squeeze," 11–14
66 Exeter Street, "Tooms," 73–75
737 26th Street, "Colony," 138–141
1222 South Dakota Street, "Grotesque," 227–228
1223 Hanover Street, Georgetown, "Avatar," 249–251
1533 Malibu Canyon, "3," 111–113
1953 Gardner Street, Winnetka, "Sanguinarium," 283–286
3702 Medlock Street, "Piper Maru," 229–231
8426 Melrose Ave., "3," 111–113

E

F

X

Onscreen
Locations Index

Index

Sanders, Owen, 274, 275
Sandominsky, Kerry, 263
Sanford, Dr. Sally, 285
"Sanguinarium," 109, 222, 260, 261, 263, 283–288
Saunders, Mark, 263
Sauve, Ron, 263
Savalas, Cindy, 66
Sayles, Carina, 249, 250
Scanlon, Dr. Kevin, 66, 314, 315, 341
Schaeffer, Jack, 246–248, 261
Schilling, Ms., 313
Schnauz, Gerald, 45, 277–279
Scully, Margaret, 115, 309
Scully, Melissa, 47, 48, 87, 115, 145, 185, 230, 309
Scully, Mrs. William, 47, 48
Scully, William, 46, 47, 202
Secare, Dr., 82, 83, 213, 354
Secona, 238–239
"731," 4, 109, 127, 128, 149, 212–214, 241, 261, 263, 330
"Shadows," 21–23, 109, 116, 128, 242, 261, 262, 287, 288, 347
Shannon, Dr., 284–286
"Shapes," 65, 67–69, 109, 110, 128, 150, 242, 262, 263, 274, 288, 308, 309
Sheherlis, Agent, 260
Shuyang Hsin, 243–245
Simmons, Joel, 38, 39, 150
Simmons, Teena, 39
Simms, Tasha, 263
Sistrunk, Reverend, 260
Skinner, Mrs., 249
Slaughter, Ruth, 263
"Sleepless," 24, 66, 100–102, 109, 127, 128, 149, 166, 260–263
"Small Potatoes," 45, 127, 149, 200, 222, 261–263, 309, 310, 337–339
Smallwood, Tucker, 272
Smirnoff, Yakov, 312
Smith, Jeremiah, 131, 257–259, 267–269, 288, 331, 341
Soames, Raymond, 3–5, 66, 131, 136–137, 329
"Soft Light," 109, 128, 163–166, 241, 253, 260–263, 288

Soona, Kenneth J., 171, 181
Sophie, 146
Sorenson, Senator Albert, 293, 297
"Space," 32–34, 127, 261–263, 308, 354
Sparks, Addie, 66, 301
Sparks, Carrie Cain, 263
Sparks, Frank, 301
Speranza, John, 194
Spiller, Nancy, 121, 260
Spinney, Doug, 70–72
Spitz, Bob, 261
Spuller, Harold, 344–347
"Squeeze," 11–14, 43, 44, 46, 73–75, 93, 96, 100, 109, 127, 128, 181, 201, 202, 211, 241, 262, 288, 308, 309, 325
Stans, Lieutenant Colonel Victor, 203–205, 263
Steen, Dr. Larry, 263
Steffen, General, 321
Stefoff, Val, 59
Stevens, Jerry, 132, 133
Stewart, Bobby L., 263
Stewart, Malcolm, 263
Stroman, Dr., 255, 261
Sugar, 240
Summerfield, Brenda J., 262
Summers, James, 47
Surnow, Dr., 79, 263
Svo, Comrade, 261
Swenson, Karen, 5
"Synchrony," 109, 128, 242, 261, 309, 332–336
"Syzygy," 5, 45, 65, 109, 110, 128, 224–226, 230, 243, 261–263, 308

T

Taber, Mr., 99
Talbot, Detective, 263
"Talitha Cumi," 127, 128, 131, 257–259, 261–263, 268, 288, 290, 302, 309, 310, 331
Tanaka, Peter, 117–119, 262
Tanner, Elaine, 307
Taylor, Sheriff Andy, 271–273
Teager, Nathaniel, 262, 320, 321, 322